POLICING THE OPEN ROAD

Policing the
OPEN ROAD

HOW CARS TRANSFORMED AMERICAN FREEDOM

Sarah A. Seo

Harvard University Press

Cambridge, Massachusetts
London, England
2019

Copyright © 2019 by the President and Fellows of Harvard College
All rights reserved
Printed in the United States of America

First printing

Library of Congress Cataloging-in-Publication Data

Names: Seo, Sarah A., 1980– author.
Title: Policing the open road : how cars transformed American freedom /
    Sarah A. Seo.
Description: Cambridge, Massachusetts : Harvard University Press, 2019. |
    Includes bibliographical references and index.
Identifiers: LCCN 2018040573 | ISBN 9780674980860 (hardcover : alk.
    paper)
Subjects: LCSH: Traffic regulations—United States—History—
    20th century. | Traffic safety—United States—History—20th century. |
    Automobiles—United States—Public opinion. | Automobiles—
    Social aspects—United States. | Searches and seizures—
    United States—History—20th century. | Discrimination in law
    enforcement—United States—History—20th century.
Classification: LCC HE371.A3 S53 2019 | DDC 363.2/32—dc23
    LC record available at https://lccn.loc.gov/2018040573

For my parents and Mike

Contents

POLICING THE OPEN ROAD

Introduction

> The horseless carriage was just arriving in San Francisco, and its debut was turning into one of those colorfully unmitigated disasters that bring misery to everyone but historians.
>
> Laura Hillenbrand, *Seabiscuit* (2001)

ON APRIL 11, 1916, eight years after the Model T's debut and just two years after the perfection of its moving assembly line, the Tucson, Arizona, sheriff's office received a call around midnight about a robbery and assault at Pastime Park, a pleasure resort just north of the city. Three officers jumped into a "public service automobile" and, on their way to the scene of the crime, saw a car that seemed to be heading toward them suddenly turn around. Suspicious, they sped up to the car and yelled "Stop!" and "We are officers!" to no avail. Deputy Sheriff Thomas Johns testified that he then fired his pistol at the wheel "to puncture the tire." He fired a second shot, Deputy Sheriff Joseph Wiley fired the third shot, and Police Officer Ramon Salazar followed with a fourth shot—all to "find out who the parties were in the car." As it turned out, Captain John Bates and his wife, Mary, innocent parties, were driving home from a friend's house.

One of the shots struck and killed Mrs. Bates. All three officers faced murder charges.[1]

At trial, Captain Bates testified that his car was "very noisy" and the road "rough," which could have described all motor vehicles and country roads at the time. The "chains which hold up the tailboard were rattling up and down on the fenders which are over each rear wheel; in fact, every time [he] hit a bump they would jump up and down; the muffler of the machine was wide open, and the exhaust [was] directly in front of the driver, underneath the footboard." The driver of the public service automobile testified that his muffler was "wide open" as well. With all the racket that the cars were making, it was impossible for the Bateses to hear the officers' shouts for them to stop. This, plus the fact of the Bateses' actual innocence, convinced the jury that the three defendants had acted beyond their lawful authority and were guilty of murder.[2]

In the case of *Wiley v. State*, which affirmed the guilt of Deputy Sheriff Johns, whose shot had killed Mrs. Bates, the Arizona Supreme Court maintained that even if the Bateses had heard the shouts and refused to stop, the officers' manner of pursuit "was more suggestive of a holdup by highwaymen than an arrest by peace officers." The court was not at all being facetious. Recognizable police cars with black and white color blocks would not exist for another two decades, and the first revolving emergency light, the "Beacon Ray," would not be invented until 1948. As late as 1934, a consultant recommended that the police department in Dallas, Texas, paint its patrol cars "some unusual color, such as fire department red or bright yellow or perhaps with a fine grade of aluminum paint." Without "definite identification," his report warned of precisely what had happened to the Bateses: it was "not inconceivable that a frightened motorist thinking he is to be robbed may attempt to run away from officers, thereby creating a situation embarrassing and undesirable at its best and which may result in a serious accident or even in the officer, through mistaken identity, actually firing on and killing a reputable citizen." At the time of the Arizona incident in 1916, it was uncommon for "public service" vehicles to be branded as such. The exceptions had either a sign the size of a license plate attached to the radiator or the initials

New York Police Department cars, circa 1925.

Courtesy of the Alfred J. Young Collection, Museum of the City of New York, X2010.11.11056.

"P.D." painted on the door—nothing that drivers could easily discern, especially at nighttime.[3]

The minuscule markings matched the small size of police forces at the time. When officers shared the task of enforcing the criminal laws with citizens and private patrol services, it would have been unfathomable that respectable citizens like the Bateses might be targets of a police chase. The law reflected this social reality. Because private citizens also pursued, arrested, and prosecuted those who had injured or wronged them, the common law clearly circumscribed the right to arrest in order to distinguish a lawful seizure of a person from a kidnapping or assault. Legal requirements ensured that arrestees would know the exact reason for the apprehension. So when Captain Bates and his wife drove home after an evening with friends, they had every reason to believe, as the court noted, that highway bandits were after them, firing away.[4]

Unfortunately, an intact copy of the officers' brief in their defense has not survived the withering effects of time, but we can hazard an educated guess as to their argument. While half of the court's opinion dealt with the different degrees of murder and joint liability, the other half discussed an officer's arrest powers. As the court recited, the common law required the showing of a warrant, but it authorized warrantless arrests when an officer reasonably believed that an arrestee had committed a felony offense. The law also allowed an officer to kill a fleeing felon. Given these well-established precedents, the defendants likely claimed that their attempt to make a felony arrest unintentionally resulted in Mrs. Bates's death. An especially persuasive attorney would also have pointed out that, with motor-powered vehicles having practically invented the getaway, a rule that officers could not stop cars with gunfire would effectively nullify their authority to arrest suspected felons speeding away.[5]

The Arizona court rejected the officers' arguments, and rather than focusing on their right to arrest, it instead elaborated on the Bateses' right to drive. The opinion declared that the officers had violated the "personal liberty of both Capt. Bates and the deceased," who, "having committed no crime, were entitled to proceed on their way without interruption or molestation." This presented a broad statement on the rights of drivers. Entitling them *to proceed on their way without interruption or molestation* necessarily included the corresponding right to decide for themselves whether officers had legal cause to stop them. If they decided that an officer did not, then they would have had the additional right to refuse to pull over. Indeed, the court made this exact suggestion when it stated hypothetically that even if "the Bateses had heard [the officers'] outcries and refused to stop, no inference of guilt could have been reasonably drawn therefrom," a mandatory inference to justify an interference with the Bateses' right "to proceed on their way." The rules of the road according to the Arizona Supreme Court would have made it extremely difficult for officers to stop a car they found suspicious. This was the world of *Wiley v. State*, when the police were few in number, easily mistaken for highwaymen, and limited in their authority over innocent citizens.

Ninety-Nine Years Later

On July 10, 2015, a Texas state trooper pulled over Sandra Bland for failing to use a turn signal. After a tense dialogue, the traffic stop quickly came to a violent end. The trooper first tried to yank the young, black woman from the car before forcing her out with a Taser gun. He then arrested Bland, who was lying face down, crying, and screaming in pain. Three days later, Bland was found dead in her jail cell. A year later, *The Nation* published an article that asked the question that had become a viral hashtag, #WhatHappenedtoSandraBland? To find the answer, the article examined Bland's life, beginning with her birth to a single mother in Chicago's West Side. The answer, according to the writer, was not just the neglectful conditions in that Texas county jail that led to her death. The answer was also unemployment, insufficient mental health care, and draconian drug laws. Bland's life story is tragic. Also tragic is that the themes of poverty and race in the criminal justice system are all too common.[6]

But another motif, although unnamed, loomed throughout the article. The automobile appeared in nearly every significant setback in Bland's life. Exorbitant traffic tickets that Bland paid for by "sitting out" in jail. Convictions for driving under the influence and arrest warrants for unpaid traffic fines that severely limited her employment options. Charges for possessing marijuana—her lawyer suspected that Bland was self-medicating—that the police discovered in her car. The automobile stood in the background in *The Nation*'s biography of Bland, but it played a prominent role as a site of violence, poverty, and discrimination.

The overpolicing of cars is a fact of life for people of color in America. Although Bland was not killed during the traffic stop, in 2015, the year of her death, 27 percent of police killings of unarmed citizens began with a traffic stop, according to one survey. Bland herself had been increasingly vocal on social media against police abuse and violence against African Americans, especially when the Black Lives Matter movement gained momentum after a police officer fatally shot eighteen-year-old Michael Brown. It turned out that what had happened in Ferguson, Missouri, on August 9, 2014, was part of a larger trend. The US Department of Justice opened an investigation of the

Ferguson Police Department and found "a pattern of unconstitutional policing" that skewed along racial lines. Most encounters with law enforcement, the report concluded, began with a traffic stop, an experience that disproportionately befell Ferguson's black residents. In 2014, its municipal court had roughly 53,000 traffic cases, compared with about 50,000 nontraffic cases. This pattern was not limited to Ferguson in the American car-dominated society. In the words of several scholars, "No form of direct government control comes close to these [traffic] stops in sheer numbers, frequency, proportion of the population affected, and in many instances, the degree of coercive intrusion."[7]

What has not changed since the days of *Wiley v. State* is that the police's authority during car stops remains contested. After Bland's arrest, the *New York Times* asked several lawyers and law professors to assess the legality of Trooper Brian Encinia's actions. Although they believed, after having watched a video recording of the encounter, that Encinia had exceeded his lawful authority, they hedged their answers. The police rarely arrest drivers for failure to use a turn signal, but the legal experts recognized that it is technically an arrestable offense in Texas. There was no evidence that the officer feared for his safety to justify ordering Bland out of her car, but the police have "complete discretion" to do so, and drivers are legally obligated to comply. While Encinia forcefully restrained Bland, the law does allow the use of force in proportion to the circumstances of an arrest, and at least one of the commentators did not think that Encinia used disproportionate force. Throughout the twentieth century and into the present, motorists, the police, and even legal scholars have been unsure about the law of car stops.[8]

But what has changed since the early years of the automobile is that everyone's uncertainty stemmed not so much from officers' attempts to exceed their rather limited powers; instead, the inconclusiveness arose from questions about what rights individuals have against the police's broad authority. The dashboard camera in Sandra Bland's case was crucial in undermining Trooper Encinia's claim that his actions were defensible. Without the recording, a judge would have been more likely to take the officer's word that the driver was "combative and uncooperative," as Encinia alleged in the arrest affidavit. For most of the twentieth century, there were no tapes. This mattered when prosecutors, judges, and juries reliably accepted the police's version of the story. But even with the video, Encinia, in the end, faced no criminal charges, revealing just how much leeway the law gave police. A grand jury indicted the trooper only for perjury based on his false statements in the arrest affidavit. Special prosecutors then dropped that charge in exchange for Encinia's agreement never to work again as a police officer.[9]

What is the history that can account for the changes from *Wiley v. State* to Sandra Bland? In the span of a century, towns and cities throughout the country—and not just in metropolitan centers—expanded their forces and professionalized beat cops, turning them into "law enforcement officers." Figures are hard to come by, but one early report indicated that in the sixteen smallest states, the number of officers as a percentage of the population nearly doubled from 1910 to 1930. In addition to adding manpower, municipalities unified the police function and increased the police's discretionary authority. Courts then sanctioned that accumulation and concentration of power. The most glaring part of this history, considering that it culminated with mass incarceration by century's end, is race. Today, it would be improbable that Mrs. Bates, a white woman sitting in the passenger seat next to her husband of social standing, would be killed in a police shooting, a tragedy that now falls mostly on minority drivers. The statistics bearing this out, as well as stories like Sandra Bland's, not only reveal a problem of discrimination and implicit bias; they also raise a troubling question about our laws that have actually enabled racialized policing.[10]

Contrary to what one might expect, the social and legal developments that made the systematic policing of minorities possible did not originate with an intention to do so. This history begins with the mass production of the automobile and the immediate imperative to regulate the motoring public. From today's perspective, it may be unexpected—incredible, even—to call attention to the democratization of policing. But this was a consequence of mass automobility. Before cars, American police had more in common with their eighteenth-century forebears than with their twentieth-century successors. What revolutionized policing was a technological innovation that would come to define the new century. This is, therefore, a history about policing cars and, thus, about policing American society as it fast became an automotive society. It is thus also about the practical, theoretical, and legal problems of policing everybody who drove. Those who became subject to regular police surveillance included not just criminals in getaway cars but more importantly, and for the first time, the respectable class of citizens who were the automobile's early adopters. The need to discipline drivers and to do so without giving offense necessitated changes to the police function and to well-established constitutional laws. Officers now required discretion to administer the massive traffic enforcement regime and deal with the sensitivities of "law-abiding" citizens who kept violating traffic laws. The law's accommodation of discretionary policing profoundly altered what it meant to live free from state intrusion in the Automotive Age. By the postwar, Cold War years, American society's dependence on the police to maintain order raised troubling comparisons with totalitarian police. Unforeseen by midcentury jurists, their solution to the potential arbitrary policing of everyone led directly to the problem of discriminatory policing against minorities. Only by considering how American society as a whole came to be policed can we more fully understand the history of American criminal justice and its troubled present.

Mass production would not have been practicable without mass adoption, and Americans eagerly embraced the "horseless carriage." Numbers provide some sense of the dramatic change. While the number of traditional carriages manufactured in the country shrank from 2 million in 1909 to 10,000 in 1923, the number of automobiles produced during those same years went from about 80,000 to over 4 million. In 1910, the number of registered passenger cars, a category that gets closer to the number of drivers since it includes secondhand cars, was just under 500,000. That figure exploded to over 8 million in 1920 and to nearly 18 million in 1925—a thirty-fivefold increase in fifteen years. In Robert and Helen Lynd's famous study of the average American "Middletown," anonymized for Muncie, Indiana, there were an estimated 200 cars in 1906; in 1923, there were 6,221, or roughly two cars for every three families. By 1925, there was one car for every 4.85 Hoosiers, compared with the national average of one car per 6.5 persons. For a more qualitative portrait of this trend, consider architecture in the suburbs, itself a development that accompanied the automobile. The overhead garage door, a commonsensical space-saving contraption, was invented in 1921, and the electric garage door opener followed five years later. "Real-estate men testify that the first question asked by the prospective buyer is about the garage," an *Atlantic Monthly* writer reported in 1925. "The house without a garage is a slow seller."[11]

Perhaps no one has better captured the automobile's transformation of American life than James Willard Hurst, professor at the Wisconsin Law School from 1937 to 1980 and trailblazer in the method of legal studies that examines the relationship between law and society (aptly called "Law and Society"). In 1949, he counted 119 "Derivative Effects of the Auto upon the Law." Some of those effects' connections to the rise of automobility are now largely taken for granted. Road trips, for example, informed no. 68 on Hurst's list: "The hotel business, with new forms such as the tourist cabin grew, giving new importance to the law of innkeepers." The necessities of manufacturing and retail appeared higher up on the list: "4. Legal devices for private economic planning—contract, franchise, parent-subsidiary corporation relationships—became important for ordering an industry that draws together diverse sources of supply." Other effects' ties to cars are still pressing, such as no. 39: "Conservation problems developed in connection with the oil industry." Or familiar, as in no. 50: "It affected the extent and types of extra-legal sex relations through the privacy and mobility it afforded." Scanning the list gives the impression that the automobile left no area of law, or aspect of everyday life, untouched.[12]

Notwithstanding Professor Hurst's insights, scholars have not studied the law or its histories through the automobile. A prominent judge skeptical of such analytical frameworks once retorted, "Isn't this just the law of the horse?" But Americans did not think of the twentieth century as the Automotive Age for nothing. Cars radically changed daily lives and aspirations, culture and the built environment, and people's relationships with each other and their communities. Even more profoundly, the automobile came to represent individual solitude and freedom. The poet Stephen Dunn described the car as a "sacred place," where one can be "in it alone, his tape deck playing / things he'd chosen." It "could take him from the need / to speak, or to answer, the key / in having a key / and putting it in, and going." These lines spoke to the hallowed privacy (*in it alone*), individual self-determination (*things he'd chosen*), and the liberating mobility (*and going*) that cars provided. Cultural productions from high art to pop culture, from Great American novels to commercials and advertisements, reinforced these widely embraced notions about driving a car. Decades before Jack Kerouac's adventures on the road, Sinclair Lewis wrote about two restless souls leaving the dullness of small-town life with an open-ended road trip in his 1919 novel *Free Air*. In 1905, Americans sang "Come away with me, Lucile / In my merry Oldsmobile / Down the road of life we'll fly." Seventy years later, Bruce Springsteen would similarly, if more desperately, belt out to Mary, "It's a town full of losers / And I'm pulling out of here to win."[13]

Movies, too, featured the automobile as a plot device or a character in its own right. *The Hitchhiker*, *Bonnie and Clyde*, and *Thelma & Louise*, to give classic examples, all portrayed road trips as a form of escape. They also depicted a darker side of freedom with these "suicide machines," as Springsteen crooned. Drivers were vulnerable to the depredations of others on the road, and lawbreakers made their getaway, whether literally to be free from the authorities or metaphorically to break free from dominant society's mores.

Despite culture's consensus, the law did not treat cars as the preeminent symbol of the right to be left alone. The regulatory and police practices that developed soon after their mass adoption were ingrained in twentieth-century American life and have remained so through the twenty-first century. Then, as now, no one could drive without taking a test, applying for a license, registering the car, and buying insurance. And that was just the beginning. Once a person set out for a drive, speed limits, stoplights, checkpoints, and all the other requirements of the traffic code restricted how one could drive. A violation of any one of these laws authorized the police to stop the vehicle, issue a ticket, and even make an arrest. If at any

FREEDOM

for the woman

who owns a Ford

To own a Ford car is to be free to venture into new and untried places. It is to answer every challenge of Nature's charms, safely, surely and without fatigue. ⸿ Where a narrow lane invites or a steep hill promises a surprise beyond, a Ford will take you there and back, in comfort, trouble-free. ⸿ Off and away in this obedient, ever-ready car, women may "recharge the batteries" of tired bodies, newly inspired for the day's work.

FORD MOTOR COMPANY, DETROIT, MICHIGAN

Ford

CLOSED CARS

Print advertisement for the 1924 Ford Model T.

Image from the Collections of The Henry Ford, THF116860.

point during the traffic stop an officer suspected drugs inside the car—or liquor in the early twentieth century—criminal procedures empowered the officer to start investigating; if the officer's suspicions were confirmed, the individual almost certainly faced arrest, a severe sentencing regime, and an "eternal" criminal record. Confronted with the authority of the police to inspect and to intrude, the automobile was not quite the unmitigated freedom machine it was celebrated to be. In fact, driving, or even just being in a car, was the most policed aspect of everyday life.[14]

This automobile paradox offers a sense of how completely cars transformed the conditions of freedom in the twentieth century. Motorized vehicles offered unprecedented mobility, but at the same time their mass adoption created mass chaos that threatened everyone's safety. Police chiefs throughout the country identified traffic as the biggest police problem of their generation—a point they repeated for several generations. Local governments passed a long list of "public rights" regulating the use of cars pursuant to their "police power," a concept, distinguished from the authority of police officers, that refers to a sovereign state's inherent power to regulate for the public welfare.[15] This response was in line with the Progressive Era's legislating frenzy. But towns and cities quickly ran into an enforcement problem: everybody violated traffic laws. Noncompliance was not a new phenomenon, but violations of the rules of the road presented a different quandary for two reasons.[16] First, drivers included respectable people, and their numbers were growing every year. Second, traffic lawbreaking resulted in tremendous damage, injury, and death, and those numbers were increasing every day. It soon became clear that the public's interest in street and highway safety required more policing. The police power not only authorized social and economic regulations; it also sanctioned the police's power. In other words, the breathtaking expansion of the police rested on the same public rights that gave rise to the modern administrative state. Without examining how cars wreaked havoc in communities throughout the United States, it is difficult to account for modern, professionalized police. Only by integrating the histories of policing and the regulatory apparatus built around cars can we capture the full scope of the police power in the twentieth century.

Certainly, policing as a mode of governance affected some groups more than others. But just as importantly, it changed the dynamic between *all* individuals and the police. Before cars, officers mainly dealt with those on the margins of society like vagrants and prostitutes. Voluntary associations governed everyone else. Churches enforced moral norms, trade groups managed business relations, and social clubs maintained social harmony. To be sure, the force of state power was palpable and vast, but the presence of the police was minimal because the "well-regulated society" of the nineteenth century, to use one historian's description, was self-regulating in that it depended largely on communal and private enforcement.[17]

Self-regulation described the domain of criminal law as well. Citizens and private groups like banks and insurance companies pursued criminal investigations and initiated prosecutions. Aside from the constable or sheriff who worked for the court and mainly executed warrants, publicly funded police figures rarely took part in private enforcement efforts. A nineteenth-century treatise on the "duties of sheriffs and constables" indicates that the bulk of their tasks was to serve summonses, warrants, and writs, as well as to supervise prisoners.[18] These were their roles even in cases of regulatory crimes that did not have a traditional victim.[19] Large cities began establishing police forces in the mid-nineteenth century, but even so, municipal coffers did not support the extent of protection that wealthier neighborhoods and business districts sought. A system of "special policemen" licensed by the government but paid for by private citizens—they were essentially private security—filled the void. As a criminal law scholar pointed out in 1936, "until quite modern times police duties were the duties of every man," meaning that communities were largely self-regulating.[20]

After the mass adoption of cars, *everyone* became subject to discretionary policing. In fact, modern policing began with the need to police upstanding citizens. The well off were among the first to buy cars, as were farmers who needed cars for more practical reasons. Even if independent farmers may not have been as wealthy as the early auto enthusiasts, as a group, they enjoyed social standing in a country with a strong sense of agrarian virtue. Driving quickly became a middle-class, or what used to be called "business-class,"

Full-page print advertisement on the cover of *Motor Age*'s March 2, 1911, issue.

Reproduced from a copy at the New York Public Library.

phenomenon by the mid-1920s, when car ownership passed a tipping point: 55.7 percent of families in the United States owned a car in 1926. Eighteen percent of those families had more than one. But even the rest of the population who did not drive and instead walked were policed, too, for the regulation of drivers on public streets also required the regulation of pedestrians on those same streets.[21]

In the age of mass consumption, when the viability of mass sales needed to standardize everyone into an average consumer, references to "Everyman" appeared regularly in cultural discourses, especially in advertisements. Everyman, and its more common variant, the "law-abiding citizen," also surfaced in legal texts and policy papers as an object of policing. That this figure showed up most prominently in these two contexts suggests how the policing of cars facilitated the buildup of police governance throughout the United States. It also pointed to a problem. Those who invoked these seemingly generic labels meant to be all-embracing. But Everyman was hardly a class-, race-, or gender-neutral figure. The term held significance precisely because it conjured a white man from a respectable class who, before the twentieth century, had largely been shielded from policing. The physician, the merchant, the salesman, the farmer, the commuter—the list went on in the 1911 Brush Runabout print ad—were now motorists whose freedom on the road somehow had to be reconciled with the necessity of police law enforcement to maintain vehicular order.

Policing cars created conundrums both profound and practical. How could a democratic society founded on self-governance depend on police governance and still be free, an especially freighted question during ideological wars against authoritarian police states? And more delicately, how could the laws be fashioned to allow the investigation of potential criminal suspects without harassing law-abiding citizens when everybody drove? This was especially challenging with standardized cars that made it hard to tell the difference between the dangerous traffic violator and the ordinary one. Judges may have preferred to avoid these thorny questions, but litigant-drivers forced courts to look past their own guilt and consider Everyman when defining the difference between democratic policing and arbitrary policing, between a free society and a totalitarian regime.

These occasions usually arose in disputes over the Fourth Amendment, which states in full:

> The right of the people to be secure in their persons, houses, papers, and effects, against unreasonable searches and seizures, shall not be violated, and no Warrants shall issue, but upon probable cause, supported by Oath or affirmation, and particularly

describing the place to be searched, and the persons or things to be seized.

Because the first moment in a police encounter is a stop, otherwise known as a "seizure" of a person, which could then be followed by a "search," the guarantee against unreasonable searches and seizures was the main provision governing the police, whether in the US Constitution or state constitutions—"the Fourth Amendment," for the sake of simplicity. In the twentieth century, when many interactions with the police took place during a vehicle stop, one of the most litigated issues in criminal procedure was whether officers needed a warrant to stop and search a car. At stake in this legal question was the very legitimacy of discretion at the heart of police governance. Requiring officers to get a warrant from a magistrate would hold up their efforts to proactively investigate crime. Conversely, eliminating the warrant requirement would allow the police to act according to their own judgment. In adjudicating Fourth Amendment car cases, then, judges were, at bottom, redrawing the boundaries of legitimate policing.

The automobile served as the main setting for working out difficult questions about the police's power not only because its mass adoption prompted the changes in policing. It also undermined the public/private distinction, the cornerstone of nineteenth-century constitutional law. Cars were private property, which should have given individuals all the private rights attached to ownership and possession, including the Fourth Amendment rule that officers have warrants for searches and seizures. But cars traveled on public roads and were subject to public rights, and early twentieth-century judges believed that the warrant requirement did not apply in the public sphere of regulation and policing. In a legal tradition that hewed to categorical reasoning, judges floundered in their attempts to protect both individual expectations of the private sphere and the public's interest in orderly and crime-free highways. The need for police protection and protection from policing collided in Fourth Amendment car cases. Judges grappled with the warrant question precisely because robust police powers and equally robust ideas about the freedom of automobility had developed, paradoxically, in tandem.

Justice Louis Brandeis embodied this contradiction. He believed, more confidently than his associates on the Supreme Court, that officers had the constitutional authority to search ships on the high seas and cars on public highways without warrants. At the same time, his dissent in the 1928 case *Olmstead v. United States* marked the first appearance of the right "to be let alone" from government intrusion in a Supreme Court opinion. Within half a century, Brandeis's "right to privacy" provided moral and legal authority for *Griswold v. Connecticut*, a 1965 case that established the fundamental right of married couples to use contraceptives, which, in turn, set off a series of cases staking rights to personal and sexual autonomy.[22] How did Brandeis reconcile a far-reaching power to govern with a visionary right of privacy? This was the great struggle in the twentieth-century United States. When American society shifted to policing as a mode of governance, the defense of liberty was not simply about restricting the police's power. When Everyman turned into a perpetrator on the road and Everyman depended on state protection from every other perpetrator, the challenge was to figure out how to incorporate policing within the meaning of freedom itself.

Examining the spate of car cases in state and federal courts that began in the 1920s and persisted throughout the century reveals a startling revelation: Fourth Amendment jurisprudence evolved not just to limit police discretion, as we have learned, but also to accommodate it. This conclusion is at odds with most accounts of twentieth-century criminal procedure. The familiar story, in brief, goes something like this: Beginning in the 1960s, the Warren Court overthrew the traditional arrangement in which federal courts left local police matters to the states in order to protect minorities and the poor. *Overthrew* is an appropriate word, considering that scholars refer to this as the Due Process *Revolution*. What was so revolutionary was the judicial creation of a national standard of criminal procedure. Put simply, the US Supreme Court began policing the police.[23]

But the standard narrative provides only half the story, not least because its emphasis on the conflict between individuals and the police overlooks the foundational shift to policing as a mode of governance. Fourth Amendment cases first shot up not in the 1960s, but in the 1920s, and not just in federal courts, but in state courts as well. A few scholars have traced the roots of the Due Process Revolution to the earlier period, and the main thrust of these accounts is that judges felt compelled to protect criminal defendants from flagrant police abuse, whether during National Prohibition or in the Jim Crow South. These histories, like the chronicles of the Warren Court, place the Supreme Court in the role of protector of individual liberty to explain the proliferation of criminal procedure rights in the twentieth century.[24]

But, in fact, American courts did more to encourage and sustain, rather than to check, the police's growing authority. This can be easy to miss if we look only at the Supreme Court's landmark cases. Instances where the police acted unlawfully and egregiously so—when, for example, they invaded a home, the most sacrosanct space in American constitutional law—presented easier cases for the Supreme Court to act boldly in the name of upholding democratic ideals. *Mapp v. Ohio*, which launched the Due Process Revolution in 1961, was such a case. More challenging were the matters where the exercise of discretion was seen as a crucial part of the police function. Once we examine the celebrated decisions alongside the underbelly of criminal procedure—the thousands of car cases that justified police action—the judicial endorsement of greater discretionary policing becomes undeniable.

To resolve the conflict between public and private rights in these car cases—to simultaneously empower discretionary policing for Everyman's safety and shield Everyman's privacy from discretionary policing—American law shifted from a binary analysis to a standard of reasonableness. Instead of deciding whether cars fell within the public or private sphere to determine whether stops and searches of cars, as a category, required warrants or not, judges evaluated whether a particular car stop and search was reasonable. Even Justice Brandeis, upon conceding that the right to privacy could ultimately be subject to the public's interest, resorted to "the reasonableness or unreasonableness of an act" to determine the boundary between competing rights. The *Wiley* right to drive "without interruption or molestation" quickly receded as a relic of the horse-and-buggy days. Captain Bates would now have to pull over, but at least he would be dealt with reasonably.[25]

But it proved difficult to pin down a definition of reasonable policing, let alone flesh out a coherent theory for determining reasonableness, when patrolling the byways and highways presented a myriad of unexpected situations and often involved split-second decision-making. What jurisprudential philosophy could both enable and limit police discretion? Rather than settling on a principle, judges deferred to the police. When faced with the exigencies of automobility—and especially when those caught red-handed, not the wrongly suspected, were typically the ones who brought Fourth Amendment challenges—judges tended to side with order and security and conclude that zealous and intrusive police action for the sake of the public welfare was reasonable and did not compromise the values of a democratic society. In case after case, throughout the country and through the decades, courts concluded that the police had acted reasonably. Every now and then, an individual defendant won. But far more often, reasonableness functioned as a deferential standard. This deference, in turn, gave the police even more power. From the perspective of cars, the Due Process Revolution was not much of an overthrow of the existing order.

But the Court's revolutionary decisions left an opening for an insurgency, even if ultimately ill-fated. Increasing numbers of criminal defendants invoked the new rights established in home invasion cases and disputed the reasonableness of police action, forcing courts to mediate their encounters with police. Over time and without a consistent method or principle, all the individual reasonableness determinations accumulated into judicial rules, which became more numerous, more specific, and more complex. Scholars refer to the body of laws accrued from legal challenges against the police as "the modern regime of criminal procedure." These laws are procedural in the sense that they direct *how* the police should police, unlike substantive rights, which secure the right to be free from government, including police, intrusion. As illuminating as accounts of the Warren Court are, they do not explain why the justices settled on procedural rights to protect individuals from the police, rather than, for example, a substantive privacy right not to have one's car searched. It is easy to understand why minorities and the poor needed more rights. But standard narratives of the Due Process Revolution have passed over the more basic question of why those rights took the form they did.[26]

In truth, more significant than the choice between substance and procedure was the decision over how Americans would govern themselves. Because substantive rights would have greatly limited the discretionary policing that the "law abiding" wanted, minorities and the poor instead received rules regulating the police's ever-growing power. The upshot, as time would tell, was not the protection of individuals' privacy in their cars but the empowerment of highway patrollers and traffic cops who could take advantage of the thicket of procedures to exercise their power in discretionary, even discriminatory, ways. This was the legacy of the Fourth Amendment from the Automotive Age. By the end of the century, the Fourth Amendment was still in search of a theory. As the automobile became a site of inequality, it was also an area of law that lacked a theory of justice.

1

A Mystery of Traffic

The supreme rule of the road is the rule of mutual forbearance.

Judge Cardozo, *Ward v. Clark* (1921)

At the base of all popular government lies individual self-control.

Elihu Root, "The Citizen's Part in Government" (1916)

AMERICA WAS NOT ready for the mass production of the automobile. At the turn of the century, thousands of motorized vehicles on Main Streets originally intended for pedestrians and horse-drawn carriages suddenly choked intersections and gave new meaning to the word "traffic." Before mass-produced cars, even New York City's Broadway had provided enough space that carriage drivers usually did not hesitate before making a turn. Afterward, they had to contend with horseless carriages for every square inch. Narrower streets, many unpaved, simply could not handle the traffic that piled up, and municipal officials were caught unprepared to deal with the chaos. "If the automobile had existed fifty years ago," one commentator wrote wistfully in 1916, "our city 'dads' would have looked at the laying out of a city from an entirely different angle." Movement stalled in every town large enough to have a commercial district, prompting then US secretary of commerce Herbert Hoover to declare a national crisis. "Are we consuming the new living conveniences faster than we can digest them?" he questioned. "Are we not like one who overeats?" While Secretary Hoover analogized automotive congestion to indigestion, another observer deemed traffic "a bugaboo, an ogre, and an everything else one could desire to call it."[1]

These "machines," as cars were sometimes called in the early years, also posed an unprecedented threat to public safety. Pedestrians accustomed to horses trotting on roads at about five to ten miles per hour were taken aback by motor-powered vehicles whose speed was limited—by law, not by mechanics—to between thirty and fifty miles per hour. Even drivers seemed surprised by how fast they could go, judging by the number of accidents that occurred from failure to slow down when turning corners. So were horses that were easily startled by the noises that cars made, which created another hazard. The previously mundane act of crossing the street or walking on the sidewalk now risked life and limb. Stories appeared regularly in newspapers of cars jumping curbs, plowing into pedestrians, and violently flinging bystanders. Automobile fatalities had become so common that by 1935, a reporter for *Harper's Monthly Magazine* declared, "In these deaths by motor cars, there was no news."[2]

Data from the National Safety Council showed that between 1913 and 1932, deaths from car accidents increased 500 percent; during the same period, the death rate for all other accidents dropped 42 percent. A more dramatic measure was to compare vehicular deaths with the American casualties of the recent Great War. In the 1920s, articles on the traffic problem frequently mentioned that during those nineteen months, the loss of life from car accidents was twice the loss of life from war. By 1930, the comparisons shifted to the crime wave. More than four times as many people died in automobile accidents as from crime, a statistic that "might be startling were it not so familiar," rued one police chief. He consulted another report that calculated the cost of accidents and traffic delays to be more than $2.5 billion a year, about the equivalent of the total estimated cost of crime. In another eye-opening comparison, this figure added up to "more money than we spent for all of our schools, colleges and universities, public and private, for the same period."[3]

The first response of local governments confronting traffic snarls and car accidents was to do what they had always done: pass laws based on their well-established "police power," a legal concept that referred to a sovereign's inherent power to regulate for the public's health, safety, and welfare.[4] That was exactly what the Fresno Board of Supervisors did when it limited automotive speed to thirty miles per hour. To enforce the speed limit, the board posted the following sign:

Speed sign in Fresno, California, 1915.

Popular Mechanics 24, no. 2 (August 1915): 241. Reproduced from a copy at the University of Iowa Library.

In 1916, the Iowa State Highway Commission lobbied for a similar enforcement plan after hearing that it was "working splendidly" in Bucyrus, Ohio, because the "reasonable motorist is ashamed to drive other than moderately." But the experiment with the honor system was short lived. Later that year, *Popular Mechanics* reported that "a traffic officer was again resorted to" in Fresno County and that the signs were "now for sale" after too many motorists "apparently interpreted [the signs] to mean that road races were in order and that their engines alone determined the speed limit."[5]

The traffic crisis lasted for as long as it did because, to offer a diagnosis with the perspective of history, the automobile introduced a massive technological innovation that wreaked disorder at the very same time that it destabilized existing institutions for maintaining order. In the first decades of the unfolding Automotive Age through the 1930s, authorities dealt with the traffic problem by reaching for familiar tools of governance, all the while grasping for new ideas. They were quickly discovering that the assumptions underlying older forms of social control—namely, the expectation that reasonable people would abide by the law out of a sense of decency or shame— were woefully archaic in the twentieth century. Nineteenth-century enforcement tools proved disastrously inadequate in the anonymous, fast, and crowded world of automobility. In the search for solutions to the death and mayhem wrought by mass-produced cars, officials everywhere grappled with a fundamental puzzle: *why did law-abiding citizens disobey traffic laws?*

In 1924, dean of Harvard Law School Roscoe Pound reminisced about the days of horses and buggies, when traffic had been governed in the same way as every other human activity. The "law said to us a very simple thing: adhere to the standard of what a reasonably prudent man would do, at your peril of liability in case you guess wrong." This common law of negligence had sufficed when the "chance of one farmer injuring another one with a lumber wagon, was pretty remote, and the chance of anybody, while driving the family horse down the road, running over anybody was pretty remote." In a slower, less cramped era, individuals worked out and enforced community norms among themselves, and when their disagreements resulted in unresolvable injury or loss, they could take it to the courts to determine who was at fault. "In the old days there was no such thing as a jaywalker," Pound recalled, because one "could cross the street wherever you pleased, subject to your liability for negligence."[6]

Pound's invocation of "the old days" betrayed a bit of nostalgic exaggeration. Even in the nineteenth century, at least in denser urban areas, local ordinances had regulated traffic, which included speed limits for horses on public streets, typically around eight miles an hour. For instance, 1870s Louisiana authorized its policemen "within the metropolitan district" to "regulate the movement of teams and vehicles in the streets and roads." In the same decade, Los Angeles also began experiencing a bit of traffic, so its police chief was tasked with "prohibiting the grazing or herding of cattle in the streets." Many towns and cities had enough carriages, carts, and wagons, on top of animals and pedestrians, that created congestion in their business districts that they delegated traffic management to the police, who even made a few arrests for speeding. For fiscal year 1902, police in Los Angeles made a total of thirty-nine arrests for "fast driving."[7]

Still, Pound's memory was generally accurate that custom and common sense—"what a reasonably prudent man would do"—dictated the rules of the road more than police officers or legislative enactments. Even in the cities, the flow of movement on streets and highways was largely self-regulated, and traffic laws appeared mainly in collision cases between private parties who argued over whether an alleged violation demonstrated negligence.[8]

The older way of coordinating social behavior fostered what Pound called a "pioneer" concept of freedom that "stressed the limitations upon interference with individual liberty." Each person judged "for himself at the crisis of action whether and how far to obey or enforce the law as it stands in the books," limited mainly by potential liability and community disapproval. The foundation of a free society was built on individual self-reliance and "self-assertion," which added up to self-government in the aggregate.[9]

But "self-reliance, impatience of regulations, and faith in one's individual judgment at the crisis of action, are not tolerable in action when displayed by drivers of motor vehicles," Pound noted. With "the advent of automobiles, motor trucks, pleasure vehicles, and motorcycles," he pointed out, "the law cannot exactly say to us, well, both of you fellows guess at your peril, and if you guess wrong, one or both of you will have to answer." To be sure, injured parties in car accidents continued to sue for tort damages, as a fourteen-volume treatise on the law of automobiles, first published in 1927, indicates. But the sheer number of cars required constant coordination even when the unrelenting chaos did not amount to litigable claims. As Pound observed, a "freedom of that kind" that had existed before now "impedes traffic, it imperils life, it creates an impossible tangle in our highways." Nineteenth-century self-regulation was unsuited for the sudden influx of thousands of fast-moving cars on the public roads.[10]

Local governments responded swiftly by enacting laws and more laws. In addition to speed limits and license requirements, new regulations mandated safety equipment, like nonglaring headlights, rearview mirrors, and, in Massachusetts, at least two brakes for cars with horsepower greater than ten. They also prohibited motorized vehicles on certain roads; determined who among cars, horses, carriages, and pedestrians had the right of way; and specified how fast a car could overtake horse-drawn coaches and trolleys. According to one legal eagle, San Francisco even regulated "the angle at which motorists should make turns from one street into another." In a short time, the number of regulations multiplied exponentially. In 1905, three years before the introduction of Ford's Model T, a treatise on municipal corporations mentioned the automobile in just one line: "Bicycles, tricycles and automobiles are ordinarily considered vehicles and entitled to the use of that part of the street or highway set aside for them." Tellingly, another treatise published just seven years later in 1912 devoted two entire sections to the regulation of "the running of automobiles." An observer in 1920 noted that the "enormously increased traffic has given birth to laws that are now almost countless," to the point that they could "fill a separate manual to overflowing and their number is added to at each session of the legislatures." "When will they end?" he groaned. "Is it to be wondered at that the adjournment of Congress and the state legislatures brings a universal sigh of relief?" another commentator wrote more sarcastically. "So numerous [were] the . . . laws regulating traffic," a police chief asserted in 1936, "that few indeed are the persons who can travel the streets or highways without violating one or many of them every hour of the day."[11]

Suddenly, misdemeanors became mainstream. Violations were committed "up town, down town, all around town," one New York paper rhymed. Another reporter from the Empire City explained this phenomenon based on his personal experience getting a driver's license in 1921. The written portion of New York's application included the following questions: "Are you thoroughly familiar with

the New York State Motor Vehicle law? General Highway Traffic
law? New York City Traffic Ordinances and Police Traffic Regulations?" The *New York Times* writer's cheeky response was: "Who
is?"—confirming the reality that no one knew, and therefore no one
could obey, all the laws. Right before his road test, a fellow applicant
advised him to watch out if the examiner "tells ye to pull up. Chances
are ye'll be 'longside a fire hydrant." "Why that?" the writer inquired
"innocently." He learned right then and there that it was against the
law to stop within fifteen feet of a hydrant. A traffic engineer for
the state of Massachusetts, extrapolating from an early 1930s study
of a typical intersection and assuming similar conditions at all other
intersections in the same city, concluded that approximately 2.5 million traffic violations occurred daily. The proliferation of traffic laws
had turned everyone who drove a car into a lawbreaker.[12]

Lawbreaking posed a great problem at a time when American society was shifting from custom-based to law-based modes of governance. Roscoe Pound perceived this shift in his 1930 tome *Criminal
Justice in America* when noting the increasing number of titles and
chapters in state penal codes. Taking Rhode Island as a representative example, he determined that the number of crimes on the books
had more than doubled from the General Statutes of 1872 to the
General Laws of 1923. Pound also reported that out of the 100,000
arrests made in Chicago in 1912, more than half were for violations
that had not existed twenty-five years earlier. If the common law established the basis of nineteenth-century society, then the criminal
laws were laying the foundation of the twentieth-century state.
Widespread failure to obey traffic codes was one manifestation of a
larger issue that bedeviled progressive state builders: the necessity
of legal compliance with positive laws that were not necessarily
rooted in moral values but that nevertheless benefited society at
large.[13]

While local governments were dealing with the traffic problem,
the country undertook the "noble experiment" with the ratification
of the Eighteenth Amendment. "Drys" believed that ending the consumption of alcohol—or at least vastly reducing it by prohibiting its
manufacture, sale, and transport—would keep families together, cultivate more productive workers, and even eliminate the corrupting

Cartoon from the October 1, 1925, issue of *Ford News*.

Image from the Collections of The Henry Ford, THF136478.

power of the brewing and distilling monopolies. When Americans defied National Prohibition by purchasing intoxicating drink, Congress made antiliquor laws harsher by passing the Increased Penalties Act. The move quickly backfired when the law's severity—it made even the mere failure to report a violation a felony—seemed only to encourage even more brazen lawbreaking. Given the national incorrigibility, a legal commentator presented the following options: If Americans were serious about drying out their communities, then they needed to spend "an enormous amount of money" to secure "a large enough police force" to ensure compliance. But if "the preservation of a good civic spirit" was more important, "then the only solution is to do away with mala prohibita"—that is, conduct that was wrong simply because the law forbid it. As it turned out, the inability to enforce antiliquor laws contributed to Prohibition's demise and called into question the promise of positive laws. One minister of the Gospel proclaimed that "there must be deeper motives to quit drinking booze than man's laws." If the preacher was right, then the governance of a modernizing, complex, and interdependent society would be crippled without solving the related issues of compliance and enforcement.[14]

Herbert Hoover, now as president of the United States, warned in his 1929 inaugural address that even more was at stake. He called out "disregard and disobedience of law" as the "most malign" danger to "government by the people." He referred not only to mobsters and bootleggers who flourished during Prohibition but also to the "large numbers of law-abiding citizens" who disrespected the law with their purchase and consumption of alcohol. "Our whole system of self-government will crumble," Hoover warned, if "citizens elect what laws they will support," for the "worst evil of disregard for some law is that it destroys respect for all law." Chief Justice William Howard Taft shared these sentiments, declaring that "every loyal citizen must obey. This is the fundamental principle of free government." According to the heads of the executive and judicial branches of the United States, liberty depended on individuals to put law above personal desires. Taft was most exasperated with the "well-to-do class, the intelligent part of the community," who were "not willing to give up something that isn't essential to their life or happiness, and insist upon violating the law because they don't like it." He indicted those who failed to exercise self-discipline as having "something of the autocratic spirit," for "he is willing to govern, but not to be governed." Many other prominent jurists and statesmen reiterated the message that a free society was a self-governing society, which required the obedience of every citizen. Pervasive defiance of both liquor and traffic laws not only dimmed optimism that positive laws could be used to improve social conditions; it also led to a breakdown of ordered liberty and threatened the workability of American democracy.[15]

There was, however, an important difference between automotive traffic and the trafficking of spirituous drink. The American public was sharply divided on the policy of prohibiting alcohol. Those who opposed the Eighteenth Amendment argued that drinking was natural—even Jesus turned water into wine, one judge pointed out. Noncompliance marked an act of protest against judgmental reformers or a daring embrace of cosmopolitan lifestyles. In sharp contrast, the social utility of regulating vehicular travel was much harder to controvert.[16]

Certainly, traffic laws, like prohibition laws, established *mala prohibita*—acts that were wrong only by virtue of statute. No inherent sense of morality deemed, for example, driving at the speed of twenty-two miles per hour a per se evil like murder or theft. Still, many traffic violations, especially when they resulted in tragedy, did incite righteous outrage. More and more, careless or reckless driving shocked people's moral intuitions, even if what constituted an obvious depravity on the road could not be pinned down as clearly as aiming a gun or filching a wallet. Some, however, thought the two comparable, pondering in "what way is the driver who races through a Safety zone different from the man who carries a loaded revolver through our streets?" Courts recognized this threat by treating certain traffic offenses as *malum in se*, an evil in and of itself. In 1930, the US Supreme Court decided that a violation of Section 9 of the District of Columbia's Traffic Act, which set a speed limit of twenty-two miles per hour on "any public highway in the District," was *malum in se*, which accordingly required a jury trial. The offense had a "serious" rather than "petty" character, the opinion reasoned, because an "automobile [was] a dangerous instrumentality, as the appalling number of fatalities brought about every day by its operation bear distressing witness."[17]

Given the fatal toll on society, it was difficult for municipal officials to understand why otherwise law-abiding citizens persisted in violating traffic laws. Even Herbert Hoover "doesn't always obey his own safety rules," the papers reported in 1925, back when he was secretary of commerce and was heading the national movement for street and highway safety. "Dressed in immaculate white flannels and blue coat," he was spotted jaywalking on H Street, near the Commerce Building, having "wormed his way thru one lane of parked cars." He stepped out "directly in the path of a big limousine," which had to slam to a sudden halt to allow "the distinguished safety expert" to "narrowly escape[] being run over." Hoover, of all people, would have known the statistics identifying lawbreaking pedestrians as one of the leading causes of auto accidents.[18]

Of course, disobedience is human nature. Even the upright slip every now and then. But transgressions of the traffic code presented a new predicament. For one thing, the magnitude of the consequences often proved disproportionate to the seeming triviality of the violation. Failure to slow down while turning, for instance, could result in the deaths of innocent passengers or passersby. These accidents were not uncommon, as statistics amply demonstrated. According to the National Safety Council, the two decades from 1909 to 1929 experienced an increase in "the number of motor vehicles by more than 8400 per cent and the number of accidental deaths by more than 2400 per cent, while the national population was increasing by about 33 per cent." Just as significantly, almost everybody disobeyed traffic laws. From his years of overseeing traffic in Berkeley, California, Police Chief August Vollmer observed countless drivers who failed to act lawfully, let alone in consideration of the safety of others, cutting in and out of traffic, failing to signal when changing directions, driving recklessly, and committing all the other "countless violations of both the legal and the moral laws of the road." Even the "drawingroom gentleman" was not immune from turning into a "road hog" who "with a smile steals the right of way." Municipal officials dealing with the sudden onslaught of motor vehicles confronted the troubling realization that normally law-abiding citizens violated traffic laws to everyone's detriment. Now the general population, drivers and walkers alike, became the problem.[19]

This was an uncomfortable fact. Notwithstanding the democratizing appeals of mass-produced cars, the media racialized drivers from the automobile's earliest years. Not many African Americans owned or drove cars in the 1910s and 1920s, although exactly how many is uncertain. No statistic on black car ownership existed until the mid-1930s, even though the US Census Bureau had been keeping track of information like "Type of Access Road Leading to Black Farms by Farm Location" (there were nine types). From this, one can surmise the relative prevalence of black drivers versus black farmers. In 1935 Atlanta, Georgia, one of the few cities that counted car ownership by race at the time, 17 percent of all black families had a car, compared with 63 percent of white families. For minorities, driving remained an elite prerogative until well after World War II. Disregarding their respectability, white journalists, travel writers, and photographers often portrayed black drivers as incapable of handling the modern technology. When, in 1910, the legendary black boxer Jack Johnson—who had just defeated the "Great White Hope" Jim Jeffries in the "fight of the century"—challenged the top-ranked racecar driver Barney Oldfield, mainstream papers, the *New York Times* among them, highlighted his traffic violations to suggest that he was a reckless driver and a public threat. In 1913, Johnson was arrested twice and ultimately convicted of violating the Mann Act for transporting—presumably driving—a white woman, a former paramour, across state lines for "immoral purposes." (He received a presidential pardon in 2018.) Black newspapers sought to counter stereotypes and bad press with profiles of successful black drivers, auto mechanics, inventors, chauffeuring entrepreneurs, and driving instructors. But most persuasive in convincing government leaders that traffic violations were not a "racial habit," as one writer admitted, was the daily display of citizens of every race, ethnicity, age, and gender who committed them. Lawbreaking was done "by children and by adults; it is done by frolicking urchins, by dignified merchants, by heedless flappers and by staid women of mature years," the reporter observed. This perhaps explains why, unlike the ideations of white culture, official documents and discourses on the traffic problem rarely mentioned race.[20]

When it came to self-reflection, most drivers did not consider themselves delinquent even when they violated the rules of the road. In the history of cars, "law-abiding" referred to upstanding traffic lawbreakers. Illustrating this belief was the response that the police often received: "I'm not doing any harm. Why don't you catch a few burglars for yourselves instead of bothering good citizens?" Even the New Yorker who wrote candidly that no citizen followed all the traffic laws still believed that "the great majority of motorists . . . are honest, law-abiding, decent folks." This dissonance was certainly not new. But in the early twentieth century, it frequently resulted in disaster, leaving policymakers bewildered that so many ordinary citizens resolutely disobeyed traffic laws.[21]

When Police Chief August Vollmer observed the main thorough- fares of Berkeley in the early hours of the day when there was no traffic, he found it "very difficult to conceive how accidents can occur on these streets." Nothing in the conditions of the roads themselves foreshadowed scenes of collisions and pileups. Vollmer also did not think that mechanical issues, like "defective brakes, defective head- lights, steering gear and whatnot," caused most accidents. From his daily observations, he came to the inescapable conclusion that the source of the problem was human.[22]

By the early 1920s, Vollmer joined the nationwide call for driver's license exams to verify mental and physical abilities. At the time, traffic studies had identified "a group of automobile drivers who are prone to accidents, due to their mentality, their habits, and their attitude toward the rights of others." Dr. Walter Bingham, who chaired the Causes of Accidents Committee at the US Department of Commerce, accordingly recommended that local governments establish clinics for reckless drivers. More feasibly, experts roundly agreed that epileptics, the insane, and the feebleminded should not be licensed to drive. They also sought exclusions based on minority of age, physical incapacitation, and illiteracy. In the age of women's suffrage, no one mentioned sex as a disqualification.[23]

But the consensus view among laypeople was that bad driving af- flicted the entire motoring population. "Some scientist should analyze" the "careless disregard for elementary caution on the highways and tell the nation what strange complex is responsible," suggested an observer stumped by this "mystery of traffic." Vollmer proposed that a peace officer vouch for the "moral fitness" of each applicant. He did not elaborate on the moral characteristics of suitable drivers, but he provided clues in his frequent declarations that most accidents resulted from "thoughtlessness and carelessness," or in other words, "just plain everyday discourtesy." After going over the findings of one study, he concluded that "it was perfectly clear that some great power was protecting [drivers and pedestrians] because so many things were done that must of necessity have otherwise led to disaster." A traffic officer shared similar testimony, confessing how he "didn't use to believe in a kind Providence, a power that watches over humanity—but [he did] now for otherwise the papers would carry headlines every day like this: 'Six Hundred Men, Women and Children Killed in Automobile Accidents on Main Street.'" Those charged with traffic duty soon learned that they "cannot overlook the fact that selfishness, one of the commonly inherent tendencies of humankind, is very largely responsible for accidents."[24]

Of course, some were worse than the average selfish human being. There were people who, in Vollmer's account, "step[ped] on the accelerator instead of the brake and crash[ed] into the pedestrian and, after knocking down the pedestrian, again step[ped] on the accelerator instead of the brake." A similar scenario actually served as a plot device in *The Great Gatsby*, when Daisy, absorbed in a love triangle, recklessly runs over her husband's mistress and flees the scene. But aside from extreme or literary examples, any traffic officer could point to mounting evidence of the "contempt for the rights of fellow men." Something inexplicable happened when a person got behind the wheel. Vollmer found that even the mildest-mannered person seemed "to lose all sense of mental, emotional, and moral balance as soon as he puts his foot on the starter of an automobile." Municipal leaders were flummoxed that motorists' personal experience of automotive freedom had somehow devolved into an "every man for himself and the devil take the hindmost" attitude.[25]

In these vertigo years of accelerating speed, Roscoe Pound wrote about how technological innovations—he dubbed them "agencies of menace"—like the automobile, the radio, and the moving picture seemed to magnify "conscious and aggressive individual self-assertion," which, in turn, increased the "points at which the claims and desires of each individual and those of his fellows conflict or overlap." Confirming Pound's opinion, the drama of clashing individual interests played out daily on congested roads and highways taken over by the automobile.[26]

More than any other technology, the automobile had enlarged perceptions of the self. Granted, other inventions had already begun to inflate people's regard of their place in the natural world. The steamboat stoked the hubris that humans could harness nature for their own purposes, electricity extended human productivity by illuminating the night, and the locomotive train enabled the conquest of vast stretches of land in comfort and style. But automobiles, as individualized carriages of transport, offered a wholly new sense of empowerment. Never before had individuals been able to outrun the fastest beast. The horse's gallop, which reached around thirty miles an hour, must have seemed like a mere trot compared to motor-powered cars with a top speed of at least sixty miles an hour, and that was in the 1920s. More importantly, unlike the steamboat or train, the automobile enabled individuals to decide when and where to go, freeing them from the tyranny of timetables and fixed routes of public transportation. Each person behind the wheel handled the machine and controlled his or her destiny, and many drivers experienced automobility as the agent of their freedom and self-determination. A 1909 *Harper's Weekly* article marveled at "the ability to go where and when one wills" in a car. Another writer at the turn of the century reveled in the ability "to really travel again, as free men, free to decide, in the free air." If the train had changed how people viewed the world by facilitating travel between great distances, then the automobile transformed how people viewed themselves by empowering them to drive to any destination of their choosing.[27]

The transformation was even more radical for underestimated and exploited groups, for whom driving demonstrated their skill, mobility, and liberation. Advertisers trumpeted the freedom—albeit a domesticated version—"for the woman who owns a Ford." The "closed car" enabled the female driver "to venture into new and untried places . . . safely, surely and without fatigue." In reality, this meant that women could travel in public in their own enclosed spaces, free from unwanted glances and touches. Still, many women felt a greater sense of independence and competence as they mastered the new technology and broadened their "sphere of action." Driving was no easy feat, especially before the invention of the electric starter in the early 1920s. Manual cranking involved not only automotive know-how but also a possible sprain to the wrist and the prospect that the engine could backfire. Aside from mechanical issues, motorists often had to maneuver unpaved roads, which could pose hazards, especially after a wet spell. "Choose your ruts carefully: you'll be in them for a long time," was one common tip. Notwithstanding these pitfalls, many women drove. Four years before the Nineteenth Amendment, *Popular Mechanics* declared that "women are as capable of driving motor cars as are men." Women had a powerful ally against naysayers: automobile manufacturers and dealers who sought to expand their markets. By 1928, one commentator remarked that anybody "who doesn't realize how completely woman has been 'emancipated,' as people used to call it, should watch the automobiles." They would have seen that about 24 percent of the driving population was female.[28]

Likewise, after World War I, a small but emerging black middle class eagerly sought the markers and privileges of their economic status. The motoring lifestyle represented racial progress, one that speedily trickled down. By the mid-1930s, even some black tenant farmers in the South scraped together everything they had to buy a secondhand car. According to an early twentieth-century sociologist, the "feel of power, even in an old automobile, [was] most satisfying to a man who owns nothing, directs nothing." Becoming "machinery wise," the ability to drive as fast as the richest planter in the county, and the opportunity to travel "incognito" in a covered car without constantly confronting the significance of their skin color gave southern blacks a taste of the mobility, freedom, and equality that otherwise had not materialized after Reconstruction. What they encountered once they stepped out into the world of white commerce was another matter. Beginning in 1936, *The Negro Motorist Green Book* helped black drivers navigate Jim Crow on the road by compiling a directory of lodgings and restaurants that would serve them.

The modern woman—in flapper dress, with short hair, and driving
a car—circa 1930.

Keystone View Company, Prints & Photographs Division, Library of Congress,
LC-USZ62-122386.

Although driving in a racist society diminished the liberating
potential of the automobile, scholars have highlighted the ways that
African Americans, as well as women, were able to use "the driver's
seat as a sort of podium from which they staked their citizenship
claims."[29]

Paradoxically, the automobile had a homogenizing effect as well.
On the one hand, its mass production made it possible for greater

numbers to drive their own cars, which reinforced people's sense of individuality. But at the same time, it was precisely the necessity of standard construction that rendered their individualities the same. As one early commentator noted, "these machines largely resemble[d] each other in construction and color." One auto company tried to capitalize on this limitation with the tag line "The Brush Runabout is truly Everyman's Car." More commercially successful was Ford's "universal car." To one judge, the sight of standardized, dark-hued vehicles parading down thoroughfares of travel conjured images of their having taken "possession of our highways in battalions." Drivers even looked the same, according to *Popular Mechanics*, with their faces "covered by masks, goggles or veils." These accessories were especially useful in the early period of uncovered cars, whose production out-numbered that of closed cars until 1925. But even through the 1930s, before the invention of mass-produced sunglasses, "heavy colored goggles" that covered one-third of the face were worn to shield the eyes from glare. In addition to physical uniformity, daily routines—leaving for work, working, returning from work—became more regimented and standardized.[30]

But Roscoe Pound argued that even standardization could feed individualism. In his estimation, "a certain inferiority complex" grew out of living a uniform life that "led to insistence on self-assertion in the form of exceptional conduct, of being different, of flying in the face of conventions, of doing shocking things." People insisted that "no two are alike," demanded special treatment, and "claim[ed] to be judged by the measure of themselves." The automobile, along with the radio and other readily available goods, fed those demands as it fueled consumption and offered "a bewildering multiplicity of diversions, demanded by all as of course." Materialism drew attention to the self with the lure of self-transformation and self-expression. By driving, the advertisements promised, one could become modern, independent, and carefree—never mind that a vast majority of Americans had to borrow money or mortgage their homes to purchase their cars. In fact, installment plans took off and consumer debt gained middle-class respectability with the automobile.[31]

In addition to heightening individual self-regard, cars played a significant role in undermining the conditions that had fostered local, custom-based methods of ensuring conformity to community norms. In the nineteenth century, self-governing associations like churches, trade unions, clubs, and fraternities maintained social order by instilling civic spirit and setting forth the rights and duties of their members. When people could not resolve disputes among themselves—and all disputes could be boiled down to disagreements about rights and duties owed to each other—judges and juries decided how the common law would govern the situation. When someone breached a social or legal norm, the aggrieved person brought the offender before a justice of the peace to settle the matter. Through this "judicial patriarchy," lives were regulated and disciplined. Both associational and common-law governance were local in scale, and proximity and regular contact among members and neighbors made accountability possible and effective.[32]

These older methods of enforcement began breaking down with cars. To be sure, nineteenth-century Americans had seemed constantly on the move. But the mobility that the automobile enabled was unprecedented. As Hoover phrased it rather poetically in 1924, "Locality has been annihilated, distance has been folded up into a pocket piece." In 1930, Chief Vollmer continued to marvel that "cities and villages one hundred miles apart today are in closer proximity than cities and villages fifteen miles apart were thirty-five years ago." People drove across city, county, and state lines in mere minutes or hours rather than days, which enlarged the spheres of work and play. Factories could hire workers who lived farther away, and many businessmen carried on their economic lives in commercial centers with one set of associates and their social lives near their homes with a different set. The result, Pound observed, was that the neighborhood ceased to be a "social and economic unit," and "neighborhood opinion" no longer served as an effective social control mechanism. Moreover, when people's jobs were located in a different jurisdiction from their place of residence, they seemed to grow more indifferent to local politics. According to Pound, the severance of the "essential relation" between the political and economic weakened institutions like guilds, which in the nineteenth century had functioned as "restraining agencies" in disciplining individuals.[33]

The new mobility destabilized local organizations not only by broadening an individual's social world but also by offering a wider array of diversions. Labor leaders complained that the "Ford car has done an awful lot of harm to the unions here and everywhere else." They grumbled that "as long as men have enough money to buy a second-hand Ford and tires and gasoline, they'll be out on the road and paying no attention to union meetings." Daylong Sunday motor trips also threatened the church. As one wayward member explained, "We've been away from church this summer more'n ever since we got our car." Ministers tried their best to compete with the "strong pull of the open road," imploring their congregations that "if you want to use your car on Sunday, take it out Sunday morning and bring some shut-ins to church and Sunday School; then in the afternoon, if you choose, go out and worship God in the beauty of nature—but don't neglect to worship Him indoors too."[34]

Despite the waning socializing influence of local institutions, leading figures working on the traffic problem stuck with nineteenth-century modes of governance. In fact, many leaders came from voluntary associations. It was these organizations that asked Secretary Hoover to organize a conference on the matter, and he did. For the very first National Conference on Street and Highway Safety, which convened in Washington, D.C., in December 1924, Hoover drew his invite list from a directory of associations that were "actively interested in traffic safety." They included the National Highway Traffic Association, the American Automobile Association, and the National Association of Mutual Casualty and Surety Underwriters, among several dozen others. Even public officials had formed associational units, like the International Association of Chiefs of Police and the American Association of State Highway Officials, and they attended as well. But voluntarism had changed. The national scope of these groups reflected the centralizing pull of automotive travel. Cars, along with other unifying forces like the radio and motion pictures, knit the nation together in common experience. So did the problems that these innovations created. National associations reflected a more bounded United States.[35]

The conference delegates had gathered voluntarily, and voluntarism remained important in their arsenal of solutions to the traffic problem. They concluded, unsurprisingly, that "cooperative work" was crucial and that "every community [had to] undertake prevention work aggressively, since it is the community that largely controls the factors that make for a reduced accident toll." Along these lines, the National Traffic Officers' Associations suggested "Safety Sunday," when clergymen of all denominations could deliver sermons on safety. Business associations could "encourage the loading, unloading and movement of trucks during the hours when other traffic is lightest, especially in congested districts." Another idea was for local automobile clubs to "perform a useful service by supplementing the work of public authorities in placing standard signs at the chief danger points on . . . highways." The sign that Buffalo, New York, erected on its busiest street was not exactly standard. The "death meter" posted the number of automobile fatalities for the day, week, and year. Its purpose nonetheless conformed to the principles of voluntarism: to serve as a reminder of "the need for a decrease in reckless driving and for greater community pride and co-operation." Perhaps the most guilt-inducing of them all was the sign put up in West Palm Beach, Florida, that read, "Obey the Law—Don't Kill a Child."[36]

The "community" also included car manufacturers, organized under the umbrella of the National Automobile Chamber of Commerce, which assured Secretary Hoover that they were doing what they could on "the matter of traffic accidents due to the use of motor vehicles." Actually, the Commerce Department had something specific in mind: it wanted the automobile industry, of its own accord, to end the advertisement of excessive speed. The federal agency communicated its wishes not through the mandates of policy but through the appeal of voluntarism. In 1926, Hoover's assistant sent a letter to the engineer for Chicago's Association of Commerce, "asking him if he could not, because of his intimate personal connection with Mr. Erskine, President of the Studebaker Corporation, persuade them to stop this kind of advertising," which had "a very adverse effect in the minds of the public."[37]

The death meter erected in Buffalo, New York.

Popular Mechanics 41, no. 4 (April 1924): 590. Reproduced from a copy at the University of Iowa Library.

Voluntarism operated through channels of subtle coercion and the persuasion of the public's mind. Individuals, whether sitting at the head of a company or behind the wheel, had to be exhorted to conduct their business reasonably, drive reasonably, step out reasonably. Belief that such appeals could work explains the thinking behind the Safety Pledge, the brainchild of several associations in California. In cooperation with the police, they solicited citizens to sign the following:[38]

The safety pledge, an effort to apply the principles of voluntarism to enforce traffic laws.

Courtesy of Herbert Hoover Presidential Library.

But these were exhortations, not laws. In that vein, enforcement efforts focused on positive reinforcement, like the Detroit Automobile Club's "courtesy campaign." According to the plan, club members would report the license numbers of motorists who exhibited "courtesy on the road," and the director would then send the considerate drivers a sticker of the slogan "Courtesy Makes Safety." The accompanying letter urged that even "though your natural modesty may dictate otherwise, we want you to display this sticker on your windshield, that other less thoughtful motorists will be encouraged to observe the rights of others." Unfortunately, drivers did not separate neatly into groups of the courteous and thoughtless. Even if the message of Safety First convinced the public of its importance, it did not necessarily mean that *all* drivers at *all* times would comply with *all* the rules of the road.[39]

On the theory that if people knew better then they would act better, government officials and community leaders also launched traffic education campaigns. Instruction began in elementary school. Junior safety councils reached juveniles. Night schools and vocational schools taught those in the trades. "Americanization schools" included lectures on safety as part of courses on citizenship. This became especially important when traffic experts identified "illiterates and foreign born" as a factor in car accidents—the rare occasion where race or ethnicity was noted in the movement for road safety. Everybody else received their lessons at churches and mass meetings, in newspapers and magazines, on posters and the radio, through motion pictures and "magic lantern slides," which were early versions of slide projectors. Ford Motor Company did its part by producing some of these films, such as *Hurry Slowly*, and awarding college scholarships to winners of safe-driving competitions. The National Automobile Chamber of Commerce sponsored essay contests on traffic to raise awareness. Teachers also wrote safety lesson plans for a chance at a prize, and hundreds of thousands submitted entries.[40]

Of course, lawbreaking drivers needed the most education, which was pointedly achieved in Highland Park, Michigan. Instead of going to jail, traffic violators had to study safety bulletins posted on the walls at the police station for a fixed amount of time. According to reports, this "new method . . . has educational value not found in other forms of punishment." This approach of inculcating safe driving habits pointed to another element of traffic schooling: shaming. A more common strategy for accomplishing these twin objectives essentially amounted to tattling. Police departments, in cooperation with various civic organizations, formed "public safety committees" or "vigilance committees" whose members, sometimes

called "the Vigilantes," would inform on traffic violators. The spe-
cifics of Northern California's program were typical. Appointed citizens, upon observing a violation, would fill out a report card and send
it to the committee, which would then mail a letter to the offender,
"calling the reported violation to his attention, pointing out the increasing number of traffic accidents, and urging his co-operation
in their reduction." A second report would trigger "a more pointed
communication," and a third report would finally prompt police action. In some towns, newspapers printed a blank cut-out form so that
anyone could report safety-first transgressions. Operating from the
assumption that people could be taught and shamed to be more cooperative, these citizen watches prioritized the cultivation of civic duty
before resorting to the penal provisions of traffic laws.[41]

Automobile associations and police departments claimed immediate
success. Reports piled in, and warning letters were mailed out, which
"were received in the spirit in which they were sent." One police
chief gushed that motorists praised the campaign and promised to
cooperate. Particularly appreciative were employers who previously had no way of checking on their drivers; now the public safety
committee did it for them. They posted the letters for all their drivers
to read and used them as an educational, and likely also shaming,
device during company meetings. The San Francisco Police Department issued a press release boasting that the number of deaths
from car accidents in the city decreased in a year when that number
increased in the rest of the state. Similarly, in 1921, when Detroit
met its goal captured in the slogan "Cut Traffic Deaths in Half," it
adopted a more ambitious slogan, "Less Than 100," for the following
year. St. Louis's Vigilance Committee also claimed to see improvement in the accident rate, prompting the Third Congress of the
National Traffic Officers' Association to recommend the program
for all municipalities.[42]

Alas, drivers were prone to recidivism. After more than a decade
of experience, officials had to concede that "traffic education, in order
to be effective, must be continuous, and not merely 'another' traffic
campaign."[43] The very idea of continuous education suggested that
people would not obey laws simply because they understood their ra-
tionales. A mode of governance that relied on personal accountability

proved increasingly futile in the anonymity of an automotive society. One's duties to a stranger were unclear, particularly if one
could zip by relatively unnoticed inside a covered car. How courteous
did one have to be? Or how antisocial and badly mannered could one
be? Unease lurked through early twentieth-century discourses about
the changes that modernity wrought. Technological advancements
seemed to have fostered selfishness to the point that even "law-
abiding" citizens endangered public safety and threatened democratic
self-government.

Roscoe Pound turned the troubles of modernity into a justification
for his brand of jurisprudence, which sought to incorporate the social
sciences into the law. Pound, like many legal scholars at the time,
questioned the concept of individual free will in favor of determinism,
the idea that heredity and environment informed human choices and
actions. If behavior was contingent on factors external to the will,
Pound argued, then lawless behavior in the frenzy that characterized the automotive society was inevitable. In an earlier time when
communities were made up of "a small group of God-fearing men,"
Pound granted that laws may have worked "by their own moral
weight" to serve as "guides to the conscience of the upright man."
But newfangled "agencies of menace" had thoroughly transformed
American society. With the "rush and turmoil of a busy, crowded
life," people did "not take time to consider how the intrinsic right
and justice of the law appeal to their consciences." Society had become so complex that at most a "high average of observance" of laws
was "the most to which we can attain." In short, Pound maintained
that law and morality had become distinct concepts in the twentieth
century. Lawlessness no longer revealed individual failing or immo-
rality. Rather, it reflected modernity. In pinpointing the roots of
self-centeredness in modern society, Pound assuaged concerns that
something had fundamentally gone wrong with the idea of democracy that was based on individual self-restraint. It was simply that
inherited models of governance had become outdated.[44]

   At first glance, Pound's progressive thinking may seem caught in
a conundrum. By his account, the conditions of modern society that

made obedience to law difficult also rendered that obedience necessary. When flocks of the upright moved to twentieth-century towns and cities, laws, especially criminal laws, replaced conscience as a tool of governance. But, as Pound also recognized, law enforcement was much harder in urban settings. Consider the alcohol problem in the years straddling the twentieth century. When efforts to reform individuals, first taken up by religious temperance asylums and fraternities like the Independent Order of Good Templars, proved ineffective, local governments implemented regulatory schemes to curb abuses of an activity that was not inherently evil but socially undesirable. Taxing liquor was one such attempt. When multijurisdictional channels of supply proved capable of bypassing state regulation, the country resorted to criminal laws. But prohibiting alcohol turned out to be a tall order, especially in cosmopolitan centers.[45]

Pound had a way out of this Catch-22. The modern era required different, better laws. Instead of case-by-case, judge-made common law, the complexities of twentieth-century society required comprehensive solutions based on the insights of economics, politics, sociology, and psychology. To write laws that people could and would obey, lawmakers needed knowledge of real-world conditions that shaped people's choices. In the twentieth century, lawlessness revealed shortcomings in the laws themselves, not in the lawbreaking public.[46]

Police Chief Vollmer came to the same conclusion as Pound, but from a different perspective. Although he deplored the self-centeredness that he witnessed on the streets and highways, he stopped short of claiming that Americans had become more selfish and less civic in the twentieth century. Selfishness was "inherent." In Vollmer's view, the persistence of dangerous driving habits reflected the failure of laws to take natural human tendencies into account and not any new deficiencies in the character of the American people. He complained that legislators seemed to be writing the traffic code in knee-jerk reaction to tragedies, and as a result, the volumes of laws made perfect adherence difficult, if not impossible. It reached a point where police officers and traffic experts alike could understand why law-abiding citizens seemed to treat traffic laws as merely advisory. Their sympathy called to mind a common complaint during the Progressive Era heyday about "the avalanche of laws, laws often self-contradictory and, at best, mutually contradictory."[47]

A perfect case in point, California's Motor Vehicle Act of 1919 contained so many provisions, many of which were not intuitive to the average driver, that police chiefs in the state agreed to "avoid making arrests except in cases of deliberate violations" for sixty days after the new laws became effective (they did not elaborate, however, how officers would determine whether violations were "deliberate"). The state legislature had amended the act so many times that it seemed to safety experts that many sections, clauses, and phrases began with "provided, however," "provided further . . . except that," or "provided further, however, anything to the contrary herein notwithstanding," all but rendering the already cumbersome language indecipherable. The experts had a point. For example, the subsection on passing street cars specified that

> vehicles shall be operated or driven on the right hand side of [street] cars and at a rate of speed not exceeding ten miles an hour and no portion thereof or of any load thereon shall come within six feet of the running board of steps of such cars . . . *provided, however,* that where local authorities have plainly marked upon the surface of the highway safety zones . . . vehicles shall not, at any time, be operated or driven within such zones; *provided, further,* that said safety zones shall only be marked at street corners or at other regularly established stations or stopping places . . . and shall not extend beyond seven feet toward the boundary of the highway from the outer rail of such railroad, interurban or street car line.[48]

To be clear, traffic authorities were not criticizing law per se. Rather, they were critical of laws that were poorly designed. This distinction pointed to a key difference between nineteenth-century regulations and progressive ideals of positive law. Pre-automobile laws could lay down a norm and then leave enforcement to individual citizens who, it was assumed, would act reasonably, with courts as final arbiters. Justice Cardozo's articulation of the "supreme rule of the road" as "the rule of mutual forbearance" epitomized this custom. A traffic specialist rebutted that if this "ideal rule" were "strictly applied . . . a great deal of brotherly feeling might be engendered," but "no great facility of movement would result." In an automotive society, laws had to take into account the interrelated problems of coordination and enforcement. Legislators accordingly needed knowledge of the circumstances and environment that would make legal compliance straightforward so that people would not even be aware that they were doing the right thing.[49]

While Pound promoted the social sciences as an aid to crafting laws, Vollmer endorsed the hard sciences, especially engineering. Various factors—traffic patterns, direction, speed, road conditions—determined the optimal amount of regulation. Too much or too little would be "worse than no control at all." The goal of any traffic-management scheme was not to penalize but to design "a thoroughly scientific engineering program" that would "arouse the people and make them constantly aware of danger when they are on public streets," so that law enforcement would not be necessary at all. Dr. Miller McClintock, the country's leading traffic engineer and the first person to write a Ph.D. dissertation on traffic, envisioned the stream of cars like "the flow of water in a river" and advocated for "foolproof roads on which the minimum of human judgment was required." One of the best examples of the efficacy of good design was the line in the middle of the road, first painted in Wayne County, Michigan, in 1911. In the words of legal scholar Willard Hurst, "The men who learned how to build hard-surfaced roads and how to draw a black line down the middle for mile after mile did more to enforce the rule of keep-to-the-right than all the police could do without these mechanical helps."[50]

Unfortunately, traffic did not always present a pure engineering problem that led to a simple engineering solution. Setting speed limits, for instance, turned out to be one of the "most important" and "most difficult" issues, according to Dr. McClintock, as well as one of the most controversial. One camp preferred definite limits, but that had some definite drawbacks. For one thing, although experts could agree that legislators often set inappropriate speed limits, they disagreed on what the limit should be. They concurred, for example, that a maximum of five miles an hour on country roads that were usually empty served only to antagonize drivers. But there was no "mathematical process" to determine the "most practical speed regulation," for a safe speed was "a relative thing" and depended on a multitude of variables like time of day and the weather. As one legal commentator explained, "A normal, sober driver can operate a car more safely at 45 miles per hour than a one-armed driver or a drunken driver at 30 miles per hour. A speed which at noon at a crowded corner would be most hazardous might not be at all dangerous or reckless at the same spot at midnight." Even "the slow vehicle" could pose "as much of a menace to safety as the speeder," Maryland's State Roads commissioner pointed out.[51]

At the third National Conference on Street and Highway Safety in 1930, a "row over speed limits" ended with a recall of the report that Dr. McClintock, then of Harvard University, had submitted on behalf of the Committee on Uniform Traffic Regulation. It had proposed to set limits "outside of business and residential districts, except at crossings, etc. 45 miles per hour; in residence districts and parks, 25 miles; business districts, 20 miles; passing schools with children, 15 miles; approaching intersectional highways, 15 miles; approaching railroad crossings with a clear view, 30 miles." The proposal unleashed criticisms that the limits were too high, too low, and too complicated, and the delegates sent it back to committee with a different traffic expert.[52]

To bypass the entire debate, another camp sought flexibility. Instead of a one-size-fits-all rule, the law would prohibit "'reckless driving,' or driving at a speed 'greater than is reasonable or prudent' or at an 'unreasonable speed.'" Before methods of clocking cars existed (speed guns for nonmilitary use were developed after World War II), proving that a driver was speeding was nearly impossible anyway. Given the legislative and prosecutorial hassles of definite speed limits, quite a few localities reverted to the flexible model. *Popular Mechanics* reported in 1921 that "earlier restrictions as to speed have . . . wisely[] been revised in many cities and states . . . to read 'at a safe rate of speed.'" But, as McClintock defended himself, this approach depended on the "impossibility of trusting individuals to use proper discretion." Ironically, an accident was often the best proof of unreasonableness.[53]

Other jurisdictions tried to combine flexibility with definiteness. For instance, one section of California's 1919 Motor Vehicle Act prohibited driving "at an unsafe and unreasonable rate of speed." Adding unhelpful specificity to ambiguity, another section described the varying circumstances for which the speeds of 10, 15, 20, 30, or 35 miles per hour would be considered unsafe and unreasonable. The problem, as with the reasonableness approach more generally, was that it was anyone's guess as to what speed would be deemed beyond prudent. One writer admitted that while "common sense" was a good rule, the hitch was that "no two men measure alike." "The big question," he put it succinctly, was "just how to write 'common sense' into traffic laws."[54]

However it was achieved, there was consensus that uniformity was the best policy when the automobile made jurisdiction crossing an everyday phenomenon. Traffic experts blamed the "hodge-podge conglomeration of laws and ordinances" for a large share of traffic violations. Secretary Hoover claimed that he "could be arrested and convicted on a dozen counts between Washington and New York" if he "carefully followed either the Washington or New York traffic regulations." When each district, town, and county had their own laws—when, for instance, one city permitted drivers to pass streetcars, the next required them to slow down when passing, and the following prohibited overtaking streetcars altogether—not only did the patchwork legal landscape make it impossible for drivers to be able to obey all the laws but, even more problematically, it thwarted the cultivation of consistent, and thus safer, driving habits. "Without uniformity," Hoover declared, "reduction in loss of life, personal injury and property damage upon our streets and highways is virtually impossible."[55]

The effort to standardize traffic laws, however, faced hurdles rooted deeply in the American legal structure. *Ex Parte Daniels* illustrates how the California Supreme Court dealt with one such obstacle. In 1919, the city of Pasadena set a speed limit of fifteen miles per hour on all its bridges. California's Motor Vehicle Act also set a speed limit on certain bridges in the state at twenty miles per hour. Earle Daniels had been driving below the state's but above the city's speed limit on the Colorado Street Bridge, which fell under both statutes, and was charged for violating the municipal ordinance. The practical necessity of uniform traffic regulations likely explains why a majority on the bench decided that Pasadena's ordinance conflicted with state law and was therefore void. But to get to that result, the judges had to maneuver around several legal issues. The majority acknowledged that according to the "usual practice throughout the United States," a municipality could not only enact traffic regulations pursuant to its police power but also provide greater protections than the general laws of the state. This is precisely what Pasadena did by imposing a lower speed limit than the state of California. To circumvent these well-established principles, the court concluded that the state legislature intended to "occupy the whole field of traffic regulation." The dissent cried foul, arguing that the legislature could not constitutionally forbid the city from exercising its police power and that a preemptive move was plainly an indirect way of doing so. Nevertheless, the majority decided that their interpretation of the state's traffic laws was valid "although there are cases holding to the contrary." The legal gymnastics to get to that conclusion were undoubtedly an attempt to navigate the bewildering tangle of overlapping and conflicting mandates that drivers faced every day.[56]

An even more firmly established obstacle to uniformity was American federalism, to which one Louisiana official howled in exasperation, "The 'Tweedle-dum-and-tweedle-dee' of 'states' rights' must not be allowed by the people whose lives and limbs are at stake." It could be argued, as this official did, that the traditional arrangement, in which states took care of local issues while the federal government handled national matters, was unsuited for dealing with individual actions that regularly extended beyond state borders. The authorities all agreed, one, that traffic was "not a problem to be solved by individual cities or even individual states" and, two, that "our motor-vehicle and traffic laws ought to be approximately the same throughout the United States." That these two propositions added up to federal action, however, was a result that many did not want to accept. As the writers of *Scientific American* thought through

the hypothetical, the federal administration of traffic would require "an enormous new clerical and judiciary machine," which
would siphon "all the money that could possibly be wrung from the
automobilist." (They had a point; in 1923, federal excise taxes on
motor vehicles constituted 5.9 percent of total US revenue receipts,
and automotive products paid 77 percent of the total special excise
taxes.) Practical questions also arose. Would the US government
appoint hundreds of thousands of traffic officers, enough for every
busy street corner and intersection throughout the country? If, instead, the officers were to come from local police forces, then would
they have to enforce federal laws and appear in federal courts? To
the rationally bent, these scenarios sounded too complicated to be
feasible.[57]

Many officials also believed that the national government could
not mandate *the* solution for the states consistent with the principles
of federalism. Uniformity "imposed by the inflexible fiat of central
power" was not the way forward, President Coolidge insisted. Secretary Hoover admitted that traffic was "intellectually an interstate
problem," but it was one "which must be solved materially and actually by the individual states acting in concert." In these helter-skelter
times, the federal government could coordinate action among the
states, much like a conductor in front of an orchestra. The United
States would not have "government from a central authority," but
government through "education of the local community to intelligent action." While Washington, D.C., would lend assistance by
"securing a spread of information and coordination in activities,"
the states would remain responsible for implementation.[58]

An example of this "new conception of government" was the National Conference on Street and Highway Safety. In 1924, Hoover
gathered delegates from state administrations, voluntary associations,
and private businesses, who together proposed "universal" solutions
from the "best remedies that have been devised." Over several conferences, they drafted the Model Municipal Traffic Ordinance and
the Uniform Vehicle Code, which included the Uniform Motor
Vehicle Registration and Certificate of Title Act, the Uniform Vehicle Operators' and Chauffeurs' License Act, and the Uniform Act
Regulating the Operation of Vehicles on Highways. These model

laws included provisions not just for consistent speed limits and street crossings but also for standardized road construction and accident reports to aid in the compilation of statistics for studying the causes of accidents. The Committee on Engineering and Construction finally determined, once and for all, that red should be used to mean "stop," green for "proceed," and yellow for "caution." To adopt this color scheme, municipalities that had been using black and yellow for "stop" would have to procure a lot of red paint, which was less available.[59]

States progressed, more or less, toward uniformity, although it would not be achieved until the passage of the Highway Safety Act in 1966. Until then, reformers in each state continued to insist that with coherent, science-backed laws, "there would be no opportunity for the conscientious vehicle operator to violate the law," which might finally reduce the toll of traffic jams and accidents.[60]

Standardization worked . . . somewhat. In 1926, two years after the first National Conference, Hoover reported that though the numbers of fatalities and accidents were still going up, the rate of increase had slowed. In 1924, there were one hundred deaths per 100,000 registered cars; in 1926, that figure was ninety-five. It was an improvement, even a significant one, especially when compared with figures from a decade earlier; there had been 178 deaths per 100,000 registrations in 1917. But in 1930, Hoover, as president of the United States, called for a third National Conference in light of the persistent fact that the "accident rate has mounted steadily despite the measures adopted as the result of the previous conferences."[61]

The realization that, in Hoover's words, "laws are of little value if they are not or cannot be properly enforced" raised a surging chorus for greater law enforcement. The Jamestown, New York, police department confirmed that severity was working; enforcing the law "to the letter" with frequent arrests had "brought about a general observance of traffic regulations." When fines proved ineffective, municipalities added workhouse sentences. Hoover's assistant Ernest Greenwood wrote to the secretary of commerce about how he had witnessed a Detroit traffic court judge sentence "a wealthy woman" to ninety days for driving while drunk. People did not disagree that severe punishment could be a compelling method of prevailing upon intractable motorists.[62]

But some still clung to the view that society had to depend on "the voluntary cooperation of law-abiding citizens." The new challenge in the motor age, they believed, was to be more scientific about sorting out those who possessed a cooperative spirit from the anti-social lot. This was the view of John Hertz, who owned the Yellow Truck and Coach Manufacturing Company, which operated taxicabs and "Drivurself" rental cars. After he hired a psychologist to screen job candidates—he employed more than 10,000 drivers—he realized a 20 percent reduction in accidents. "Of course, that's good business," Hertz acknowledged, but "it means more than business to me," he insisted. The experiment persuaded him that "we must arouse the whole nation to a spirit of responsibility and a genuine instinct for the rights of others." But the unrelenting traffic and the stubbornly high rate of accidents cast doubt on Hertz's conviction.[63]

From 1933 through 1937, Yale law professor Underhill Moore studied people's behavior while parking and driving around a rotary inter-section. For five years, and presumably longer if funding had not run out, Moore recorded how long people left their cars parked, both be-fore and after time limits had been put in place; whether ticketing by the police affected adherence to time limits; and whether drivers kept to the right in a rotary intersection under a general regulation requiring vehicles to keep right versus when the words "Keep Right" were painted at the entrance of the intersection. He was so focused on the project that when an acquaintance met him on the street with the greeting, "I haven't seen you in years," Moore gruffly responded, "Don't bother me. Can't you see I'm busy counting these cars?" He was aware that the "legal lights" at Yale dismissed his work as trivial, but he tried to ignore the ridicule, telling confidants that he was "not writing for them." He hoped that a "hundred or five hundred years from now a kindred soul may find in my crude researches some clue to the solution." Motivating Moore's dogged observation of drivers in search of that solution was the question, under what circumstances do legal rules change people's behavior?[64]

Believing that the "problems of jurisprudence [were] psychological problems," Moore approached this question by applying psychologist

Clark Hull's learning theory to determine "the quantity and degree of conformity to rules of law." The theory reduced all human behavior to learned behavior. And to learn behavior, a person must want something ("drive"), notice something ("cue"), do something ("response"), and get something ("reward"). To put it simply, Hull explained that people learned behaviors when their actions were reinforced by a satisfaction of their wants. Armed with Hull's theory, Moore hypothesized that laws were *cues* and that people *responded* by obeying the laws when the *reward* for doing so met their *drive*. For his experiment, Moore conceived of the drive as the reduction of anxiety that was "based on a fear of the consequences of 'violating' the ordinance"—namely, the fear of being "subjected to the regular police procedure." To state this plainly, Moore suspected that people obeyed the law to avoid police action.[65]

After five years, Moore concluded that, indeed, New Haven motorists exhibited learning patterns in accordance with Hull's thesis. Moore's traffic study never gained much scholarly traction, in part because the report of his findings was almost unreadable for a seemingly simple experiment. The following is one representative sentence in his 136-page article, "Law and Learning Theory: A Study in Legal Control":

> After many trials, during which every relationship which suggested itself was tried, it was judged that the closest relationship between a measurement of the location of each of the Points and some other significant measurement in each of the studies was the relationship between the location of the Points, as measured by the cumulated percentage of the respective unregulated distributions to the left of such Points, and the ordinance times, that is, the parking limitations stated in each ordinance, as similarly measured by the cumulated percentage of the respective unregulated distributions to the left of each ordinance time.

In the fog of the scholarly gobbledygook, Moore made this point clearly: compliance with traffic laws was relative, not absolute. The tagging experiment, for instance, demonstrated that people whose cars were ticketed obeyed the parking ordinance more frequently than people whose cars were not. In other words, policing made a difference in encouraging lawful behavior.[66]

This conclusion seems obvious today. But Moore was a serious academic, and his project offers insight into how a legal scholar in the 1930s grappled with the problem of enforcement. Moore's perspective came at the tail end of a transition in American governance, when self-regulation seemed inadequate to enforce positive laws. His experiments, along with public education campaigns and the honor system, took place at a time when police law enforcement was not assumed. Earlier in this transition period, in 1916, lawyer and statesman Elihu Root declared that it was "not fear of the policeman or the sheriff that keeps the peace in our many cities; it is the self-control of the millions of inhabitants enabling them to conform their lives to the rules of conduct necessary to the common interest." Fearing that such self-discipline was in decline, an Illinois judge proposed a "code of ethics for the public." This was a period when local governments were beginning to rely more on police officers to execute the state's police power. Tellingly, Moore called his experiment an "administrative" study rather than a study of policing. By the time he finished his research, police experts were declaring that "it is quite often natural that enforcement officers should be needed." The point of Moore's investigation was to determine whether they were right.[67]

His findings were a foregone conclusion not because of any inherent flaw in human nature but because of how Moore devised his experiment. He focused on traffic. Something about automobility—the impatient entitlement encouraged by individualized speed or the tendency of each motorist to discount the harm of their free-wheeling driving or to overestimate their driving skill—made it difficult to coordinate social behavior on the road. It was "my belief," Secretary Hoover proclaimed in 1926, "that much of the solution of the present high accident rate on our city streets and rural highways lies in the enforcement of the law by the police." Striking a contrary note, President Coolidge, under whom Hoover served, declared that the "utmost ingenuity on the part of the police powers will be substantially all wasted in an effort to enforce the law, if there does not exist a strong and vigorous determination on the part of the people to observe the law." "Such a determination," he continued, "cannot be produced by the Government"; rather, "it is furnished by religion." At first glance, the two men seem to be at odds. But they were talking about different topics, and only one of them was referring to vice. What Hoover was speaking of, and what Moore's "administrative" experiment confirmed, was the necessity of police to enforce *traffic* laws. When such laws lacked an inherent moral force compelling obedience, and when efforts to endow those laws with a moral obligation to obey proved inadequate, reliance on the police appeared to be the only option left.[68]

In 1921, the special deputy police commissioner in charge of the New York Police Department's Traffic Division anticipated the shift to policing in an article about the "tower flash system" that regulated the flow of traffic. The city had constructed what resembled lookouts in the middle of intersections along Fifth Avenue. Each had a box where a policeman could stand, and above each box was a set of lights, a prototype of a traffic signal. A flashing yellow light indicated that traffic was moving north and south; a flashing red light meant that traffic had changed directions to east and west. Based on the topic of the article, one might have expected a dry description of technical information. But Dr. John Harriss had a poetic bent, which at times came out in convoluted passages. He extolled at length the "splendor" of the flash, which he described as "a most remarkable thing," like the "magnificence of a setting sun," which could "rivet the mind." His praise betrayed the pride of a creator in his handiwork. Harriss worked for the police department not for pay, but out of "love" and a passion for finding efficient ways to regulate traffic. A millionaire, he also personally paid for all the traffic projects that, according to the papers, "would put some municipal treasuries into bankruptcy."[69]

Dr. Harriss was pleased to report that the traffic towers worked marvelously. Eventually, the flash had become part of people's "daily routine when on the streets," and they knew immediately that a flash was "a command for something." The way this worked was both scientific and mysterious. The key was that the towers represented "the great big policeman." Even though drivers could not see the police officer who may or may not be sitting elevated many feet above

"Flash System-Traffic Tower" at Gay and Union Streets in Knoxville,
Tennessee.

National Police Bulletin 1, no. 4 (October 31, 1921). Reproduced from a copy at the
New York Public Library.

"Flash System-Traffic Tower" at Fifth Avenue and Thirty-Fourth
Street in New York City.

National Police Bulletin 1, no. 1 (June 6, 1921). Reproduced from a copy at the New York
Public Library.

the ground, they believed that one was up there. The traffic towers sustained the impression of constant surveillance, which made it work as "a great big giant of regulation."[70]

Harriss was essentially describing a panopticon, a circular prison designed by the eighteenth-century philosopher Jeremy Bentham. A tower in the center permitted a single guard to observe all the inmates, who could not tell whether they were being watched or not. Michel Foucault later analyzed the panopticon as an architectural metaphor for modern disciplinary mechanisms that control human behavior with a visible but unverifiable power. The tower (or traffic light) is always visible, but the prisoners (or drivers) cannot confirm whether they are being observed. According to Foucault, this motivates self-discipline, which enables the exercise of power to become automatic.[71]

Viewing signal lights as a type of panopticon highlighted the kind of governance that an automotive society seemed to require. In an increasingly anonymous world, the gaze of the police, or at least the perception that the police were watching, gradually replaced the observation of neighbors and members of one's community as a method of social control. By 1920, one reporter comparing Yankee traffic cops with their French equivalent bragged, "Every driver and every foot passenger in American cities keeps an eye on the man bossing the traffic. We have been trained until we keep the regulations of our own accord." Her boast threw into sharp relief the contours of freedom as early twentieth-century Americans experienced it. Whatever free will was—a term that was difficult to define at a time when many educated persons subscribed to determinism—it did not always encompass freedom from police surveillance.[72]

Apparently, New Yorkers found this means of control agreeable— as evidenced by the thousands of letters that the police department received—so much so that after a few months, the police were "now concerned with making [the traffic towers] artistic . . . in keeping with the architectural beauty" of Fifth Avenue. The winning design, out of a hundred that competed for a prize—again, funded by Harriss—had a granite base, bronze columns rising twenty-three feet, and an upper compartment enclosed in glass. A traffic officer who occupied one of these beautified structures quipped, "They'll be putting silk curtains in the window before they get through." "And maybe a bit of lace," another cracked. The lighthearted affair suggested that no one seriously protested the new structures of discipline. Even the press applauded the "imperious towers" that served as "pillars of luminous cloud by day and of changing fire by night." The *New York Times* acknowledged that though the towers may "stand in restraint of liberty, . . . on the whole, they make the pursuit of happiness through this most attractive and crowded of earth's avenues less hazardous to life." This sense of relief at having found a solution to the risks of automotive travel revealed how much the management of traffic had started to modify older notions of American freedom.[73]

This change in the meaning of freedom was perhaps even better explained by a justice of the Ontario Supreme Court. While presiding at the Criminal Assizes in 1919, he had detected "a phenomenon not quite new but exhibiting a new phase." Although his observations were based on the Canadian experience, his thoughts described developments in the United States as well. In eight vehicular murder cases, both defendants and jurors alike were astonished to learn that a person could be guilty of a crime even while driving at the lawful speed. The justice continued that under tort law in Canada "as well as in England and many of the United States," the contributing negligence of the other party provided a perfect defense against liability, a principle that had been ingrained in the public's understanding of relative right and wrong. "But in the criminal law, the rule is different," he explained. Everybody had a duty "in preserving the life and limbs of every citizen," and the negligence of the victim offered no defense. This seemed hard to swallow for automobilists, whose outlook the justice summed up as, "I look after myself; you look after yourself; if you don't, so much the worse for you." They were discovering that in the Automotive Age, "Cain's jibe, 'Am I my brother's keeper?' [had become] outworn," and "when the King, i.e., the People, charges any one with killing one of the people, he is made to understand that he *is* his brother's keeper." As the management of traffic migrated from the tort system to the criminal justice system, responsibility for the greater good was redefining individual freedom.[74]

Another glimpse of this shift from the individual to the collective in freedom's orientation came from Walter Crosby, a civil engineer by training. In 1926, having attended the International Road Congress in Milan, Italy, he sent his friend Herbert Hoover his thoughts on "European ideas of Safety." They certainly did things differently there, reflected in their concept of safety that was "broader" than how Americans conceived it. In Europe, the "attitude on the whole" regarded safety as the "integrity" of traffic, rather than the well-being of the individual. Europeans accordingly pursued measures that sought to secure as uninterrupted a flow of vehicular movement as possible. They focused on "engineering expedients," such as road construction and the layout of traffic routes, which were supplemented with general regulations that penalized any interferences to safety writ large. For Crosby, the "Parisian practice" of arresting the pedestrian run over by a car for "disturbing traffic" encapsulated the continental model.[75]

The approach stateside was the opposite. The American unit of analysis was the individual, and efforts to promote safety likewise centered on "individual or personal selfishness." The honor system, safety pledges, and the unending education campaigns all reflected this perspective. Crosby recalled that highway safety in the United States had its origins in the "Watch your Step" slogan of the New York City subway, which was intended to safeguard "the financial interests of . . . corporations against liability for personal damages." It was this individualistic mindset, steered through the tort system and directed at personal appeals, that had laid the groundwork for traffic management in the United States. But Crosby recognized that his country was moving toward the broader conception of safety, which was "undoubtedly due to the 'National Conference on Highway Safety.'" Like the Europeans, conference delegates were proposing ideas like standard grade crossings and intelligently designed road systems, as well as stricter criminal penalties for traffic violations.

For the Progressive Era, a time when ideas about governance frequently crisscrossed the Atlantic Ocean, it may not have been remarkable that Crosby found himself "impressed" with the European model. Still, it is worth noting that he thought that a system that governed for the collective afforded the motorist a "greater degree of individual liberty and freedom" than the American system. To boot, it "seemed to develop a high degree of skill among the drivers there." The embrace of criminalization and police law enforcement to protect people against "the abuse of liberty" called into question the American tradition of self-governance. Revealingly, when praising the National Conference's work on the model traffic ordinance, a pundit exclaimed, "A self-governing people we are, are we not?" What was meant to be rhetorical instead suggested doubt.[76]

The automobile introduced new tensions in the way Americans understood and experienced freedom. Pulling in one direction was the autonomy of the individual that driving emboldened. Tugging in the opposite direction was the mandate of public safety. What was freedom in a modern, automotive society that depended on the police to maintain order? Self-determination would have to be redefined to include adherence to rules that promoted conformity. Autonomy would acquire new meaning to encompass obedience motivated by the specter of the police looming above in a tower flash system or by the side of the highway. How would the necessity of policing be reconciled with the requirements of freedom? That, ultimately, was the question that Americans grappled with in the automotive century.

2

From Lumbering Foot Patrolmen to Motor-Mounted Policemen

Courtesy—Service—Protection
> Iowa State Patrol motto, adopted in 1935

Courtesy—Professionalism—Respect
> New York Police Department motto, adopted in 1996

In 1905, August Vollmer began his career in police work as the twenty-nine-year-old "boy marshal" of Berkeley, California, with big ideas. He immediately ordered his men to don uniforms. Previously, they had worn only a bright star pinned to their lapels. "Berkeley was putting on airs," one local newspaper gibed; the college town, "still bucolic with many a big hayfield within its limits, was trying to be citified." Actually, Vollmer was trying to professionalize his force. When uniforms first appeared in the largest cities in the mid-nineteenth century, criticism ensued about their antidemocratic look. Uniformed officers, also called "bluecoats," resembled either military men or liveried servants. However controversial they had once been, Vollmer embraced them as the symbol of modern police.[1]

Officers riding around on bicycles, another first for the Berkeley police, drew even more guffaws. "It was new, and therefore ludicrous,"

August Vollmer as the "boy marshal" of Berkeley, California, in 1905.

The *Oakland Post Enquirer*, June 2, 1938. Reproduced from a copy at the California State Library.

explained a reporter. Among the many innovations he introduced, Vollmer garnered the most enthusiastic support for a signal-and-recall system, for which the townspeople approved a $25,000 municipal bond in 1906. The apparatus was essentially a prototype of a pager. Consisting of little more than electric lights installed on telephone poles with callboxes, it was a game changer in patrol duty by enabling the marshal to contact his officers out making the rounds instead of waiting for them to check in at headquarters. The communication system played a key role in one of the stories Vollmer was fond of telling. Spud Yarrow, the notorious burglar whose modus operandi was to prey on the rich while they entertained guests, had arrived in town. When the station received a call that Yarrow had made a visit during a dinner party and had just fled the scene, Vollmer sent out a message via signal: "All men move south . . . surround district E . . . burglar." Two officers on bikes soon found Yarrow waiting on a corner for a streetcar to Oakland, leaving him completely mystified by how quickly they had caught up to him. Police departments throughout the country found this method for calling cops on the beat "invaluable . . . in case of burglary, fire or accident."[2]

Vollmer served as the forward-thinking leader of the Berkeley Police Department from 1905 to 1932, with a brief stint as the police chief in Los Angeles in 1923. His career overlapped an era when progressive reformers tackled political, social, and moral problems with confidence in science and human effort. This period began in the late nineteenth century, when millions of people had followed the flow of capital, industry, and culture into cities where they sought new opportunities, work, and political and cultural havens. But these boom years for metropoles also came with growing pains. Industrial accidents, housing shortages, changing family structures, and the increasing visibility of ethnic, racial, and class enclaves prompted a flurry of reforms. Discovering that the interdependence of people, the city, and the environment required fresh solutions, progressives applied their knowledge of the social sciences to address the new problems. State and local governments regulated everything from the fat content of milk and the construction of factories to the sale of securities and the payment of child support. Though their projects

The signal-and-recall system in Berkeley, California.

The American 18, no. 1 (1918): 42. Reproduced from a copy at the
University of Iowa Library.

were diverse, progressives shared a worldview that the complexities
of modern society required nonpartisan specialists to manage a rationally organized state. Expertise became the raison d'être for the
various professionalization movements that flourished at the turn of
the century.[3]

Vollmer stood at the forefront of the campaign to professionalize
the police, insisting that they "take their place with other branches
of public administration." The historical irony of Berkeley as a
laboratory of police modernization makes more sense in the context

of its underlying progressive impulses. At the twilight of the Coolidge prosperity years dominated by big business, Vollmer boasted that the "modern police department is an up-to-date business institution conducting its affairs on a solid business basis, and to the fullest extent utilizing principles of the several sciences and gradually developing principles peculiar to police service." He accordingly referred to himself as a "police executive." Others called him a "scientist of the law." So it was with pride when Vollmer contrasted the police in 1905, when he first became marshal, with the police in 1932, when he retired as police chief, and concluded that it was "much like comparing modern civilization with the civilization of the Stone Age." Vollmer may have overstated his case when he declared that the "days of the brutal and stupid policeman are gone forever." But he was not exaggerating too much when he observed that the "alert and fast motor-mounted policemen" of the twentieth century seemed an "altogether different type of official" compared to the "heavy, lumbering, foot patrolmen" of the past.[4]

By the 1920s, Vollmer had gained a national reputation. He was among the first police chiefs to put his officers on bicycles (1910), then on motorcycles (1912), and finally in Fords (1913). He also received credit for establishing the first police school, promoting crime laboratories, and using the lie detector. In addition to these achievements, Vollmer aspired to the grander goal of thoroughly reorganizing his profession. He sought more men who were college educated if not specially trained for fighting crime, employed full-time with competitive salaries and pensions, and united under a single state force modeled after the "G-men" of the US government or the centralized police found in Europe. The police ultimately took form largely as Vollmer had envisioned, for which he earned the title "father" of modern policing. To be sure, in the nineteenth century, big cities like Philadelphia, New York, and Boston had formed police departments that focused on crime prevention and law enforcement. But the transformation of the police into its modern version is a twentieth-century story that happened in urban centers as well as in smaller towns. Vollmer's ambition in realizing that change is understandable at an individual level, and he was fortunate that his university town was sufficiently prosperous and willing to pay for many of his ideas.

SCIENTIST OF THE LAW

August Vollmer, profiled in the *Oakland Post Enquirer* in 1938.

The *Oakland Post Enquirer*, May 28, 1938. Reproduced from a copy at the California State Library.

The larger question is, *why did towns and cities throughout the United States invest in his vision?*

As early as 1924, Chief Vollmer declared that traffic was "the police problem of today." Notwithstanding his progressive optimism, he did not think that it could possibly be solved within his lifetime. The police chief of Evanston, Illinois, echoed his concern, citing traffic as "the greatest single problem confronting the Police Department." When the new commander in Duluth, Minnesota, took the helm in 1920, he realized that the first issue he had to tackle was traffic, a realization that came to police leaders throughout the United States. The chief of Buffalo, New York, reportedly thought about it "every spare minute of the day," such that the *National Police Journal* described him as someone who placed the traffic problem "close to [his] heart." For others, it gave them their biggest headache.[5]

Making people obey traffic laws required a disciplining presence, as Underhill Moore at Yale Law School would conclude in his rotary and parking studies in the 1930s. But even before Moore had begun his research, experience had led traffic authorities to the same conclusion: mass automobility required more police. "Automobile congestion is developing a new type of police officer, the Traffic Cop," one commentator observed in 1920. And the phenomenon was spreading. "His burly form appears not merely on crowded city streets," he continued, "but many smaller cities find him necessary to pilot the profession of gas riders." An official in the US Department of Commerce made the same observation in 1924: "Yesterday traffic officers were a class of community officials unknown. Today the budget of practically every police department in the United States contains a plea for more of them." "More men needed" was the appeal heard wherever cars gained mass adoption, and it came not just from police chiefs. Traffic engineer Miller McClintock also claimed that in many cities, "a traffic division possessing twice the present number of men would not be fully prepared to deal with existing traffic demands." Business owners petitioned for more crossing officers "to regulate the constant streams of humanity and vehicles." Even the National Automobile Chamber of Commerce and the National Conference on Street and Highway Safety—voluntary organizations that touted self-governance—requested more police law enforcement.[6]

Municipal governments complied as much as possible. Buffalo started with ten traffic patrolmen in 1894 and by 1918 had sixty, not including those detailed to traffic duty in the outer precincts. In 1919, nearly 20 percent of Detroit's force, 300 out of 1,370, were assigned to manage traffic, while in Cleveland, that percentage was 15. But—and here was the important point—those figures were not enough. Cleveland's police chief wanted to more than double the number of men, which would cost the city an additional $225,000 a year. Newark's traffic squad jumped from 47 to 157 in 1921, but the director of Public Safety declared that even that was insufficient; fifty to seventy-five more were necessary for the night shift. Pittsburgh's city council authorized an increase of more officers to the traffic unit, a total of thirty-six, than to any other unit. Even in pedestrian-dominated New York City, dedicated traffic police increased more than 50 percent from 1,400 in 1921 to 2,200 three years later, with experts recommending an additional thousand. A description of Seattle's traffic division, as one that was "rapidly growing both in volume of business and in importance," could have been said of any traffic division in the country.[7]

The numbers, however revealing, do not tell the whole story, for even the officers not part of the traffic crew still had to deal with cars. The difference between "traffic patrol" and "general police patrol" was a matter of degree when, according to the *National Police Journal*, the latter could "be either specially assigned to traffic or have such work included as a part of their general police duties." It explained that "so great has this movement of traffic become, and so closely is it associated with the daily life of all of us, that a big percentage of *every* policeman's activities is connected in some way with the automobile." From the average town of Berkeley, Chief Vollmer confirmed that "the urgency and the volume of traffic regulation and control have compelled the shifting of large numbers of men from their beats and their assignments to special traffic duty." To put it simply, a part of every regular officer's daily grind came to include the management of vehicular traffic.[8]

The bean counting is further misleading because officers in special departments had to attend to traffic's ancillary matters. In Columbus, Ohio, for example, the detective bureau investigated "all accidents in which persons were injured," which included automobile accidents. In some places, while directing traffic fell within the domain of the accordingly named traffic division, a separately identified "auto patrol" or "motorcycle unit" pursued speeders, the number one traffic violator. This segregation would soon disappear as almost all traffic patrolmen became "motorized."[9]

Although traffic justified more cops, this reason did not suit Vollmer's professionalizing mission. In his opinion, police work ought not to include the enforcement of traffic laws. The "less police are burdened with traffic," he argued, "the more successfully will they perform" their core duties: fighting crime. A Columbia professor of criminology went so far as to claim that putting the police in charge of traffic raised crime rates because it diverted the police's attention "from actually running down criminals." Reforming police chiefs called for the creation of a separate agency for traffic so that they could focus on crime. Vollmer pointed out that the federal government established separate bureaucracies to administer different laws. The Treasury Department had secret service agents, the Post Office had inspectors, and the Department of Justice had its own investigators, "all having separate duties and all performing their duties satisfactorily."[10]

The US government had also formed the Bureau of Prohibition, a delegation of responsibility that Vollmer surely approved. In 1920, the Eighteenth Amendment criminalized what had previously been dealt with as a regulatory or spiritual matter. But throughout the decade, Vollmer still thought of antiliquor laws—along with laws outlawing prostitution, gambling, and narcotics—as distinct from criminal laws. He considered "the suppression of vice" more in line with "sanitary and health inspections" than with the pursuit of murderers and thieves. Actually, there was legal basis for the blurred categories. The state's police power to govern for the public welfare authorized the regulation, even to the point of criminalization, of a wide range of behaviors, from drinking to personal hygiene. But for Vollmer, regulatory offenses seemed different in kind from antisocial conduct like murder and theft. At a time when police forces were coming into modern age, it was confusing that all government regulation fell under the concept of "police." Vollmer wanted to keep things straight, and in 1928, he published an article with a title that captured his view: "Vice and Traffic—Police Handicaps." The "control of traffic, vice and crime presents entirely different types of problems," Vollmer wrote, and having to deal with all of them hindered the police.[11]

In the article, Vollmer fixated on one particular reason for eschewing morals enforcement. He chronicled a grand narrative about the corrupting reach of politics, with a cast of characters that included "thieves, prostitutes, gamblers, bootleggers, narcotic users and peddlers, professional bondsmen and shyster lawyers." This "indolent, unscrupulous, parasitic group" bought the protection of a "political boss" who publicly promoted reforms and "big police shakeups" while allowing rackets to continue. "Honest policemen" who enforced the law too earnestly would suddenly find that they had been demoted or fired for trying to clean up the city, while the "crooked or morally weak policemen" were rewarded. Vollmer concluded the story with "police morale shattered" and the city "left to the mercy of the human vultures."[12]

Vollmer was not just telling a simple morality tale dressed up with dramatic embellishments. He was also venting about his own experience as the Los Angeles police chief in 1923, which ended with his resignation after just one year. He was probably even referring to the City of Angels when he divulged that in "one large city in this state the political boss agreed to allow three gamblers to name the three chiefs of police for the following three elections." In Vollmer's observation, morals regulation inevitably led to well-funded attempts to thwart enforcement and undermined the integrity of policing as a science, which explains his insistence that vice suppression should not be part of police work. Professional police conducted their business according to "a sound business or scientific basis" rather than beholden to political benefactors, Vollmer stressed. Nothing inherent in the investigation of liquor or gambling violations rendered it incompatible with the police function. Rather, the vulnerability to corruption made the police unsuited for vice control. If professionalization required autonomy from politics, and if political meddling went hand in hand with vice, then it followed that professional police officers should not deal with vice.[13]

Regardless of Vollmer's principled reasons, many police departments did not bother with liquor violations. Some lacked resources, others did not care about cracking down on alcohol, and many found bribes too tempting to resist. Consequently, civic leagues and their army of citizen volunteers picked up the slack. This posed a two-front problem for Vollmer. First, the excesses of vigilante enforcement raids, which often received the blessing of Prohibition agents, triggered backlash against police as a whole. Second, as Vollmer had expected, police nonenforcement, often purchased with dirty money, scandalized the nation just as much as the activities of bootleggers and gangsters. The situation crested into a national hysteria, prompting President Hoover to establish the first national crime commission, headed by Attorney General George W. Wickersham, to determine the causes of law enforcement failures and to make recommendations for reforming the entire administration of justice.[14]

The Prohibition fiasco confirmed Vollmer's concern that the police could never claim the respect due professionals as long as they were tasked with enforcing vice laws. One way out of this predicament would require municipalities and states to establish new bureaucracies dedicated to antiliquor enforcement, as the federal government had done with the Bureau of Prohibition. But this strategy depended on each and every jurisdiction doing its part, an impossible feat of cooperation that had required the Eighteenth Amendment in the first place. Another option was decriminalization, which would eliminate the need for policing vice. In fact, many Prohibition supporters had begun to doubt the viability of the "noble experiment" in light of flagrant police misconduct and corruption. One of the Wickersham Commission's fourteen reports, *Lawlessness in Law Enforcement*, bolstered arguments to reverse course.[15]

Instead, the commission provided an opportunity to boost law enforcement at its most vulnerable moment. Vollmer turned the criticisms of the police into an urgent petition to raise the standards for hiring officers, to invest in new technology and criminal record-keeping, to centralize the police function, and to eliminate politics—basically, to professionalize the police in line with his vision. In 1931, he authored the Wickersham Commission's *Report on Police*, which recommended the very changes that he had urged ever since becoming town marshal. Even the report specifically on Prohibition adopted Vollmer's proposals for "improvements . . . in the organization, personnel, and equipment of enforcement." In short, the commission's solution to the abuses of law enforcement was not to cut back on policing by repealing the Eighteenth Amendment. Rather, it sought to throw even more money at the problem. One stunned commentator exclaimed, "How the recommendations could have been drawn from the facts is beyond me." But for the commis-

sioners, the benefits of Prohibition proved too valuable to give up altogether. The report maintained that abolishing alcohol "increased
production, increased efficiency of labor, . . . and decrease[d] industrial accidents." It also cited social workers who noted a "distinct improvement in standards of living" with the "closing or substantial
closing of the old time saloon." In the end, the Wickersham Commission remained hopeful that the benefits would outweigh the costs,
especially if the costs could be addressed by strengthening law
enforcement.[16]

Although the commission did not give up on Prohibition, the
people did. Just two years after the publication of the Wickersham
reports, the country ratified the Twenty-First Amendment to undo
the Eighteenth. For the voters who changed their minds between
1919 and 1933, repeal was about regret. National Prohibition made
clear the need for law enforcement, but Americans discovered an
aversion to the police. The misdeeds that they read about in the papers was not the only source of their misgivings. Ethnic and racial
minorities, a growing constituency, resented the bigotry underlying
the selective enforcement that targeted them while turning a blind
eye to the drinking going on in fashionable speakeasies. Mainstream
Americans were outraged at the corruption that infested local politics. Elites were horrified that police lawlessness was eroding respect
for the rule of law. And few wanted to pay more for even more
police, especially federal agents, to try to make Prohibition work.
Eyes popped when the commissioner of Prohibition informed a congressional committee that his bureau needed $300,000,000 to do the
job. The message of repeal was that the people had had enough.[17]

This lesson, however, did not apply to traffic. Some actually did try
to propose a prohibition on car sales when no amount of regulation
or punishment seemed to reduce automobile accidents and fatalities. In 1916, the Iowa State Highway Commission queried, "Is it
not time for Iowa to prohibit by law . . . the sale or use of motor vehicles, pleasure or commercial, capable of a speed greater than 25 or
30 miles per hour?" After all, "the statute books [were] full to the
brim of regulative and restraining laws to prevent danger or menace
to human lives." But this was merely a thought experiment born of
desperation. Americans had already come to view their cars not just

as a luxury, but as a necessity. As early as 1921, President Harding proclaimed that "the motor car has become an indispensable instrument in our political, social and industrial life." A few years later in 1924, soon-to-be president Herbert Hoover declared that traffic was "here to stay." Unlike liquor, the automobile could "not be ruled out of existence." Not only were Americans unwilling to give up their automotive way of life, but they also decided to build more roads to make room for more cars, which meant more traffic, which meant more police. "The completion of miles of new boulevards and streets adds to the duties of the Traffic Bureau," the LAPD reported in its 1913 *Annual Report* as it requested more men. The problem only got worse. Two decades later, the department was still making the same case, pointing to the "6000 miles of paved highways included in the city's 453 square miles."[18]

Despite his view that managing traffic should not be the police's job, Vollmer reluctantly accepted that it had landed "at the door-step of police departments." Since the nineteenth century, some states, like Louisiana, had charged municipal officers with overseeing "the movement of teams and vehicles in the streets and roads." Adding motor vehicles to that list followed logically. After all, the policeman's duties were to preserve the peace, maintain order, and protect life and property. The mass volume of cars disturbed peace and order, endangered life, and destroyed property. Although local governments could decide not to enforce Prohibition, they could not ignore the unrelenting disruption and destruction of traffic. Reflecting these priorities, Toledo, Ohio, assigned six officers to the vice squad, the second largest "special duty" unit, which paled in comparison with the traffic squad of sixty-eight. As a whole, Ohioans seemed not to care much for vice enforcement. In 1929, their senate introduced a bill to abolish the prohibition department and, in exchange, enlarge the safety department, which handled traffic.[19]

The problems of motor-powered transportation not only justified greater municipal forces but also supplied an argument for the creation of state police. Vollmer wanted to combine the myriads of village, town, city, and county police units into "a well-organized State Police" that replicated the gendarme systems in European states. He explained in a 1935 radio interview that the current decentralized arrangement had not evolved much from the era of "night watches of Medieval England and Europe a thousand years ago." Back then, "policing was a purely local problem and could be handled adequately by small, independent organizations." Woefully, he continued, "America has been almost oblivious" to how cars had transformed the political landscape. With the automobile, distance no longer posed the same limits for criminals who did not respect county or state boundaries. He spoke of one gang that proceeded from Los Angeles, up the San Joaquin Valley to Berkeley, then to Portland, and finally to Vancouver, robbing banks along the way. Another criminal partnership worked in no less than eleven different states. Sophisticated auto-theft rings divided their operations strategically, stealing cars in one state and selling them in another. While criminals "rove at will from one part of the country to another," Vollmer explained, the police, on the other hand, were "largely confined to their own territories, have no authority outside of their own backyards, and can't always get cooperation from their fellow officers in other backyards." They were fighting crime like "a football team without a quarterback."[20]

Vollmer was well aware of the many obstacles to his "ideal program," which included the difficulty of amending state constitutions. He did not have to mention the ideological objections. Even as progressive Americans were looking across the Atlantic to European models of administration, they still feared the inclination of centralized police to turn into the private force of the political party in power. Many also worried that state police would be used for union-busting, just as Pinkerton's strikebreakers had intervened in labor disputes on behalf of industry, often using violence.[21]

In an attempt to overcome this formidable resistance, Vollmer hitched the crime control rationale to traffic. In 1935, Vollmer and his acolyte Alfred Parker published *Crime and the State Police*, which, notwithstanding the title, really dealt with motor vehicles. The most obvious reason the authors gave for statewide police forces was traffic control. Vollmer and Parker described the "regulation of traffic on rural highways" as "twentieth-century problems" that required police with authority in multiple jurisdictions. Their other two reasons for state police, the "crime problem" and the need for "rural police protection," also arose from automotive travel. Cars facilitated the "flowing of city life into the country," dispersing criminal elements into sparsely populated regions. In short, the automobile spawned interconnected issues that rationalized the creation of state police. Nevertheless, people sought more roads. Decades before the federal government funded the interstate highway system, private groups and local and state governments were breaking ground for new freeways and highways. Each project sprouted new suburbs and connected farther-flung towns and counties, generating a need not just for more traffic cops but also for multijurisdictional patrollers. In 1936, New York's governor spoke of the inevitability of police consolidation in a special message to the legislature, emphasizing the need to "strengthen the police defense of the state in rural areas and on the great arterial highways." Regardless of their intertwined developments, the conveniences of automobility exceeded the drawbacks of state police. The Federal Bureau of Public Roads began studying the feasibility of a superhighway system, which would culminate with the 1956 Federal-Aid Highway Act, at the very same time that governors and law enforcement officials were promoting police unification because of cars.[22]

States, however, did not unify all the local police departments under one agency as Vollmer preferred; instead, they organized their own forces. According to Vollmer and Parker, in 1905, only Connecticut, Massachusetts, New Mexico, Pennsylvania, and Texas had state police. By 1932, they counted twenty-seven states with highway patrols under a department of motor vehicles, eight that were under the state police, and five with county patrols. Only eight had no form of centralized police—yet. By the end of the decade, almost every state had its own force, and nearly all of them specifically cited traffic as their mandate. For example, in 1935, Iowa's first female secretary of state established the "Iowa Highway Safety Patrol." Secretary Ola Babcock Miller, undeterred by previous failed attempts, succeeded by crusading against reckless driving, which she called "Public Enemy Number One." The legislature gave her funding for fifty officers and three commanders. Miller boosted those numbers by redefining the job description of the inspectors who handled motor vehicle registrations and sending them out to patrol Iowa's highways.

Officials who had previously dealt with cars as a regulatory matter—literally as paperwork—were transformed into patrollers, which aptly reflected the progression from regulation to police governance that attended mass automobility. It is difficult to calculate precisely how much of the growth in police forces at the local and state levels stemmed directly from the need to manage traffic and its accompanying problems. But it would not be an exaggeration to characterize it as a dominant factor.[23]

Not every jurisdiction could afford to keep pace with the influx of cars. In 1921, the superintendent of the police in Minneapolis sought one hundred additional men, but the city council authorized only twenty-five more. So he pursued the next best option, the time-tested solution to manpower shortage: special policemen. These officers were not publicly employed like their regular counterparts. Although the police department licensed them, citizens contracted privately for their services. Special policemen were essentially private security. But in terms of historical lineage, special policemen, also referred to as "watchmen" or "citizen policemen," hailed from old English traditions of the constable, the night watch, and the hue and cry that relied on the mandatory service of all adult males in the community. Over time, these institutions lost their voluntary character as rich men hired deputies to serve in their place. American towns and cities continued these practices even after they began forming public police forces in the mid-nineteenth century. Through the early twentieth century, many municipalities deputized a stable of special policemen to patrol the wealthy districts. In 1903, for instance, the Los Angeles Chamber of Commerce requested that the Police Commission expand "the system of registration and inspection of special policemen." "Even if the number of municipal policemen were doubled and then doubled again," the merchants pointed out, the increase would not be sufficient. They concluded that "the only way that the citizen can secure thorough protection is by private watchmen, each covering a small beat." The Police Commission continued to use this rationale a decade later to justify its appointment of 200 citizen policemen. Following this custom, the Minneapolis police superintendent appointed several hundred special policemen, "all responsible professional and business men who drive their own automobiles." This "civilian police squad" mainly ticketed cars that were parked illegally or were in noncompliance with safety-equipment regulations.[24]

Other cities tried different variations of voluntarism. The Boston Automobile Dealers' Association offered to do traffic duty and was credited for performing "wonders in a trying position." In Passaic, New Jersey, the police chief organized the "Junior Traffic Police" staffed with "older boys, preferably members of Scout troops," who were assigned to school zones. They wore arm bands with police insignia and were empowered to make arrests, but their primary job was to help younger students cross the street. "Street boy patrols" caught on in cities from coast to coast, especially after the Education Committee of the National Conference on Street and Highway Safety approved such programs for every town. The committee reasoned that not only did the junior patrols provide "a very practical outlet" for the students to apply safety lessons in the real world, but they also gave "actual assistance to traffic policemen." Vollmer added that giving juvenile delinquents a "star and a little authority—everything but a gun"—was a better reform strategy than arresting them.[25]

Instead of young boys, Washington, D.C., relied on "coppets," a volunteer corps of women. Unlike the junior traffic police, they wore a simple white band above each elbow and did not make arrests themselves. Instead, coppets took down the license plate numbers of violators and turned them over to the traffic department. Within the first few weeks, one hundred women signed up. It was the rare win-win-win situation. The city saved money, children took to the "mamma policeman," and volunteers found meaning in the work. To boot, a prominent doctor recommended the activity for all of his female patients on the advice that there was "nothing . . . that will give health like regular outdoor exercise and the feeling of helping others."[26]

That local governments resorted to recruiting even women and children to enforce motor vehicle laws indicated that the problem of traffic had reached a crisis point. As the number of cars kept growing, so did the need for cops. No amount of displeasure with the police could wean Americans from their freedom machines. More

Precinct 15 junior police with Captain J. F. Sweeney, circa 1915–1920.
George Grantham Bain Collection, Library of Congress, LC-DIG-ggbain-21682.

damningly, their inability to govern themselves on the road had made police law enforcement necessary.

Cars profoundly altered the relationship between citizens and the police. Before automotive traffic, the police had focused most of their attention on beggars, drunks, and those who seemed out of place. Now, because so many people drove, a vast and mostly "law-abiding" population suddenly became subject to policing. Even the rich were not immune. The *National Police Journal* frequently heaped high praise on the patrolman who showed "no partiality while in the performance of his traffic duties." For instance, it commended Patrolman Albert Kasbaum of Tonawanda, New York, for arresting "some of the wealthiest people in this country." Vollmer's men recalled that in Berkeley, even state senators received traffic citations. Hauling arrested citizens into court for minor traffic violations was common enough that people referred to the procedure as the "bawling out system." Police officers were no longer mere service providers who kept the streets clear of riffraff, although they still performed that task. They now stopped respectable people on the streets and in their cars, told them what they had done wrong, and meted out consequences for violating the law. This proved to be a job so challenging that it would fundamentally change the police function.[27]

Although the traffic problem certainly arose from too many cars on streets originally meant for nonmotorized vehicles, it was the human aspect of traffic that stood out in the minds of those working the pavement, or dirt. In 1920, the *National Police Journal* ran a story asking, "What does a traffic cop think about?" He tried not to, was the answer. What else could one do with "women drivers insisting they are on the right side of the street when they're on the left"? With "retired farmers changing the dusty color of the air to a dark blue because they are forced to wait a few minutes"? When tired and cranky businessmen were hurrying home, "sweet young things" were "zig-zagging down the middle of the street," and hordes of pedestrians were demanding "the heads of those who own automobiles"? As one traffic officer explained, "It's just a matter of standing there like one of the immortals and not worrying about whether you hurt the feelings of some woman shopper." The ire against women was especially pointed. In another officer's opinion, "Women especially think they're fortified against all danger when they're in a car. Invincible as the rock of Gibraltar is their idea of the automobile they're driving." Criticisms were more gender-neutral when it came to the walking lot, who tried to squeeze themselves into any "space of three inches between two moving automobiles" instead of waiting for their turn. *That* was what brought traffic to a halt. To be fair, pedestrians' walking customs became an issue only when cars showed up on the same roads.[28]

Enforcement of traffic laws to the letter aggravated drivers and even encouraged willful disobedience, posing a dilemma. To state the obvious, Vollmer asked rhetorically, "Where is the individual who does not resent the presentation of a traffic tag for one of the many possible violations?" Who did not resent having their names written in the public arrest book for a "trifling traffic violation"? Drivers began to direct their anger at the police, especially when they were pulled over while other equally culpable drivers were getting away. The department lost so much of its goodwill that, according to Vollmer, "some of the community's best citizens [became] actual enemies of the police." He lamented that normally law-abiding people were boasting about their traffic transgressions at cocktail parties. Juries reportedly acquitted defendants out of sympathy despite the "careful, honest, and impartial presentation of evidence and guilt by the police." Maintaining the public's support while at the same time managing traffic constituted "one of the police department's most serious problems." Efforts to uphold the law threatened the rule of law, putting the police in a double bind.[29]

To allay contempt for law enforcement and encourage obedience, officials tried to persuade the public, to the point of lecturing, to be more understanding. A New York City police commissioner appealed to citizens' better nature by suggesting that they were "often wrong" in allowing themselves "to be impatient when individual policemen err." To explain why, he provided some context. "The traffic man is expected not only to enforce the regulations upon the roughest, most reckless specimens who may be driving along the street." At the same time, the officer was expected, "very likely within the next few seconds, tenderly and courteously to help a feeble, timid old lady across the street." It tested the limits of human nature "to adjust itself to such changes quickly and with unruffled equanimity of temper." In this difficult situation, the public could help the police. If the people "will unfailingly treat the policeman with the politeness which [they expect] from him, some of the bad effects of his contact with the dreary, outcast sides of life will be neutralized," the commissioner guaranteed.[30]

Magistrate Judge Bruce Cobb of New York's Traffic Court also addressed the public's role in a 1923 pamphlet, *Making the Road Safe*. He gave a copy to every defendant who appeared before him. Copublishers the *Evening Telegram* (one of the city's dailies), the Automobile Club of America, and the National Automobile Chamber of Commerce also helped with distribution. The handout implored drivers not to "sass" even the unreasonable officer, no matter the situation. Then Judge Cobb let them in on a secret: if they were "attentive to the traffic officer," they would find that the officer would "then be more considerate" of them. The judge also warned against using "real or pretended 'pull'" to get out of a ticket or summons. If the officer was "the right sort," such antics would hurt the driver's case; if the officer caved, then the driver would be complicit in "undermining [the officer's] standards of duty and impartiality." The citizen's duty to drive safely apparently included an obligation to uphold the police's composure and integrity.[31]

Of course, primary responsibility for maintaining the high expectations of public service fell on the police, and government officials realized that the sensitive task of controlling the respectable classes in their freedom machines required a special person. It required a professional. A traffic cop, Vollmer once quipped, needed "the wisdom of Solomon, the courage of David, the strength of Sampson, the patience of Job, the leadership of Moses, the kindness of the Good Samaritan, the faith of Mary, the diplomacy of Lincoln, and the tolerance of Confucius." Dealing with the motoring public was too stressful of a job, and it was too much to ask of private citizens. Safety experts agreed that not every person had "the personal qualities necessary to succeed as a traffic control officer." Certainly, not every patrolman could handle the pressure, which sometimes manifested in unbecoming conduct that did nothing to get traffic moving. Launching into an unproductive tirade against the out-of-towner for making a wrong turn confused the driver and succeeded only in stalling traffic even more than letting the unwitting offender pass. Too many officers "cussed out" citizens as a matter of habit. No doubt, the police were unpopular because of encounters like these. Police leaders worried that motorists often drove away with the view that traffic cops were "arbitrary, irritable and frequently inclined to hale them into court for trifling infractions of law." The combustible nature of daily contacts between police officers and citizen-drivers obliged local governments to supervise those regulating traffic more closely.[32]

Ultimately, Vollmer's ideals for his profession became a reality on the concrete roads of automotive travel. One of the first steps toward professionalization involved a process of exclusion, a way of prohibiting laypeople from providing the services of specialists. This was precisely why Vollmer's first action item as marshal was to put his men in uniform. Not only did he want to instill professional pride in his force, but he also wanted to set his officers apart. He railed against special policemen who threatened his professionalizing project. "Ingenious schemes have been suggested to displace patrolmen," he warned, including the proposal that "police patrol work may be done by the employment of private watchmen . . . [or] organized citizens' police—reverting to the old watch and ward system." Vollmer claimed, with some anxiety and without proof, that "it has always been found that there is no substitute for good patrol service by professional policemen." The argument was not as convincing when it came to general crime control. It was hard to persuade the public to pay more taxes for more officers. They had gotten used to letting the wealthy districts hire their own watchmen. No one complained that insurance companies often had to take it upon themselves to recover stolen goods.[33]

Traffic, however, affected everyone, even those who did not drive and were content to walk, and traffic cops served the entire public. Recruiting volunteers to help schoolchildren cross the street was one thing. A more trying matter was finding people to manage the grown-ups. For this, it was quickly becoming clear that relying on do-gooders or private patrolmen would be untenable. After observing civilian police in action, traffic expert Miller McClintock concluded that "amateur direction is usually worse than none at all," so much so that if uniformed officers were unavailable, then "drivers should be permitted to exercise their own discretion."[34]

The increasingly penal nature of traffic laws provided another reason to bring everyone managing traffic under the full control of the police department. This became especially necessary when unremitting defiance of the law convinced municipalities to reinforce the patrolman's authority. In 1924, the Committee on Municipal Traffic Ordinances at the National Conference on Street and Highway Safety recommended making it "unlawful for any person to refuse or fail to comply with any lawful order, signal or direction of a traffic or police officer." Violators of this mandate, as with any other provision, would be guilty of a misdemeanor. Criminalizing disobedience to traffic commands shifted the balance of power between officers and citizens. To similarly unsettle relations among fellow citizens would have been all the more socially disruptive. Kansas City, aware of the potential problems, instituted rules for its civilian force, the "Vigilante Committee," which included the stipulation that the group's members were not to make arrests. If they invoked their common-law authority to make citizen's arrests, then they would be "personally and financially liable for the false arrest in case there should be an acquittal." By disclaiming liability, city officials were distinguishing the authority of citizen volunteers from that of full-time police. In the end, relying on the police exclusively or not at all, as McClintock suggested, presented the least hassle.[35]

The ability to exclude, in turn, entailed the prerogative to select. The requirements for one of the nation's premier traffic divisions, in New York City, were exacting. To be eligible, the candidate had to be at least six feet in height (most "progressive" departments required a minimum of five feet, ten inches) and be of "good appearance." These were more than vanity qualifications, according to McClintock. An ideal officer had to be tall enough to look above pedestrians' heads, be strong enough to wave his arms for hours at a time in all weather conditions, and have a fair enough countenance "to lend authority to his directions." Even in the smaller college town of Scranton, Pennsylvania, the sergeant who led the traffic squad "carefully selected" his twelve men. When Secretary Miller posted the draft for Iowa's first State Patrol, she received over 3,000 applications for fifty positions. In the first round, Miller picked one hundred who stood above five feet, ten inches tall and were at least twenty-five years of age. Former athletes and college graduates had an edge.[36]

Most importantly, Miller looked for "good moral character." When making the final cuts, the secretary personally conducted the interviews, searching for the "moral courage to do what is right regardless of political or other pressure." This was important because officers who could be bribed or swayed by power jeopardized highway safety. Corruption weakened support for Prohibition, but the country could not similarly eliminate automotive traffic to eradicate corruption on the highways. So cars necessitated perhaps the most important criterion of professionalism—that is, independence from politics. To manage traffic, police chiefs had to pick the most suitable men for the job, based not on political connections but on objective measures.[37]

Intelligence was another qualification because officers needed to be able to learn all the traffic rules and regulations, which was not always a straightforward assignment considering how simultaneously detailed and ambiguous the codes were. One Iowa State patrolman ticketed a driver for driving on the wrong side of the road. The fellow hired a lawyer, who argued that there was no "wrong side" because the law required vehicles to pull to the right only when meeting oncoming traffic. He won. Along with vindication, the Iowan probably also felt indignation for the trouble, both on the road and in court. To avoid encounters that irked the driving public and wasted state resources, officers had to master the laws on the books as well as judges' interpretations of them.[38]

Such mastery was required not just from Iowa's patrollers. The National Conference on Street and Highway Safety recommended specialized education for all traffic officers. At police academies that cropped up throughout the country, significant chunks of the curriculum dealt with traffic. For instance, at the New York State School for Police, traffic lessons took up 15 percent of the total class hours. Courses included twenty hours of state highway and motor vehicle laws, eight hours of municipal traffic ordinances, and four hours of parking regulations. The rest of the hours were not spent on cutting-edge investigatory methods as Vollmer had envisioned.

The police school that Vollmer founded in 1907 taught techniques and subjects relevant to pursuing criminals. Guest lecturers gave weekly presentations on topics ranging from toxicology to microscopy to handwriting. Students were also trained to use lie detectors, identify fingerprints, and analyze blood. They studied chemistry, physics, biology, sociology, and anthropology. Schools in the mold of Vollmer's model caught on slowly. The trainees, many of whom were not used to intense academic environments, seemed disinterested as well; they did, however, enjoy "making plaster and moulage casts of parts of their own and fellow officer's [sic] anatomies." In most schools, however, recruits focused instead on learning court procedures, writing accident reports, and practicing first aid—skills useful in dealing with all aspects of traffic mayhem. In smaller cities such as Toledo, the police school was affiliated with the traffic division in the most literal symbol of the connection

between automobility and police professionalism. Even if most police schools did not conform exactly to Vollmer's ideal, and even if
most police officers were not "trained . . . in exactly the same manner
that teachers, doctors, lawyers and engineers are trained for their
professions" as Vollmer had insisted, traffic enforcement more or
less fulfilled his demands for specialized education.[39]

Indicative of the importance of traffic in police work, Vollmer's
protégé O. W. Wilson, who would later serve as the chief of the Chicago Police Department during the tumultuous 1960s, spent his
early career in the 1930s directing the New England Traffic Officers' Training School and working with the Bureau for Street Traffic
Research at Harvard University. A more infamous police commissioner had a similar start. Lester B. Sullivan attended Northwestern
University's Traffic Safety Institute, a well-regarded school that
educated police officers from around the country. He would later
gain national notoriety as the supervisor of the Montgomery, Alabama, police department that arrested Martin Luther King Jr. four
times. One of those arrests was for speeding.[40]

Police training meant more than giving recruits technical instruction to do their job effectively. According to San Francisco police
chief Daniel O'Brien, it prepared officers "for the part he is to play
in American life." Now that policing had become an inescapable fact
in an automotive society, Americans had to figure out how citizens
and the police would get along. When Chief O'Brien argued that
only proper education could foster "a closer union" between the two,
he was keenly aware that he was witnessing a turning point in the
history of policing, nay, of US history. In the past century, people
may have expected the stereotypically illiterate, lazy, and pugnacious
cop who got his appointment as a political spoil. But now "we have
arrived at a period of American civilization," O'Brien declared, when
citizens demanded "the calm analytical judgment" of law enforcement officers.[41]

"Calm analytical judgment" actually contained a host of ideas,
some conflicting. First, the word "calm" referred to a pleasant, cool-
headed demeanor. For most drivers, it meant courtesy, a commonly
invoked word whose etymology traced back to the old-fashioned gesture of respect, "curtsy." In 1932, Los Angeles County's grand jury

convened to address numerous complaints about "a lack of courtesy" on the part of police officers. Although this body of esteemed citizens lacked jurisdiction to bring indictments in these instances, it did have the authority "to make recommendations which appear proper for the public service and the conduct of public servants." On that basis, the grand jury issued a report suggesting that the police department should "make it their business to see that the members of the police force are *courteous* in their dealings with the citizens." Although the report did not specify the circumstances of the complaints, they must have arisen in the context where the respectable citizenry most often encountered the police: in their cars. The report alluded to the "distinction between the class of offenders that every officer well knows" and advised that it was "this distinction that should be kept in mind in the handling of persons who come in contact with the police departments." In plainer terms, the grand jury's recommendations did not apply to "dangerous and known criminals," but to "the average citizen." By directing officers to be considerate of the general motoring public but not the criminally suspect, the mandate of courtesy implicitly acknowledged the police's increasingly discretionary authority to discern the difference between the two.[42]

Courteous cops soon became a hallmark of professionalism, which would later be enshrined in the Law Enforcement Code of Ethics that the International Association of Chiefs of Police adopted in 1957 ("I will enforce the law courteously . . ."). In the earlier period of automobility, the most explicit expression of this norm appeared in the name of South Dakota's highway patrol, which was called the "Courtesy Patrol" before its rechristening as the "Motor Patrol" in 1937. Colorado similarly had the "Highway Courtesy Patrol," which did not change its name until 1945. The association between traffic, courtesy, and professionalism permeated the culture of police progressives. Chief James W. Higgins, who seemed to have matched Vollmer's ambition, sought to create a professional force worthy of national attention by making his traffic squad the "pride of Buffalo, [New York], and the best in the country." Shortly after taking office, Chief Higgins visited several cities "with a view of seeing what improvements he could make in the movement of traffic." He made "some radical changes" upon his return, but the only one mentioned in a profile of him in the *National Police Journal* was how the traffic patrolmen had now been "trained to be alert, to be considerate of the pedestrian, to take pride in the reputation of their 'corners,' and to be courteous at all times." To emphasize that Chief Higgins had thoroughly professionalized his men, the article declared that the "days of the bully traffic 'cop' are gone in Buffalo."[43]

It was the same story in Philadelphia. Courtesy was an aspect of the "extensive reforms" that the new superintendent of the Bureau of Police introduced. At the start of the summer season when the city expected more visitors than usual passing through on their way to and from the New Jersey shore, he issued an order stating, "Firmness and politeness in handling all cases is expected and demanded . . . and discourtesy and profane language will not be tolerated from any member of this Bureau, no matter what may be his rank or position." Many citizens welcomed these reforms, but not everyone appreciated them. When New York City's traffic squad of 2,200 men was sent to "courtesy classes," one paper scoffed that a better way of dealing with the "wild, erratic and dangerous" category of drivers was to punish them to "a long, quiet contemplation of the inside of a city jail" instead of telling them "thank you" and "please." Penalties did get stricter for reckless driving, but so did courtesy and professionalism become indelibly linked.[44]

Courteous conduct segued to the next word in the phrase "calm analytical judgment." Indianapolis police captain Michael Glenn frequently went over the relationship between *calm* and *analytical* in his daily "policeman etiquette" lessons. His lectures followed a certain formula: The police were to enforce the laws, but with "courtesy and kindness." Applying this precept to "the proper way to make arrests" sounded simple coming from Captain Glenn. "If you find some motorist violating the law, arrest him and then present the evidence to the judge." Under no circumstances was the arresting officer to "try the case [him]self" by arguing with the arrestee. "Let the judge do that," Glenn instructed. Here was where "analytical" became relevant. When enforcing the law, officers needed to do so without passion and prejudice. They were to examine the situation and apply the right law, no less and no more.[45]

Michigan State Police Training School, 1940.

Image from the Collections of The Henry Ford, THF136474.

But Captain Glenn's clear-cut guidelines obscured the complexity of traffic law enforcement that many of his peers were describing in the same pages of the *National Police Journal*. The mechanical execution of the laws could not guide officers in determining when to stop a traffic violator, whether to issue a citation or make an arrest, and whom to treat courteously. In other words, "analytical" ran counter to the third keyword, "judgment." Traffic experts and police chiefs alike were stressing the importance of using "discretion and judgment in handling all violations of the motor vehicle laws" because for one thing, the large number of laws made perfect enforcement impossible, and for another, individuals became peeved when they were selected for enforcement.[46]

Before the innovation of the ticket system, which became more common in the late 1930s and early 1940s, a violation of the traffic code was treated like any other crime. Offending drivers were arrested, taken into custody, and brought before a magistrate, which initiated full trial procedures, unless the defendant pleaded guilty. Because it was impractical for traffic cops to leave their corners to take offenders to court, many jurisdictions began to rely on summonses, which were notices to appear in court at a later time. This practice may have started in New York City. A 1910 treatise on the "Law of Automobiles" noted that the city offered "persons of good character" a photo identification card; pursuant to statute, its bearer could "not lawfully be arrested in the city of New York for any violation of the motor vehicle law" and instead would receive a summons, which was "returnable not more than 48 hours after it [was] issued." By the early 1920s, other cities began experimenting with early versions of citations or traffic tickets, which differed from a summons in that rather than having to appear in court and go through the criminal process, the individual could simply pay the fine at the police station. Even with these simplified procedures, the deficit of manpower compared with the sum total of traffic violations meant that selective enforcement was unavoidable and, thus, antagonism from the public inevitable. Safety officials worried that while the deterrent value of prosecuting to the fullest extent of the law might be minimal, the wrath that it engendered would prove more lasting.[47]

When Chief Vollmer consulted police departments throughout the country on how not to alienate the citizenry, he advised them to "recognize the limitation of the law of legislators." This meant that arrests, even though the law called for them, could be counterproductive to the ultimate goal of public safety. Reflecting this view, some departments adopted a "golden rule" policy of refraining from arresting first-time offenders of nonviolent misdemeanors, which was controversial to be sure. Even the Cleveland police chief who expected his officers "to rigidly enforce all laws" relented and allowed for a limited application of the golden rule, but only for certain traffic offenses.[48]

Like his mentor, O. W. Wilson also had a side gig as a consultant, and he, too, recommended that officers ratchet down the penalties for traffic violations. Instead of an arrest for defective automobile lights, for example, they could serve a "defect notice," which would require only that the driver make the necessary repairs. Instead of citations for moving violations, which carried heavy fines, offenders could receive warnings. In certain cases, Wilson allowed that the police might not even attempt enforcement, especially if the public was not prepared to have the law enforced. He did not elaborate how exactly the public's attitude would be determined and who would make that determination. But his recommendations for effective law enforcement, like Vollmer's suggestions and the golden rule, instilled in patrol officers that they had discretion and that in many circumstances it would be wise for them to exercise their judgment.[49]

Traffic cops were aware of their discretionary power even without being told they possessed it. Every hour on patrol, they chose some individuals for the criminal process while letting others go scot free for equivalent transgressions. They experienced control whenever they stopped out-of-towners who could ill afford to spend a day in court far from home. As late as the 1940s, many cities had a policy of arresting nonresidents because they were unlikely to collect traffic fines once the violator had left the state. Many untold passing tourists surely submitted to any demand in order to continue their journey without further ado. Because of the potential misuse of power, one traffic expert's guidelines for police specified that "no amount of abuse by the offender should influence the officer to give an appearance notice if it was originally decided to give a warning notice." And yet, his very next instruction underscored that "all traffic violators cannot and should not be handled in exactly the same manner." This was the reality of traffic law enforcement. Officers knew that they possessed the power of choice and that they could change their mind on a whim.[50]

Chief O'Brien, who coined the phrase "calm analytical judgment" to describe the qualities of the twentieth-century policeman, detected an even more radical change in the police function. While the police's traditional "sphere of activity" involved serving "as the protector of the people's lives and properties," that sphere had expanded in the Automotive Age. According to O'Brien, the officer now also served "as a judge and a jury upon many trivial matters"—that is, on traffic—"which he is expected to summarily decide." The growing trend of assessing punishment without trial through some sort of ticketing or tagging system eliminated the judicial portion of the criminal process and transferred the role of judge or jury in adjudicating guilt to the traffic cop. To be sure, defendants could request that their cases be transferred to court where they could stand trial. But most people preferred to pay the assessment at the police station and be on their way without the hassle of appearing in court. The upshot was that cops determined guilt on the road (which would later raise confusion about whether a traffic stop constituted an arrest). Notwithstanding the separation-of-powers issue, local governments approved streamlined methods of handling traffic violations. Because tickets lowered the stakes of being prosecuted, the police also endorsed them as a way to minimize arguments spewing on the streets between citizens and the police.[51]

These benefits of routinizing traffic procedures seemed to have caused Chief O'Brien to gloss over the full import of the police's simultaneous duties to protect and to judge. His lack of further reflection is striking in the light of widely publicized accounts that critically described the police in Germany and Austria, where they reportedly exercised judicial functions. According to the 1916 study *European Police System*, which was reprinted in the *National Police Journal* and advertised in several issues, "the extensive judicial powers in the hands of the police [were] easily capable of abuse." Its author, the well-known police reformer and scholar Raymond Fosdick, concluded that from "the standpoint of any democratic government or any liberal political creed," the continental scheme was "greatly to be deprecated" for its tendency to infringe "fundamental rights." Notwithstanding comparative studies like Fosdick's and the stream of news from abroad, police leaders did not ponder the implications of traffic law enforcement in the United States. Regardless of whether police chiefs like O'Brien and Vollmer were aware of it or not, the mass chaos of automobility, the volumes of traffic laws, and the need to cultivate a relationship of mutual respect with the driving public had expanded the range of police discretion to the point of encroaching on the magisterial role.[52]

So it was that traffic accomplished the goals of professionalization and even made it seem crucial and uncontroversial to do so. The ability to exclude and to select, autonomy, specialized training, the commitment to public service, standards of ethical behavior, and the exercise of judgment: these tenets of professionalism became essential not because Vollmer was particularly persuasive about reforming the police. His vision became a reality in part because law-abiding citizens were incapable of governing themselves on the road, and in part because they were too unmanageable for just anyone to deal with them. It may be that police as an institution had existed "everywhere and at all times" because "in every society disorder has been a threat to survival," as a criminal law scholar once asserted in 1953.[53] But the police of the twentieth-century United States took on its specific characteristics in response to the particular need to discipline the motoring public.

Traffic duties also helped Vollmer fulfill his wish list for the accoutrements of professional crime fighters. In 1905, the boy marshal of Berkeley had ordered his reluctant men to wear uniforms to inaugurate the new police. By 1924, patrolmen throughout the United States put on bluecoats for the "beneficial effect on the discipline of motor traffic," according to the National Highway Safety Council. Nobody minded. Officers preferred being clothed with the authority of the uniform when patrolling the highways. The public wanted the police in blues because otherwise, they were unable to tell whether they were being stopped by a highwayman posing as a law enforcement officer.[54]

The most sought-after accessory was the patrol car, which public safety experts universally deemed indispensable. After all, cops in motorized vehicles were the most effective way to go after speeders, the largest category of traffic lawbreakers and one of the main causes of accidents. At first, motorcycles were more common because they were cheaper than cars, but four wheels eventually phased out the two-wheelers. Even though motorbikes were more maneuverable in traffic, they were useless in bad weather and on bad roads. Officers preferred to be in an enclosed car that shielded them from rain that hit their skin, which felt just as painful as gravel that hurtled onto their faces.[55]

But Vollmer never cited traffic as a reason to put policemen in patrol cars because his idea of policing focused on crime control. In

Police officer on a bicycle, stopping a car, undated.

Image from the Collections of The Henry Ford, THF136479.

his view, officers needed cars because speed had become the "all-important factor in police work," for no modern invention revolutionized the cat-and-mouse chase like the automobile. It was its facilitation of rapid, individualized travel that made the getaway car such an elusive target. By enabling criminal suspects to abscond at any moment, in any direction, and at unprecedented speed, cars eliminated the need to wait around for public transportation, which had been Spud Yarrow's undoing, and made escape that much faster. The modern motorcar had become, in the words of William Howard Taft, "the greatest instrument for promoting immunity of crimes of violence . . . in the history of civilization." A Michigan judge noted that cars had "a capacity for speed rivaling express trains" and provided "a disguising means of silent approach and swift escape unknown in the history of the world before their advent." Another commentator described "the average policeman, on foot, horseback or depending upon a jitney . . . about as powerful an enemy of a man

The original caption was "Chicago Officers Apprehending Obstreperous Speeders."

The *National Police Journal* 6, no. 5 (August 1920): 5. Reproduced from a copy at University of California, Berkeley, Library.

Highway traffic officer, sometime before 1920.

The Department of Agriculture, Bureau of Public Roads, Washington, DC. Courtesy of New York Public Library, image ID 92677.

in a high[-]powered car as would [be] Don Quixote grappling with an American tank." Foot patrolmen, they all argued, were ill-equipped to pursue criminals in this motorized world. Vollmer thus arrived at the conclusion—in fact, the conviction—that officers must be "motor-mounted."[56]

In 1910, Vollmer ordered his officers to replace their bicycles with motorcycles; four years later, he put them in Fords. The city paid for gas and compensated each patroller an extra $27.50 a month for the use of his own machine. By local accounts, the Berkeley force became the first in the world to motorize its men. Notably, these reports did not count the early electric-powered patrol wagons, the size of buses, that had debuted in the 1890s to transport prisoners and equipment. What Vollmer had in mind was different: he envisioned each officer patrolling his beat in his own personal automobile.[57]

But simply putting an officer in a patrol car was not enough to overcome the fleeing lawbreaker's head start. Without a nearly instantaneous system of communication—or, as Vollmer put it, without the "means which is at all in proportion with the speed afforded to the criminal in his getaway, through the use of the automobile"—the police would never be able to catch up. Traveling speed alone proved insufficient without also speed in the exchange of information. In 1921, both Berkeley and Detroit announced a breakthrough. Installing a two-way radio transformed the patrol car into a mobile receiving station and enabled the officer, no matter where he was located, to communicate instantly with headquarters. On their own, the radio and the automobile had limited potential for police service. But outfitting cars with radios compressed the time between alarm and arrest into a "matter of seconds and not of minutes, hours or days as was true in the past," Vollmer raved.[58]

As his disciples moved on to command police departments of their own, Vollmer's first piece of advice was to "motorize your force." He sent the following recommendation to Wilson, who in 1928 had become the police chief of Wichita, Kansas: "Mount as many patrolmen as you can as soon as circumstances will permit. Bicycles are preferable as a preliminary step in this direction." The final step in Vollmer's plan was "complete motorization." The mastermind of police professionalization even tried to get those who had never benefited from his guidance to follow suit. In 1930, Vollmer wrote letters to all police leaders of cities with a population greater than 100,000.[59]

But Vollmer often argued in vain. Many chiefs responded with regret that, with the economic depression, their departments could not afford to buy more cars or to equip existing ones with radios. In Boston, the new mayor had required all agencies to reduce their budgets by 15 percent at a time when police expenses had doubled. Its police chief wrote back to Vollmer that with municipal funds severely depleted, it was impossible to purchase radios. Vollmer granted that it "may be months and it may be years," but he guaranteed that "all the money that you have spent for equipment will be returned to you with interest" because "the city without up to date communication methods is bound to suffer from depredations by criminals."[60]

Vollmer's relentless advocacy met with some success. Despite the financial crisis gripping the country, he reported that more than forty departments had provided their motorized policemen with radios. Vollmer commended them for recognizing the necessity to "speed up" just to catch up. "The radio and automobile in police work," he declared, "has assured a brilliant future." Along with these grand pronouncements, Vollmer relished retelling stories of "criminals [who] have been apprehended by radio-equipped policemen before they have had an opportunity to escape from the scene of their crime." He reveled that "murderers have been caught, figuratively speaking, with the blood of the victim on their hands."[61]

Still, headline-grabbing cases, even if they sustained the impression of a surging crime wave, were hardly typical. The President's Research Committee on Social Trends in 1933 submitted a sober analysis that should have allayed any hysteria about the crime rate. Most police forces accordingly had a few cars, which were stationed at headquarters, ready to be deployed when needed. For example, the Dayton, Ohio, police department's "Ford squad" consisted of just two cars that were "constantly on duty answering emergency calls."[62]

Also, within the universe of serious crimes, the murders that inspired Vollmer's police innovations or the sensational escapades of mobsters and bank robbers during the Prohibition Era were not very common. At the turn of the century, when people talked about crime, they were talking about theft. With the mass production of cars, it was auto theft. As a police chief put it in 1919, "The highwayman, the burglar, the pickpocket of the past have been almost superseded by the automobile thief." The LAPD's "Daily Bulletin" for November 27, 1922, to pick a typical day, gives an idea of the sorts of crime that occupied a Los Angeles cop's investigatory hours: besides the names of missing and runaway children, which were two separate categories, descriptions of burglars and a much longer column of "unrecovered" autos filled the entire sheet. On this particular day, the police were also apprised of a patrolman's lost badge.[63]

If we can trust one 1920 report, thieves and joyriders were stealing one out of every ten cars manufactured each year. This high percentage stemmed from the obvious fact that the object of theft also provided an instantaneous means of escape. To compound the problem, at a time when most cars were standardized—which facilitated the black market of stolen auto parts—no one could tell "whether or not the person who is getting into the automobile is the rightful owner," an insurance investigator observed. As a Michigan court noted in 1922, motorcars were constructed "as covered vehicles to standard form in immense quantities," making these machines much harder to distinguish than the "slower, animal-driven vehicles, with their easily noted individuality." The fact that most cars looked alike provided a successful defense for one defendant, who claimed that he was in the wrong Ford because "both cars are Fords, and all Fords look alike, not only to me but to their owners." In a 1931 Mississippi case, the court ruled that the description of a car as a Ford "that might be occupied by negroes" was not specific enough to justify the issuance of a warrant.[64]

Especially before colorfully painted cars became common, trying to spot a particular car in a sea of drab shades must have seemed like a search for the proverbial needle, prompting police chiefs to call for a numbering system to identify automobiles that would be detectable even when a car was traveling the average thirty miles per hour. Others trained their men to tell cars apart by focusing on small details, like the shape of the hub caps. Some people adopted the fad of monogramming radiator caps.[65]

THE DAILY BULLETIN
DEPARTMENT OF POLICE, CITY OF LOS ANGELES

CHIEF'S OFFICE   Monday, November 27, 1922   Vol. 15 No. 6391

POLICE COMMISSION
Geo. E. Cryer......Ex-Officio Chairman
J. H. De La Monte....621 Laughlin Bldg.
      Phone 64691
C. A. DeCoo...........467 P. E. Bldg.
      Phone 820286
L. D. OAKS............Chief of Police
    Police Court Schedule
This week: Judge Richardson, Dept. 4
Next week: Judge Chesebro, Dept. 5.

The Daily Bulletin was omitted on Saturday, Nov. 25.

MISSING

JOSEPHINE HOGE, age 16 yrs., blonde, blue eyes, very pretty and attractive, wearing a fuzzy, turned-up all around, dark blue hat and imitation plush coat with strip of gray fur on collar.

This girl disappeared from Fallbrook High School Tuesday night, Nov. 21, 1922.

Supposed to be with DAVID LAURENCE of Fallbrook, California, who is said to be 17 yrs., of age, large boy, dark hair, weighing about 140 pounds; driving a gray or blue stripped-down Ford.

If located, detain and notify Detective Bureau.

RUNAWAY BOYS

2347
    EDWIN SCHULTZ, American, 16 yrs., 5 ft. 9 in., 145 lbs., blue eyes, light brown hair, fair complexion and heavy build. Wore brown checked Mackinaw, dark brown suit, brown shoes and mixed grey cap. This boy formerly attended the Stockton School of Commerce, Stockton, Cal. (Juvenile Bureau.)

2348
    ALIOS GALLUN, American, 10 yrs., 3 ft. 8 in., 65 lbs., blue eyes, blond hair, fair complexion and medium build. Wore blue overalls. This boy formerly attended the Cahuenga School. (Juvenile Bureau.)

JACKSON MORGAN, stage name Perry Smith, negro, 11 yrs., 5 ft. 5 in., 90 lbs., brown eyes, black hair, medium build. Wore gray suit, tan shoes and cap. This boy recently arrived here from Detroit, Mich. May be found at Culver City. (Juvenile Bureau.)

RUNAWAY GIRLS

2349
    JUNE CARR, American, 17 yrs., 5 ft. 5 in., 135 lbs., blue eyes, dark brown hair, fair complexion and medium build. Wore tan coat, blue suit, lavender sport hat. (Juvenile Bureau.)

2350
    ELEANOR AGUAYA, 15 yrs., 5 ft., 110 lbs., olive eyes, brown hair and complexion, slender build. Birthmark over right eye. Wore pink dress fur neck piece, black slippers and stockings. This girl ran away from Santa Ana, Cal. (Juvenile Bureau.)

LOST BADGE

Patrolman's badge, No. 372, has been lost. Finder will return same to the Inspector's office.

WATCH YOUR BEAT!

Twenty-eight yrs., 130 lbs., 5 ft. 6 in., dark clothing. Burglar who entered room near 800 S. Flower about 5 p. m.

No. 1, 5 ft. 8 in., 150 lbs. Wore dirty overalls and jumper.

No. 2, 5 ft. 11 in., 160 lbs. Wore dark clothes, very slender. Two Negro prowlers who were shot at by officer near 1st and Anderson. One probably injured.

Negro, 23yrs., 5 ft. 8 in., 150 lbs., gray suit, gray cap, well dressed. Apartment burglar who entered place near 700 California about 11 a. m.

Unrecovered Autos from Nov. 1 to Nov. 20, 1922

Make	Type	License	Engine	Date Stolen
Ford	Coupe	828846	6434226	11- 1-22
Ford	Tour.	414121		11- 3-22
Ford	Tour.	820530		11- 3-22
Ford	Tour.	674948	2533253	11- 4-22
Ford	Speed.	654583	1005838	11- 5-22
Ford	Coupe	788098	5913849	11- 5-22
Ford	Coupe	?	5873018	11- 6-22
Ford	Coupe	825609	6416097	11- 6-22
Ford	Coupe	765456	?	11- 8-22
Ford	Coupe	827109	6434082	11- 8-22
Ford	Tour.	743856	5808046	11- 8-22
Ford	Coupe	836103	6569940	11- 9-22
Ford	Coupe	838753	6578084	11-10-22
Ford	Bug	776090	630472	11-10-22
Ford	Coupe	840424	5610908	11-10-22
Ford	Road.	762441	6095674	11-11-22
Ford	Road.	?	?	11-12-22
Ford	Road.	454907	5352465	11-12-22
Ford	Tour.	373222	3939961	11-13-22
Ford	Coupe	?	6563561	11-13-22
Ford	Road.	348625	3599885	11-13-22
Ford	Tour. Dia.	E 7103	5354934	11-13-22
Ford	Coupe.	?	?	11-18-22
Ford	Tour.	733191	4839128	11-18-22
Ford	Road.	296222	5631450	11-18-22
Ford	Tour.	719206	?	11-18-22
Ford	Tour.	720802	?	11-18-22
Ford	Coupe	368876	4597136	11-18-22
Ford	Tour.	820468	?	11-18-22
Ford	Coupe	834892	6540303	11-19-22
Ford	Sedan	?	5698628	11-20-22
Ford	Tour.	?	4848504	11-20-22
Ford	Coupe	840282	6666030	11-20-22
Ford	Tour.	753480	MVD-22474	11-20-22
Ford	Road.	380230	5500340	11-20-22
Ford	Rd.Del.	770422	6231782	11-20-22
Buick	Road.	671367	225211	11-10-22
Chand.	Chy.	407130	38129	11-20-22
Chev.	Tour.	766227	F-47279	11- 5-22
Chev.	Tour.	485443	B-51452	11- 8-22
Chev.	Road.	744306	?	11-16-22
Essex	Coupe	438304	50820	11-12-22
Essex	Coach	767357	81541	11-16-22
Hud.	Speed.	822375	140554	11- 3-22
Hud.	Sedan	473055	13267	11- 7-22
Hud.	Tour.	464720	67159	11-10-22
Hud.	Coupe	682716	?	11-17-22
Moon	Tour.	719390	10283	11-19-22
Mar.	Chy.Rd.	?	?	11-17-22
Reo	Spd. Trk	?	MF-50946	11-19-22
Stude	6Rd.	373135	BG-61427	11-10-22
Stude.	Big 6 Tour. 7P.	550669	25391	11-19-22
Harley-Dav.		7721	?	10-28-22
Harley-Dav.		8274	20-T-12324	11-16-22
		(Detective Bureau.)		

L. D. OAKS,
Chief of Police.

Parking lot near Soldier Field in Chicago, Illinois, for the Notre Dame–USC football game in November 1929.

Prints and Photographs Division, Library of Congress, LC-USZ62-45643.

Parking on Main Street in Brawley, California, circa 1920.

Prints and Photographs Division, Library of Congress, LC-USZ62-41893.

Car thieves also benefited from ignition and door locks that re-mained shockingly inadequate until 1965, when regulatory pressure finally prompted General Motors and Ford to redesign lock mech-anisms. Until then, a vigilant watch seemed to provide the only guarantee against theft. But as an insurance investigator pointed out, when an "automobile is left by the owner on the street," the owner "can't stay with it and [it would be] impractical to hire someone to see it is not stolen." Another insurance representative recommended that "when dining in a public restaurant the driver of the car should be seated in such a position that he can observe his car." Following this line of reasoning, one company sold the "Collapsible Rubber Driver," which was advertised to fool a would-be thief into thinking that "a real, live man" was sitting in the driver's seat.[66]

The impracticability of maintaining constant guard and the un-realistic threat of the modern scarecrow left owners with no defense against the experienced swindler, as statistics confirmed. In 1932, based on numbers that the US Department of Justice had begun compiling, for every 100,000 persons in the United States, 363 auto thefts were reported, compared with 85 robberies, 291 burglaries, and 615 larcenies. It would be fair to assume that the automobile played a role in the other crimes counted in the 1932 statistic. That was also the estimation of an insurance investigator who in 1921 had figured that 75 percent of all crimes involved a motorcar. Similar data from that year prompted the Chicago Crime Commission to propose a law that would "make the use of an automobile in the commis-sion of a crime a separate offense." This was after the federal gov-ernment had already passed the 1919 Dyer Act, which criminalized interstate trafficking in stolen vehicles. Other states attempted greater deterrence with stiffer penalties. Virginia, for example, re-classified auto theft as a felony in 1920. Cars undoubtedly contrib-uted to an overall increase in crime, and patrol cars seemed crucial to meet the exigencies of a newly motor-powered world. "What the police need," the *National Police Journal* stressed in affirmation of Vollmer's position, "is means to meet the modern thief on even terms."[67]

But the curious fact was that recovering stolen automobiles, which took up more of the police's time than any other crime, did not

necessarily involve a car chase, for the police did not usually go
after a car thief right at the moment when the bandit was driving
off. More often, they received a call from a suddenly carless owner,
and by then it would have been too late for any motor-mounted officer
to set off in pursuit. The standard protocol that the Toledo, Ohio,
police department used to recover stolen vehicles, which was similar
to the one that the Auto Theft Committee of the International
Association of Chiefs of Police adopted, did not even rely on patrol
cars. Checking bills of sale and car titles, verifying license applicants'
cars, and maintaining an up-to-date index of stolen autos proved
more effective. These records contained descriptions, such as the
make, the model, and even the factory numbers for different car
parts. So crucial were identification numbers—*any* number, whether
for the car itself or a part thereof—to solving auto theft cases that
one police chief recommended that states make the destruction,
effacement, or alteration of such numbers a felony, as it was for the
analogous crime of forgery.[68]

Indeed, much of the work of dealing with numbers and papers was
done in an office. By midcentury, the LAPD had organized its procedures for handling auto thefts into an assembly line of sorts, performed mostly by women, behind the scenes, in the Records and
Identification Division. The department's 1956 annual report included a pictorial diagram of the "chain of events . . . from the time
the theft is reported to the police until the time the car is returned to
its rightful owner." Five of the eight pictures showed women
typing, filing, or searching files. The other pictures, all of men, depicted an officer in a patrol car talking into a radio for a license check
(presumably consulting with one of the women back at headquarters),
another impounding a car, and a third checking a claimant's proof
of ownership. Most events in this sequence, even the ones with male
officers in action shots, did not exactly comport with Vollmer's idea of
crime fighting.[69]

What little that cops on the beat could do did not require patrol
cars, either. The Toledo Police Department's procedures had its officers match out-of-town license plates with registrations on file with
the state. They also checked under the hoods of cars parked around
the plants or on the streets at nighttime for altered factory numbers,

a telltale sign. Inspecting all the cars parked in the business district between ten and eleven o'clock at night appears to have been the practice in Enid, Oklahoma. Police detectives in Buffalo, New York, visited auto repair shops and garages daily, which reportedly restored most stolen vehicles to their owners. Foot patrolmen managed these tasks as well as, or even better than, motor-mounted ones.[70]

Since a high-speed chase for murderers or auto thieves did not happen every day, Vollmer also highlighted the number of square miles a beat officer could patrol in a squad car. In his calculation, the more locations an officer visited in a shift, the more he could spread his crime-deterring effect. By transporting them from place to place more quickly than if they were on foot, a car allowed the police to attend to more areas without having to increase the size of the force. According to one chief's estimate, "the mounted officer is six times as effective as a foot patrolman and instead of protecting two to four blocks, he covers an area of over three square miles." Vollmer claimed that in residential neighborhoods where buildings were more spread out than in business districts, an officer without a car proved "utterly useless"—never mind whether the more sparsely populated quarters required a regular roving police presence.[71]

Even though the efficacy of a patrol officer depended just as much on qualitative factors, Vollmer insisted on computing efficiency in terms of distance over time. His emphasis on quantitative measures is perplexing in light of what he had written in a 1929 draft of *The Police Beat*, which presented a more nuanced understanding of good policing. The treatise, which was eventually published in 1939, may have set a high bar, but it provides an indication of what Vollmer thought officers were supposed to do. According to the father of modern policing, a conscientious officer knew his beat, which meant that he knew "the character, occupation, and habits of every resident on his beat so that when inquiries are made concerning any person living within the boundaries of his beat he will be able to supply his commanding officer with correct information without delay." He was also intimately familiar with the businesses, buildings, streets, and hidden alleyways so that any suspicious activities would be immediately obvious to him. He knew when something was out of the ordinary, when the shades of a shop had been fixed differently from previous nights, when a family was traveling on holiday by the pile of mail he had to remove before it caught the attention of a prowling burglar. He visited junk shops, pawnbrokers, bawdy houses, saloons, dance halls, and other known resorts for notorious characters to take note of who was who. At night, the scrupulous officer looked for stolen vehicles in parking lots. On his evening walks, he tried doors and windows of business shops to make sure they were locked. He lighted street lamps and removed obstructions on sidewalks and streets that could cause accidents. In short, the beat officer served as the eyes and ears of his commanding officer and the greater community. Clearly, to do the job well required careful attention to one's surroundings, which would have been difficult for an officer driving a vehicle, especially since Vollmer strongly recommended "one-man cars." His case for "complete motorization" undermined the intuitive aspects of the beat patrol that Vollmer himself had described.[72]

Even Vollmer's own students questioned his advice. He conceded in a letter to Wilson, "Obviously, in a city constructed after the plan of Wichita, it is impossible to completely eliminate foot patrolmen in the downtown areas." He continued, "You are better informed, and if you believe that foot patrolmen are necessary, of course your judgment should prevail." Still, Vollmer defended his position, clarifying that his "only purpose for recommending complete motorization [was] that in periods where mobilization is necessary, or in periods of temporary emergencies, great service can be rendered effectively, and with great dispatch." Even without reading Wilson's letters, the reason for his doubts about "complete motorization" is evident in Vollmer's response. Some aspects of policing simply worked better with the officer walking about rather than driving a car. The Baltimore Crime Commission would report in 1940 that "law enforcement officials have discovered that [patrol] cars can never replace the peculiar type of service rendered by patrolmen." Another decade later, in his 1950 textbook *Police Administration*, Wilson would note that "automobile patrol has some disadvantages because, while driving, the patrolman has less opportunity for observation and for contact with citizens than when on foot, and consequently he is less useful in furnishing information to citizens and in serving as the eyes and ears of the department."[73]

The efficiency argument sometimes had unintended consequences. Persuaded, some municipalities reduced police budgets once they provided patrol cars. In 1922, Portland's Tax Supervision and Conservation Committee announced that because it had approved the new expenditures, it would deduct $72,000 from the police department's budget. Since the equipment cost $30,000, it meant that the department actually had $102,000 less for the following fiscal year. Port Huron, Michigan, planned to add more automobiles and, in exchange, eliminate seventeen positions from the force. Many towns and cities were willing to subsidize the expensive machinery not necessarily to match the crime rate that fearmongers declared was escalating but to save money.[74]

To be sure, Vollmer did have valid reasons for putting officers in cars. Automobiles spread communities farther apart, connected only by ribbons of highway. According to the National Automobile Chamber of Commerce, home building increased 53 percent in 1922 because of cars. With more and more people living in the suburbs, the police, in turn, had to reach these outer areas more quickly. And it did make sense that at least some officers should drive cars for "periods where mobilization is necessary," as Vollmer pointed out to Wilson. But Vollmer went too far when recommending "complete motorization" and listing it first among the action items "tremendously important for [Wilson's] success" as a new police chief. In light of the expense, it is even more remarkable for Vollmer to have sought cars with two-way radios for every officer just in case, for "periods of temporary emergencies." As one police veteran wryly recalled decades later, reformers had "painted pictures of how crime was certain to disappear with the advent of the radio-equipped patrol car." Vollmer had overargued his case, which suggests that police cars served another function besides crime control.[75]

Vollmer's increasingly strident call for a fully motorized police force was not so much a repudiation of traditional beat patrols but was more a reflection of his aspirations in a society that had itself become motorized. His lifelong mission was to raise the standing of the police on par with "teachers, doctors, lawyers and engineers." He had a specific idea of what it meant to be a professional, and the patrol car helped to reshape the police into the image of a crime fighter.

The automobile, in other words, was a key element of Vollmer's professionalization strategy. For one thing, the patrol car erected a barrier to entry that distinguished public officers from private security. The expense would have been prohibitive for many one-man shops offering patrol services; indeed, many departments at first could afford only a few radio-equipped cars. As cars became more readily available at lower costs, police chiefs lobbied for laws not only equipping official vehicles with sirens and other special markers but also requiring nonofficial vehicles to remove them. More importantly, the patrol car functioned as an ideal symbol of professionalism because of its public presence. Other modern tools of policing, such as machines to analyze blood or identify fingerprints, were utilized in crime labs where no one could see the experts at work. In contrast, the value of a patrol car lay precisely in its visibility, which served as an important reminder to the public that, Vollmer lamented, had "not yet awakened to the fact that police work has grown from the cobble-pounding cop to a profession"—a profession that pursued criminals, that is.[76]

Vollmer routinely singled out cars among the various "modern devices" used in police work as the difference between "old style" police and the new generation of professional police. In 1928, when motor vehicles had become common throughout most of the United States, Vollmer remarked, in an obvious exaggeration to make a point, that the old-timers "haven't learned that the world has progressed; in fact, they don't seem to even know that automobiles are running on the public thoroughfares." The hyperbole may have seemed hypocritical to some, for Vollmer himself never learned to drive. Nonetheless, in Vollmer's mind, this emblem of progress could modernize, and thus professionalize, the police. Offering allowances for patrol cars as a perk also did not hurt in recruiting qualified men who could serve as the face of the new police.[77]

The link between cars and professional law enforcement was also evident throughout the pages of the *National Police Journal*, which featured a "modern" department in every issue. To demonstrate a police force's progress, the profiles mentioned how many motorcars it had and would be adding. The automobile even became a metaphor for the Newark police: "From an old-fashioned, ambling, easy-going sort of police force, it has developed into a high-geared, well-oiled, powerful modern machine, as nearly perfect as a police department can be." Several other cities, in addition to Berkeley, claimed to have been the first to use cars for police work, which goes to show that many progressive police chiefs shared Vollmer's view.[78]

Although the mandate of crime control proved insufficient in convincing local and state governments to endow Vollmer's vision of professional police, the imperative of traffic law enforcement gave the police their patrol cars. With the automobilization of American society and the triumph of the doctrine of professionalism, the beat-pounding patrolman almost disappeared. From the 1930s to the mid-1950s, a period when crime rates were actually decreasing, all police departments would adopt two-way radio patrol cars, and by midcentury, almost every officer would be motor-mounted except in the densest northeastern cities. In 1971, a police scholar would characterize the "uniformed officer who patrols the streets in a distinctively marked patrol car . . . [as] the most visible and direct representative of law enforcement, of the specific department for which he works, and of the entire criminal justice system." With near complete motorization, the police no longer focused on the kind of beat patrol that Vollmer had once described. In the late 1960s, reformers trying to develop "a closer rapport" between inner-city residents and the police would rediscover the virtues of the walking patrol cop for the same reasons that O. W. Wilson had explained to Vollmer back in the 1930s: cars kept officers from getting to know their beat as well as when they were on foot.[79]

It was also traffic that aided the police in their criminal investigations. As crime became more mobile, traffic and criminal law enforcement began to overlap. This development was most obvious with state highway patrols. In a few states, the power of patrollers at first remained limited to enforcing motor vehicle laws. But these states soon joined the others that conferred on patrollers the full powers of the sheriff. When this happened in Virginia in 1932, its "inspectors" of the highway patrol became "troopers" of the state police. The representative case of Alabama also illustrates the progression from traffic regulation to crime control. The state's highway patrol was established under the Department of Public Safety in 1935.

Then in 1939, its officers received not only statewide arrest powers but also semiautomatic shotguns, Thompson submachine guns, and long-range rifles. In 1945, they were, for the first time, charged with alcohol control; drug enforcement would soon be added to their mission. As Vollmer generalized this development in Alabama, "with the increasing necessity of traffic law enforcement, it was not long before state governments realized that the highways were often being used by criminals." The governor of Missouri likewise explained that even though the highway patrol was "chiefly a traffic regulatory body, almost daily its members capture men who are wanted for various crimes." New York's governor was more outspoken in recommending that the state police's criminal investigation unit be enlarged.[80]

The merging of duties was evident at the municipal level as well. As early as 1912 and through the 1950s, the LAPD routinely reported that it had "wisely avoided overspecialization of the traffic divisions" because they "greatly supplement[ed] the work of the regular patrol forces." Significantly, the department identified "the most important police officer" as "the patrol, investigation and traffic officer"—a revealing statement that described order maintenance, crime control, and traffic enforcement as the duties of one official. Law enforcement officers elsewhere were discovering the same benefits of unification. When in 1921 New York City launched a campaign "to lessen the automobile menace" by having its officers stop and examine cars for safety violations, the police realized that while at it, they could also look for evidence of auto theft. Traffic officers on duty near the ferry entrance in Edgewater, New Jersey, got the same idea, as did officers throughout the country on the lookout not only for stolen vehicles but also for liquor, which was criminalized throughout the country in 1920. With the motorization of the getaway, criminal investigations increasingly took place on the road, and often as part of a vehicle stop.[81]

The consequences of traffic management went beyond multitasking traffic cops. Local governments discovered, as the LAPD tallied in 1920, that the "revenue derived by the city from the traffic division [had] made it practically self-supporting." Fines funded a hiring bonanza that, in turn, enabled police departments to do more routine patrolling. For example, the LAPD in 1912 reported that

Table 2.1. Los Angeles Police Department Arrest Statistics, 1902 and 1912

Year	Population	Number of patrolmen	Patrolmen per person	Number of order-maintenance arrests	Order-maintenance arrests per 100 people	Number of traffic arrests	Traffic arrests per 100 people
1902	120,000	98	1 per 1,200	5,077	4.23	39	0.03
1912	347,550	392	1 per 900	21,303	6.13	2,386	0.69
Percentage increase			33 percent		45 percent		2,200 percent

Sources: LAPD, *Annual Report* from 1902 and 1912.

while directing traffic was "one of [its] largest tasks," the traffic squad nevertheless "assisted in the general work of the Police Department." A comparison of arrest statistics between 1902 and 1912, shown in Table 2.1, corroborates the department's reports that more traffic enforcement specifically led to more policing generally. From the turn of the century, when "fast driving" arrests referred to horseless carriages, to ten years later when the police agonized that "the automobile-motorcycle problem . . . is before us day and night," the ratio of patrolmen to residents increased from one patrolman for every 1,200 residents to one for every 900—an increase of one-third. Traffic arrests obviously went up—by over twenty-fold. More significantly, the same period also witnessed a 45 percent increase in arrests for order-maintenance types of offenses (begging, drunkenness, disturbing the peace, and vagrancy). In short, the automobile served as the justification and the modality for scaling up police law enforcement as a method of governing all of American society, drivers and vagrants alike.[82]

Policing had become a profession because of traffic, but the public's perception of the police function narrowed to crime control. The professionalization movement, with reformers like Vollmer leading the charge, played a part in this. These leaders repeatedly reminded citizens that the police's job focused on crime. As the association of professional police and crime-fighter became indelible, the traffic origins of modern police receded from historical memory. But its regulatory beginnings would provide legal justification for expanding the police's authority to enforce the criminal laws beyond even Vollmer's loftiest dreams.

3

The Automotive Fourth Amendment

> Everything was either masculine or feminine, man or woman. . . . Was it possible to live outside language?
>
> Arundhati Roy, *The Ministry of Utmost Happiness* (2017)

> I suggest that in the interest of coherence and credibility we either overrule our prior cases and treat automobiles precisely as we do *houses* or . . . treat searches of automobiles as we do the arrest of a *person*.
>
> Justice Byron R. White, *Coolidge v. New Hampshire* (1971)

On December 15, 1921, three federal Prohibition agents and an officer from Michigan's Department of Public Safety were on the prowl for bootleggers on Pike 16, the country road between Detroit and Grand Rapids. When a flashy Oldsmobile Roadster drove by—the 1920 model was more than triple the price of a basic Model T—one of the agents, Fred Cronenwett, had an inkling that George Carroll had passed them. They had met a few months earlier during what turned out to be a failed sting operation. Cronenwett had introduced himself as "Stafford," an employee at the "Michigan Chair Company," who wanted to buy three cases of whisky from Carroll. They settled on the price of $130 (over $1,500 today) per case.

Carroll, along with two accomplices, agreed to return with the goods and left in an Oldsmobile Roadster. They never returned, presumably because the "Carroll brothers" had caught on to the ploy. But they were now on the Feds' radar.[1]

About a mile later, after debating whether Carroll had just driven by, the officers turned around, sped up, and drew up to the Roadster. Cronenwett leapt onto the running board and called out for Carroll to stop the car. John Kiro, who was driving, did. Carroll recognized Cronenwett and called him by his real name, not Stafford. The officers proceeded to search the car and at first found nothing. They were about to let the duo go when Cronenwett struck something hard, so hard that it "was practically solid," in the cushion of the back seat. He tore the fabric and, according to the indictment, found sixty-eight bottles of whisky and gin. Carroll offered all the cash he had on him "to make it right." Spurning the bribe, the officers seized the bottles and arrested the men for violating the National Prohibition Act, also known as the Volstead Act.

After a jury found them guilty and the judge imposed a fine of $500, Carroll and Kiro appealed their convictions all the way up to the US Supreme Court, arguing that the search of their car, the seizure of seventy-three bottles of alcohol, and their arrest—all without a warrant—were unlawful. (The other five bottles not counted in the indictment seem to have mysteriously disappeared.) The government, represented by Solicitor General James M. Beck, defended the officers' actions by relying on the Volstead Act, which, in addition to outlawing the sale of alcohol, provided that a law officer who "shall discover any person in the act of transporting" illegal liquor in "any wagon, buggy, automobile, water or air craft, or other vehicle" had a "duty to seize any and all intoxicating liquors," "take possession of the vehicle," and "arrest any person in charge thereof."[2]

The petitioners contended that the government's interpretation of this provision to permit the warrantless stop and search of their car violated the Constitution. Specifically, the Fourth Amendment provided:

The right of the people to be secure in their persons, houses, papers, and effects, against unreasonable searches and seizures, shall not be violated, and no Warrants shall issue, but upon probable cause, supported by Oath or affirmation, and particularly describing the place to be searched, and the persons or things to be seized.

When Carroll and Kiro were forcibly stopped on the road, they were seized, their lawyer argued, and the Fourth Amendment required warrants for "seizures" of persons, also known as an arrest. To be sure, they could be arrested without warrants under the common law if the officers had knowledge, based on personal observation, that they had committed a misdemeanor offense or probable cause for a felony. But one of the agents had testified that they "had no reason to believe that the [defendants] were transporting liquor" before stopping and searching the Oldsmobile. And without a lawful seizure or arrest, the officers could not conduct a warrantless search.[3]

The government did not contest the defense's legal analysis. Instead, and more astonishingly, the solicitor general urged the Supreme Court to uphold the convictions by revising the centuries-old common law of arrests. The "use of such motor vehicles by criminals . . . demands that our ancient law be so amended as to cope with these modern facilities," Beck pleaded. He argued that a lower standard than even probable cause was necessary when cars were involved. In response, lawyers for the petitioners warned that "searches of vehicles on the highway will if promiscuously permitted lead to great abuses." They predicted that warrantless, groundless car stops and searches "will extend to everyone," so that even the "doctor making his rounds, the milkman on his route, yea even the rural postman will be forced to stop and submit to indignities." Every driver—"everyone," they argued—could be stopped and searched whenever a Prohibition agent had a hunch.[4]

The parties' dispute highlighted the problem that cars posed for the Fourth Amendment. Because cars provided both the getaway and a cover for hiding things, officers not only had insufficient time to get a warrant but also usually had only mere suspicion, short of probable cause or knowledge, that a car was transporting illicit goods. And because so many people drove and their cars looked, well, standardized, any rule on the police's authority when applied to the automobile would affect the lawbreaking and the law-abiding alike. The democratization of automotive travel required rules that would allow law enforcement to investigate the suspicious-looking without bothering the innocent—a particularly thorny task when it was often difficult to discriminate between the two when traveling at motorized speeds. Throughout the country, courts wrestled with a question that was now before the Supreme Court: *how would the Fourth Amendment adapt to the modern motorcar?*

Carroll v. United States, decided in 1925, was the Supreme Court's first car search case. The nation's highest court had seldom heard Fourth Amendment cases because, until National Prohibition, the federal government did not have many law enforcement agents who needed to conduct searches, other than customs officials.[5] Even state courts had few occasions to expound on the states' analogues of the Fourth Amendment. Before the proliferation of state prohibition laws, theft had been the most common crime that required searches. Since private citizens usually prosecuted their own cases, the victim was often the one who confronted the alleged thief. Nineteenth-century cases involving stolen goods suggest that suspects sometimes agreed to a search as a way to maintain innocence. If consent was not forthcoming, the accuser could swear out a warrant. The wrongfully accused, in turn, could bring a countersuit for trespass if there was no consent or warrant, or for libel and malicious prosecution if the warrant contained false statements. State or federal Fourth Amendments did not come up in these lawsuits.[6]

After the police began taking over criminal investigations but before the mass adoption of cars, officers typically had ample time to get a warrant even if a suspect was skipping town, since most people walked or took public transportation. Case in point, Berkeley police officers finally caught Spud Yarrow, the notorious burglar of Northern California, while he was waiting for his getaway: the streetcar to Oakland. Because trains and boats followed set schedules and routes, officers knew how much time they had to catch up to the suspect. If they came up short on time, then they could contact law enforcement at the next stop. Horse-drawn wagons on mostly dirt roads were not fast enough to outrun officers on horses. Those on horseback themselves had a good chance of getting away, which may explain why there are no reported cases involving a search of a horse-riding suspect.[7]

When officers did not have warrants, they could, with varying degrees of coercion, get consent to search, especially when those who were policed were not likely to challenge authority or have the means to do so. Even if an individual had the gumption to bring a lawsuit against an officer, the incentive to litigate was essentially non-existent. Before the twentieth century, the only real recourse for a violation of the Fourth Amendment was a civil action. Most lawyers knew that even if successful, damages usually amounted to little or nothing—and probably not enough to pay their fees. The lack of remedies reflected the absence of a problem: officers did not go around bothering respectable citizens with searches.[8]

Before the twentieth century—that is, before Prohibition, modern policing, cars, and adequate remedies for constitutional violations—police searches rarely became a Fourth Amendment issue. Several coinciding developments changed that. First, antiliquor laws dramatically increased the incidence of possessory crimes. While Prohibition created a law enforcement need to conduct more searches, the mass production of cars created the need for searches without warrants. Many bootleggers and moonshiners were caught while transporting illicit liquor in everyone's preferred mode of moving goods under cover. To enforce the dry laws, officers had to stop and search cars for contraband. But the automobile's speed and the motorist's newfound ability to drive off on a whim made it difficult to secure a warrant in time. The getaway became especially problematic for law officers who could not follow suspects outside their jurisdiction. Once in a foreign municipality, county, or state, police no longer had the authority of law. Rumrunners clearly understood the advantages of the multijurisdictional United States. To address this "abnormality, so contrary to all justice and reason," state attorneys general, legislators, and police leaders formed the Interstate Commission on

Crime in 1935. One of their first acts was to draft the "Uniform Act on the Fresh Pursuit of Criminals across State Lines," which granted "a member of a duly organized peace unit" the right to make an arrest for a felony occurring outside the state during a "pursuit without unreasonable delay." An intrastate version followed in 1942 to permit hot pursuit across county and municipal lines. But before then, criminal suspects knew to head straight for a border.[9]

The salience of borders may explain why in the early car search cases, before National Prohibition, defendants relied on the commerce clause of the Constitution, which courts interpreted to prohibit local legislation that implicated activities in other states. As an example, the Supreme Court invalidated state laws that placed restrictions on out-of-state distillers and brewers as a violation of Congress's powers to regulate commerce "among the several States." In turn, the drys turned to the same commerce power to justify national legislation that could wipe out the interstate alcohol shipping industry. Bootleggers also sought shelter in the interstices of interstate commerce by arguing that they had not intended to sell liquor in the state where they were arrested but were merely transporting liquor to sell in the next state over where, presumably, alcohol had not yet been prohibited. At the time, everybody thinking about liquor thought about the commerce clause.[10]

Another common defense arose during forfeiture proceedings. Typically, the owner of the automobile, who was not in the car at the time of the search, tried to reclaim the property by claiming ignorance that the driver would use the car to transport alcohol. Clearly, people trafficking liquor had ingenuity, a minimum sense of entitlement, and, importantly, the means to mount a vigorous defense. They included wholesalers and producers, many conducted business in multiple states, and some also owned several cars. Even small-timers were not exactly the downtrodden who rarely challenged their fate in the criminal justice system. In siding with a bootlegger, the South Carolina Supreme Court described him in a way that would arouse the most sympathy in agrarian country: as the "young, white farmer."[11]

In 1920, the Eighteenth Amendment criminalized nationally what had previously been dealt with as a local, regulatory, and spiritual matter. It was significant that Prohibition's offenders were not limited to the unsavory sort. John Wigmore, dean of Northwestern University Law School from 1901 to 1929 and an expert in the law of evidence, explained that before Prohibition, "the usual classes of persons" subject to law enforcement scrutiny were "forgers, panderers, gunmen, get-rich-quick schemers, fraudulent bankrupts, and the like" who were "of course, limited in number." After 1920, he noticed that "a potential field of vast extent has been added" that included "many not ordinarily deemed 'undesirable citizens.'" That even the desirable citizenry violated the Volstead Act made police searches more visible. Being searched was "a comparatively new experience to American citizens," an assistant US attorney noted in 1923. What he meant was that these probes were new to people not used to being policed. They might have been accustomed to prying neighbors who "policed" norms in self-regulated communities of the nineteenth century. But police surveillance was an altogether different and more invasive phenomenon.[12]

Notwithstanding greater resources and feelings of indignity, it would have been pointless to bring a Fourth Amendment challenge without an adequate remedy. Before the enactment of National Prohibition, some states had already adopted the exclusionary rule, which prohibited prosecutors from using evidence obtained in violation of a constitutional right. In jurisdictions that permitted this remedial rule, which had the potential to derail a prosecution for insufficient evidence, defendants now had reason to question the lawfulness of warrantless searches. The US Supreme Court began excluding ill-gotten evidence with its 1914 decision in *Weeks v. United States*. The case was about a different vice, lottery tickets, but it opened the floodgates for federal Prohibition cases to come.[13]

The convergence of Prohibition, the mass production of the automobile, and the rule of exclusion raised one of the most contentious questions in twentieth-century criminal procedure: when did the Fourth Amendment require a warrant to stop and search a car? This question became so common that in 1926, Asher Cornelius of the Detroit bar published a treatise spanning more than 1,000 pages on the "Law of Search and Seizure," stemming from "wide-spread violations of the state and national prohibition laws."

In 1936, an Oklahoma court expressed frustration that the issue of car stops and searches "has been before this court so many times." (The state remained resolutely dry, with the exception of beer, until 1959, when it finally repealed state prohibition.) It was not entirely a coincidence of history that the Supreme Court's first car search case involved rum-running.[14]

According to one federal prosecutor, it took a few years after the Volstead Act had made it into the law books for a critical mass of lawyers to conceive "the idea of questioning any Federal Government agent's right to search for and seize contraband liquor as he felt inclined or as his suspicions directed." But once litigants throughout the country seized on the idea, the national debate over alcohol turned into a showdown between two constitutional provisions. "Of all the legal topics in which interest has been stimulated by the Eighteenth Amendment and the Volstead act," the prosecutor continued, "none has claimed public attention to a greater degree than that of search and seizure" under the Fourth Amendment. The exclusionary rule soon proved as divisive as Prohibition itself. In fact, the procedural question of exclusion became synonymous with the substantive matter of outlawing liquor.[15]

The drys believed that without permitting the use of evidence found in warrantless searches, enforcement would be impossible and Prohibition would fail. One court predicted that strict adherence to the Fourth Amendment would "nullify the practical working of the Eighteenth Amendment." Legal commentator Frederic Johnson put it baldly: "To make these statutes effective, convictions are, of course, necessary. To secure convictions the prosecution must introduce incriminating evidence. . . . Frequently, however, the means themselves used to secure evidence which will convict are unlawful, violating constitutional rights, especially the guarantee against unreasonable search and seizure." Johnson thus argued that the Supreme Court should "recognize frankly that the 4th Amendment is inconsistent with the 18th" and "that the 4th Amendment has actually been repealed." The wets identified the same constitutional conflict, noting that "a large amount of searching and seizing is indispensable to thoroughgoing sumptuary legislation." But they came to the opposite conclusion that "the price we pay for prohibition," which included "summary haltings of automobiles," was "too high."[16]

Since the Supreme Court did not make the *Weeks* rule applicable to state prosecutions, argument over the exclusion of evidence turned up wherever defendants fought their prohibition charges. For instance, in a 1925 case before the Mississippi Supreme Court, Judge Ethridge insisted that "the great weight of modern authority supports the doctrine that evidence illegally obtained by an officer cannot be received." In dissent, his colleague Judge McGowen cited cases from thirty-four states proving otherwise. In truth, it was hard to tell which way the authorities were heading. Influential jurists like Professor Wigmore and Judge (later Justice) Cardozo opposed the exclusionary rule. New York's highest court rejected it in 1903 and again in 1926 in an opinion in which Cardozo famously quipped that under the rule of exclusion, "the criminal is to go free because the constable has blundered." But disregarding this controlling case law, New York's lower courts regularly excluded illegally obtained evidence in liquor cases.[17]

Other state cases also indicate that alcohol may have influenced the outcome. While thirty state courts rejected the exclusionary rule, sixteen adopted it by 1927. All but two of those sixteen did so in prohibition cases. Nine state courts had to overrule precedent to follow the federal rule. While it may be, as historians have argued, that the war on alcohol provided the blueprint for the twentieth-century state's war on drugs, the changes in criminal procedure at the time suggest that Americans were ambivalent about the development of aggressive police law enforcement, at least when it came to their drink.[18]

The squabble over liquor created a patchy state of the law, sometimes even within the same jurisdiction. One of the first state cases to apply the exclusionary rule, even before National Prohibition raised the political temperature to a fever pitch, was *Town of Blacksburg v. Beam*, which came before the South Carolina Supreme Court in 1916. The defendant had bought whisky from a dispensary in the town of Union and packed it in his suitcase to take home. At a stop in Blacksburg on his return rail trip, the police chief of that town "without any process" searched the defendant and—this part was disputed—somehow came into possession of the key to the suit-case and searched that as well. The majority affirmed the dismissal of the case against Beam, deeming the search unlawful because it was "fundamental that a citizen may not be arrested and have his person searched by force and without process in order to secure testimony against him." To apply the exclusionary rule, the court overturned its own precedent.[19]

The following year, the South Carolina court, composed of the exact same judges, declined to apply the new *Beam* rule in *State v. Harley*, an appeal of a conviction for running a lottery. The court did articulate grounds for distinguishing the cases—here, there was "voluntary surrender" (one wonders how voluntarily) of the key to the room where the evidence was stored. But the opinion went on to state hypothetically that "even if" the books and papers in question were illegally seized, "they nevertheless would have been admissible in evidence." For this dictum, the court distinguished *Blacksburg v. Beam* as "not rest[ing] so much upon the question whether there was a violation of . . . the Constitution, which provides that the people shall be secure from unreasonable searches and seizures." But *Beam* had clearly rested on that question! The same bench had maintained just a year earlier that "it is a serious thing to arrest a citizen, and it is a more serious thing to search his person; and he who accomplishes it, must do so in conformity to the laws of the land."[20]

What is particularly striking about the South Carolina example is that the judges, except for the one who had dissented in *Beam*, did not seem troubled by their own inconsistency. The same court re-jected the exclusionary rule again five years later in a case involving an attempted rape of a twelve-year-old girl. It is understandable that judges would wish to admit every relevant piece of evidence, no matter its unconstitutional origin, in the prosecution of an alleged child rapist. But it is less clear why a defendant accused of a lottery offense was more objectionable than an accused bootlegger and thus undeserving of the exclusionary rule's protection. Certainly, rampant police abuse in prohibition enforcement swayed judges who believed that excluding evidence was the only way to uphold the Fourth Amendment guarantee. But investigations of bookmaking could be just as intrusive as inspections for liquor. Arguably, the invasion of privacy was just as great or greater in *Harley*, when the police ransacked an entire room, than in *Beam*, when the police rummaged through a suitcase.[21]

The real difference, perhaps, was that the criminalization of gambling never received the same outcry as Prohibition. No one could claim a natural right to wager. But people claimed a natural right to drink. A North Dakota judge cited literature and religion that "Robinson Crusoe [exercised] his natural right to make and use wine and strong drink" and that "turning grape juice or water into wine [was] the very thing that was done by Jesus Christ." Many judges held the sentiment, like many of their fellow citizens, that violating Prohibition did not transform ordinary folks into criminals. As one New Yorker put it, most people seemed to have a "favorite bootlegger" or at least a "favorite club or gathering place" where the topic of conversation always circled around to "how to get 'it,' make 'it,' keep 'it,'" "it" being "that newest of American playthings, 'hooch.'"[22]

The debate over Prohibition and the exclusionary rule soon reached the Supreme Court. The *Carroll* appeal first appeared on the docket for the 1923 term, but the justices asked the parties to argue the case again the following year. In their brief on reargument, petitioners exclaimed that they could "not believe that this court [was] contemplating overruling the principle announced in *Weeks*," the principle of exclusion.[23]

But for Chief Justice Taft, the case did not present a simple choice between the exclusionary rule or no exclusionary rule, between supporting Prohibition or opposing it. The difficulty of the case for Taft stemmed from the fact that the Eighteenth Amendment was the law of the land. The American people had voted to make it part of the US Constitution. Certainly, the police had to respect constitutional limits on their actions. But citizens had to obey the law as well. On the one hand, the Fourth Amendment was on the line. On the other hand, noncompliance eroded the Eighteenth. Many judges, including Taft, were originally against National Prohibition. But once it was ratified, they believed that the rule of law demanded obedience, which, it quickly became clear, depended on greater police enforcement. At stake was the rule of law. The dilemma was that it cut both ways.[24]

Solicitor General James Beck, who argued *Carroll v. United States*, tried to sidestep the choice altogether. With the possibility that Prohibition's unpopularity might jeopardize the convictions, he reframed *Carroll* as a case not about liquor but about how the automobile had completely transformed American society. In his brief to the Supreme Court, Beck asserted that the fact that "this is a liquor case is accidental." The import of the case reached "far beyond the incidental problem of enforcing the liquor laws" to "the invention, the rapid development, and the general use of automobiles as a means of transportation." He described how cars had "produced a more profound effect upon social conditions than any other invention of modern times." Although this was a case about the illicit haul of alcohol, the next case could involve a murderer or robber fleeing in a getaway. The revolution in the commission and pursuit of crime, Beck argued, compelled the Court to reconsider "the well-settled rules of the common law" regarding an officer's authority to search and to seize.[25]

The government would win the case. In fact, every court in the country, albeit with vocal dissents, eventually changed long-established laws to adapt to the modern motor car. In making his argument, however, Beck—a classical conservative who felt "no great pride" in having to defend Prohibition's interference with personal liberty and property—did not know that the automobile would also unsettle the classical foundation of Fourth Amendment jurisprudence.[26]

Nineteenth-century jurists interpreted the Fourth Amendment according to what legal scholars refer to as classical legal thought. This way of thinking ordered the world into two spheres, public and private. This division, in turn, determined the scope of legitimate state action vis-à-vis individual rights. Put together, government could regulate the public sphere, but free men (and they were *men*) enjoyed the right to be left alone and do as they pleased in the private sphere. Applied to the Fourth Amendment, officers could not probe the private sphere without a warrant specifying "the place to be searched, and the persons or things to be seized." In contrast, no constitutional requirement hampered law enforcement efforts in the public sphere. One read the text's enumeration of what fell under its purview— "persons, houses, papers, and effects"—to discern a boundary between public and private. In this jurisprudential context, it made sense that an action in trespass served as the remedy for violations of the warrant rule; they were unwanted intrusions into the private sphere. Although historians have debated just how hegemonic classical legal thought has been, it was the dominant approach in Fourth Amendment doctrine.[27]

The 1886 case *Boyd v. United States*, the Supreme Court's first significant interpretation of the Fourth Amendment, provides an illustration of classical legal thought in operation. During forfeiture proceedings for nonpayment of import taxes, US Attorney Elihu Root obtained a subpoena ordering Edwin A. Boyd of Platt & Boyd to produce an invoice that might prove his guilt. His lawyers argued that compelling the production of commercial papers violated the Fourth Amendment. The Supreme Court agreed by distinguishing contraband from a person's papers. It reasoned that stolen or forfeited property differed "toto coelo"—that it was "diametrically opposite"— from a commercial receipt, even if the latter could prove the former. In "the one case, the government is entitled to the possession of the property; in the other it is not," the opinion explained. In formalist fashion, the Court categorized the nature of an invoice as private, and from there applied the rights that attached to that classification. In this case, that meant that the government could not force Boyd to hand over his invoice as evidence against himself. To put it another way, individuals had a fundamental right to the privacy of their business documents.[28]

Boyd demonstrated that the public or private nature of a thing was not self-evident and sometimes had to be litigated. The dualistic thinking also did not preclude reshuffling between the categories. In other words, private rights were not absolute. Parties argued, and courts weighed, competing public and private interests to decide questions of constitutional interpretation. For instance, in 1928, a New York City police commissioner defended aggressive, even unlawful, police tactics on the ground that "any man with a previous record is *public* property." More authoritatively, in his classic 1886 treatise *Limitations of Police Power*, Christopher Tiedeman employed similar sphere-shifting to justify warrantless arrests. The "general rule," he began, was "that there can be no arrest without a warrant." After all, the Fourth Amendment included "persons" under its protection. But Tiedeman granted that for "*public* reasons," which arose in cases where "the requirement of a warrant would so obstruct the effectual enforcement of the laws, . . . the personal security of the citizen is subjected to the further liability of being arrested by a police officer or private individual without a warrant."[29]

Tiedeman was, in fact, summarizing the common law of arrests, which one could describe just as accurately as the common law of warrant exceptions, for the main point of this body of law was to dictate when officers could seize—that is, arrest—a person without a warrant. One such situation arose when an officer had reasonable grounds to believe that a person had committed a felony. For misdemeanors, the common law required more: the officer had to actually see the offense take place, and in some jurisdictions, the offense also had to amount to a breach of the peace.[30]

Even the home, the classic private sphere, sometimes had to open its doors to the public. Yes, individuals enjoyed the inviolability of their proverbial castles—at least until what they did inside their homes affected the "public interest." The need to prevent fires, for instance, justified building codes, which also authorized inspectors to enter dwellings to check for compliance. The public's interest in morality persuaded judges to condemn bawdy houses as a "public nuisance." Once a home became a "disorderly house," regulations permitted inspections, searches, seizures, abatement, and even prosecution.[31]

Notwithstanding the state's ability to cross the threshold for the public interest, a key difference distinguished houses from persons. An officer could arrest a person without a warrant based on his own determination of legal cause, and the arrestee would then receive due process after the fact, which began with a prompt hearing before a magistrate. In contrast, any government action regarding a home had to go through legislative or judicial procedures first. Lawmakers passed building codes; judges heard nuisance cases. In the Fourth Amendment context, officers had to go to a magistrate and get a search warrant. The home occupied a special place in constitutional law. Although the Fourth Amendment listed houses along with persons, the law treated a man's [*sic*] castle differently. While the common law provided warrant exceptions for persons, there were none for houses.[32] Tiedeman's treatise contained a section on warrantless arrests, but it had no provision for warrantless searches of a home. While not impenetrable to state action, the home nonetheless represented the preeminent private sphere.

It was this public/private framework that Solicitor General Beck invoked when he posed the question in *Carroll* as "whether the same rule which applies to a man's dwelling shall also apply to his automobile." The alternative, of course, was to treat cars like people, which would then raise the possibility of a warrant exception for cars. A house or a person: these were the two Fourth Amendment archetypes that would determine the issue. But the automobile proved difficult to place within the organization of classical legal thought. As the government put it in its brief in *Carroll*, "with the advent of the motor car, property has taken a form . . . which has not heretofore existed." What kind of property was a car?[33]

On the one hand, cars were private property. As one prolix judge pointed out, "the automobile would fall within the meaning of either" "effects" under the US Constitution or "possessions" under the Mississippi Constitution. Another judge found in the Constitution "no such distinction, and no more than a comma[,] between the security afforded houses of persons and their papers and possessions." A plain reading, he concluded, required warrants to search a car just as a warrant was necessary to search houses and papers. (It is worth pointing out that this textual analysis proved too much. The judge failed to mention that no more than a comma also separated persons from the rest of the list, but people could be seized without warrants when the public interest required it.) It was also a literal interpretation of the Fourth Amendment that prompted a federal appellate judge to recite the truism "A 'man's house his castle'" when describing the automobile.[34]

That cars were private in the same ways that a home was private seemed obvious to these judges. It was a common assumption. Many early twentieth-century Americans experienced the automobile not just as a mode of transportation but also as a new private space. Early on, advertisers marketed, and consumers adopted, the "closed car" with its "four walls" as a space akin to a home or even a "boudoir." For many families, it functioned like a domestic hearth. When Robert and Helen Lynd studied the typical life of a "representative" American town in the 1920s, they found that the automobile served as the "agency holding the family group together." One mother reported, "I never feel as close to my family as when we are all together in the car." Less wholesomely, cars also replaced the parlor for courting couples. A hit 1905 song asked "Lucile" to go "Automobubbling you and I," promising her, "You can go as far as you like with me / In my merry Oldsmobile."[35]

And yet, while cars provided a new way to experience privacy, they also traveled on public roads and accordingly were subject to all sorts of laws enacted for the benefit of public order and safety. The government in *Carroll* pointed out that as "soon as the motor car appeared upon our highways it was recognized as a dangerous instrumentality, and thereupon the public asserted its right to declare upon what conditions such machines might use the public streets." These public rights were indeed extensive. "Can any one [*sic*] doubt," the government posed rhetorically,

> that in granting a license the State may constitutionally provide, as in fact it does provide, that every operator of a motor vehicle may be stopped at any time by an officer and made to exhibit his license card, and may even be compelled to write his name in the presence of the officer for the purpose of establishing his identity, or that any vehicle may be stopped by an officer for the purpose of inspecting it as to its equipment and operation and for securing "such other information as may be necessary?"

Of course not. The government lifted these particular examples from the Laws of Pennsylvania.[36]

The government also cited numerous state and federal court decisions that relied on the pervasive regulation of cars to classify them as public for Fourth Amendment purposes. The Michigan court in the oft-cited decision *People v. Case* acknowledged that although "a

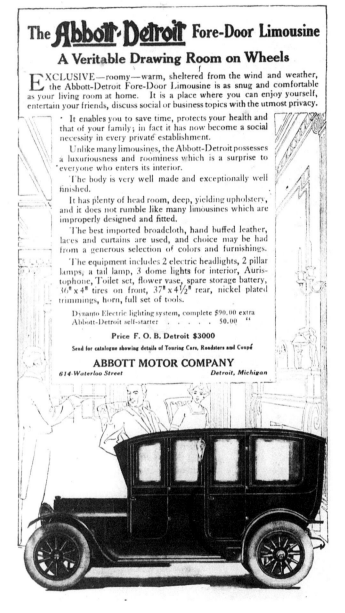

Print advertisement describing the car like a home.

The *Saturday Evening Post* 184, no. 34 (February 17, 1912): 42. Reproduced from a copy at the University of Iowa Library.

possession in the sense of private ownership," the automobile had all the hallmarks of public property, for it was "but a vehicle constructed for travel and transportation on highways." In another frequently cited case, *Commonwealth v. Street*, the Pennsylvania court explained that even though cars were privately owned property, they were sui generis because of their mobility, because the state regulated their operation, and because their ordinary use was almost entirely on public roads. It continued that because "life and society would be hopelessly imperiled" without government control over vehicular "travel," cars were in "an entirely different position" from other Fourth Amendment effects. By emphasizing vehicular *travel*, the court shifted the analysis from a noun to a verb. This linguistic maneuver made it easier to categorize the car as public. While "natural rights" to private property existed "entirely independent of government," the opinion went on that "no one [had] a natural or inalienable right" to drive. Rather, the use of a motor vehicle on the public highways was a privilege that was "derived wholly from the state." The driver's license was proof positive of that fact.[37]

Whether the automobile was public or private made all the difference. That the conservative Justice McReynolds sided with the Carroll brothers reflected his strict adherence to a traditional conception of property rather than any personal views on alcohol. While he voted against the government in *Carroll*, he voted for the government in *Olmstead v. United States*, another Prohibition case that allowed warrantless wiretaps. In the three years between the two cases, McReynolds did not change his mind about Prohibition. He joined the majority in *Olmstead* because the opinion clearly specified that neither the agents nor the wiretaps had trespassed on the defendants' houses.[38]

On the other side, the progressive Justice Brandeis voted for the government in *Carroll*, which reflected his robust views on public rights—robust to the point that the public interest could justify regulations that destroyed all economic uses of private property and even voided private contracts. That Brandeis placed the car within the public sphere of regulation and policing explains his position in *Carroll*. His concurring opinion in *Maul v. United States*, decided two years after *Carroll*, revealed even more clearly his position on the state's power to police vehicles. While the majority was content to rely on statutory authority to uphold the Coast Guard's warrantless seizure of a vessel on the high seas, Brandeis went further to assert that there was "no limitation upon the right of the sovereign to seize without a warrant vessels registered under its laws."[39]

Although McReynolds and Brandeis were ideologically at odds, they shared a classical worldview. While McReynolds held private rights as a trump against the public interest, Brandeis prioritized the public over the private. That both the conservative and the progressive saw the world in terms of the public/private dichotomy goes to show how profoundly the dualism shaped how legal minds conceived and articulated arguments for individual rights or state action. Indeed, that Brandeis, one of the more forward-thinking justices on civil liberties, granted state officials a near limitless power to search reflected the dominance of the public/private distinction in Fourth Amendment jurisprudence.

Brandeis's stance in *Carroll* has puzzled legal scholars, especially in light of his visionary dissent in *Olmstead* in which he identified the "right to be let alone" and the corresponding value of privacy as the essential principles underlying the Fourth Amendment. Why did Brandeis appreciate the privacy implications when the government eavesdropped on a phone conversation but not when it searched a car? One partial answer is that Brandeis's understanding of "the right to privacy," as he elaborated further in the *Harvard Law Review,* was not absolute. In delineating "the limitations of this right," he specified that the "right to privacy does not prohibit [action] which is of *public* or general interest." In Brandeis's explication, even individual privacy, which we tend to think of as a fundamental right today, had to be amenable to overriding societal claims. In most cases, it did not take much for Brandeis to side with the public's interest.[40]

This was especially so when it came to cars. It may be an underappreciated detail that Brandeis never owned a car and preferred walking for short commutes and taking the train for longer distances. He rode a horse-drawn buggy well into the 1920s, and after that, a car and driver were arranged to take him where he needed to go. A Luddite, Brandeis feared how new technologies, like telephones and wiretaps, were eviscerating individual privacy. He once mistakenly believed that "with the advent of television . . . it will be possible to peer into the inmost recesses of the home"—a line that almost went into his *Olmstead* dissent until his law clerk convinced him that televisions did not work that way. Brandeis's resistance to the automobile was in line with this antitechnology outlook, but more importantly, the sense of privacy that cars offered many others did not resonate with Brandeis as much as their threat to public safety. When the Supreme Court heard argument for the second time in *Carroll*, Secretary of Commerce Herbert Hoover was across town, hard at work with the National Conference on Street and Highway Safety. Diehard pedestrians like Brandeis were particularly adamant that the government regulate motor vehicles that had overtaken shared public spaces. As prescient as Brandeis was about the importance of privacy in twentieth-century constitutional law, he failed to anticipate the hallowed place the automobile would occupy in American society and culture.[41]

Brandeis, like many judges, decided that the public's interest in highway safety also encompassed the right of officers to stop and search a car without a warrant to enforce the criminal laws. As the Philadelphia court in *Commonwealth v. Street* declared:

> The right to stop and search an automobile for liquor is no different from the right to stop and search an automobile to see whether or not it contains an infernal machine, opium or a bandit concealed beneath a laprobe [*sic*], or, indeed, to discover whether or not the operator of the vehicle has in his possession the license card provided by the automobile statutes of the State.

The import of placing cars within the public sphere is difficult to overstate. For instance, *People v. Case* held that it was entirely permissible for the sheriff and his deputies to investigate an unattended Ford truck parked on the fairgrounds, enter it, discover bottles and jugs of whisky, and seize the vehicle and its contents—all without a warrant or even a justifiable suspicion that the car contained illicit liquor. "Police surveillance," the Michigan court explained, was "generally recognized as essential to the orderly conduct" in public spaces. This situation, the opinion continued, was entirely different from the "invasion of private premises."[42]

But these judges' easy distinction between cars and houses did not ensure that the analogy between cars and persons would be as simple. Even if courts classified the automobile as public, the common law of arrests still placed some requirements on the police, and jurists strained to explain how officers satisfied them when it came to cars. In one attempt, a federal judge suggested that because "from time immemorial" an animal or an inanimate object was deemed capable of committing crimes like a person, it could also be subject to legal consequences like a person. Therefore, an officer who had grounds to believe that an automobile was transporting contraband could stop and search the car without a warrant as if making a felony arrest. Another court went so far as to personify the automobile as an "inanimate 'outlaw'" when used in the bootlegging business. But this reasoning did not quite work. Before a car search took place, an officer had no idea whether he would find evidence of a felony or a misdemeanor. This exception applied only for felony offenses, but most antiliquor violations were misdemeanors, not felonies.[43]

To meet the stricter requirements for misdemeanor arrests, several courts concluded that when an officer stopped a vehicle that was transporting liquor, the officer was, in fact, observing a violation of the law. As *Commonwealth v. Street* explained, since "every revolution of the wheels of the trucks was a part of the perpetration of the offence [*sic*]," the defendant was "then and there in the midst of committing the crime of the illegal transportation of intoxicating liquor" before the officers' very eyes—even if those eyes had not yet seen the liquor inside the car. Dissenters saw the flaw in this logic right away. When an officer personally observed a misdemeanor, as the common law required, it meant that he had knowledge that a crime was afoot. But when an officer saw a car on the highway, he could only guess, with varying degrees of certainty, whether that car contained alcohol, since it was usually concealed inside. Applying the misdemeanor exception to this situation, dissents pointed out, was tantamount to "a hunt for cause to arrest or make seizure." Efforts to justify warrantless car searches under the common law could not get around the inconvenient fact that officers did not have legal cause *before* searching the car. They acquired sufficient cause only *after* the search had been conducted and the contraband found.[44]

Rather than stretching the common law of arrests, other courts relied on Prohibition's forfeiture laws that provided that "any receptacle or container" used to transport liquor was "forfeited to the state." They took this to mean that at the very moment a person placed prohibited goods in a car, ownership of the car transferred immediately to the government—even if an officer could not confirm that a forfeiture had taken place until after the search. So when the state stopped and searched a car carrying alcohol, the Michigan Supreme Court concluded that it was searching and seizing "its own" property, not the defendant's. The court accordingly held that there had been no search or seizure at all. Relying on this logic of forfeiture, a federal district court in Montana maintained that "the United States without process could recover possession by force," no matter how "irregularly the officers proceeded," just like "any other owner of property." In the case, the officers did proceed with certain force. They had waited for the defendants on the highway from Canada, and when they finally caught sight of the defendants' car at 3:30 in the morning, they flashed their lights, fired shots at the tires, overtook the car, mounted the running board, drew their guns, and ordered the defendants out.[45]

Rumrunners challenged this attempt to turn Prohibition's forfeiture procedures into a license to search. If interpreted to permit warrantless searches and seizures without even probable cause, then, they argued, the Volstead Act had essentially created an unlimited sanction to stop and search any car. As Judge Wiest pointed out in his dissent in *People v. Case*, the "officer in this case had no warrant, unless we consider the liquor law his warrant. If the liquor law is considered as his warrant, then he acted under general warrant." By invoking the general warrant, Wiest summoned the history of liberty. His dissent amounted to a twenty-seven-page disquisition on arbitrary searches and seizures from the "unsavory Star Chamber" in seventeenth-century England, through the American war for independence, to the ratification of the Bill of Rights. He pointed out that the revolution began with protests against Parliament's efforts to collect taxes by enacting general warrants that granted customs officials the power to search anyone and anywhere for smuggled goods. As Wiest quoted John Adams, "American independence was then and there born." By the time that it was drafted and ratified, the Fourth Amendment stood as a statement against the arbitrary power of legislatures tempted to confer broad authority to search and seize any persons or things. Upon highlighting the similarities between Parliament's revenue-collecting methods and antiliquor laws, Wiest declared that warrantless car stops and searches were "un-American, arbitrary, and despotic."[46]

The analytic gymnastics required to justify warrantless car searches showed how the public/private structure dominated—we might even say limited—everyone's thinking. The court in *Commonwealth v. Street* claimed that it was trying to adapt the "vital principles" of the Constitution to "changing conditions," but it fell back on traditional understandings of private rights and public order. To determine the relative rights of individuals and the state, it emphasized the public nature of cars and disregarded the ways in which they were private. In a similar way, Judge Wiest failed to put forth counterarguments to the necessity of governing automobility. Categorizing cars as public accommodated the police too much, while classifying them as private ignored the novel problems they posed for law enforcement. Many judges seemed unable to conceive of the automobile as a new, private object of regulation. While the *Street* court had deemed the automobile as public, it was still "not prepared to say that there are no limitations of the power of the state even under such circumstances." But it left the task of specifying what those limits might be for another day. Unable to think outside the public/private duality, courts struggled to balance the competing claims of individual privacy and the public interest.[47]

Judges who were committed to a jurisprudence of formalism but could also see that both sides of the dichotomy had a point were even more at a loss. This turmoil was evident in Chief Justice Taft's opinion in *Carroll v. United States*. He relied as much as he could on categorical reasoning, noting with approval that the Volstead Act had made "a distinction between the necessity for a search warrant in the searching of private dwellings and in that of automobiles." Although he had taken the first step in the methodology of classical legalism, Taft ultimately did not rely on the public/private framework. If he had done so, then the logical conclusion that followed would have been that a stop and search of an automobile, classified as public, did not require a warrant. Many jurists, including Justice Brandeis, had come to this very conclusion. But Taft could not grant that an officer *never* needed a warrant, believing that it "would be intolerable and unreasonable if a prohibition agent were authorized to stop every automobile on the chance of finding liquor." He recognized that people, "entitled to use the public highways, have a right to free passage without interruption or search." Individuals had some rights in their cars even when they traveled on public roads. Although not quite private, cars were not entirely public either.[48]

Classical legal thought proved unhelpful when cars simultaneously demanded greater policing for the public's safety and heightened individuals' expectations of privacy. The public/private division provided no principled way for determining whether a warrant would be required whenever an officer suspected that a car contained contraband. It offered no straightforward guidelines for balancing individual rights and the public welfare in all the myriad, spur-of-the-moment encounters on the road. That Taft ultimately abandoned formalist thinking reflected the fundamental incongruity of nineteenth-century jurisprudence in an Automotive Age.

By unsettling the public/private structure of classic legal thought, the automobile disrupted the law of searches and seizures. It also necessitated a new theory for determining when the personal freedom to drive had to accommodate law enforcement. The text of the Fourth Amendment, which prohibited "unreasonable searches and seizures," suggested one possibility. Noting that warrantless searches and seizures "have long existed in practice," *Commonwealth v. Street* pointed out that the "only limitation prescribed in the Constitution is that such searches and seizures shall not be 'unreasonable.'" This was, in fact, a familiar notion in case law. Back in 1886 in *Boyd v. United States*, the Supreme Court had explained that "not all searches nor all seizures are forbidden, but only those that are unreasonable."

Before cars, the common law of arrests contained all the reasonable warrant exceptions. Now, the concept of reasonableness offered a new way to consider both the public and private aspects of the automobile. This then raised the question, for car stops and searches, what was reasonable?[49]

Chief Justice Taft's answer to this question began differently from where he ultimately landed. He started with the pronouncement that individuals enjoyed the "right to free passage without interruption" and, accordingly, that a warrant "must be used" if securing one was possible. Conversely, it would be reasonable to dispense with the requirement if getting a warrant was "not practicable . . . because the vehicle can be quickly moved out of the locality or jurisdiction in which the warrant must be sought." Here, Taft articulated a definition of reasonableness that depended on the exigencies of the situation.[50]

If time had been the measure for reasonableness, then warrantless car searches would not have been allowed in situations like the 1925 Mississippi case *Moore v. State*. One of the points that the dissent made was that the police chief had had plenty of time to secure a warrant. He had received a telephone call from an officer in the next county over, informing him that the defendant was headed toward the Pearl River Bridge in a car transporting liquor. The officer also provided a description of the automobile and license number. Upon receiving this information, the police chief immediately headed to the bridge in wait instead of first walking over to the police justice's office in city hall—the same building where his own office was located—to make out a warrant. The dissenting judge also pointed out that there were two other justices of the peace within two or three blocks of city hall as well. "There is no showing in the record that a search warrant could not have been obtained," he charged, and clearly, time was not the problem. Taft at first seemed to embrace this dissent's perspective that reasonableness turned on whether the officer had enough time.[51]

But in formulating the rule of reasonableness, Taft took Fourth Amendment jurisprudence in an entirely different direction. *Carroll v. United States* held that a warrantless search and seizure was lawful if the "officer shall have *reasonable or probable cause for believing* that the automobile which he stops and seizes has contraband liquor therein which is being illegally transported."[52]

As Taft admitted in a letter to his son, this holding established "some rather new principle." Even more revealing of his intentions, Taft wrote to Justice Van Devanter, "I note what you say about brother Butler and I shall try to steer away from the suggestion that we are introducing any new law and new principle of constitutional construction, but are only adapting old principles and applying them to new conditions." The *Carroll* rule did sound like eighteenth-century laws authorizing warrantless searches and seizures in the enforcement of import duties, and the opinion did analogize the Volstead Act to the Customs Act. But Taft's private admissions were closer to the truth that *Carroll* had created an entirely new rule.[53]

For one thing, allowing officers to seize a car and then search it with *reasonable or probable cause for believing* that the driver may be violating Prohibition laws, many of which were misdemeanor offenses, went beyond what existing laws permitted. Under the common law for misdemeanors, warrantless arrests required actual knowledge through personal observation, not cause *for believing.* The difference in adding the phrase "for believing" was the difference between knowledge and suspicion. Outside the context of a car, an officer needed to witness a misdemeanor crime taking place. But when a car was involved, *Carroll* now authorized officers to take action if they believed that the situation at hand called for it. And with a suspicion-based seizure of a car and its driver, the same officer could then conduct a warrantless search. The *Carroll* rule thus established the "automobile exception" to the Fourth Amendment, for it not only dispensed with the warrant for the search and seizure of this traveling "effect." It also relaxed the standard from knowledge to belief.

Another way to think about *Carroll* is that it created a new category of seizures short of an arrest—the vehicle stop—which solved several law enforcement challenges. It was nearly impossible for officers to have knowledge of illegal activity, based on personal observation, when evidence was usually hidden inside what were essentially movable containers. This explains why Taft did not craft a warrant exception based only on whether an officer had time to get a warrant. He also wanted to enable Prohibition agents to investigate suspicious situations. *Carroll* addressed the lack of both time and legal cause with a lower standard that empowered officers to pull over any car that seemed reasonably questionable to them. In short, the *Carroll* rule constitutionally legitimized police discretion.

With *Carroll*, the reach of patrol officers now far exceeded the search powers of customs officials. The new rule affected the entire motoring public. Any person in a car could encounter *Carroll* on the roads and highways, not just at the ports at the periphery of the nation. Law-abiding citizens could also experience the automobile exception in a more forceful, harrowing way than a customs inspection. At a time when local governments were earnestly expanding their police forces to meet the demands of traffic law enforcement, the *Carroll* rule created "a dangerous predicament," the prominent lawyer Zechariah Chafee warned. "Ordered by strangers to stop, [the nocturnal motorist] runs the risk of being shot by prohibition officers if he goes on, and of being shot by bandits if he halts," he explained. This was precisely the situation that had confronted Captain Bates just a decade earlier in *Wiley v. State*. Roaming highwaymen still posed a real, and frightening, danger. Now with *Carroll*, overzealous federal agents seemed the more likely threat.[54]

Even more consequential, *Carroll* delegated the judicial inquiry of probable cause, at least in the first instance, to the police. Judge Wiest spelled out the implications of the new rule in his dissent in *People v. Case*: "Remove the restraint, and we will have officers running where no warrant could take them, speeding about in a search for probable cause, usurping the magisterial function of determining such cause." He demanded to know, "Where does the Constitution depute to police officers the office of the magistrate in determining probable cause?" By referring to the constitutional principle of separation of powers, Wiest alluded to the common fear that merging judicial and executive duties in one office preceded tyranny. An Oregon court conceded this point. "As a practical matter," it stated, "administrative and executive officers are often called on, in the performance of their duties, to exercise judgment and discretion"—that is, to perform "functions of a quasi judicial character." Indeed, police chiefs and safety experts were constantly reminding traffic cops to use "discretion and judgment in handling all violations of the motor vehicle

laws"—and, for all intents and purposes, determine guilt and innocence on the road—since they could not possibly arrest and prosecute every offender. But this was a matter of policy. By contrast, the
reasonableness standard "clothed" the police with "discretion or judiciary power" as a matter of constitutional law. Nonetheless, the
Oregon court insisted that the standard did not delegate to officers the
"exercise of judicial powers, strictly speaking," for requiring suspicion
to be based on "reasonable grounds" offered a limiting principle. This,
the court maintained, was the difference between warrantless car
searches and general warrants. The requirement that an officer have
"reasonable ground to believe" that a car contained liquor, which
could later be reviewed by a court of law, ensured that "there is no opportunity or place for arbitrary and tyrannical action."[55]

One pundit, upon reading *Carroll*, identified a weak spot in the
reasonableness standard: "What would prevent an unscrupulous and
lawless agent from manufacturing 'reasonable and probable cause'?"
Reasonable belief left room for the possibility that the belief could
be wrong, which meant that it could also be fabricated. Even without
an intention to lie, the commentator continued, the standard could
"be stretched by the hold-up officer to cover any set of circumstances." Since an officer's word was likely to receive "judicial
charity," the aftermath of *Carroll* was to put the highways "in the
power of reckless prohibition agents." Much of the legal commentary likewise criticized the ruling for giving "discretionary *carte
blanche*" to prohibition officers. When a Mississippi judge denounced
the *Carroll* decision as "erroneous" and argued that it "should not
be followed by the state court," he also gave a warning: authorizing
warrantless searches and seizures would "make petty tyrants of policemen," "harass and discommode" citizens, and "speedily become
intolerable."[56]

Whether the reasonableness standard would truly serve as a restraint on arbitrary policing depended on how closely courts would
scrutinize the police's actions. Taft's assessment in *Carroll* suggested
that courts did not have to be too attentive. The government had
submitted that its agents were certain of the Carroll brothers' iden-
tities; that they knew the defendants drove an Oldsmobile Roadster;
and that they saw the car coming from the direction of Canada, a

well-known source of supply, on the road between Detroit and Grand Rapids, which was well tread by the transport of alcohol. "Had any reasonably cautious man known the same facts," the government stated in conclusion, "he would have inferred that these men when they passed the officers on this highway were bringing with them a cargo of contraband liquor." Taft incorporated these facts into his determination of probable cause and also took judicial notice that Grand Rapids was about 152 miles from Detroit, a thriving center for trafficking spirits.[57]

But Taft overlooked the gaping hole in the government's case. When the Prohibition agents stopped the defendants on the Detroit– Grand Rapids country road, they had no reason to suspect that the bootleggers were *at that instant* carrying on their illicit trade. This had been the defense's point all along. Agent Scully had testified that his team "had no reason to believe that the [defendants] were transporting liquor" before they searched the Roadster. As the pundit had put it, "judicial charity" appeared to be the guiding principle in *Carroll*. In excoriating the majority's finding of probable cause, Justice McReynolds exclaimed, "Has it come about that merely because a man once agreed to deliver whisky, but did not, he may be arrested whenever thereafter he ventures to drive an automobile on the road to Detroit!" That Taft sided with the government signaled that courts could and would defer to officers' claimed need for an investigatory search rather than perform a vigorous, independent review. This deference acquired the force of law in cases like *Tranum v. Stringer*, a 1927 Alabama case holding that "the fact that the automobile upon search is found to be transporting contraband liquors is of decided weight in passing upon the reasonableness of the search without warrant." The outcome, not the propriety of the search itself, would justify the means.[58]

Carroll marked a turning point in criminal procedure. It shifted Fourth Amendment jurisprudence from a categorical analysis—is the automobile, as a category, public or private?—to an individualized determination of reasonableness—was this particular search reasonable?—to determine the warrant question. Moreover, the new inquiry centered on the officer's point of view, on *his* reasonable belief, which reflected an increasing reliance on proactive policing. Rather than making the warrant requirement the default rule for car searches with a limited exception for exigent circumstances, the Court authorized individual officers to use their judgment in every car case. And thus *Carroll* heralded the beginning of the problem of police discretion in constitutional criminal procedure. To be sure, discretionary policing as a practice existed long before *Carroll*. But after *Carroll*, judges had to decide whether an exercise of discretion was reasonable under the Fourth Amendment—a bedeviling question that would be litigated time and time again. And over time, courts' interpretations of the reasonableness standard would make space for the police's power to grow.

As the United States became an automotive society, the *Carroll* exception had ramifications beyond cars. To be sure, the policing of loiterers and vagrants—a classic, public-sphere regulatory function—predated the policing of cars. But the law governing car stops and searches developed *before*, and would come to inform, the law on the police's authority to stop, question, and search people. Notwithstanding the fact that cops and lawyers today refer to *Terry* stops and *Terry* frisks, in reference to the Supreme Court's 1968 decision in *Terry v. Ohio* that authorized stop-and-frisks, the legal history of the practice goes further back.

In the 1930s, even after the repeal of National Prohibition in 1933, the rule of law still seemed to be at a crisis point to legal Brahmins who could not deny ample evidence that the police routinely disregarded the law of arrests. One prominent state judge suspected that "in nearly all, and probably in all, American cities the police regularly violated the law in making arrests." If he were to put a number on it, he "hazarded the guess that over 75% of all arrests [were] illegal." One possible response to this problem could have been to reform the police. But the Interstate Commission on Crime, an organization of government officials established with the progressive goal of "modernizing the administration of criminal justice," had a different solution in mind. When modern society depended on more policing than what existing laws allowed, there was a way to uphold the rule of law without requiring the police to change their ways: amend the laws instead.[59]

In 1939, the commission launched a task force and assigned Sam Warner, a Harvard Law School professor who had worked on the Wickersham Report, "to make a study of the law of arrest to ascertain whether the police did, or could, operate within its limitations and, if not, what changes were necessary to make it both a practical standard of police conduct and a safeguard of personal liberty." To study the law of arrests in action, Warner spent weeks shadowing the police in Boston, Chicago, Los Angeles, San Francisco, and Portland, Oregon. He discovered "very few police practices that did not seem to have a good deal of practical justification, but a large number that were illegal." In other words, the police had to violate the law to do their job.[60]

An example of a practice that was not lawful but nevertheless useful was police questioning. "Every day in every city of the United States," Warner reported, "large numbers of persons are questioned by the police," which was "essential to proper policing." By way of illustration, Warner described a scenario of a man who "looks around furtively, tries the door of an automobile, steps in and seems unfamiliar with its mechanism." A brief inquiry would resolve any suspicion of an auto theft in progress before he drove away. But the common law permitted investigatory detentions only at nighttime. Aside from this limited timeframe, stopping a person even just to ask a few questions constituted an arrest if conducted with the authority of law. But a valid arrest required probable cause, not mere suspicion. To address this gap in the law, some courts had begun to recognize a legal distinction between a stop for questioning on the one hand and an arrest on the other. According to Warner, however, these decisions were "insufficient to establish unequivocally an American common-law right to question and detain suspects."[61]

To be sure, constables, watchmen, and other nineteenth-century police figures had long confronted vagrants and other suspicious persons without much pushback. But toward the end of the century, as smaller communities became larger towns and as strangers began to outnumber acquaintances, disputes over officers' authority to interrogate nonvagrant individuals arose more frequently. A story from fin de siècle Los Angeles illustrates this development. In March 1898, the Board of Police Commissioners convened what turned out to be one of the stormiest meetings it had witnessed in months. C. A. Power of Russell & Power, owner of the Westlake stables, brought charges against "special officer" Charles Foster, a privately employed patrolman licensed by the police department. Power accused Foster of repeatedly stopping his employees on their way to his customers' homes to bring the horses in for the night. In one instance, Foster had even stopped *him* and "in a very officious and ungentlemanly manner demanded to know where he was going, who he was and what business he had upon the streets at that hour." Even after Foster, who was not in uniform, identified himself as a policeman, Power "denied [Foster's] right to accost him in that manner." Power petitioned the board to order Foster to cease harassing him and his men.[62]

Foster responded with a speech defending "what he considered the rights and duties of a policeman." He claimed that as an officer, he "had a right to stand people up on the streets in a right manner at night in a residence district." The mayor and the board ended the matter by dismissing the charges on the ground that "nothing very serious had been proven" except that Foster had been "over-zealous." By the 1930s, as American society shifted to police governance with traffic law enforcement, that zealousness had not only become more common, but it also appeared to Sam Warner to be a serious technical violation of the law of arrests.

Warner also found that the "most common illegal police practice connected with arrest" was "frisking." A frisk, which he defined as "passing one's hands over [suspects'] outer clothing to ascertain whether they are carrying any deadly weapons," amounted to a search. The legality of a search of a person, in turn, depended on a lawful arrest. But most suspicious circumstances that made a frisk necessary for the officer's safety were not sufficient to justify an arrest under the common law. Because the law did not permit searches of individuals who were not under arrest, it was, Warner observed, "universally violated by police officers and must be violated by them if they are to perform their duties."[63]

Warner relayed several stories to illustrate this predicament. On one occasion, shortly after midnight while he rode along with the police, gunshots had startled him from his half doze. From inside the patrol car he saw an officer pointing his gun down an alley. The officer had come upon two burglars prying open a cash register, and the parties had exchanged fire before the men escaped. The best description the officer could give was that they were young—"not valuable information as nearly all gunmen are young"—and that one wore a dark blue sweater and the other a light blue sweater. Warner and his guides drove a little over a block when they spied a young man with a blue sweater standing inside a doorway. The officers jumped out, frisked the man, and ordered him to the back seat of the police car. When the man asked why, the officers hurriedly answered, "Never mind, we'll explain later. Jump in quickly." And he did. A couple of blocks later they found another young man in a blue sweater. "Into the back seat he was hustled." They apprehended one more suspect wearing a blue sweater, and with the car full, they headed to the station. Other patrol officers had brought in four more suspects. Warner was amazed that there were so many young men in blue sweaters within a few blocks of the shooting.[64]

After the lineup, two were charged with the crime, leaving the police with five innocent men on their hands. Because they had technically been arrested, the "legal way to dispose of them" was to charge them, lock them up for the night, and explain the situation to the judge the following morning. But to save the men the trouble, the sergeant thanked them for cooperating with the police and offered to drive them home. Three accepted the token of gratitude. The sergeant also asked all of them to sign a release of their right to sue the police, which they did.[65]

On another occasion, the officers Warner was observing had received a radio call about "a negro with a gun . . . in a certain saloon." They "lined up all the negro customers, 'frisked' them and arrested those whom we found illegally armed." Upon concluding this story, Warner proceeded to tell another one about two men walking down the street with huge bulges in their breast pockets. The officers jumped out of their car and asked the men to open their coats. Instead of a concealed weapon, each pocket contained a quart of

scotch. To Warner's astonishment, the police wished them a happy
new year, the men replied that they intended to have one, and both
groups "went on their way in a good humor." For Warner, the incident at the saloon was not troubling because of the patrons' race;
rather, frisking "the negro customers" presented the same problem
as approaching the New Year's revelers. A frisk constituted a search,
which required an arrest. To arrest based only on a hunch was unlawful, so the frisks were unlawful as well. To Warner, it seemed
"outrageous to have so treated the unarmed negroes in the saloon or
the two men bent on celebrating the new year with Scotch."[66]

At the end of his survey, Warner concluded that the source of police lawlessness was not the police themselves. They violated the law
because "strict compliance with the law would hamstring the police
in their efforts to protect society." The law of arrests had "under-
gone practically no revision since its formulation in England in the
seventeenth and eighteenth centuries," and reforms were long
overdue. Frisking, for instance, was unlawful not because the people
found the practice undesirable but because of "historical lag." In an
earlier time, requiring a valid arrest based on probable cause before
searching the arrestee was reasonable; the "constable could then
stand a few feet from a suspect while questioning him and protect
himself with his staff if the suspect drew a dagger." But now with
"hoodlums with four-inch pistols," a quick frisk presented a more
prudent course of action.[67]

Warner was also concerned that outdated laws created confusion
about what exactly the police could and could not do, which gener-
ated ill will against them. As late as 1960, a federal judge noted that
most people just assumed that police questioning without probable
cause was permissible. But not everybody, like Mr. Power of Los Angeles, made that assumption, which left officers vulnerable to false
arrest claims if they happened to stop an innocent person who turned
out to be litigious. Warner discovered that the police protected themselves from potential lawsuits with release forms or else by formally
charging the person with "some misdemeanor" and then requesting
a discharge from the magistrate. But subjecting an innocent person
to the criminal process, which entailed considerable expense and humiliation, just to shield officers from liability undermined trust in

the justice system. One law professor lamented that criticisms of the police arose from their mistreatment of "respectable persons" who "sometimes get caught in the enormous mill" and consequently "join the thousands of individuals of inferior economic status in their hostility to police." This was not uncommon when the false positives of proactive policing meant that sometimes an upstanding person might be mistaken for a suspicious person.[68]

Upon conclusion of Warner's study, the Interstate Commission introduced the Uniform Arrest Act in 1942 as a model statute for the states' consideration. In functional terms, the act narrowed the definition of arrest by taking out detentions, interrogations, and frisks. Arguably, these actions could constitute an arrest under the act's definition—"the taking of a person into custody in order that he may be forthcoming to answer for the commission of a crime"—depending on the interpretation of the word "custody." In one old English case as quoted by the Vermont Supreme Court, Lord Hardwicke explained that an arrest could be made even without touching the person, "for if a bailiff comes into a room, and tells the defendant he arrests him and locks the door (upon him), there is an arrest, for he is in custody of the officer." But the Uniform Arrest Act distinguished custody for arrest and nonarrest purposes. It gave the police the right to "stop any person" and "demand of him his name, address, business abroad and whither he is going" if the officer "has reasonable ground to suspect" that the person "is committing, has committed or is about to commit" some crime. If the person failed to answer questions to the satisfaction of the officer, the act also gave police the right to detain the person for further investigation for up to two hours. Warner recognized that this provision seemed "closely akin to what is ordinarily considered an arrest." But for the sake of "not calling it such even when it includes taking the suspect to the police station for further inquiry," Warner included a subsection that spelled out that "detention is not an arrest and shall not be recorded as an arrest in any official record." In addition, the act permitted a frisk without an arrest "whenever [an officer] has reasonable ground to believe that he is in danger if the person possesses a dangerous weapon."[69]

The Interstate Commission hoped that by providing more certainty on the respective rights of citizens and officers, an updated law of arrests would also allay any misgivings that the public may harbor against the police. But the issue was not so much that existing laws were unclear. Rather, twentieth-century police had outgrown the limits of well-established laws and often found themselves working on unsettled legal terrain. When the commission charged Warner with revising the common law of arrests, it had in effect asked him to redraw the boundaries of lawful policing. If adopted, the Uniform Arrest Act would mark an important shift in the relationship between citizens and the police. By taking away interrogations, stops, and frisks as a potential basis for false arrest suits, Warner sought to legitimize greater police action than what Americans in the past were used to. With these legal changes, Warner expected that "the innocent person who is 'frisked'" would be "less likely to feel that he has been unjustly treated." The new rules, in other words, would inform citizens that proactive policing was not an unreasonable constraint on their personal liberty.[70]

To justify these changes to the centuries-old law of arrests, Warner cited just one authority. *Carroll v. United States* was about cars, but Warner interpreted it more broadly as a case about the need for the law to adapt to modern society. He explained that in *Carroll*, the relevant question was "not whether [the Volstead Act] extends the powers of peace officers beyond what they were at the time the Constitution was adopted, but whether the extensions are reasonable." If the constitutional scope of police practices was based not on historic practices but on reasonableness in light of contemporary conditions, then the Uniform Arrest Act "should certainly be constitutional," Warner submitted. Strikingly, he viewed the pervasiveness of existing police practices as "extremely pertinent" in determining their reasonableness and, further, their constitutionality. That police officers regularly questioned, detained, and frisked suspects proved to Warner that such practices were essential and—the keyword—reasonable.[71]

Warner recognized that the Uniform Arrest Act represented a matter of principle and would not make a practical difference. He admitted that the new laws "would probably have no effect on police practices" because the police were already stopping and frisking notwithstanding their present illegality. But for midcentury reformers, legal infractions by the police created problems disproportionately greater than their mere technicality. In the words of Warner, the "existence of one common situation in which it is obviously necessary to violate the law reduces their respect for all law." It was important to Warner that the law reflect the needs of police officers rather than work against them, which only encouraged lawbreaking by the very people tasked with law enforcement. Prohibition's still recent failure had demonstrated that police lawlessness had the potential to subvert the legitimacy of government. As one legal commentator put it in 1932, "usurpative conduct of public officials is one of the greatest breeders of hatred and disloyalty toward law and even government itself."[72]

The Uniform Arrest Act failed to gain widespread adoption. Only two states, New Hampshire and Rhode Island, updated their laws. By 1951, one more state, Delaware, had ratified it. The rest of the states left the citizen-police encounter in a state of flux. In a 1945 foreword to a treatise on the law of search, seizure, and arrest, Milwaukee's police chief acknowledged that "few law enforcement officers . . . were ever as sure of themselves as they might have been concerning the extent of or limitations upon their authority." The treatise apparently did not clarify matters. In 1953, a professor of government researching warrantless arrests found "little general information on this subject," and so he reached out to the American Civil Liberties Union. In response, the ACLU admitted that it did not know much either and requested "a copy of your analysis when it is completed." Around the same time, another study of arrest practices in Philadelphia, which was modeled on Warner's survey, also noted that police officers sought "certainty in the law so that they may know the limits of permissible conduct" and accordingly recommended that "the procedural law under which the police operate must be set out in unmistakable terms in a comprehensive code." Of course, what the police wanted was not just clarity but, more importantly, legal changes authorizing their crime prevention methods.[73]

In 1955, Los Angeles district attorney S. Ernest Roll was heard making the same arguments. With "the invention of automobiles, radio, television, airplanes, photography, burglar alarms and other electronic devices, the police officer is faced with a complex and entirely different set of conditions to consider than in 1872," Roll pointed out. In his invocation of modernity, Roll echoed the appeals of the father of modern police. The prosecutor declared that the "19th century law of arrest has become outmoded by 20th century law enforcement" and argued for legal reforms that would make August Vollmer's vision for the police profession consistent with the rule of law. It is noteworthy that Roll also favored the exclusionary rule. He did not mind that the constable's blunder would make it harder for him to prosecute a case if the rule of exclusion could ensure that the police stayed within the law's parameters. At the same time, though, Roll thought the law ought to give the police more leeway to do their job.[74]

Notwithstanding these arguments, the status quo lulled most states to inaction. At the time, thirty states had rejected the exclusionary rule, so illegal arrests and searches would not have thwarted criminal prosecutions in those jurisdictions. The majority of the states chose not to go through the trouble of updating their laws for the sake of an abstract rule-of-law principle, especially when the public did not mind technical violations when it came to solving crimes. It was this state of affairs that planted doubt in some of the more liberal jurists who opposed the Uniform Arrest Act's expansions of the police's powers. An ACLU lawyer conceded that if officers were going to keep breaking the law and the people were going to let them, then their position seemed like "doctrinaire antagonism" for preferring "widespread illegality as against proposals to regularize some police practices which are arguably unobjectionable (for example, on-the-street questioning)." Some reformers eventually came around to the view that only by legalizing brief seizures and frisks could the law at least regulate practices that were going to continue anyway.[75]

The impetus to update the law came unintentionally. In 1955, the California Supreme Court adopted the exclusionary rule, and within two years, the state passed a law "to 'modernize' its laws on arrest and search and seizure." After the US Supreme Court imposed the rule of exclusion on all states in 1961, New York immediately responded by enacting a law "to clarify the rights of police to frisk suspects," as Governor Rockefeller explained. The possibility that the exclusionary rule could frustrate law enforcement had finally prompted legislative action. Advocates of law and order were on guard, watching for the judiciary's, especially the Warren Court's, next moves. It was now their turn to reluctantly consider legal reform. In the mid-1960s, during the height of the Due Process Revolution, the President's Commission on Crime recommended adopting the reasonable-suspicion standard for detentions, interrogations, and frisks, anticipating another defense-friendly opinion that might prohibit the practices altogether. If the legislative branch acted first, then perhaps it could preempt more drastic constraints that the liberal court would surely place on the police. So they believed.[76]

In 1968, the Supreme Court constitutionally sanctioned stop-and-frisks in *Terry v. Ohio*, and it did so in the exact same way that Warner had done with the Uniform Arrest Act, which was what Chief Justice Taft had done in *Carroll v. United States*. The Court first distinguished a "stop" from an arrest and a "frisk" from a full-blown search, and then applied the standard of reasonableness. Like his predecessor, Chief Justice Earl Warren crafted a rule that split the baby. He accepted the state of Ohio's position that the police practice in question was not an arrest, but he also took the petitioner's position that it nonetheless constituted a "search" and a "seizure" under the Fourth Amendment. He rejected the more stringent standard of probable cause, but he also declined to let the police act based on their mere suspicion, which was no standard at all. Warren, like Taft before him, created an intermediate police option just short of arrest. In fact, *Terry* cited *Carroll* in holding that when "a police officer observes unusual conduct which leads him reasonably to conclude"—a phrase that was reminiscent of *Carroll*'s "reasonable or probable cause for believing"—that "criminal activity may be afoot and that the persons with whom he is dealing may be armed and presently dangerous," the officer could stop those persons to make "reasonable inquiries" and conduct a "carefully limited search of the outer clothing." To pare this down, *Terry* created another category of searches and seizures that did not require the police to have actual knowledge but only "reasonable suspicion."[77]

To search the private sphere, the police still needed a warrant based on probable cause. But in the public sphere, whether in a car or "on the street" as was the case in *Terry*, the rules had changed. "Unquestionably," citizens were "entitled to the protection of the Fourth Amendment" when "walk[ing] down the street," Warren declared in *Terry*, just as Taft had maintained in *Carroll* that those "entitled to use the public highways[] have a right to free passage without interruption or search." But those rights had to yield when the police reasonably believed that a stop or frisk, or both, was necessary. While courts would review the police's reasonableness determination after the fact, the imperatives of impromptu policing meant that individual officers would have to be the judge in the first instance.[78]

That the Warren Court adopted the same standard in the Uniform Arrest Act drafted over two decades earlier, which adopted the same standard that the Taft Court had set forth nearly two decades before that, raises a question about history's trajectory. Would the law have changed to allow stop-and-frisks, and changed in the same ways, even if *Carroll* had not been decided? Imagining this counterfactual history involves more than assuming away *Carroll*'s existence. It also requires putting aside the history of how cars not only led to modern police but also democratized policing. A United States without cars would have been a society without police as a mode of governing everyone. If policing had remained focused on those on the margins of society, one could imagine that stop-and-frisks might have stayed under the radar or that the law would have allowed the practice based on an officer's mere suspicion instead of reasonable suspicion. In the automotive society that did come to pass, cars altered the calculus between individual rights and state power in an unprecedented way—it raised demands for both. Personal mobility cultivated expectations of privacy at the same time that mass mobility justified greater law enforcement for the public's safety. Moreover, the mass adoption of cars, unlike that of any other technology, rendered the status of the private sphere—of private property and ownership—useless in delineating the boundaries of the police's power. When social status could no longer guide the officer's judgment, the law's decisionmakers required that the exercise of power be reasonable.[79]

Fifteen years after *Terry*, Justice Blackmun expressed concern with what appeared to him to be "an emerging tendency on the part of the Court to convert the *Terry* decision into a general statement that the Fourth Amendment requires only that any seizure be reasonable." By the 1980s, Fourth Amendment public-sphere cases seemed to be discarding the warrant requirement and going straight to a determination of the reasonableness of the police's actions, a question that was usually decided in their favor. The police noticed this trend too. An early 1970s textbook, *Police Patrol: Tactics and Techniques*, asserted that the "system of criminal justice abundantly provides for broad use of discretion by its law enforcement officers." In support, it pointed to "specific sections of the criminal codes" that incorporated police discretion through the word "reasonable." These observations reflected a breathtaking change since the days of bootleggers and speakeasies. The core of the Fourth Amendment had shifted from a question of warrants to a jurisprudence of reasonableness.[80]

One of the first cases to refer to reasonableness as the "touchstone" of the Fourth Amendment, a characterization that the Supreme Court often used when justifying a warrantless search or seizure, was *Pennsylvania v. Mimms*, decided in 1977. The case held that during a traffic stop, the police could order a driver out of the car, even without any suspicion that the driver was armed and dangerous. For the proposition that this police action was constitutionally reasonable, the *Mimms* opinion cited *Terry*. In an automotive society, case law on policing the public generally and case law on policing cars specifically built on each other. While *Carroll* provided precedent for *Terry*, the case about on-the-street police encounters, in turn, provided precedent for later cases involving vehicles and their passengers. In fact, the first case to "give some flesh to the bones of *Terry*" involved the frisk of a person sitting in a parked car. The automobile had become such "a central, constitutive feature of American life," as one poet phrased it, that the laws on the police's authority to search the person or a car were mutually reinforcing.[81]

Neither Sam Warner nor Chief Justice Warren seemed to foresee the full consequences of the legal changes they had accomplished. Although both considered a stop as a separate act from an arrest, in the real world, the line between the two could be hazy. Warner expected that in most cases, a few questions would clear up any

suspicion of wrongdoing, that the citizen would cooperate, and that
the officer could then let the innocent person go. This scenario
easily maintained the distinction between a short detention and an
arrest. But Warner failed to think through the situation where police questioning *did* unearth inculpatory information. A stop could
end with the suspect in jail if an officer came to have probable cause
after a round of questions or a pat-down. That an arrest could begin
with suspicion amounted to an astounding expansion of the police's
power. But Warner was untroubled because he was not primarily
concerned with the guilty; his aim was to enable the police to investigate criminal suspects.

Minority Americans, however, were troubled by this legal development. "The defect is exposed . . . at the point where the *Stop-Frisk
Model* meets the real world of streets and courts," the NAACP wrote
to the Supreme Court when it was deliberating *Terry*. The attempt
"to establish some third state of police powers" between a lawful arrest and unlawful policing "has the allure of sweet reasonableness
and compromise," it granted. But this, it cautioned, was a mirage.
"The rub is simply that, in the real world, there is no third state; the
reasonableness of theory is paper thin; there can be no compromise."
The NAACP brief explained that on the "ghetto street," any standard
less than probable cause would disappear into the police's "concept
of the Negro as a savage, or animal" who posed mortal danger "even
in the absence of visible criminal behavior." When even racist cops
received "judicial charity," as the Prohibition Era pundit had anticipated upon reading *Carroll*, requiring suspicion to be reasonable
actually allowed the police to "accost and detain citizens at their
whim." When the American Law Institute proposed a similar change
to the common law, the NAACP's executive director objected on
the ground that it "will be found to be an exceedingly mischievous
one, if not one fraught with the danger of violent outbreaks." His
warning was based on history. In the American experience, riots had
followed police abuse. Even if protest did not ensue, the social cost
of community alienation, the NAACP implored, was not worth the
benefits of preventive patrol.[82]

In 1968, at the end of a decade singed with urban riots and smol-
dering with mutual antagonism, the *Terry* opinion recognized that

stop-and-frisks were "a major source of friction between the police and minority groups," particularly when "motivated by the officers' perceived need to maintain the power image of the beat officer." Still, it was an observation made only in passing. The reality of race, which the NAACP had described, was relegated to a footnote, and the opinion ignored the fact that the arresting officer in the case was white and two of the three suspects were black. Guiding the Court's decision in *Terry* was the logic of *Carroll* that the transformations in modern America necessitated a new relationship between citizens and the police.

4

It Could Happen to You

> You think any goddam private eye is going to quote law at me over this, mister, you got hell of a tough time coming your way. There ain't a police force in the country could do its job with a law book.
>
> Raymond Chandler, *The Long Goodbye* (1953)

> Indeed, if put to the choice, one might well prefer to live under Soviet substantive law applied in good faith by our common-law procedures than under our substantive law enforced by Soviet procedural practices.
>
> Justice Robert Jackson, *Shaughnessy v. United States ex rel. Mezei* (1953)

AT A TIME WHEN it was unremarkable for mainstream Americans to think of the American Civil Liberties Union (ACLU) as a communist front, J. Lieberman of Los Angeles wrote a letter to its Southern California branch. He wanted to know, "Has a police officer the right to stop an individual under circumstances in no way suspicious and not only question him but search him for concealed weapons, as well?" He was not a lawyer, but it seemed to him that "such a practice constitutes a violation of civil rights."[1]

156

The incident that prompted Lieberman's inquiry occurred in July 1948. He and two friends went for a drive to Elysian Park when two patrolmen pulled up next to their car and ordered them to stop. The officers than launched into an interrogation and asked the friend who was driving to see a bill of sale for the car. Lieberman found the intrusion annoying, but he conceded that it was within their "line of duty" since the car was brand new with Wisconsin plates. But he could "see no excuse for what followed." After he had informed the officers that he lived nearby and had given his address, the officers directed all of them to get out of the car and subjected each to a "personal search," which would soon become more commonly known as a "frisk." Lieberman referred to it as "an uncalled for personal outrage."

Uncertain of the law and flustered by the unexpected aggression, Lieberman and his friends submitted to the "procedure." But he did manage to get his wits about him to ask the officers whether it was "their custom to stop people indiscriminately." One answered that it was done for their own protection because the park was "a notorious crime area." Even so, Lieberman could not make sense of it. It seemed wrong "that in order to find the guilty, people at random have to be treated as guilty until they are proven innocent." He wanted to know if he was right. Did the citizen have any rights in this situation?

The Reverend Albert Heist, who received the letter, confirmed Lieberman's legal intuition. He responded that the police, "of course, have no right to do the sort of thing that you describe." But they were also "perfectly well aware that the chances of your getting enough out of them to pay for a lawyer are rather remote." Because organizations like the ACLU could "not afford to take anything except the special, strategic case," the police effectively and routinely got away with unlawful conduct.[2]

Lieberman's letter nonetheless moved Heist to write a letter to the Police Commission, one of many that he sent during his tenure as director of the ACLU branch office. "I am well aware of the probable results of whatever 'investigation' will be made under your present set-up in which the Personnel Department 'investigates' the complaints with regard to members on the force," he chided. Still, he wanted to hear "the police version of the story."[3]

Heist received the department's curt version: "The officers in the performance of their duty conducted themselves at all times in a courteous and gentlemanly manner."[4]

Heist tried once more. He wrote back clarifying that he "did not raise any question as to the courtesy or gentlemanliness of the officers in their handling of Mr. Lieberman." Rather, he "raised the issue of their constitutional right to order him out of his car and subject him to a search." He added that, in his view, the "Police Department is taking the position of 'getting away with it.'" To this, Heist received no reply.[5]

The exchanges between Heist, the Police Commission, and Lieberman reflected the range of viewpoints on the police's power before 1968, when the Supreme Court settled the constitutionality of what we now call stop-and-frisks. Under the common law before *Terry v. Ohio* was decided, all searches of persons required a valid arrest, which, in turn, required probable cause. This informed the legal activist's position that both the car stop—a "seizure" in Fourth Amendment terminology—and the "personal search" based on mere suspicion were unlawful. But law enforcement viewed the law as honored in the breach, feeling more than justified in stopping, questioning, and searching occupants of a car with out-of-state license plates in a "high frequency crime area." The contested legal status of stop-and-frisks left the hapless citizen in the middle. Having experienced the police action personally, he was dubious, but unsure of where the law stood.

At stake in this dispute was not just a matter of constitutional law. At issue was the very definition of arbitrary power. Policing had become a prevalent method of enforcing social order in the United States at a time when people were obsessively comparing democracy with totalitarianism. By the Cold War era, the police had claimed so much authority that even respected jurists could think about American police in the same sentence with the Gestapo or the Russian secret police. In 1955, Justice Robert Traynor of the California Supreme Court, widely regarded as one of the greatest judges never to sit on the US Supreme Court, wrote that unlawful searches could turn a democratic society into a police state. This was not an abstract worry. Traynor observed that it was "one of the foremost public concerns" considering "recent history" that "demonstrated all too clearly how short the step is from lawless although efficient enforcement of the law to the stamping out of human rights." Even for criminal law scholar and democratic theorist Jerome Hall, it was difficult to deny that the police in America often acted in ways that seemed comparable to "domination by sheer physical force unlimited by law" characteristic of authoritarianism.[6]

Most Americans believed that they lived in a free country, but their increasingly frequent encounters with the police in their freedom machines tested that faith. The central place of cars in the "American Way of Life" magnified the tension.[7] The automobile's mass production democratized the ability to travel to wherever one wanted, whenever one wanted. It fueled the postwar capitalist economy. In film, song, and literature, the car represented freedom. And with its mass adoption, automobility literally became a way of life in the United States. The contradiction of the automobile as both the preeminent symbol of American values and an object of extensive policing threw into sharp relief the vexing conundrum of discretionary policing in a society based on the rule of law. For the fast-growing numbers of people who endured a traffic stop, the difference between the United States and a police state began to seem all too thin. Their doubts betrayed a lingering fear that the distance between illegal and efficient law enforcement was too close, as Justice Traynor fretted. When society's reliance on police collided with the freedom of the open road, the difficulty was in defining *what, exactly, constituted arbitrary policing?*

In the October term that began in the fall of 1948 and ended in the spring of 1949, the US Supreme Court decided two cases on the Fourth Amendment. By prohibiting "unreasonable searches and seizures," it was the constitutional provision that most directly applied to the police.[8] (It was not a coincidence that a search and seizure were at issue in Lieberman's encounter with the LAPD.) The justices were clearly thinking about *Wolf v. Colorado* and *Brinegar v. United States* together. They heard argument for the two cases on the same day in October, and they issued decisions in both cases on the same June day.

Just as evidently, the justices struggled to come to a resolution; even though the cases were argued early in the term, the opinions came out on the very last day before they broke for summer recess. The challenge, at bottom, was to figure out how a free society could depend on the discretionary authority of the police and still be free. The horrors of Hitler's Germany, the foremost example of arbitrary rule, loomed throughout the opinions in both cases. *Wolf* declared that unlawful searches "did not need the commentary of recent history to be condemned as inconsistent with the conception of human rights enshrined in the history and the basic constitutional documents of English-speaking peoples." Justice Jackson's prosecutorial experience at the Nuremberg trials prompted his declaration in *Brinegar* that "uncontrolled search and seizure is one of the first and most effective weapons in the arsenal of every arbitrary government." But these were straightforward statements to proclaim. It was much more difficult to reconcile the demands of security with the requirements of liberty.[9]

The Court faced this difficult task in *Wolf* and *Brinegar*. Juxtaposing the two cases reveals a jurisprudential map of how the Court ultimately drew the boundary between arbitrary police power and lawful discretionary power. It shows that the distinction between houses and cars mattered when the justices determined what the police could and could not do. In other words, the constitutional definition of arbitrary policing would depend on whether or not the police were policing cars.

The first case, *Wolf v. Colorado*, involved a classic Fourth Amendment violation: the warrantless search of private property and papers. Law enforcement officers received an anonymous telephone call about a woman suffering from a botched abortion. Investigators from the district attorney's office found the woman, who gave them the name of the chiropractor who had performed the operation. The investigators, two district attorneys, and a deputy sheriff then raided Wolf's office, identified a few patients listed in his appointment book, and questioned them for information to charge the doctor with conspiracy to commit abortions. All nine justices concluded that the "knock at the door . . . as a prelude to a search, without authority of law"—that is, without a warrant—"but solely on the authority of the police" violated "the concept of ordered liberty."[10]

By describing the nefarious deed as beginning with a "knock at the door," the *Wolf* opinion conjured the image of a home, which carried a lot of weight in Fourth Amendment doctrine. Doing so protected even an abortionist's office at a time when performing such procedures was a criminal offense. Not a single justice argued that the criminalization of abortion placed the entire matter within the public sphere of government control and, accordingly, outside the purview of the Fourth Amendment.[11] Arguments like this had been made before.[12] And although a place of business could arguably be distinguished from houses in a literal interpretation of the Fourth Amendment, Supreme Court precedent going back at least to the 1928 case *Olmstead v. United States* collapsed any differences with one sentence: "There was no entry of the houses or offices of the defendants."[13]

Of course, the Fourth Amendment did not seal off the private sphere from all policing. According to *Wolf*, any intrusion needed the "authority of law" in the form of a warrant, which served to ward off "arbitrary intrusion by the police." *Arbitrary* power, not police power in its entirety, was anathema to a free society. It was not per se the entry into a home, actual or metaphorical, that was reminiscent of Nazi Germany and totalitarian rule. It was police action carried out without the *authority of law*. The Fourth Amendment's warrant requirement, all the justices agreed, erected an important legal constraint on the police's power. Before entering a house, officers had to appear before a magistrate, make out the case for probable cause, and get a warrant.[14]

Despite the consensus on the sanctity of the private sphere, the *Wolf* decision provoked strong dissents. Justice Murphy lamented that he found it "disheartening to find so much that is right in an opinion which seems to me so fundamentally wrong." What was right was the decision to take the constitutionally momentous act of "incorporation." That meant that although the Fourth Amendment did not directly apply to the states, it would be applicable through the Fourteenth Amendment's guarantee that no state shall "deprive any person of life, liberty, or property, without *due process of law*." In other words, according to *Wolf*, the due process clause encompassed the right to be free from unreasonable searches and seizures. Granted, the incorporation of the Fourth Amendment did not make much of a difference, since all states already had an equivalent right in their state constitutions. Still, it was an important statement, which all nine justices embraced, that the "security of one's privacy against arbitrary intrusion by the police" was "basic to a free society."[15]

But what was so "fundamentally wrong" with the majority opinion, in Murphy's view, was that the Court's ruling left Wolf without a remedy for the violation of his constitutional rights. It was clear that the sheriff and his colleagues had acted without the authority of law when they barged into the doctor's office without a warrant. Should not the Court provide some sort of relief? When confronted with arbitrary power, what must a government of laws do to keep from turning into an authoritarian government?

Although all the justices agreed that an adequate remedy was crucial in deterring violations of the Fourth Amendment, the majority sided with Justice Frankfurter that the issue was amenable to "varying solutions which spring from an allowable range of judgment." It was up to the individual states to establish their own remedial schemes and not for the US Supreme Court to mandate one for all. At the justices' first conference, Frankfurter emphasized that *Wolf* was not about forbidding the police the "right to do anything they please"; rather, the issue was whether states had to "provide *the remedy*"—that is, the exclusion of evidence taken from unlawful searches. States could choose, instead, to provide civil or statutory damages or to establish internal disciplinary procedures. The fact that most states rejected the exclusionary rule proved to Frankfurter, tautologically, that it was not a "fundamental right" and, thus, not essential to due process. The Court accordingly affirmed Colorado's judgment against Wolf despite the arbitrary actions of law enforcement.[16]

While Frankfurter considered most states' rejection of the exclusionary rule as proof that it was not basic to a free society, the dissenting justices viewed those rejections as effectively nullifying the Fourth Amendment. "Alternatives are deceptive," Murphy argued, for they conveyed "the impression that one possibility is as effective as the next." But in reality, he continued, there was only "one alternative to the rule of exclusion. That is no sanction at all." Murphy's dissent focused on a particular deficiency in the American legal system: it provided insufficient remedies for lawless policing. "Self-scrutiny is a lofty ideal," he observed, "but its exaltation reaches new heights" if the Court believed that police departments would discipline one of their own. Even district attorneys could not be relied on to prosecute their law enforcement associates for constitutional violations. Victims were more motivated to sue, but civil remedies were "illusory." In most cases, it made little sense to bring a lawsuit because damages were usually limited to actual injury, which often amounted to very little in monetary terms. Even if the sum were not insignificant, the chances of satisfying a judgment depended on the policeman's personal finances. Many legal scholars had accordingly concluded that these shortcomings in the system of torts and damages actually encouraged the police to flout the Fourth Amendment. Considering the bleak prospects, Murphy pleaded, unsuccessfully, that the procedural remedy had to be part and parcel of the substantive right itself; otherwise, he warned, arbitrary policing would continue.[17]

What constituted arbitrary policing was itself a question up for debate. While the justices agreed that the warrantless entry and search of a private space fell on the side of arbitrariness, they could not come to agreement when it came to the warrantless stop and search of a car. The second case that was also decided in 1949, *Brinegar v. United States*, raised the "crucial question," according to the Court, whether the officers had probable cause to invoke the automobile exception set forth in *Carroll v. United States*.[18]

The "basic facts" of the two cases were "very similar," according to the *Brinegar* opinion. In *Carroll*, Prohibition agents had stopped and searched an Oldsmobile Roadster based mainly on the fact that its occupants had once agreed to sell them liquor. In *Brinegar*, federal investigators from the Alcohol Tax Unit recognized a Ford coupe belonging to Virgil Brinegar, who had a "reputation for hauling liquor." Based on his notoriety and their observation that the car's rear end appeared "weighted down," the agents pulled him over by crowding the car to the side of the road. One of them greeted Brinegar by asking, "How much liquor have you got in the car this time?" Brinegar admitted—one wonders how freely—"Not too much." The officers then proceeded to search the car, finding one case on the

front seat under a lap robe and twelve more in the back. Brinegar
was subsequently charged with violating federal laws prohibiting the
importation of liquor into a state that outlawed it. After a jury found
him guilty, he was fined $100 (a little over $1,000 today) and sen-
tenced to thirty days' imprisonment.[19]

At first glance, it may be puzzling that the Supreme Court agreed
to review the case. According to the opinion, *Brinegar* was "indis-
tinguishable" from *Carroll* "on the material facts." The nation's
highest court typically did not hear cases involving straightforward
applications of precedent—that is, unless the justices had reservations about the precedent in question. Indeed, they were conflicted
about how much power the police had claimed under *Carroll*'s automobile exception. The flip-flopping votes reflected their uncertainty.
Three justices ultimately changed positions. For starters, Justice
Jackson's dissent had begun as the majority opinion. Surprisingly,
given his forceful criticism of the officers, Jackson had initially voted
to affirm Brinegar's conviction. Justices Douglas and Rutledge had
originally voted to reverse, but eventually decided against it. Strikingly, Rutledge had indicated at the first conference that he "would
overrule" *Carroll*, but he ended up writing the opinion for the Court.
Months after "occupying both" sides, Rutledge "regretfully" informed Jackson that he believed "*Carroll* is controlling here . . .
contrary to my initial view."[20]

The quandary centered on probable cause, the minimum quantum
of facts that an officer needed to support the belief that a car was
transporting contraband, as *Carroll* required for warrantless car stops
and searches. At least five of the justices believed that the federal
agents did not have sufficient cause to force Brinegar's car into the
ditch by the roadside and bring it to a halt for inspection. As Jackson
wrote in a memo to the justices that later wound up in his dissent,
this conduct "was a form of coercion and duress under color of official authority—and a very formidable type of duress at that." Even
the trial judge had believed that the agents lacked probable cause.
So, seemingly, all that the Court had to do was to hold that the lower
courts had erred in concluding that even if the initial stop was unlawful, Brinegar's admission that he had "not too much" alcohol justified the subsequent search.[21]

The problem, however, was that the case for probable cause in *Brinegar* was largely the same as the case for probable cause in *Carroll*. To reverse judgment in *Brinegar*, the justices believed that they had to either overrule *Carroll* or distinguish the two cases in some way. Jackson's first draft sought to differentiate *Brinegar* from *Carroll*, which was how he lost Justice Rutledge. Rutledge conceded that Jackson's "last circulation does as good a job of distinguishing the cases as can be done," but he had "come to feel" that "the distinctions taken are not controlling." Try as he might, Rutledge could not get over the dilemma that evidence of probable cause in *Brinegar* furnished "support quite as strong as that made in the *Carroll* case, indeed stronger in some respects." Justice Frankfurter agreed with that last thought, believing that "*Carroll* went to the verge for me on prob[able] cause—maybe beyond it." To these two justices, any effort to distinguish *Brinegar* and *Carroll* seemed disingenuous at best. Worse, lower courts might interpret any distinction as a de facto repeal of the automobile exception.[22]

Even though Rutledge had initially entertained overruling *Carroll*, such a course, he realized, was not a practical option. All the justices viewed *Carroll* as standing "chiefly for the proposition that there must be probable cause in every search without warrant, even of a moving automobile." *Carroll*, in other words, placed a limit on warrantless searches. Justice Burton wrote a separate opinion indicating that he would have been satisfied with an even lower standard than probable cause to grant federal agents a "positive duty to investigate," otherwise known as proactive policing. But he was alone in that view. For the other justices, the *Carroll* standard struck the perfect balance between the need to give law enforcement some flexibility to meet the exigencies of automobility on the one hand, and individual freedom to drive on the other. "Requiring more" than probable cause "would unduly hamper law enforcement," Rutledge wrote. "To allow less," he continued, "would be to leave law-abiding citizens at the mercy of the officers' whim or caprice." In the perspectives of the sheltered judges, *Carroll* established a restraining principle. As Justice Murphy wrote privately to Jackson, he did "not think any one [sic] would insist on over-ruling *Carroll*—after all it is a good case for the citizenry opposed to the constablulary [sic]." It did not occur to him that those citizens might actually have preferred the warrant requirement over the automobile exception.[23]

The disconnect between the justices' understanding and Brinegar's preference stemmed from the discrepancy between law on the books and law in action. The crux of *Carroll* depended on how trial judges would interpret the nebulous concept of probable cause. In most cases, they adopted the police's account of probable cause, which, over time, expanded their discretionary power. Indeed, it was not the standard itself that caused disagreement among the justices deciding *Brinegar*. Their differences came down to their application of the standard. What minimum proof would be required to constitute probable cause? Would it be enough that a person who had previously transported illicit liquor was driving from the direction of a source city? The *Carroll* majority had answered in the affirmative. But twenty years later, that conclusion seemed mistaken to the Vinson Court.

A majority of the justices came up squarely against *Carroll* and backed down. They feared that disturbing *Carroll*'s probable-cause determination might undermine the automobile exception. As Rutledge wrote for the Court, "the *Carroll* decision must be taken to control this situation, unless it is now to be overruled." So notwithstanding his initial misgivings, Rutledge concluded that the officers had acted within reason. Today, courts still cite *Brinegar* for its aphorism that in "dealing with probable cause . . . we deal with probabilities." Using this lax calculation, the Court upheld the warrantless search and seizure of a car that amounted to unrestrained policing. Its opinion acknowledged just as much. Allowing that the "troublesome line posed by the facts in the *Carroll* case and this case is one between mere suspicion and probable cause"—a stunning admission that the facts in both cases may have fallen just short of probable cause—the Court decided to draw that line in deference to the officers' "act of judgment." After all, the agents' suspicions were dead on: Brinegar was, in fact, transporting illegal liquor. So were the Carroll brothers.[24]

To defend this ends-justify-the-means logic, Rutledge explained that *Brinegar* and *Carroll* involved the "freedom to use public highways." When in their cars, citizens had "to give fair leeway" to officers "enforcing the law in the community's protection." In this public sphere, "room must be allowed for some mistakes on [officers'] part," an acceptable accommodation, Rutledge wrote, because "no problem of searching the home or any other place of privacy was presented." Here, then, was the boundary between arbitrary and non-arbitrary police discretion: it followed the divide between the public and private spheres.[25]

While the majority distilled *Brinegar* as a case about a car traveling on the public highway, Jackson argued that "when a car is forced off the road, summoned to stop by a siren, and brought to a halt . . . the officers are then in the position of one *who has entered a home*." Even the dissenters understood the Fourth Amendment within the public/private framework, but they drew the "troublesome line" differently. By analogizing to a house, Jackson sought to give drivers some protection from discretionary policing. This might have meant that the warrant requirement should apply to cars as it did to houses. But Jackson did not go that far, concluding only that "the search at its commencement must be valid and cannot be saved by what it turns up." The dissenters did not want to rescind the automobile exception. They simply wanted the probable-cause standard to have some bite, fearing that *Carroll* had "been too much taken by enforcement officers as blanket authority to stop and search cars on suspicion."[26]

But for the majorities in both *Carroll* and *Brinegar*, the exigencies of crime control took priority. Their deference to law enforcement indicated that the public's interest in a crime-free, and alcohol-free, community far outweighed a vigorous review of the police's actions when they investigated cars. It is hard to overstate the implications of the *Brinegar* decision. By finding that the federal agents had probable cause to bring Brinegar's car to a screeching halt and to search it, the Court concluded that the officers' conduct did not violate the Fourth Amendment and, consequently, was not arbitrary. Placing *Brinegar* and *Wolf* side by side, as the justices surely did, it was clear that the line between public and private, between cars and houses, not only mattered for deciding when the Fourth Amendment would require an officer to get a warrant. It also determined when discretionary policing crossed into arbitrary policing.

Arbitrary policing was not simply about police lawlessness. One takeaway from the *Brinegar* decision was that actions that skirted the boundary of illegality might not count as arbitrary if the police got the right person. One could deduce from this lesson that arbitrariness also encompassed the idea that lawless policing could affect anyone, particularly the innocent. Justice Jackson expressed this notion in his dissent, perhaps recognizing that Brinegar's guilt was swaying his colleagues to side with law enforcement. He understood their dilemma. After all, he himself had initially voted to affirm the conviction. But Jackson ultimately concluded that courts had to scrupulously defend the Fourth Amendment, and not necessarily because of the intrinsic value of upholding the Constitution even when the defendant was guilty. Rather, it was because of the importance of protecting the rights of the innocent.

According to Jackson, the guarantee against unreasonable searches and seizures was not only one of the first rights to succumb to an authoritarian government but also "one of the most difficult to protect." In comparison, the freedom of the press and speech typically involved suppression of the kind for which an individual could request an injunction before the violation could occur. Judicial oversight protected other rights, such as the right to an impartial jury or the assistance of counsel. But unlawful searches and seizures, especially of a car, were usually "perpetrated by surprise" and "conducted in haste." Once pulled over, the individual had "no opportunity for injunction or appeal to disinterested intervention."[27]

Not only was there no "advance protection," Jackson continued, there was also very little recourse after the fact. Justice Murphy's dissent in *Wolf v. Colorado* already explained the inadequacy of civil action. To that Jackson added the fact that innocent citizens did not make Fourth Amendment arguments in criminal cases. Such claims arose when a search unearthed evidence of a crime that led to an arrest in a jurisdiction that applied the exclusionary rule. In short, only guilty people contested unconstitutional searches and seizures.

That was the problem. The innocent experienced lawless policing too. But unlike the guilty, they had nothing to suppress, which meant that they had no remedy at all.

So when a police officer stopped a car, the "citizen's choice," Jackson laid out, was "quietly to submit to whatever the officers undertake or to resist at risk of arrest or immediate violence." Considering the lack of options, Jackson was "convinced" that there were "many unlawful searches . . . which turn up nothing incriminating, in which no arrest is made, about which courts do nothing, and about which we never hear." Thus, a "search against Brinegar's car," Jackson pithily stated, "must be regarded as a search of the car of Everyman." Although Brinegar was guilty, he represented every innocent person who had been pulled over and searched without lawful reason. The idea of Everyman suggested that implicit in the definition of arbitrariness was a distinction between the guilty and the innocent. In other words, to become a problem of arbitrary policing, it had to affect the law-abiding.

Also central to the concern with arbitrary policing was that any group, and not just a particular group, could experience police lawlessness. To be sure, midcentury Americans recognized, to varying degrees, that the police picked on racial minorities. Organizations such as the NAACP were calling attention to police lawlessness against black citizens. Still, most jurists understood arbitrary and discriminatory policing as distinct concepts: arbitrariness selected its victims at random, whereas discrimination targeted specific groups. Many, like Justice Jackson, seemed to consider arbitrary power more troubling. He was not concerned that most states lacked an exclusionary rule—he joined the majority in *Wolf*—because, in his words, "local excesses or invasions of liberty are more amenable to political correction." This rationale was strikingly oblivious to the wrongs that state and local police perpetrated against African Americans. Jackson elaborated further that the Fourth Amendment "was directed only against the new and centralized government, and any really dangerous threat to the general liberties of the people can come only from this source." That was why he was adamant that the Constitution ought to protect people in cars from *federal* agents, while at the same time, he believed that the Fourth Amendment did not require *states* to apply the exclusionary rule. As a federal judge, Jackson worried more about centralized arbitrary power, not localized discriminatory power.[28]

Another example comes from the well-respected criminal law scholar Jerome Hall's 1952 public lectures at the University of Chicago Law School, titled "Police and Law in a Democratic Society," which was published the following year in the *Indiana Law Journal*. Hall began by listing examples of law enforcement abuses from ancient Greece through the Middle Ages, from the American colonies to Nazi Germany, "not to minimize the evil of race antagonism, but to encourage persistent realistic dealing with perennial problems." He devoted just two short paragraphs to "discriminatory law enforcement." On that topic, Hall noted that the "relatively high rate of arrests of Negroes" possibly reflected their "actual criminal behavior" or else was "accounted for by the fact that the Negro is also allocated to the impotent, underprivileged classes whose legal rights may be infringed upon with impunity." Although Hall found this situation unfortunate, he did not consider illegal arrests, committed against mostly this class of citizens, to be "vicious or brutal"; instead, he considered them to be "well motivated." According to Hall, such arrests served "a social need"—namely, the maintenance of order, especially when dealing with "vagrants, drunkards, and derelicts." His inattention to the particular problems facing black Americans is all the more jarring because his lectures were part of a conference on police and racial tensions. Clearly, arbitrary power in general troubled Hall more than discriminatory policing specifically.[29]

The fixation on arbitrary policing perhaps explains why race leaders often articulated their concerns in Everyman terms, maintaining that "brutality, lynching and all that grows out of it work against all people as well as against Negroes." Sometimes they tried reaching out to white America. Police discrimination, as one citizen wrote to Pasadena's City Hall, "make[s] us all feel extremely insecure for it is a very short step from such encroachments on the rights of minority racial groups to the complete breakdown of law and order [and the] Gestapo-like rule of the police." Nevertheless, most mainstream jurists focused on the plight of the average law-abiding citizen, whom they imagined as someone like themselves.[30]

This averaged figure appeared pervasively, and not only in judicial opinions or scholarly articles. In the 1950s, several state bar associations and the ACLU began distributing booklets, which had some variation of the title "If You Are Arrested." These "bust books," as they would come to be called, explained a person's rights when arrested, such as the right to contact a lawyer and the right not to answer questions. Newspapers publicized the pamphlets by highlighting the possibility that anyone could find themselves in trouble with the law. "Even the well-meaning individual," one paper cautioned, "may at any hour find himself trapped in a net of circumstances that land him in court, guilty or not." So it was "worth getting, even if you never expect to clash with the law." The *Boston Herald* likewise warned, "Even though you are sure you will never commit a crime, you cannot be certain that you won't be arrested and charged with one. It happens to a great many innocent people every year."[31]

Everyman captured the idea that arbitrary policing could harm any and every citizen; the automobile made that notion conceivable. In a 1949 article titled "It Could Happen to You," published in *The American Magazine*, investigative journalist Frederick Brownell reported that police lawlessness was occurring throughout the country and against "ordinary law-abiding people." The police got away with it, according to Brownell, because most citizens believed that "you've got to grant the cops a little leeway in dealing with crooks and racketeers" and, in any case, "it could never happen to you or me." To prove otherwise, one of the opening illustrations featured two football referees who were driving to Ithaca, New York, for a Cornell game when they were pulled over for speeding. "When one of the men failed to get out of the car fast enough," Brownell recounted, "the policeman hit him over the head with the butt of his gun. It took six stitches to close the wound." The egregiousness of the police's actions suggests that the men might have been African American, but Brownell did not mention their race, presumably so that the story would resonate with a general audience. The reporter may have anticipated that his readers would find the incident improbable anyway, for he went on to declare that an illegal car search was one of the "most common forms of police lawlessness." As an example, he mentioned how the Los Angeles police had recently "descended upon each of a dozen busy traffic intersections, set the lights red in both directions, and jammed up cars for blocks . . . to search both cars and occupants."[32]

Brownell was referring to the "secret roadblocks"—secret because they were unannounced—that the Los Angeles Police Department had introduced the year before. At each checkpoint, scores of officers, sometimes numbering over sixty, stopped every vehicle for questioning and inspection, and not just for public safety purposes, but primarily to look for criminals. The police hoped to find concealed weapons and narcotics, and they planned to show recent crime victims a photo lineup of all those found with incriminating items. The Reverend Heist, ever vigilant, wrote several letters to the Police Commission about this encroachment of the Fourth Amendment. As Heist described the operation, officers "arbitrarily" determined which cars and occupants seemed suspicious enough to be further detained to a side street so that they could search the car and "frisk" the driver and passengers. The police hailed the first "crime-crusher blockade" a success, netting seventy-two suspects and more than fifty weapons. But the fifth roadblock ended with just one arrest, that of a solitary drunk. Another one the following month ensnared 4,800 cars, but the police made only a few arrests. The enforcement of the traffic code proved more successful; the police issued 114 traffic citations and fifty mechanical warnings.[33]

The police department tried to bolster the legitimacy of its program by giving credit to August Vollmer, the father of modern police in the United States. It was similar, the police said, to the plan that Vollmer had instituted when he had been police chief back in 1932. But they failed to mention, as one news report pointed out, that police blockades were "long considered a last-resort measure" rather than a routine procedure. When Vollmer's successor set one up after the 1933 shooting of newspaper publisher Crombie Allen, he had assured the public that "he had no intention of inconveniencing citizens." But the latest iteration in 1947, which backed up traffic for hours, seemed to have no such intentions.[34]

To be sure, some citizens did not mind. The International Association of Chiefs of Police informed Heist that state highway patrols had been using roadblocks throughout the country "with very effective results," and the Southern California ACLU was the first to call in a complaint. Even in the de facto capital of American car

The April 19, 1947, blockade resulted in the arrest of thirty-one
suspects.

Daily News, American Civil Liberties Union of Southern California records (Collection
900). Library Special Collections, Charles E. Young Research Library, UCLA.

The April 14, 1947, blockade on Sunset Strip.

Daily News, American Civil Liberties Union of Southern California records
(Collection 900). Library Special Collections, Charles E. Young Research Library,
UCLA.

culture where Heist and his fellow activists were raising objections, not everyone opposed the measure. The annoyance of some people provided security for others. Romaine Poindexter of Pasadena was "thankful this is done and only wish[ed] it could be more thorough." It did not surprise him that the ACLU, which he believed "stands for subversive activities definitely linked with Communism in the minds of most people[,] would be such an organization which would try to block" the roadblocks.[35]

It would be safe to assume that Poindexter did not experience what Merrill Mead did. The twenty-one-year-old Stanford graduate student was arrested at the June 25 blockade, which Police Chief Horrall personally led. During the search, two officers found an unloaded Colt automatic inside a suitcase in the trunk. Mead explained that he had borrowed the gun from his father for target practice during naval training and that he was on his way to Fresno to return it. The officers dismissed his explanation and took him to the Hollywood police station, where they booked him for "suspicion of robbery." The police refused him his phone call and instead handed him a release form waiving his right to sue the city for any damages suffered from the arrest.[36] Continuing the nightmare, Mead discovered that he had to pay five dollars to retrieve his impounded car and a dollar for storage. To add insult to injury, the fender was dented and some items that had been in the car were missing.[37]

By the 1950s, more people were becoming aware of the police's discretionary power, and not only because the civil rights movement was drawing attention to police abuse. They were also experiencing it for themselves, in their cars.[38] In police encounters on the road, they began to question how the law, as interpreted by its high priests, distinguished arbitrary and reasonable policing. They doubted the line that courts had drawn between public and private. They expected dignity and privacy in the public sphere of the automobile. The discretionary policing that judges condoned seemed to them unreasonable. It seemed arbitrary because it could affect Everyman.

In 1950, the New York City chapter of the ACLU sent a questionnaire to various churches, temples, homeless shelters, labor groups, and community organizations like settlement houses and the YMCA to survey "irregular police practices." The cover letter identified "physical brutality and illegal entry into private homes" as "all too common practices." To "bring the offenders to trial," the ACLU sought any complaints regarding the police, "especially in the man-handling of jobless or intoxicated people."[39]

This letter illuminated three aspects of a liberal perspective on the police problem at midcentury. First, the ACLU's historic role in de-fending laborers—*jobless or intoxicated people*—informed their framing of the issue primarily in terms of class. Second, the letter pinpointed particular practices—*physical brutality and illegal entry into private homes*—as especially problematic. Finally, defending civil lib-erties required a legal strategy—specifically, a *trial*.

But when the Police Committee of the ACLU chapter looked at the responses to its inquiry, it discovered that the main problem did not concern laborers, beatings, or warrantless searches of private homes. Rather, the police appeared to be targeting minority youths on public streets. The committee identified what seemed to be a "po-lice policy" of rounding up young adults congregating on sidewalks and dropping them off at their homes without filing any charges. Ac-tually, this policy was neither new nor confined to New York City. In 1937, the LAPD wrote glowingly about its efforts to "straighten the bending twig." One measure was to question "youngsters . . . loi-tering on the streets" and, if necessary, taking them home "where matters [were] discussed with the parents or guardians." The goal was to prevent juvenile delinquency and maintain orderly streets. But by the 1950s, teens in minority enclaves experienced more coercion than discipline.[40]

The survey results highlighted a problem that was of a different nature than the issues that the ACLU traditionally pursued. From its beginnings, ACLU lawyers had challenged law enforcement methods that infringed on constitutional rights. In 1920, they re-ported that raids of "homes, offices, or gathering places of persons suspected of radical affiliations" were carried out "without warrants or pretense of warrants" in violation of the Fourth Amendment. When President Hoover established the first national crime com-mission in 1929 at the height of Prohibition's crime wave, ACLU director Roger Baldwin successfully lobbied the Wickersham Commission to look into police practices as well. At Baldwin's suggestion, the commission delegated this part of the study to ACLU-affiliated lawyers. Their headline-grabbing *Report on Lawlessness in Law Enforcement* was an exposé on the third degree—"that is, the use of physical brutality, or other forms of cruelty, to obtain involuntary confessions or admissions"—which, they argued, violated the Fifth Amendment. The 1950 questionnaire that focused on "police brutality and illegal entry into private homes" mirrored the concerns of the ACLU's founding era.[41]

But the harassment of teenagers, according to the ACLU's understanding of the law, did not necessarily violate constitutional rights. Actually, reformers, experts, and government officials tended to view adolescents idling in the streets as a social problem. Later, in the 1960s, young people would argue that their activities in public constituted speech or expressive action that ought to be protected from police interference. But not in the 1950s. "Gee, Officer Krupke" from the 1956 musical *West Side Story* captures the earlier perspective in song. The characters—street gang members, a beat cop, a judge, a psychiatrist, and a social worker—sing about the variety of factors contributing to "juvenile delinquency," including "It's just our bringin' upke," "Society's played him a terrible trick," and "Deep down inside him, he's no good." No one sings about a legal right to be on the streets. At the time, not even ACLU lawyers grasped the constitutional dimensions of what teenagers were doing.[42]

To be sure, while the Fourth Amendment's warrant requirement did not apply in the public sphere, other legal constraints did. The ACLU's evolving approach to challenging vagrancy laws illustrates the various civil liberties that could be implicated in public-order maintenance. In the early 1950s, the organization's lawyers argued that the police were using vagrancy charges to silence "soapbox orators" in violation of the First Amendment. Later in the decade, they added the argument that the police, in attempts to circumvent the probable cause requirement, resorted to vagrancy arrests when they did not have sufficient evidence for some other crime. Even in the public sphere, the police had to abide by the Constitution and the common law of arrests. But outside of those well-defined perimeters, the police could exercise a great deal of discretionary authority, and the harassment of minority teens hanging out on streets and sidewalks did not seem to cross any clear legal boundary.[43]

Nonetheless, the ACLU recognized police mistreatment as a "serious problem" even if it did not amount to a legal one. According to the Police Committee, the "relationship between the police and the citizens in those sections of our city where there is a concentration of population of minority groups" had become "increasingly characterized by mutual antagonism, distrust, and a mounting fear of the police by the people in those neighborhoods." In worst-case scenarios, these reciprocal suspicions combusted into riots. During periods of peace or order, citizens "who should normally have turned to the police department" instead went to the NAACP, churches, or other private organizations. When people "felt that they needed protection from the police" instead of being able to rely on the police, the committee reported, it "militate[d] against the efficient functioning of the police department." Significantly, concern for *the efficient functioning of the police* revealed an acceptance of law enforcement's role in maintaining social order. For liberal activists, what distinguished a free society was not the absence of police. Rather, it was the nature of their relationship with the citizenry. As the ACLU's Southern California branch explained, those who lived in a democracy "respect and honor their police," in contrast to totalitarian states where "the police have earned only the fear and contempt of the citizens." While holding on to an ideal of democratic police, ACLU lawyers deplored the "bullies, brutes, and bigots" in uniform who acted like little despots and undermined the police's ability to protect citizens.[44]

Aggressive policing compromised the legitimacy of American police in the eyes of minority citizens, but from the ACLU's perspective, if it did not end in a beating or an arrest without probable cause, then it did not present a constitutional problem. Instead, it was a matter of best practices when governing the public. Because mere harassment could not be litigated, the committee proposed a "Program for Police Training in Human Relations," which focused on developing officers' interpersonal skills. To this end, the recommendations included not only the hiring of Spanish-speaking officers but also consulting "specialists in the human relations field" who could educate officers about "sociologically acceptable patterns of action in the exercise of their duties," "minority group behavior," and the "causes and manifestations" of prejudice.[45]

The committee circulated its recommendations at a time when police professionals themselves were recognizing "the importance of training in human relations as well as in the detection of crime." They issued their own reports, written on the heels of riots that erupted in several cities throughout the country in the 1940s. Although the titles used general phrases like "race relations" or "minority problems," these publications dealt specifically with preventing race riots. Notably, law enforcement's solutions were nearly identical to the ACLU's proposals. As an initial matter, the police manuals insisted that all recruits "receive a thorough indoctrination in the civil rights laws which they must uphold." While the ACLU focused on Fourth and Fifth Amendment rights, the relevant constitutional principle in the context of minority relations was the Fourteenth Amendment's equal protection clause. In an era of formal equality—*Brown v. Board* overruled the principle of separate but equal in 1954—"equal protection of the laws" had a double meaning. For one thing, it meant that police services, like other government resources, had to be equitably distributed; black victims deserved police protection just as much as white victims. It also meant that the police had to enforce the law equally. As Professor Jerome Hall wrote, an "officer who arrests rioters of one group and closes his eyes to the aggressions of the other, is violating the equality of democratic law."[46]

Police reformers recognized, however, that fostering positive relations required more than equal protection and enforcement. They also had to cultivate a "'human' approach" to their work, and laws did not provide any guidance for this task. To imbue police-minority encounters with humanity, they sought to train officers in human relations and to debunk commonly held prejudices. Recruits would learn that "scientists have found that no group has biological or racial tendencies toward criminality or delinquency." The manuals also explained that "Negroes and Mexican-American youths" were "oversensitive" to policing not because of any inherent criminality but because of persistent racism. That they would respond to the indignities of bigotry with antagonism was a "universal human reaction" and not meant as a personal affront to individual officers. These lessons in human relations were precisely what the ACLU's Police Committee had in mind as well. Because American society relied on the police to govern the public sphere, the ACLU's solution was not to challenge policing but to improve it. The Philadelphia chapter perfectly captured the organization's attitude toward policing in its 1951 slogan, "Cooperate While You Conflict." More accurately, the ACLU cooperated with the police in the public sphere while it conflicted by litigating invasions of the private sphere.[47]

The understanding that police conduct that stayed within the bounds of the law did not amount to a civil rights issue, no matter how offensive or obnoxious, guided the ACLU's responses to individuals inquiring whether the police had violated their rights. Significantly, when staff lawyers answered with a definitive "no," the incident transpired in the most prominent public sphere at midcentury: the automobile.

By 1950, 71 percent of US families owned at least one car. Also noteworthy is that half of all car owners were between the ages of twenty-five and forty-four. In short, the people who could have encountered the police in their cars came from a more general population than the urban minority youth that the ACLU surveyed. This larger group also included those in less densely populated areas as the nonstop construction of highways and freeways connected urban centers to sprawling suburbs. More pavement in turn led to more cars, which led to more drivers, which led to more police. So it was to be expected that complaints about the police would go up as well. As one editorialist wrote in 1946, "We ALL of us, at some period in our lives, have had a 'peeve' against some certain 'Cop,'" probably for "a Traffic 'Citation.'"[48]

Like the teenagers in New York City, many drivers felt that the police had treated them too harshly, and some harbored enough doubts about the legality of the confrontation that they sought advice from the ACLU. But the lawyers' analysis of traffic stops followed the same reasoning that led them to conclude that police harassment was not an infringement of constitutional rights. The letter writers had been pulled over, not arrested; thus, there was no violation of the law of arrests. They were spoken to roughly, not beaten; thus, no violation of their person. They were in their cars, not in their home or office; thus, no violation of the Fourth Amendment.

In 1959, Melvin Wulf, who would become the national legal director of the ACLU in 1962, replied to one Robert Arends that since a traffic stop did not amount to an arrest, his rights were not violated. On an August evening, the twenty-year-old veteran of the US Marine Corps and a sophomore at the Illinois State Normal University had driven to Thawville, Illinois, with a friend. On Tuesdays, the town screened a free drive-in movie, which filled the neighborhood with people and packed the streets with cars. After the show, as Arends and his friend were making their way home, they attracted the attention of an officer. The officer pulled Arends over and demanded to see his driver's license. Bewildered, Arends asked, "What for?" The conversation immediately turned hostile. The officer again repeated his demand without giving a reason. Believing that he "was being done wrong," Arends walked over to the police car, where the officer was in the middle of contacting the county sheriff's office to check for outstanding warrants. Arends asked again, "Why have I been arrested?" When the officer barked, "You'd better get back in that car and stay there before you get in trouble," Arends complied. The officer finally ordered Arends to "quit driving around town and . . . get out of there." Arends persisted in asking for an explanation for the treatment until the officer threatened to have the mayor sign a complaint if Arends "didn't hurry up and get out of there."[49]

Shaken and angry, Arends walked over to two bystanders, one of whom was a town councilman, who had witnessed the incident. According to Arends, both "admitted that they saw no reason for me to be stopped" and even "consented to appear in court and testify to that effect." In his letter to the ACLU penned the next day, Arends asked "if this is actually false arrest or something encroaching my civil rights."[50] Wulf answered that what Arends had experienced was not an arrest, but "an example of a police officer merely throwing his weight about and interrogating you out of curiosity rather than on the basis of a belief that you had violated any law." "Unfortunately," Wulf continued, "this kind of thing goes on," and there was "no remedy for the ill treatment."[51]

T. R. Mathews, a self-identified "old stock American, of the old school" from Birmingham, Michigan, wrote about an argument with a cop over a ticket for parking his car just six inches over a yellow line "for a moment in front of property owned by me." He first tried to reason with the officer "to no avail," then "words ensued," and finally the officer threatened jail three times. Mathews strongly suspected that the cop's "brute instinct was likely aroused" because he was "dressed like a tramp" (perhaps this was why he had introduced himself in the letter as an "old stock American"). The ordeal concluded five months later with a jury finding Mathews liable only for the parking violation and overturning the other two tickets that the officer had written out in retaliation.[52]

Staff attorney Alan Reitman informed Mathews that "unfortunately there is no civil liberties issue involved in the case" without "evidence of physical maltreatment"—a violation of one's person, which would have been a classic ACLU matter. Reitman explained further that "despite the policeman's nasty attitude, he is permitted to give you the tickets." The only solution, Reitman offered, was "urging local police departments to sponsor human relations institutes and better training programs." Without an unlawful arrest, police misbehavior simply did not rise to a legal or constitutional problem. This must have been cold news to someone who had repeatedly been threatened with arrest and received two unjustified tickets because he had argued with a police officer. It must have disturbed him even more to read Reitman's reply that what he experienced was a "generic problem."[53]

Duncan E. Hilton's exchange with the ACLU demonstrated that there were obstacles to redress even when an unlawful arrest had taken place. He wrote to see if the Southern California branch "could be of any assistance to those being victimized by the local traffic police." According to Hilton, the police had a practice of waiting around drive-ins to "make illegal arrests of drivers who have no witnesses nor the time and money to go to court." Hilton thought that "if the police knew that many of these arrests would be contested by competent lawyers, we should have fewer of them." So he urged the ACLU, an organization he commended "for protecting individuals who can not [sic] defend themselves," to sue the police. He was not seeking counsel for himself; rather, what he had in mind was a class action. "Most of my friends and acquaintances have reached the same conclusions," Hilton wrote, and they all wondered "if they can contribute to a fund that would be used exclusively for such a purpose."[54]

Executive Director Eason Monroe replied that the problem Hilton identified was "a difficult one to remedy." "General propositions that the police are incompetent, that they harass citizens, that they must fulfill quotas, are not suitable to take to court." Of course, Hilton's allegation that the police also made false arrests could be litigated— assuming that there was an arrest and not simply a traffic stop—but, Monroe explained, "the only relief secured is for the individual directly affected." Another option was to bring the issue "to the attention of administrative authorities." Even then, the evidence had to be "conclusive," which effectively ended the matter if, as Hilton claimed, the police picked on drivers who had no witnesses. The LAPD's stock responses to citizen complaints seemed to confirm Monroe's assessment. The department's internal investigations would reliably inform the complainant that "the allegations made by you could not be clearly resolved due to the absence of disinterested witnesses."[55]

Reflecting the democratizing effects of automobility, many letters to the ACLU came from individuals who could represent the mid-century Everyman: white, male, and law abiding. They revealed a sense that American society had fundamentally changed if the police could mistreat upstanding citizens without good reason. They were respectable people, as they pointed out in both subtle and not-so-subtle ways. Arends began his letter by stating his year at the university and indicating his veteran status. Mathews not only identified himself as an old-stock American but also added that another police officer had to tell the offending cop "who I was." A corporate executive from Philadelphia wrote his letter on company letterhead and included his title as vice president under his signature. Their letters conveyed a struggle to make sense of police authority in what was supposed to be a free society. The executive wrote that it was "a shame for one officer to hurt the dignity and respect which the Philadelphia Police Department deserves," suggesting that the problem might have been a few bad apples. But he must have been aware that the officer's behavior fell within a broader pattern of police misconduct. After all, he had sent a copy of his letter to the ACLU (the originals went to the mayor and police commissioner) so that the organization could include his story in its investigation into systemic abuses of the police's power.[56]

Of course, black motorists experienced the police's imperious ways as well. Beginning in the late 1930s and with increasing frequency each decade, they wrote to the NAACP about traffic stops for minor or fabricated charges that left them terrified. These letters described flagrant transgressions of constitutional limits. African Americans were falsely arrested, beaten, or shot. On top of these Fourth and Fifth Amendment violations, traffic cops were also targeting rights activists. In Florida in 1946, a nearly successful attempt to lynch Thurgood Marshall had begun with a pretextual traffic stop. A decade later, NAACP leaders in Florida, Mississippi, Alabama, and Texas reported a "southwide pattern" of arresting "Negroes active in the civil rights movement" and fining them for minor traffic infractions. In 1956, the president of the Florida branch was "handcuffed, beaten, kicked and arrested" for double-parking his car in front of the local NAACP office. Newspapers compounded the problem by providing the public with only the police's account; the local press did not bother to contact the president or the NAACP before running the story.[57]

Whether they were leaders of the freedom movement, respectable members of the community, or anonymous travelers, black citizens had to anticipate the possibility of encountering an abusive officer. Dr. Herman Barnett, the first black graduate of the University of Texas Medical School, was arrested for speeding and, while handcuffed, beaten on the head with a pistol by a Texas highway patrolman. Dr. Joseph Hayes of Los Angeles was yanked out of his car, knocked to the ground, and informed that this treatment was "the law" because he was "a colored boy driving a big automobile in a white neighborhood, and [he] had on dirty clothes [that] didn't match [his] car." The officers refused to listen to his explanation that he was wearing jeans because he had been horseback riding. When the doctor protested that the handcuffs were too tight, one of the officers replied that if he was a medical doctor as he claimed, then he should know that his hands would not be damaged from twenty minutes without blood circulation.[58]

When the Reverend G. W. Jones and his family were driving back to Arkansas from the Sesqui-Centennial Celebration of African Methodism in Memphis, Tennessee, he was pulled over for overtaking two cars with white passengers. The officer immediately began spewing vile names at the minister, interspersed with blows to his face with such force that they knocked off his glasses. When his wife got out of the car to help him, she was slapped and kicked as well. The punishment ended with a $32.50 fine for reckless driving. All this for violating the norms of segregation on the road.[59]

Jim Crow's dictates were well established. In a letter to his friend Thurgood Marshall, the *Informer*'s general manager Carter Wesley had to account for his delay in confirming last-minute changes to Marshall's visit to Houston. Wesley had just gotten out of jail after two highway patrolmen stopped him for waving at a car that he had passed. "No, there wasn't any woman with him, so there was no question of mashing," Wesley preemptively explained. He had not even waved at anybody, but the officers would not give him a chance to defend himself. Instead, they gave him "a good beating" and threw him in jail for twenty-four hours. Then, "to protect themselves for the beating, they filed a charge of resisting arrest." "No, I wasn't impudent to them," Wesley again preemptively maintained. It was just the way things were. Wesley did not need to point out that even if Jim Crow were followed to the letter, it offered no insurance against police abuse.[60]

In many cases, it was unclear which norms had been slighted. Sixteen-year-old William Owens was choked and beaten by a Georgia state trooper while he was driving his white employer, who described the incident as "the cruelest thing I ever saw happen except a hanging once." When the *New York Post* asked the trooper for a statement, he replied, "It was just an ordinary day's work and that's all I got to say about it."[61]

Unlawful stops, physical assaults, and false arrests did not happen only in the South. In 1953, Frederick North was killed on the Cross Island Parkway in Long Island, New York, by a Nassau County policeman. The officer alleged that North was speeding and driving while under the influence of alcohol, an allegation that North's friend, who was in the car at the time of the shooting, emphatically denied. Walter White of the NAACP asked the organization to double check the facts because "it [seemed to him] that this is a cock and bull story by the policeman to get him out of what appears to be a cold-blooded murder." Death at the hands of the police happened with such frequency that some referred to it as a "One Man Lynching."[62]

These extralegal executions started happening early on. In 1937—just a year after the *Negro Motorist Green Book* launched its inaugural issue—Stanley Jackson, an employee at a service station next to his home in Perth Amboy, New Jersey, decided to take one of the serviced cars for a spin. Near Trenton, a state trooper started his siren and brought the car to a stop by shooting the left rear tire. Even though the local paper, giving the police's side of the story, reported that Jackson "stole" the car for the pleasure ride, many people, including police officials, did not consider juveniles who took unattended cars for "joy rides" to be real criminals. Whether or not New Jersey officers agreed with that assessment, Jackson's moment of teenage rebellion surely did not warrant what followed. Upon reaching the immobilized car, Trooper Bull told Jackson, "I ought to kill you," and proceeded to shoot point blank. Jackson survived the shooting, but the bullets lodged in his body gave him lead poisoning. About a month later, the police transferred Jackson from the hospital to jail, where he sat for two charges, resisting an officer and reckless driving.[63]

Accumulating evidence indicated that these acts of violence at the hands of patrol officers added up to more than isolated events. By the early 1960s, a Newark hospital employee was convinced that police abuse was "rampant" after seeing so many victims treated there. The NAACP's Detroit branch examined the situation more methodically. After studying all 103 police brutality complaints it had received from January 1956 to July 1957, it confirmed that what had happened to Stanley Jackson and Frederick North was part of a larger pattern. In every case that the Detroit office processed, the policeman exhibited "a total disregard . . . for the comp[l]ainant's rights as a citizen." At the top of the list was the "searching of citizens in public streets for minor traffic violations," followed by the "use of racial slurs" and "physical assault." Ninety percent of the victims were "working people without a previous police record" whose only sin, the report supposed, was that they had neglected to respond with "Yes sir and no sir when answering a white man." This failure could unleash a torrent of abuse, which often began with the accusation of being "one of those smart niggers."[64]

William T. Phillips of Los Angeles shared his ordeal with the NAACP. While making a turn at Seventh and Grand, Officer Reeves stopped him, and in "very abusive language," berated him for not sticking out his arm. Because mechanical signals became common only in the late 1940s, when Phillips was pulled over in 1953, the custom—in many places enforced by law—was to use hand signals.[65] Next time, Reeves growled, he would write out a ticket "that would take . . . a month to pay." When Phillips asked for a reason for the officer's gruff manner, Reeves decided to issue citations for "as many violations of the code as possible." The officer also put him in handcuffs and repeatedly called him "a smart aleck nigger." Eight days after Phillips had filed a complaint with the Board of Police Commissioners, two plainclothes policemen came to his home twice— once without a warrant and a second time with one to search the apartment. Later that day, they came to his place of employment to arrest him for the made-up charges of battery and disturbing the peace. Officer Reeves had warned him against contacting the Police Commission. This was payback.[66]

Both the fear of retaliation and the all-but-certain futility of receiving justice kept many African Americans from seeking redress. For one thing, it was easy for officers to concoct a defense. To explain why he fired five bullets into Earl French, who was being brought in for drunkenness, the officer testified that he thought French "was going to try to kill me in the car." According to black papers, it was "nothing unusual" for police to shoot and then afterward claim that the victims "resisted arrest" or "drew a deadly weapon." Prosecutors often accepted these stories at face value, which explained why grand juries were unlikely to return indictments against officers. Coroners reliably cleared policemen of guilt, and judges routinely dismissed cases. Even if a case made it to trial, the jury might be biased, too. When an all-white jury in Mississippi freed a sheriff in just twenty-three minutes—even though four witnesses saw him beat a black man to death—newspapers reported how he had rejoiced, exclaiming, "By God, now I can get back to rounding up bootleggers and damn niggers." The criminal justice system was insurmountably stacked against the black American such that newspapers referred to "whitewash" as a noun. Whitewashing or, just as often, stonewalling also rendered administrative channels a dead end. A New York City lawyer told Thurgood Marshall that "from bitter experience in the past, I have come to have very little faith in the sincerity or effectiveness of the so-called Departmental Hearings or Trials." The most that victims could hope for was to clear their good name of bogus charges.[67]

In one 1949 episode, an off-duty cop in civilian clothes fatally shot Herman Newton during a traffic dispute, and a Brooklyn grand jury declined to bring an indictment. The NAACP and the American Jewish Congress petitioned the court—and appealed to the court of public opinion—to open the grand jury minutes, arguing that the district attorney could not be trusted. While the prosecutor claimed that there were no eyewitnesses to the shooting, the NAACP had located eight of them. Their pleading described a "reign of terror" in Brooklyn that was just as frightening as "in some of the most lynch-ridden places of the South," where officers uttered threats like "Down here we never try an officer for manslaughter. . . . We try the dead man to see if he should have been killed." It was demoralizing that even up north, "officers can and do murder and assault Negro citizens with utter impunity."[68]

Although the criminal justice system failed to bring justice to Newton's family, the NAACP helped his estate file a civil lawsuit against the police officer and the city. The circumstances of Newton's wrongful death were so clearly egregious that a jury awarded $53,837 in damages, and the state's two appellate courts unanimously upheld the judgment. Nonetheless, within two years of the final ruling, the police department promoted the trigger-prone officer to the rank of detective.[69]

Sometimes, the federal government stepped in, as in the case of Officer Paul Minnick of the Homestead, Georgia, police force, who shot Emmet Jefferson on Christmas Day while the latter was being arrested for allegedly reckless driving. When the county grand jury refused to indict Minnick, the FBI ordered an investigation and turned the case over to a federal grand jury. The Civil Rights Act, enacted after the Civil War in 1866, was intended precisely for situations like this, when a local justice system refused to protect the rights of its citizens. But a design flaw doomed many of these cases: the same local population supplied the federal jury pool. Although the Department of Justice (DOJ) prosecuted Minnick, a jury acquitted him. In another federal case that illustrated "Alabama justice," the story was the same. The feds brought charges against a white officer for shooting a black veteran in the back, leaving him paralyzed. After a quick deliberation, an all-white jury came back with a verdict of not guilty.[70]

African Americans could not always rely on the federal government, either. Furor erupted in 1953 with the exposé of a secret agreement between the DOJ and the New York Police Department. When top brass complained that federal investigations into police abuse were "destroying morale" and providing fodder for communist propaganda, the assistant attorney general agreed to "give the Police Department an opportunity to conduct its own investigations and launder its own linen." No wonder that the local NAACP had detected "a definite and alarming increase" in complaints. In calling for the resignation of the police commissioner, the NAACP pointed to the numerous charges of "killings, permanent serious injuries, illegal arrest and other violations of the rights of citizens" that it had brought "to no avail." It was a shock to come upon smoking-gun evidence that "the nation's greatest city," north of the Mason-Dixon line to boot, had perpetrated the cover-up, effectively condoning police abuse of minority citizens.[71]

Because legal and other official avenues were unavailable to black citizens, the NAACP along with the ACLU lobbied for independent civilian review boards. Not surprisingly, the police opposed the measure. This "kangaroo court," critics called it, was redundant; police departments already had an "investigative machinery," they pointed out. A forum for laypeople to second-guess the police—after the justice system and the department had already cleared the officer in question—violated the civil rights of police officers, they argued. Detractors also characterized review boards as "an expression of nonconfidence in the police force" that was "bound to damage police morale." Only communists, who capitalized on civil disorder, would favor such harm, they suggested. A Los Angeles police sergeant alleged that the "scheme" came directly from "a page right out of the Communist handbook" that denounced the police as "enemies of communism." Actually, rights activists believed that citizen review boards could strengthen the police's legitimacy by providing opportunities to regain the people's trust in the police. But law enforcement viewed these panels as a bid to undermine their authority. Suffice it to say that most cities declined to establish review boards. New York City's experiment lasted only four months. Philadelphia's Police Review Board agreed to change its name to "Police Advisory Board" as part of a settlement with the Fraternal Order of Police, but it, too, folded in 1969.[72]

Better training received broader support. For law enforcement, investing in qualified officers had been a goal of police reformers ever since August Vollmer had put his men in uniform. For legal activists, instruction in human relations addressed behavioral issues that did not rise to a constitutional violation. For black Americans, educating officers about the consequences of discrimination offered a possibility that the police might stop abusing them and start protecting them. For everyone else, it offered a disappointing solution when the police offended their sense of common decency.

Attuned to these complaints, officer training manuals on the prevention of race riots emphasized that "a professional attitude" went a long way to bolster the police's legitimacy. A variety of adjectives described this professionalism: "calm, cool, and collected." But one word, which harkened back to the early days of the street and highway safety movement, captured this ethos: courtesy. In some departments, like San Francisco's, acting "in a courteous manner" was official policy. Even if not mandated, in 1956, it was instilled in the Law Enforcement Code of Ethics that the officer was to "enforce the law courteously." Likewise, police manuals encouraged "professional courtesy . . . in our contacts with the general public." Since these publications focused on the specific subject of minority relations, they also stressed that "the best rule of conduct for any police officer is to be equally courteous to all. The majority demands it; the minority is entitled to it."[73]

One example of courtesy in action in California's *Police Training Bulletin* was to "avoid use of insulting terms and names." In case an officer did not know whether or not an expression was offensive, the bulletin helpfully listed the objectionable ones. It also advised that, according to a consultant from the NAACP, "a Negro would rather be called a 'black sonuvabitch' than a 'nigger.'" Moreover, while the "term 'Negress,' [was] technically accurate"—in fact, an NAACP lawyer discovered that both the NYPD and the FBI had a policy of using this term, per *Webster's* dictionary—it was found "to be offensive to Negro women." To explain why minorities would react badly to such name-calling, the bulletin tried to elicit empathy: "Policemen feel the same way about derogatory names applied to their group. We don't mind calling each other 'cops' or 'flat-feet,' but we don't want other people to do it." It also tried out a hypothetical: "What would police officers think of a condition which (a) required all policemen to be in uniform at all times, and (b) prohibited policemen from ever leaving the profession?" Developing sensitivity to the minority perspective, police reformers believed, might help to professionalize their line officers. This awareness also reflected a new dimension in the call for courtesy. In the 1920s and 1930s, courteousness seemed like the best way to handle Everyman in the enforcement of traffic laws. By the late 1940s, it served to manage minority relations as a way to prevent riots.[74]

But even as the manuals underscored equal and considerate treatment, police officers were receiving an entirely different lesson when learning how to conduct vehicle stops. They were taught to view every driver suspiciously, to be hypervigilant, and to constantly keep in mind that any action they took could very well be their last. This ominous message pervaded the California Highway Patrol's training video on "routine" traffic stops. The narrator began with the shared understanding that "we all know that the number of attacks on law enforcement officers has risen sharply." So it was imperative, he continued, that officers "not take anything for granted . . . because death only takes a second under the right circumstances." This warning applied to every motorist, of every race and gender. In fact, the actors playing the roles of Driver 1 and Driver 2 were, respectively, a stocky white man and a young white woman. The narrator warned that even if the person seemed "like a fairly ordinary guy," patrollers should remain "suspicious of him" until the traffic stop was over and the driver back on the road. With an alert frame of mind, officers were to approach the car as though a violent criminal sat behind the wheel, to make sure to glance into the back seat for weapons, to keep the gun hand free at all times, to always stand behind the driver to keep him off balance, and, again, to keep every traffic violator "on the suspect list." In the realm of civil rights, training manuals preached courtesy and equality. But when it came to the public sphere of cars, there was no mention of courteous conduct, no reminder of equal treatment, and no admonition that minorities were not inherently criminal. No wonder, then, that the police often treated drivers roughly and black drivers even more viciously.[75]

For those who suffered the police's suspicion-fueled aggression during traffic stops, the lack of legal solutions to overweening or abusive conduct raised troubling comparisons with totalitarian governments. A victim of the Los Angeles roadblocks, upon reading the Fourth Amendment, exclaimed, "I don't know whether that means anything or not." But "it had better," he warned, "or we'll soon have the same situation here that they had in Germany." When the law abiding encountered the police in their cars, they grappled with an unsettling question: shorn of political labels, what kind of society had the United States become? The "hatred that Americans can bestow upon others for no crime at all," the old-stock American wrote, had made him "afraid of my own Nation." He implored the ACLU to "do something that is tangible to prevent the inward destruction of our Nation." These drivers were beginning to form their own ideas about democratic policing, or at least what it was *not*. What they experienced, they concluded, was *not* policing that represented a free society. In conflicts with the police that unfolded daily on the streets and in their cars, many individuals sensed that something was fundamentally, constitutionally wrong. The problem was not just lawless police. The problem was also a legal system that provided insufficient remedies for innocent victims of arbitrary policing.[76]

Since *Wolf v. Colorado* left the remedial question for the states, the debate over the exclusionary rule continued unabated.[77] So did violations of the Fourth Amendment, making the case for exclusion increasingly compelling. But a sizable contingent still maintained that, as the New York police commissioner declared, excluding evidence would disrupt "the delicate balance between crime prevention and civil liberty." Unsurprisingly, home invasions proved more persuasively than car searches that the "delicate balance" should shift toward individual rights. That was the case for the California Supreme Court, the first to follow the US Supreme Court's lead in 1955.[78]

In *People v. Cahan*, officers sneaked into the home of a suspected bookmaker and placed a microphone under a chest of drawers, all without a warrant. Concern for Everyman suffused Chief Justice Traynor's opinion. It "bears emphasis," he stressed, "that the court is not concerned solely with the rights of the defendant before it, however guilty he may appear, but with the constitutional right of *all of the people*." Traynor made this point repeatedly, emphasizing that the "*innocent* suffer with the guilty" and that the exclusionary rule was thus "primarily for the protection of the *innocent*." By using the guilty as the guardian for Everyman, Traynor acknowledged that criminals like Cahan would go free. But that was "preferable . . . than that the right of privacy of *all the people* be set at naught." Only this tradeoff, Traynor maintained, could prevent a "government of laws" from turning into "the police state."[79]

As expected, *Cahan* prompted outcry from law enforcement quarters. Los Angeles's police chief and city attorney denounced the court for impeding police work and warned that the exclusionary rule would lead to more crime. By 1958, the police department was claiming that its predictions had come true; its annual review insinuated that the "fact that crime increased in both Los Angeles and the state of California, immediately subsequent to the Cahan decision in 1955, appears to be more than a mere matter of statistical coincidence." But *Cahan* had its supporters as well. Superior Court Judge Stanley Mosk and the district attorney both refuted the charge that crime had gone up since the decision came down.[80]

The two sides clashed over an episode of *Dragnet* that became the subject of an ACLU memorandum. In the show, Sergeant Joe Friday and his assistant Ben were looking for a narcotics dealer who reportedly had six to eight ounces of heroin and intended to sell it to young children. They happened upon Sam, a known dope user, who was about to enter a car. They ran over and immediately searched him and found the heroin. They also searched the car and found two dozen cashmere sweaters that had been stolen. "Just why the cashmere sweaters came into the picture is puzzling," the ACLU memo noted. But those sweaters had a point to make. When Friday returned the goods, the shopkeeper, who had previously disliked the police, heaped praise on the sergeant's ability to solve the crime before he had even noticed that his merchandise had been stolen. The cashmere sweaters served as a plot device to deliver the message that society benefited from proactive policing.[81]

The controversial scene came next, when the district attorney informed Friday that because of "a new court ruling in California," the case "may not stick." Friday then exclaimed, "If we are wrong in making an illegal search, it costs the citizen nothing except some time and trouble; if we are right, the people are better off." The prosecutor responded that *they* would have been better off if they had arrested Sam before searching him. Friday replied that an arrest with insufficient evidence would have subjected them to a false arrest suit and that they could not have obtained an arrest warrant because they did not know who the suspected dealer was. "What do we do?" Friday asked. "You will get him sooner or later," the district attorney answered. The episode ended with Friday despairing, "Until we do, how much more dope will be peddled?"

Cahan's defenders were up in arms. *Dragnet* held itself out as an objective portrayal of the LAPD. But the episode was clearly part of Police Chief Parker's "one man campaign" against *Cahan*. ACLU lawyers charged that it was "a loaded presentation" that showed the exclusionary rule in its harshest light. They were especially miffed that "missing from the show was any statement or action pointing out the importance of the right to be free from illegal searches and seizures and its historical significance." If the program accurately reflected the LAPD's attitude, then it was incontrovertible proof that even the higher ups disdained the constitutional right. One police commissioner in a "big Eastern city" expressed this sentiment more directly: "I've sworn to protect this community against crime. If there has to be a choice between violating my oath of office and violating the Constitution, I'll violate the Constitution every time."[82]

Both sides could agree that the exclusionary rule made a difference. For one thing, the police applied for warrants more often than they had before. According to Judge Mosk, before *Cahan*, he had had only one request for a search warrant in the thirteen years that he had been on the bench. He did not mention how many warrant applications he had signed since *Cahan*. But the police certainly found the process to be such a hassle that they sought an end-run around the exclusionary rule. The Sheriffs, Peace Officers, and District Attorneys Associations in California issued a resolution endorsing bills to legalize stop-and-frisks, the very illegal action that Sergeant Friday took when he approached the heroin dealer. Notably, law enforcement groups did not seek to authorize warrantless searches of homes, the unlawful act that was at issue in *Cahan*. They knew better than to cross a clear-cut, historic constitutional line. Although judges were concerned with defending the private sphere, the police focused on maintaining order and security in the public sphere. Within two years of the *Cahan* decision, the political will finally materialized to update the common law of arrests, and California approved stop-and-frisks.[83]

Wolf did not end debate on the exclusionary rule at the US Supreme Court either, in part because of personnel changes on the bench. Between 1949, when *Wolf* was decided, and 1961, when the issue came up again for a second time, there were five new justices: Tom Clark, John Harlan, William Brennan, Charles Whittaker, and Potter Stewart. There was also a different chief justice. The case that provided the new Warren Court with the opportunity to revisit the exclusionary rule began when Cleveland, Ohio, police officers stormed Dollree Mapp's home. They pretended to have a warrant to search for evidence in connection with the bombing of the home of

Don King, a well-known boxing promoter. Instead, the officers found several books they believed were obscene. Mapp was ultimately convicted for possessing "lewd and lascivious books" in violation of state law.[84]

The Supreme Court granted certiorari on the constitutionality of the state's obscenity statute under the First Amendment but ultimately decided the case by incorporating the exclusionary rule under the Fourth Amendment. The memos between Justice Clark, who drafted the opinion, and Justice Harlan, who was blindsided by the switch, indicate that the justices simply rehashed arguments previously exchanged in *Wolf v. Colorado*. Harlan protested that the Fourth Amendment did not require the remedial rule and that the Fourteenth Amendment certainly did not require the states to adopt it as well. Clark's response evoked Justice Murphy's *Wolf* dissent: "We cannot carve out of the bowels of that right the vital part, the stuff that gives it substance, the exclusion of evidence." He intended *Mapp v. Ohio* to "do what *Wolf* didn't do."[85]

In the same year that it sought to protect Everyman's guilty representative with the exclusionary rule, the Supreme Court also made it easier for the innocent to obtain redress directly under Section 1983 of the Civil Rights Act.[86] The Reconstruction Congress had created a statutory claim for damages against local and state officials who violated a person's Fourteenth Amendment rights while acting "under color of" state law. But since its passage in 1871, the provision had remained largely unused, in part because the Court's stinting interpretation of the phrase "under color of" encompassed only actions that were authorized by state law. In other words, an officer who violated the law of arrest—for example, by entering a home without a warrant—was not considered to be acting "under color of" state law.

Nearly a century later in 1960, James Monroe, his wife, and his six children petitioned the Supreme Court to hear their case under Section 1983 because, according to their lawyer, it presented a novel factual situation: the Court had never considered the application of Section 1983 to police officers who had violated the Fourth Amendment rights of innocent people. Thirteen Chicago police officers broke into the Monroes' home early in the morning, roused the parents from bed, forced them to stand naked in their living room, and ransacked the house for evidence of a murder that the father did not commit. The officers had no warrant. Mr. Monroe was then arrested, detained at the police station, and interrogated. The police did not take him before a magistrate and did not permit him to call a lawyer.[87]

As a case that involved, at a minimum, a warrantless home invasion, *Monroe v. Pape* did not present any difficult Fourth Amendment question. The greater challenge was to persuade the Supreme Court to reverse a hundred-year-old precedent on the meaning of "state action" that had precluded claims against officials for abuse of discretionary authority that was not explicitly authorized by state law. The ACLU, which represented the family, could have framed the case in several different ways. The Monroes were African American, so the case might have been about police discrimination and unequal protection of the laws. After all, Section 1983, which was enacted right after the Civil War, was intended to address precisely these problems.

But in constructing the legal narrative, the lawyers downplayed race as a factor and highlighted the unauthorized violation of the home. Along with their main brief, they submitted a separate "Memorandum on the Historic Significance of the Individual's Right to Privacy in His Home." The memo marshaled quotes from a who's who list of founding-era patriots, distinguished members of Congress throughout the nation's history, and esteemed justices of the Supreme Court, all declaring the sentiment that "one of the most essential branches of English liberty is the freedom of *one's house*." ACLU lawyers clearly understood the importance of the home on the cusp of the Due Process Revolution.[88]

In a case that was fundamentally about police abuse of minority citizens, Everyman loomed throughout the arguments, especially on the question of municipal liability. The family sought damages not only from the individual officers but also from the city. Without "a financially responsible defendant," their lawyers contended, then "for practical purposes" the innocent person "has no remedy at all." Unlike the guilty, they argued, the Monroes had no charges to confront and nothing to suppress. This reasoning would have been familiar to the Court; Justices Murphy and Jackson had made the same points a decade ago in *Wolf v. Colorado* and *Brinegar v. United States*, respectively.[89]

Although the justices rejected municipal liability, the Warren Court resurrected Section 1983 by holding that an officer's abuse of his or her position satisfied the "under color of law" requirement. Together, *Monroe v. Pape* and *Mapp v. Ohio* upended the traditional relationship between the states and federal courts on matters involving local police. Based on these cases, the Supreme Court went on to establish a national standard of criminal procedure that regulated the police and, in the process, triggered a rights revolution that included the *Gideon* right to a lawyer and the *Miranda* warning that begins memorably with "You have the right to remain silent. . . ." But in terms of legal arguments, *Monroe* and *Mapp* were closer to the end of a series of cases that began in the late 1940s. The predicament of the law-abiding citizen had figured prominently in debates about the incorporation of the exclusionary rule as well as officer and municipal liability. It could be said that the Warren Court launched its Due Process Revolution to protect Everyman's private sphere from arbitrary policing.

Did the justices anticipate the flood of cases after *Mapp v. Ohio* and *Monroe v. Pape* that crested with a revolution in criminal procedure? Certainly, they intended to motivate the police to get warrants. It worked in New York City, where the number of warrant applications went from virtually zero before *Mapp* to over 5,000 two years later. The deputy police commissioner who headed the city's legal bureau admitted that "nobody bothered to take out search warrants" until the exclusionary rule forced them to. A lawyer at the Massachusetts Defenders Committee also confirmed that "the use of search warrants was almost unknown" before the rule. According to researchers studying arrest practices in 1950s Philadelphia, "all of the police interviewed freely admitted that the warrant has fallen into disuse." *Mapp* and *Monroe* undoubtedly revived the practice.[90]

But the "Due Process Revolution"—a phrase coined a decade after *Mapp* and *Monroe*—does not refer to the warrant process or the number of warrants issued. Given judges' tendency to rubber-stamp warrant applications, "modern" criminal procedure, characterized by judicial oversight of routine policing, did not develop primarily in cases where the police had to get warrants. It occurred mainly in cases where the police did not need warrants or when it was unclear whether a warrant would be required. These were the cases when a litigant would ask the court to review an act of police discretion. Based on how the Court decided *Brinegar v. United States*, which remained (and still is) good law, it is unlikely that the justices expected defendants to dispute warrantless action in the public sphere where Fourth Amendment doctrine allowed discretionary policing. Regardless of official doctrine that distinguished the public from private, cars from homes, disgruntled drivers nevertheless claimed the newly expanded rights that the Supreme Court had set forth in home invasion cases. As Table 4.1 shows, the number of Fourth Amendment cases generally, and car cases specifically, exploded after *Mapp* and *Monroe*, in both state and federal courts, and has continued to grow ever since.[91]

One of the first cases that took advantage of *Monroe v. Pape*'s reinterpretation of Section 1983 involved a car stop gone awry. As is typical in such cases, the parties gave two different accounts of what had happened. According to Billy Ray Stringer, it all began when he criticized Officer Roger Dilger's conduct as a state highway patrolman during a roadblock check. Some days later, Dilger saw Stringer's car and followed him for about six miles before stopping him for failing

Table 4.1 Fourth Amendment Cases by Decade since *Mapp v. Ohio* (1961)

	State Courts		Federal Courts	
Decade	"Fourth Amendment"	"Automobile"	"Fourth Amendment"	"Automobile"
1951–1960	265	112	465	145
1961–1970	2,011	930	1,738	618
1971–1980	6,835	2,926	4,849	1,503

Source: Westlaw searches of all state cases ("All States") and all federal cases ("All Federal") for the phrase "Fourth Amendment" and a search within those results for the term "automobile" provide a rough approximation of Fourth Amendment car cases.

to dim his lights. When Stringer could not produce his driver's license, Dilger proceeded to arrest him. He pulled Stringer out of the car, forced him into an armlock, and then began to hit him with a blackjack. After several motorists stopped at the scene, Dilger stopped beating him, and Stringer reluctantly submitted to the handcuffs. This was Stringer's version.[92]

Other evidence, however, cast doubt on Stringer's allegations. Stringer himself admitted that on the day of his arrest, he had had about six beers and a mixed vodka drink on an empty stomach. One of the passing motorists testified that Officer Dilger flagged down her car, hoping that a man was inside to help him subdue Stringer; that Dilger's shirt was torn and his clothes were dirty "as though he had been in a scuffle"; that Stringer's walk was staggered and speech slurred, leading her to believe that Stringer was "abusively drunk"; that Dilger requested that she stay as a witness to the still unfolding events; and that Dilger said, while trying to handcuff Stringer, "There are witnesses here now. We are not going to have any more of that." This was strong, impartial testimony that should have made at least one juror skeptical of Stringer's story.[93]

But every single juror believed Stringer, not Dilger. They unanimously granted damages for Stringer's tort claims for assault and battery as well as his Section 1983 claim for the deprivation of his constitutional rights. A possible explanation for the verdict is that the jurors identified with Stringer. He was not a social outcast, but a regular guy. A World War II veteran who liked drinking beer. A white, working-class miner with a wife and five kids. He was not rich—his friends had to help pay his $350 fine—but not poor, since he could afford payments on a new car. And perhaps the jurors had had their own unpleasant experiences with the police on the road, when they felt that an officer wielded his power needlessly. They probably believed that Stringer may have had one drink too many and that he may have resisted the arrest a bit more than necessary. But the bigger danger in the view of the members of the jury may have been abusive police authority without accountability.[94]

The district judge, however, set aside the verdict on the constitutional claim. Unfortunately, the basis for the judge's ruling was not recorded. But because he had read the *Monroe* opinion, which the

Supreme Court had issued just two months before Stringer's trial, the judge most likely concluded that Dilger did not violate the Constitution because the officer had probable cause for the car stop and subsequent arrest.[95] The judge could have relied on a number of facts, including Stringer's own testimony that Dilger had pulled him over for failure to dim his lights, which Stringer did not dispute. Stringer also did not have his driver's license, which would have given Dilger another cause for arrest. If these offenses seemed too trivial, then surely Stringer's drunk driving provided sufficient cause. As for the physical force that Dilger used to subdue Stringer, well, Stringer's drunken resistance to the valid arrest would have justified that.

On appeal, the Tenth Circuit reinstated the verdict, concluding that "the jury could well determine," among other things, "that Stringer was arrested without probable cause; that excessive force was used in making the arrest; [and] that his automobile was unlawfully seized." The cursory opinion did not explain the three-judge panel's reasoning. But the appeals court accepted Stringer's rendition of the facts, and Dilger's disproportionate response to the traffic violations, tinged with retaliatory intent, was probably central to its decision. The court cited *Monroe* three times in its short opinion, suggesting that the Warren Court's bold interpretation of Section 1983 to address police abuse of discretionary authority was on the judges' minds.[96]

Individual rights in one's automobile did not keep pace with the dynamic changes in Fourth Amendment law regarding the house, and the justices may not have sought revolution. But they ended up fomenting one. In case after case, drivers demanded private rights in a space that the law considered public. Although they did not always succeed, they forced courts to mediate their confrontations with the police. In the process, they created havoc in Fourth Amendment doctrine, with the potential to subvert the public/private framework and challenge the law's definition of arbitrary policing.

5

The Right to Privacy in Public

The most powerful elements of American society devised
the official maps of the culture: inscribing meaning in each
part of the body, designating some bodily practices as
sexual and others as asexual, some as acceptable and others
as not; designating some urban spaces as public and
others as private. . . . Those maps require attention because
they had real social power, but they did not guide the
practices or self-understanding of everyone who saw them.

George Chauncey, *Gay New York* (1994)

Although Meg still could not move her arms or legs she was
no longer frightened as she lay in her father's arms, and he
carried her tenderly towards the trees. For the moment she
felt completely safe and secure and it was the most beautiful
feeling in the world. So she said, "But Father, what's wrong
with security? Everybody likes to be all cosy and safe."

"Yes," Mr. Murry said, grimly. "Security is a most
seductive thing."

"Well—but *I* want to be secure, Father. I *hate* feeling
insecure."

"But you don't love security enough so that you guide
your life by it, Meg."

Madeleine L'Engle, deleted excerpt
from *A Wrinkle in Time* (1962)

In 1966, Charles Reich, then a professor at Yale Law School, wrote about his "disturbing number of encounters with the police," particularly the "many times" while driving his car. The traffic stops happened in several states, from New York to Oregon, and "always in broad daylight" and not during the more suspicious hours from dusk till dawn. The officers would ask to see his license and wanted to know "where I was going, where I was coming from, and my business." Each time, Reich asked why the officer had "flagged [him] down with siren and flashing light," only to receive the dismissive reply, "Just checking." When one officer informed Reich that he "had the right to stop anyone any place any time—and for no reason," Reich decided that he "had better write an article." "Police Questioning of Law Abiding Citizens" was subsequently published in the *Yale Law Journal*.[1]

Justice William O. Douglas cited Reich's essay in his 1972 opinion in *Papachristou v. City of Jacksonville*, which invalidated a vagrancy ordinance that prohibited the "wandering or strolling around from place to place without any lawful purpose or object." Although ostensibly about the right to amble, to loiter, to just *be* on the streets, the case was fundamentally about the freedom of automobility. Margaret Papachristou and her three companions were in a car on their way to a nightclub at the time of their arrest for vagrancy, or more specifically, "prowling by auto." The Supreme Court consolidated four other cases along with *Papachristou*, and two of them also involved cars. In one, the police arrested Henry Heath and his friend and searched the car after Heath pulled up the driveway to his girlfriend's house. In the other, the police arrested Thomas Campbell when he reached his home, purportedly for speeding. In the third case, although Jimmy Lee Smith was not in a car at the time of his arrest, he had been waiting for a friend who was going to lend him one so that he could drive to a produce company to apply for a job. In each of these cases, the automobile provided the means to pursue a life and livelihood, from socializing with whomever one wanted, to looking for employment, to coming home.[2]

Both *Papachristou* and "Police Questioning" confronted the seemingly boundless power of the police. Douglas faulted vagrancy laws for giving officers "unfettered discretion" to bother just about any-body. To place some limits on the police, Reich articulated a "spe-cial need for privacy in public." This inside-out claim invoked the public/private framework of classical legal thought, and Reich was thinking of the legally constituted private realm when he wrote that the "good society must have its hiding places—its protected cran-nies for the soul." Only in these sanctuaries, hidden from the intrusive gaze of the state, could individuals live freely. By "hiding places," Reich referred not to the sanctity of one's home but to the automo-bile. This was an odd claim as a matter of law. Ever since Henry Ford perfected the mass production of the Model T, courts had held that cars fell within the public sphere of regulation and policing, which was why officers could stop and question Reich as they pleased.[3]

For Reich, who had been struggling in secret with his sexuality at a time when every state but one still had sodomy laws on the books—Illinois was the first to repeal its law in 1961—the private sphere rep-resented suburban domesticity. Attempts to conform to society's ideals of marriage and family life stifled him, so Reich escaped with long, solitary drives. When the police questioned his whereabouts in his car, they were prying into the most intimate parts of his personal life. Reich was neither the first nor the only person to write critically about police surveillance. But he was a best-selling author and an adminis-trative law scholar, and no one else wrote so poignantly about the reg-ulatory foundation of the police problem. Also, not many others were regular walking companions with the Supreme Court justice who authored the opinion about the vagrancy policing of motorists.[4]

To protect his dignity, Reich sought to reclaim the automobile as a private hiding place. For many Americans and not just Reich, driving had become more than a necessity; it was a manifestation of their freedom. But constitutional law's dualistic mode of analysis made it difficult to extend private rights to cars. The challenge for Reich and Douglas was to figure out, *what kind of rights could protect individuals from the police in the public sphere?*

In 1954, after completing a J.D. from Yale Law School and a Supreme Court clerkship with Justice Hugo Black, Reich began practicing law at Arnold, Fortas & Porter, a white-shoe firm in Washington, D.C. Even though he had earned the highest accolades in his profession and a promising career lay ahead of him, Reich had misgivings about his path. Visiting a friend who had the life that society thought enviable—family, suburban home, respectable job—sent him into a depressive state. That life was also within his reach, but it did not appeal to him. Reich dated several impressive women, but his heart was not in it. He saw no way out of his despair. During the Cold War when the nuclear family formed a bulwark against the threat of communism, and especially during the "lavender scare" in the nation's capital when even a rumor that someone was gay could end careers and ruin lives, Reich's longings for a different life seemed an impossible fantasy.[5]

To lighten the burdens of his secret, Reich went for long drives. As he later recalled in his memoir, *The Sorcerer of Bolinas Reef*:

Driving around was always something special. In the first place, unlike anything older people did, it was always unpredictable. I never knew where we were going next, and David [his crush at the time] simply let the ideas come to him. We might suddenly veer off our route to ring the front door of a friend's house, spend a few minutes, and then zoom away. We might stop unexpectedly for jelly doughnuts.

For Reich, driving became freedom. It gave him the ability to be spontaneous and independent, to decide what to do on a whim rather than according to the dictates of social convention. Reich also associated driving with rock 'n' roll, which was always playing in his car and represented "the glimmer of an authentic opening to greater freedom." Even on his solitary walks in the middle of the night, feeling "intense depression," Reich could find comfort when passing an Esso station:

It had good smells and good associations. I liked the pungent smell of gasoline and the smell of tires. I thought of long trips with my car, the surge and the rhythm of driving especially at night on unfamiliar highways, brief stops at turnpike gas stations in the blazing sun, checking the tires outside the motel on a fresh morning, something going wrong with the car and the satisfying feeling of successfully getting it fixed. The gasoline smelled like outboard motors, lakes and summertime without city staleness.[6]

The autonomy that driving summoned, the roads to new adventures, and the fresh, upbeat music all stirred in Reich a "real feeling" and energy that renewed his faith in the possibility of a full, vibrant life. It was liberation. Reich had not always felt this way about driving. The native New Yorker's first memories of cars were not fond ones. They were a dangerous nuisance in the city, and he resisted getting a driver's license for as long as he could. But Reich came around after a road trip with his younger brother and two friends when he was eighteen. They ventured as far as the Grand Canyon and Glacier National Park. The journey deepened his lifelong love of the mountains and changed his mind about cars.[7]

The walks and drives, however, were an escape and not a lasting salve. So in 1960, Reich left D.C. to see if a different career would help. He quit corporate law for academia, joining the faculty at his alma mater. He loved teaching, but social life in New Haven was more or less the same as in Washington. The other professors were married. They liked to socialize by getting dressed up for dinner parties in each other's large homes and engaging in banter. Reich was still single, lived in an apartment, and never enjoyed the "acid way of speaking" that many of his colleagues affected. He always felt like an outsider at these gatherings and struggled to enjoy them. Reich knew no one like him, and the effort spent trying to hide his sexuality and to be a respectable member of the faculty worsened his depression.[8]

Reich drove a lot in New Haven, too, which had become a "necessity" and the only way he could experience "real freedom." Throughout his memoir, the automobile featured prominently in Reich's "consciousness-raising" passage from oppression in a society that viewed man-and-wife as natural to freedom as a gay man. While on academic leave in San Francisco in 1971, Reich discovered cruising—defined, according to a *Webster's* dictionary that he consulted, as, "to go about the streets, at random, but on the lookout for

possible developments"—as a way to explore the city's gay subcul-
ture and publicly acknowledge his sexuality, albeit tentatively.
Cruising literally became Reich's first step as a free person.[9]

Reich felt constrained in the traditional private sphere of the home,
which was laden with conventional expectations, and instead felt
more liberated out in the public sphere. For him, being free—to
do the unexpected, to buck social norms, to be oneself—required
a great "release of energy" that tumbled out into the open.[10] He
embraced the 1960s social and cultural revolutions that redefined
the public. During this time, Reich was working on a book celebrating the youth, which in 1970 would become the *New York Times*
bestseller *The Greening of America*. For Reich, young people seemed
to understand freedom better than the adults. Rather than placing
"unjustified reliance" on "organizational society for direction, for answers, for the promise of life," students were beginning to question
authority and "to see life in very different terms." With a fresh outlook and with their consciousness raised, they were generating a new
creative culture spanning the arts, fashion, literature, and music—and,
importantly, many of these activities were happening in public. Teenagers were creating "a new use of the streets, the parks, and other
public places," Reich observed approvingly.[11]

To be sure, a similar attitude had existed even before the 1960s.
Parks in particular have a long history as places where people con-
gregate to rebel against social rules and familial obligations, especially for the immigrant working class and wage-earning young
people, and the youth that Reich admired took part in that tradition. But the world of automobility seemed altogether new. For one
thing, cars transformed thoroughfares of transportation into another usable space for private or semiprivate pleasures. Moreover,
the counterculture claimed the public in a more openly daring way.
Previously, in early twentieth-century New York, for example, gay
men used select public spaces as a meeting place for sexual assigna-
tions, but this "Gay New York" nevertheless existed on a subterra-
nean level, invisible to the dominant city. In contrast, in the latter
half of the century, experiencing freedom in public presented an
outright challenge to prevailing societal norms and a demand that
the police stop harassing nonconformists.[12]

Reich endorsed the countercultural attitude when he argued that strolling, cruising, and being out in public were not trivial, that they in fact deserved constitutional protection. "If I choose to take an evening walk to see if Andromeda has come up on schedule," Reich maintained, "I think I am entitled to look for the distant light of Almach and Mirach without finding myself staring into the blinding beam of a police flashlight." He continued just as resolutely, "If I choose to get in my car and drive somewhere, it seems to me that where I am coming from, and where I am going, are nobody's business."[13]

These were lines from "Police Questioning" that Justice Douglas quoted in *Papachristou*. Much of the opinion's content and language also evoked the essay, which was just as much about driving as it was about walking. The differences between the two "are practical," Reich wrote, but "the similarities are ones of principle," and he treated both "almost interchangeably." For Reich, walking and driving fostered "independence, boldness, creativity, [and] high spirits"—a list that Douglas had in mind when he wrote that the activities under threat of police surveillance in *Papachristou* "have been in part responsible for giving our people the feeling of independence and self-confidence, the feeling of creativity."[14]

Self-confidence, high spirits, creativity—this was an unorthodox association of words to describe the kind of rights that the Constitution protected. But these feelings reflected a radical change in how twentieth-century Americans experienced personal liberty. The automobile, by transforming how people moved, changed how people lived. In the process, mobility came to mean more than leaving a place for good and moving on to a brighter future, as it had for the Joad family who trekked to Depression-era California in a Hudson truck in John Steinbeck's *The Grapes of Wrath*. Mobility now meant the ability to live a full and independent life in the present. Poets did not sing of the automobile's virtues because it transported people to their jobs. They spoke of the satisfaction of a deep desire that was vital to human flourishing. In *Papachristou*, Douglas connected the routine activity of walking with the very liberty undergirding the spirit of political freedom, "the right of dissent." In the social context of the 1960s and early 1970s, dissent held greater meaning than simply voicing political opposition. In his paean to mobility, Douglas elevated the choices of nonconformists as an act of independence. This was precisely the meaning of freedom that Reich imagined and associated with the automobile.[15]

The revolution in automotive freedom coincided with an equally unprecedented expansion in the police's discretionary power. One legal tool that facilitated that expansion was vague vagrancy laws that had been on the books for ages, which the police used to suit their purposes. The ordinance in *Papachristou* was ambiguous enough that the police could arrest the petitioners for "prowling by auto" even though none of them fit the law's definition of vagrant as "rogues and vagabonds, or dissolute persons who go about begging." Two had full-time jobs, one as a teacher and the other as a tow-truck operator; another was a part-time computer assistant while attending college; Papachristou herself was enrolled in a job-training program at Florida Junior College. Although the police denied it, the fact that Papachristou and her friend were white women with black dates likely raised suspicion. The additional fact that the interracial couples were in an automobile, an enclosed space amenable to romantic rendezvous, probably posed a dangerous proposition in the officers' minds. None of the petitioners was even arguably a vagrant, but a vague law gave officers wide latitude to harass, arrest, and discipline anyone who seemed suspicious to them. By the mid-twentieth century, those suspects included not just vagrants in the common meaning of the word and interracial couples but also communists, civil rights activists, antiwar protestors, and individuals with indicia of nonconformity like men with beards. They were policed because of their poverty, race, or political views or, increasingly, because they wanted to live a life that offended the mores of dominant society.[16]

In addition to broadly worded vagrancy laws, the volumes of public rights enacted for the well-being of both the individual and society also contributed to the police's growing power. In the 1960s, Reich sounded the alarm in a series of law review articles. "The New Property," the most cited of his publications, warned about the encroaching state as individuals relied increasingly on what he called "government largess," or more commonly, public benefits. Reich argued that this dependence empowered the state to monitor even the most intimate aspects of its citizens' lives. He captured this phenomenon pointedly in the title of a 1963 article, "Midnight Welfare Searches and the Social Security Act." Reich exposed the "common practice for authorities to make unannounced inspections of the homes of persons receiving public assistance," often "without warrants and in the middle of the night" to check for "an adult man capable of supporting the family." The specter of the police invading the privacy of one's home in the middle of the night must have been a harrowing thought for Reich. His own fears that someone might suspect his "secret homosexual feelings" undoubtedly sharpened his observations of the modern state.[17]

Though these surveillance practices certainly seemed like the tactics of a totalitarian regime, Reich never used the phrase "police state." He wanted to provoke his readers, mostly judges and fellow academics. But he would not have risked controversy associated with such a loaded term in the middle of the Cold War. He later recalled that as a member of the Yale Law School faculty, he was careful not to leave "the slightest left-wing or activist thing" on his record. Reich first learned this lesson during his third year of law school. Two Harvard Law School students had invoked the First and Fifth Amendments and refused to testify before the Senate Subcommittee on Internal Security. Jonathan Lubell was subsequently ousted from the *Harvard Law Review* at the behest of the dean, and his twin brother, David, was removed as president of the student newspaper. This incident convinced Reich that dissenters would suffer immediate and severe consequences. The crackdown had not lifted during his professorial years. To be sure, "The New Property" did critically discuss a 1960 Supreme Court decision with an explicit Cold War context; *Flemming v. Nestor* was a case about an immigrant who was deported and denied his Social Security benefits for having once been a member of the Communist Party at a time when Congress had not yet made such membership a ground for deportation and loss of retirement proceeds. But given the prevailing political culture, Reich tempered his indictment and referred to the society formed from the mound of government largess not as a "police state," but as the "public interest state." Semantics not-withstanding, he charged that it was not being "faithful to American traditions."[18]

Reich sought to show that the state threatened the privacy of everyone and not just welfare recipients or former communists. In "The New Property," he pointed out that the "gigantic syphon" of the administrative state dispensed a wide variety of benefits, including government contracts, licenses, and more. Nearly everyone received some sort of entitlement, which rendered them beholden to the state. To make his case even stronger, Reich described the state's regulation of the automobile. By the 1960s, driving and riding in a car had become a way of life in the United States, especially for the middle class and well-to-do. By the start of the decade, close to 80 percent of American families had at least one car; that figure was 95 percent for those in the top 40 percent of income earners. Clearly, cars could provide a salient illustration of the reach of the police power. Reich began by noting that driving, which many Americans had come to see as a birthright, actually depended on a bevy of public benefits like roads and highways. He cited a court opinion that maintained that as "an elementary rule of law . . . the right to operate a motor vehicle upon a public street or highway is not a natural or unrestrained right, but a *privilege* which is subject to reasonable regulation under the police power of the state in the interest of public safety and welfare." The legal distinction between a right and a privilege, in conjunction with the "gratuity principle" that a giver could rescind a handout, enlarged the government's power over drivers just as in other welfare contexts.[19]

Reich illustrated this heavily lopsided relationship with the administration of driver's licenses. No one could drive without one, and so the state's control over its distribution magnified its power. Reich pointed out that the New York Supreme Court had upheld a law requiring motorists to submit to sobriety tests, thereby forcing them to waive their right against self-incrimination or else lose their licenses.[20] The court had reasoned that because "highway safety is a matter of great concern to the public, it may not be held that it is unreasonable or beyond legislative power to put such a choice to a motorist who is accused upon reasonable grounds of driving while intoxicated." New York also revoked the driver's license of any motorist convicted under the Smith Act, a federal law often used in the 1940s and 1950s to go after suspected communists and Party leaders for advocating the overthrow of government. In New Jersey, the director of the Division of Motor Vehicles could suspend a license even if a court of law had acquitted the individual or, in the event of conviction, affirmatively decided not to take away his or her license.[21]

Considering how much of American life revolved around the automobile, the revocation of a driver's license had the impact of a criminal sanction that restricted the freedom of movement.[22] Indeed, mobility increasingly came to mean automobility in the twentieth century. Road trips, Sunday outings, and commutes—significant chunks of daily routines—depended on the ability to drive. Without a car, maintaining a social life would have been more difficult. With limited public transit options, financial stability would not have been within reach as jobs and homes moved ever farther apart. As commercial areas became segregated from residential neighborhoods, people had to drive to run errands, go shopping, and take care of the business of everyday life. In the American automotive society, driving a car had become essential.[23]

Some jurists did recognize this fact of American life. In 1953, when the First Circuit reviewed a claim against the Massachusetts Department of Motor Vehicles for suspending the appellant's driver's license, it declared that it had "no doubt that the freedom to make use of one's own property, here a motor vehicle, as a means of getting about from place to place, . . . is a 'liberty'" protected by the Fourteenth Amendment." Nonetheless, the court found that the government had observed sufficient procedures before taking that liberty away. In 1972, Justice Powell asserted that "losing one's driver's license is more serious for some individuals than a brief stay in jail," and he suggested that he would consider making the *Gideon* right to state-funded counsel available for indigent defendants facing that loss. But only one other justice joined him on that position. More commonly, courts characterized driving as a mere "privilege," thus enabling the state to punish violators without the full due process rights that they would have had in a criminal case. In the twentieth-century administrative state, the police power appeared more punitive than regulatory.[24]

Granted, most people had never been convicted of a crime or advocated the overthrow of government, so they had little reason to fear that the state would revoke their licenses. But many did share an experience that demonstrated the force of the state's police power: traffic stops. It may be that Reich suffered more than his share. Although nothing about him outwardly revealed his internal desires—he made sure of that—a single man driving around aimlessly may have aroused suspicion. A 1963 article in the magazine *Police* on "field interrogation procedure" listed the cast of "unusual" characters for close observation; among the top fifteen was "lone male sitting in car."[25]

Even if the number of times Reich was pulled over was above average, the traffic stop had become a common police practice. In addition, roadblocks for inspection of vehicles and driver's licenses had morphed into what Reich called "institutionalizations" of police questioning that "have grown up around the automobile." In his "Police Questioning" essay, Reich described the legal uncertainties surrounding these encounters, which further bolstered the police's leverage. He found no reported court decisions that addressed whether an officer could stop an innocent person, on which subjects the officer could inquire ("Name? Address? Occupation? Age? Marital status?"), whether a citizen could refuse to answer, and what actions the officer could take if an individual attempted "to claim some rights." Reich discovered that within this legal lacuna, the police were able to claim tremendous discretionary authority and often used that authority in the manner of petty tyrants.[26]

Reich was apparently unaware of decades of legal scholarship and reform efforts to update the law of arrests to clarify his confusion. Admittedly, Reich was not a scholar of criminal law and procedure. He analyzed the problem of police discretion as he experienced it personally, as an administrative law scholar and closeted gay man. And what was evident to him, but not necessarily to the experts in criminal law, were the regulatory roots of that problem. Reich's insight was that the police and the modern state had grown in tandem.[27] Public rights to the automobile—namely, all the rules that regulated its use—in combination with officers' power to arrest anyone who violated those rules augmented the police's discretion. In fact, the multitude of traffic laws that everyone disregarded at one point or another gave the police what amounted to a general warrant to stop anyone.

Reich pointed out that the justifications for a car stop were not limited to suspicion that a crime was afoot. The motorist could "always be charged with having faulty equipment or an obstructed window, or with careless driving." For Reich, it did not matter whether an officer's charge would lead to a conviction. The mere possibility of "arrest, delay, a night in jail, frantic calls to relatives and lawyers, the expense and trouble of a trial, and the undeniable uncertainty about whether a local magistrate's court might, in fact, convict" posed enough of a threat and hassle that it made Reich "think twice" before he told an officer that the reason for his being out and about was "none of his business." The regulation of cars had ended up creating opportunities for the policing of drivers.[28]

In Reich's view, the police's "virtually unlimited sanction" made a difference in their interactions with citizens in seemingly small but important ways. At the top of his list of "fundamental issues" was the officer's tone of voice. He recalled one occasion when a policeman pulled him over near Boston and, after inspecting his driver's license, asked, "What were you doing in Boston, Charlie?" Reich identified "something deeply offensive in familiarity which is deliberately used by a person in authority for the purpose of causing humiliation." This insult was not just a matter of discourtesy. Reich pointed out that the traffic stop constituted the "chief point of personal contact between the individual citizen and the law." At stake in this brief encounter, then, was the relationship between citizens and their government.[29]

Notably, "Police Questioning" did not pay much attention to how race aggravated the problem of police discretion. Minimizing Charles to Charlie was a fraction of the denigration of black men when the police called them "boy" or worse. As the NAACP educated the Supreme Court in its amicus brief in *Terry v. Ohio*, "in the ghetto," an officer "almost invariably" initiated a stop with, "Hey, there, *boy*." A member of the NAACP's Detroit Branch recalled a meeting where he had asked representatives of the Police Officers Association, "Why is it that police officers invariably refer to Negroes by their first names or with such terms as 'boy'?" The curt answer, "We just do it," revealed a stunning depth of power.[30]

Black citizens were also policed in their cars, but the experience for them was often much more terrifying than a series of nosy questions. In 1965, the year before Reich published "Police Questioning," the country witnessed black Los Angelenos' grievances against police abuse erupt. The Watts neighborhood revolted when a routine traffic stop devolved into a physical assault on the driver, his brother, and their mother. Just when the situation seemed to have cooled, another incident nearly reignited hostilities. In August 1966, a twenty-five-year-old man was shot when he was stopped for speeding. Leonard Deadwyler was driving his wife, who was in labor, to the hospital. One of the cops managed to hear him utter his last words, "My wife is having a baby," as he collapsed into her lap.[31]

In 1968, the documentary *Black on Black* aired on CBS, making the same points that Reich did in "Police Questioning," but through the voices and lives of South Central Los Angeles. To a nation with memories of Watts still fresh, a film about "what it is to be black in many cities in America" was a revelation. It began with the main narrator driving a Mercury Comet on "Tobacco Road," which could be "any black negro ghetto in America," he explained. From there, different residents talked about their lives, from feeling secure whenever they returned to the ghetto, to the definition of soul. They spoke about the prosaic too. How people got around was a daily question and indignity. Those who waited around at the bus stop for the "bus man" who refused to stick to the schedule were "never going to get there." So "if you don't have a car, you can't even begin to move." The narrator continued, "You have to have an automobile before you can even think about getting a job, or getting to find a job, or getting anywhere in town. A car is mandatory. You have to have transportation."[32]

While a car was mandatory, a "ride" was altogether different, according to another. It was "something luxurious." Ideally it would be a new car rather than a junky old machine bought from a used-car lot. But more importantly, a ride had attitude. It was the demeanor and philosophy of young people who wanted to stand up and stand out. A "flashy paint job" declared their individuality. Riding low, they could care less. This was the generation that "figured they ought'a govern themselves and not white society," and they wanted to be heard, to be noticed. And they were. When the officer came to the ghetto and saw a lowrider, "there [was] always a ticket."

According to the narrator, the tickets almost always came down to an "economic reason." There was no law against a lowrider attitude, but there were many other laws, reams of laws meant to ensure public safety, that the police could enforce. A car "might smoke like hell." It could have "one wheel on and one wheel off." This was "where most of the law [was] broken." When "John's making a dollar and a quarter . . . an hour . . . how can John afford to put a tire on the car?" the narrator asked. "But do [the police] stop and think how much money John's making?" he continued. No, they just "bust 'em." And there was always something. "They'll pull us over there to check our brakes. They check our tires. Their seats are too low. They check our windshield wipers. And then our brake lights, and they check our dimmer switch to see about bright lights and . . . any kind of hazard." The law mandated so many safety requirements that it was "almost impossible to go without getting a ticket." But forgoing driving was not an option. Even if not a *ride*, a car was a necessity. It was impossible to live without one. So it was impossible not to be harassed.

In the aftermath of a ticket, the economics of the situation spiraled into a deeper hole. The worst luck was to get picked up and sent to jail on a weekend. The authorities would "release you anytime they want to on Monday," and those who had a job probably would not have one for long. When "your boss asks you where you've been . . . and you tell you've been incarcerated for the weekend, . . . next thing you don't have a job, and you're back on the streets again." This cycle did not help John afford that tire. It was "hard to keep your life," the narrator sighed, "because you're watched so closely by the police."

The police could torment them because of their financial vulnerability; the police targeted them because of their race. To the narrator, the black lowrider always seemed to catch the police's attention, while "the white boys can ride all day long" without so much as a glance. "A black is forever looking over his shoulder," he explained, "because practically everything we do is considered wrong from the police's point of view." So whenever he saw a patrol car, it triggered a sense of "self-defense," a feeling that he was looking straight at "the enemy," "the one who inflicts the pain." It was not surprising that the Watts riot or rebellion—the word choice depended on one's perspective—began with a traffic stop turned violent.

Watts happened just one year before "Police Questioning" was published. In the essay, Reich did acknowledge that "the police are far more likely to stop a Negro than a white man; far more likely to question a shabbily dressed man than one in an expensive suit." But to the extent that Reich noticed discriminatory policing, it was further evidence of the same problem that affected people like him, people he knew like his psychiatrist brother, and people who were the "law abiding citizens" in the title of his essay. Reich's fears did not emanate primarily from the concerns of race or class. If anything, the "one minority group" that, in his opinion, "deserve[d] special mention in connection with police questioning" was not African Americans who were fighting for equal rights. It was "teenagers" who had "insufficient privacy at home" and so spent a lot of their time in public where they were "easily identified and easily harrassed [sic]" by the police. Reich's inattention to racialized policing stemmed from a life lived mostly in the white and male world of elite lawyers and academics. Although his analysis sounds out of touch today, Reich's point, still an important one, was that policing affected everyone in the modern administrative state.[33]

At midcentury, Reich observed that the governance of automobility had amounted to more than bureaucratic inconveniences for drivers. Public rights to cars and to vehicular travel had served as the handmaiden to a new kind of society that seemed less bound by law and more subject to the whims of police discretion. It was a society in which the state, through its police agents, crept ever more forcefully into spaces that people experienced as a realm of freedom.

"Caught in the vast network of regulation," Reich wrote, "the individual has no hiding place." Public rights seemed to have swallowed up private spaces altogether. "If public and private are now blurred," Reich reasoned, then "it will be necessary to draw a new zone of privacy," a new "hiding place from the all-pervasive system of regulation and control." If the private had become public in the twentieth-century state, then Reich suggested turning the public into the private as a way to reclaim the sphere of freedom and put some limits on the state.[34]

Reich first made this groundbreaking argument in "The New Property." To protect individuals who relied primarily on "government largess" for their livelihood, Reich proposed transforming that largess—that is, *public* benefits—into *private* property. He implored that "we must try to build an economic basis for liberty today—a Homestead Act for rootless twentieth century man." Extending the protective functions of private property to government benefits would be no different fundamentally from the nineteenth-century grant of federal land and could fend off the administrative state's attempts to overreach, Reich argued. He was not seeking to be a revolutionary who advocated for the annihilation of property rights or massive redistribution. Rather, Reich was thinking like a good lawyer by applying old legal categories in familiar but new ways and upholding the values of private property. This was probably why Reich's colleagues, whom he feared would censure the "slightest left-wing or activist" gesture, received his new property analysis with enthusiasm. During the Cold War, Reich offered an idea for social change without resorting to Marxism. The Supreme Court also embraced his proposal in *Goldberg v. Kelly*, the landmark 1970 case that extended due process rights to welfare termination proceedings.[35]

Two years later, Reich renewed his argument. The "public interest state" he wrote about in "The New Property" and the "security" state in "Police Questioning" were, in fact, one and the same.

Likewise, the "new property" rights to public benefits were analogous to his appeal for "privacy in public." To guard against invasive policing in what the law deemed public but in what he experienced as private, Reich sought to make the automobile a new private space.

By referring to the public/private distinction, Reich followed a traditional way of thinking about rights. His invocation of classical legal thought during the golden age of legal liberalism is peculiar. The older worldview that placed rights into fixed categorical boxes of public and private had fallen out of favor during the Progressive Era with the rise of legal realism, a jurisprudential theory that sought a more flexible approach to address the problems of modern society. The early twentieth century was a time when many civic and political leaders argued that a rigid notion of rights—in particular, the property rights of employers and corporations—prevented government from responding to industrial accidents, market failures, and other consequences of private action that threatened the greater good. Legal realists aided progressive efforts by expanding legal analyses, and even expanded the concepts of law and rights themselves, to take account of broader social costs and benefits. Then, at midcentury, as reformers turned their attention to racial discrimination and the challenges of an unequal society, legal liberals looked at constitutional rights through a new lens, finding novel ways of reading eighteenth-century texts for twentieth-century problems. Judges of liberal stripe decided, for instance, that land ownership did not include the right to eject nonprofit service providers seeking access to migrant farmworkers on the property or that tenants did not have to pay rent when landlords violated housing codes, even if this remedy was not written in the lease agreement. To promote a more just society, judges rejected traditional interpretations of the Constitution and formalistic understandings of private property and contracts and gave greater weight to the public policy implications of their decisions. During this heyday of liberalism, Reich harkened back to a formalist mode of argument, which was especially odd given that he espoused living constitutionalism, a legal philosophy that, in his words, demanded "adherence to the spirit and objectives of the Bill of Rights, rather than to any particular interpretation of its provisions." Reich's reliance on property rights as an antidote to the abuses of the "public interest state" stood in tension with his intellectual inheritance of New Deal liberalism.[36]

In "The New Property," Reich addressed this apparent conflict by revisiting the "old debate" between property and liberty. He wrote that progressives, in their attacks against property rights for thwarting social reform, had swung too far and forgotten "the basic importance of individual private property." In their optimistic fervor, neither progressives nor legal realists had set forth principled limits on state power, which had real consequences. The midnight welfare searches of beneficiaries' homes were one example. In the Anglo-American legal tradition, as Reich called to mind, property performed "the function of maintaining independence, dignity and pluralism in society by creating zones within which the majority has to yield to the owner." Reich sought to revive this positive aspect of property rights to protect individuals, not big corporations.[37]

Although he relied on an orthodox theory of jurisprudence, a radical bent lurked in Reich's idea of privacy in public. As the legal basis for this right, he cited "the Connecticut Birth Control case." That was *Griswold v. Connecticut*, decided the year before Reich wrote "Police Questioning." To invalidate a state law forbidding married couples from using contraceptives, the Supreme Court for the first time recognized a constitutional right of privacy. According to Justice Douglas, who wrote the opinion, this prohibition had a "maximum destructive impact" on the marital relationship, a bond that fell "within the zone of privacy created by several fundamental constitutional guarantees." Finding "repulsive" the possibility that the police may "search the sacred precincts of marital bedrooms for telltale signs of the use of contraceptives," the Court kicked the state out of that private sphere. In *Griswold*, the right of privacy worked substantively—that is, by designating decisions within marriage as a regulation-free zone, the Court held that married couples had a fundamental right to contraceptives.[38]

Inspired by *Griswold*, Reich wanted "to see the constitutional right of privacy . . . expand to form a protective shield for the individual against an increasingly intrusive world." The personal nature of his essay makes it undeniable that he sought to extend the "protective shield" surrounding married couples to himself, a closeted gay man.

By basing the right of privacy in public on the same foundation that Douglas laid down in *Griswold*, Reich seemed to be suggesting a fundamental, substantive due process right, the right to be free from policing, in his car.[39]

But when it came to describing how "privacy in public" would work in practice, the right withered into a list of detailed rules regulating police conduct, which were procedural, not substantive in nature. Instead of demarcating the car as an area beyond the reach of police as *Griswold* did with the marital bedroom, Reich allowed the police to continue exercising their discretionary authority so long as they followed some guidelines. The police, Reich concluded, "must live under rules," and he proposed a few.[40]

Reich began his list with the stipulation that the "police should not be allowed to stop anyone unless something particular about him, as distinguished from the mass of people, *gives cause to believe* that he has committed a crime." Notably, this was the same standard that *Carroll v. United States* established in 1925 for warrantless car stops and searches. It was also the standard that the 1942 Uniform Arrest Act used for police stops short of an arrest. In 1968, two years after Reich's "Police Questioning," Chief Justice Warren would also apply the standard of reasonable belief to legitimize stop-and-frisks. Remarkably, Reich beat the Warren Court in granting police the authority to conduct brief investigatory stops as well as searches of persons "if [the officer] reasonably believes that he (the officer) is in danger." In the history of twentieth-century criminal procedure, jurists applied the reasonableness standard to empower, not to limit, police discretion, and Reich was a part of this history.[41]

Strangely, Reich did not specify *which* crimes could justify a stop, an omission that is surprising given that his essay analyzed how a long list of traffic offenses gave the police carte blanche to stop anyone, anytime, anywhere. Perhaps Reich meant for "crime" to refer to violent crimes or nontraffic crimes. He did not say, but the silence revealed enough. Although Reich was critical of how traffic regulations led to overpolicing, he never questioned the substance of traffic laws themselves. He did not argue that there were too many laws, that they overcriminalized minor offenses, or that they should not provide the basis for a vehicle stop. In other words, Reich accepted the traffic regulatory and enforcement regime that lawmakers had cobbled together.

After ceding the police's authority to stop individuals with sufficient cause, Reich's guidelines became increasingly detailed. The next rule mandated that when "a person is stopped, the officer should identify himself, and explain, with particularity, his reasons for stopping the person." In turn, the "person may be questioned, but the person cannot be required to answer." If "the person stopped desires to continue on his way," then "the officer may not detain him unless he has probable cause to arrest him for a crime." With one exception, every one of Reich's rules incorporated familiar legal principles on the police's powers—hardly the makings of a revolution in privacy rights. That one exception was the general guiding principle that an officer "must conduct himself in a manner that would be proper in ordinary business relationships between equals." But this, too, called to mind the well-established directive, at least since the automobile's early years, that officers treat citizens courteously. Reich admitted that "these guidelines are a beginning" and that "there is much room for working out details." Even if incomplete, Reich believed it essential to have ground rules of engagement, or in other words, to proceduralize everyday encounters with the police.[42]

From one perspective, Reich's rules may seem like substantive laws that set forth what officers can and cannot do and, conversely, what rights individuals do and do not have.[43] But rules regulating police conduct were qualitatively different from substantive private rights, which would have greatly limited, or even prohibited, discretionary policing. For instance, the rule of *Griswold* meant that there was no longer a law on the books to justify the police entering the marital bedroom, at least for the purpose of searching for contraceptives. In contrast, codes of conduct like Reich's allowed policing *so long as it was reasonable*. Reich's guidelines were procedural in that they attempted to specify *how* the police should exercise their discretion, rather than to create zones where they could not. For a brief moment spanning a few sentences, Reich had come close to articulating a substantive right based on *Griswold*, but he ultimately fell back on procedure.

In the end, Reich accepted society's need for safety. Although he wrote pointedly that under "the pitiless eye of safety the soul will wither," he conceded that "safety is important and that safety requires measures." Pedestrians needed protection from motor-powered cars, drivers needed protection from reckless drivers behind the wheel, and everyone needed protection from everyone else on the road. Even ACLU lawyers concluded that roadblocks "for questioning and examination of vehicles or licenses is, on the whole, not unreasonable."[44]

With the word "safety," however, Reich was not just referring to the prevention of crime and car accidents, though that was part of it. Central to his understanding of safety was the mandate of conformity. "We live in a society that is increasingly concerned with safety," he wrote, and that was "a society that presse[d] toward sameness and safeness." Reich had a critical stance toward safety and convention that did not necessarily reflect the sentiments of the wider public. For many Americans, safety—or its more common variant *security*—had its advantages in the postwar, Cold War, atomic age. It meant economic security after years of depression. It was associated with the warmth of home and family after a period of wartime separation. It meant the end of race and class conflict at home and peace abroad. Security entailed conformity, but that was not necessarily bad. In fact, threats to security seemed more dangerous. For those in the mainstream, the police served an important social role when they questioned men with long hair, racial minorities in the wrong neighborhood, political rabble-rousers, and soapbox orators protesting the social order. In one way or another, the police were policing difference, and that provided safety.[45]

This was, of course, an irony. Conformity was what Americans hurled against communists. When *A Wrinkle in Time* described Camazotz as a place where all the houses were identical and whose inhabitants lived identical lives and thought identical thoughts, readers took it as a critique of the Soviet Union. But a deleted excerpt, quoted in the epigraph, suggests that Madeleine L'Engle understood, as Reich did, that the United States was also vulnerable to the dual dangers of security and conformity. Camazotz could just as well have represented suburbia, the organization man, and the American age of consensus. The internal threats to individualism and freedom appeared in other outlets as well. What L'Engle penned in narrative, Malvina Reynolds sang as satire. Her song "Little Boxes," which became a hit in 1963, also lamented the conformity of "little boxes made of ticky tacky" that "all look just the same" and "the people in the houses" who "all look just the same."[46]

During the throes of the Cold War, Reich knew that outright challenges to the values of order and security would have discredited his argument. By his own account, he had censored himself from making any left-leaning remarks as a Yale law professor. He taught at a time when the Vietnam War had not yet reached its most divisive stage, when American society widely accepted the demands of security. In fact, the *Yale Law Journal* issue that published "Police Questioning" also included a symposium on the "legality of United States participation in the Viet Nam conflict" in which its two participants debated, in a detached and legalistic tone, the merits of the State Department's arguments for intervention. Although Reich's essay may have been too "anti-law-and-order" for his colleagues, he did not stray too far from the fold. Despite his powerful appeals to be free from the intrusive gaze of the police, he gave in, however reluctantly, to the need for discretionary policing.[47]

So did Justice Douglas. In *Papachristou*, a unanimous Court held Jacksonville's vagrancy law to be unconstitutional. Even though wandering and strolling were "not mentioned in the Constitution or in the Bill of Rights," Douglas identified them as "historically part of the amenities of life as we have known them." He initially sought to invalidate the vagrancy ordinance as a violation of a fundamental, constitutional right. But Douglas struggled to articulate the contours of that right and ultimately abandoned the substantive approach. Notwithstanding its celebration of the freedom of mobility, the opinion did not establish, for instance, a right to sit in a parked car or to stand on a sidewalk without police interference. Nor did the decision recategorize the automobile or the sidewalk as private spaces and require the police to get a warrant before intruding and searching.[48]

Instead, *Papachristou* invalidated the vagrancy law based on the procedural void-for-vagueness rationale. According to this reasoning, the problem with vague laws was not their substance; it was their lack of clarity. As Douglas explained, laws that were unclear placed "unfettered discretion" in the hands of the police by failing to articulate what, exactly, they criminalized, which meant that the police often got to decide what the law prohibited. This basis for decision did not question discretionary policing as a mode of governance; rather, it opposed *unfettered* discretionary policing. Indeed, after the *Papachristou* decision, the Florida legislature revised its vagrancy law, which still criminalized loitering and prowling, but now—and this was the constitutionally required specificity—"under circumstances that warrant a justifiable and *reasonable* alarm or immediate concern for the safety of persons or property in the vicinity." The statute's reasonableness requirement belied a truly substantive remedy in *Papachristou*. The Court left intact the discretionary authority to police those who loitered and prowled. But after *Papachristou*, officers had to meet the procedural hurdle of articulating reasonable cause.[49]

In the post–Warren Court era, legal scholars have endlessly debated the efficacy of due process rights in promoting a just and equal society. But more significant than the choice between substantive or procedural rights was the question of how Americans would govern themselves. Douglas and Reich's capitulation reflected a larger development underlying constitutional criminal procedure: the transition to police law enforcement as a mode of governing for the public welfare. It would not have been easy for any respected jurist to fight the long arc of proceduralism. The Due Process Revolution is said to have begun with *Mapp v. Ohio* in 1961, but a broader perspective makes clear that the turn to procedure did not begin in the 1960s. It went back to the early years of mass automobility, with the appearance of the traffic cop who soon turned into a law enforcement officer. Litigants had been seeking judicial mediation of their disputes with the police, in both state and federal courts, in sizable numbers ever since the 1920s in the early car cases. What *Mapp* did was to eliminate one hurdle in those state courts that had not yet adopted the exclusionary rule, unleashing a second avalanche of Fourth Amendment cases that gave judges even more opportunities to formulate rules.

The twentieth-century law-enforcement apparatus and the Due Process Revolution both grew out of regulations for the public's safety and welfare that were at the heart of the administrative state. But a disciplinary boundary separated those who studied administrative law and those who studied the police. Most elite legal scholars focused on the roles of bureaucrats and judges and formulated procedural guidelines to ensure that those officials' discretionary decision-making conformed to rule-of-law principles. Henry Hart and Albert Sacks's groundbreaking 1958 casebook *The Legal Process*—one law professor deemed it "the most influential book not produced in movable type since Gutenberg"—did not include criminal procedure in its nearly 1,500 pages. As an exception that proves the rule, in 1963, the University of Wisconsin Law School hired Herman Goldstein, who never went to law school, never practiced law, and at the time was working as executive assistant to Chicago's police chief O. W. Wilson. But Willard Hurst, the famed Law-and-Society scholar, taught at Wisconsin, where, Hurst informed Goldstein, "there is challenge and excitement in the notion that we might bring police operations within the domain of administrative law." Hurst's recruitment letter continued, "It is disturbing testimony to the limited imagination which has confined works in administrative law that up to date there has been practically no law school effort to come to terms with the operating values in police activity." Perhaps the doctrinalists were not interested because the police function seemed too unmanageable or too run-of-the-mill for legal scholarship. In any case, they left the study of policing to the criminologists, who traced their genealogy to August Vollmer and his police school. Rarely did the two disciplines meet.[50]

Reich was unusual in his interest in both administrative law and policing, and his efforts to bridge the two exhibited a real struggle of someone in the legal realist tradition troubled by how the state's police power had expanded the power of police officers, so much so that he looked to classical legal thought. Most law professors ignored the issue or were not as worried about it, which may be why Reich's colleagues at Yale Law School did not like "Police Questioning" as much as they appreciated "The New Property." To be fair, Reich did not engage theories of legal process in his examination of police discretion, perhaps for the same reason that legal academia generally was not interested in policing. Police work seemed too different from the work of judges and bureaucrats, and process theory, which emphasized "reasoned elaboration" in decision-making, seemed inapplicable to the split-second actions often required of officers on patrol.[51]

Reich may have taken a step back from legal realism, but he did not follow through with classical legal thought either. Notwithstanding his desire to reclassify the automobile as a private space, by the end of "Police Questioning," he retreated from proposing a truly substantive right. Delineating bright lines between public and private rights in what was really a hybrid space, where individuals demanded freedom and the public's interest depended on discretionary policing, proved untenable. The very nature of police discretion made it impossible to formulate a fundamental right to be left alone. Indeed, the main theories of jurisprudence in the twentieth century failed to provide a principled method to both justify and limit the police's powers. Classical legal thought was too restrictive; legal realism not restrictive enough; and process theory inapposite. And so Reich was left with a standard of reasonableness and a request for courtesy. The automobile never became the new private; it became the new public. Not privacy rights, but proceduralism—that is, the process of hashing out rules determining the bounds of reasonable policing—would protect individuals in the refashioned public sphere.[52]

Whether or not Reich held deep reservations about it, his shift from substantive rights to procedural rules was a compromise, and one with implications that Reich seemed not to have fully grasped. Worried about police invasions of his privacy, Reich raised doubts about whether patrol officers were best suited to ensure highway safety, arguing that "better engineering of cars and roads" would be more effective. Although this point appears to be concerned with the efficacy of safety measures, it was more motivated by the fact that safer cars and well-designed roads did not invade individual privacy like police surveillance. Reich repeated this idea another way. Even supposing that "we had electric eyes and computers which could catch *every* traffic violation," he posited, the relentless pursuit of safety could not serve as the basis of a "good society," he concluded. Following this thought experiment through to its logical end reveals an astounding position. Reich passed on technologies that would have attained perfect enforcement, and he refrained from proposing a substantive right to privacy that might have mandated no enforcement at all. He rejected the two options that could have eliminated the necessity of selective enforcement. Instead, Reich sought *less* enforcement—a strategy that police chiefs had adopted ever since the beginning of vehicular traffic. Whether departments opted for the "golden policy," concentrated on accident-prone areas, or simply let individual officers decide whom to stop and where and when, selective enforcement depended on discretionary policing. Rather than challenging the basic system that governed the American automotive society, Reich argued for more of the same, resorting to rules of conduct that would inject more civility into his run-ins with the police. To put it another way, Reich's demand for courteous behavior was a way to make traffic stops acceptable to law-abiding citizens like himself when the imperatives of public safety made such police action seem necessary. This might have been sufficient for nonconformists like him, but it would prove woefully insufficient to minority motorists. Reich's notion of proceduralism, in other words, would largely benefit whomever could pass as Everyman.[53]

One year after the *Yale Law Journal* published "Police Questioning," a journalist wrote an essay with similar themes that appeared in a different periodical with a wider distribution. In July 1967, *Playboy* published "The Fuzz," whose author, Kenneth Rexroth, identified himself, like Reich, as "an exemplary law-abiding citizen." "Recently," the article began, "police activity began to impinge upon my own life." But unlike Reich, Rexroth did not live a secret life; he lived in "San Francisco's Negro district" and openly described his political views as "subversive." He did not, however, see himself as being inconsistent in equating the subversive stance with the law-abiding status. In his day, Rexroth argued, an entirely new moral code was gaining acceptance with "the democratization of what was once the privilege of an elite of radical intellectuals." Emma Goldman, "free lover and anarchist, was quite a sufficient bother to the police of her day," Rexroth explained, but today, "there are millions of Emma Goldmans, members of a new kind of middle class." He continued, "Half of Madison Avenue seems to take the subway home to Greenwich Village at five P.M., shed the gray-flannel suits and basic blacks and get into costumes that the police believe are worn only by dope fiends." Not only did the daytime suits start wearing hipper fashion styles, but they were also normalizing what had once been radical. Beatniks were no longer the only ones who grew beards; so did the graduate student of nuclear physics. Racially mixed couples were not just more common; they were "far more likely today to be students or professional people than denizens of the underworld." To Rexroth, everyone seemed to be smoking marijuana, and people seemed more tolerant of sex outside of marriage, even gay sex. While Reich may have felt alone in the staid world of Yale Law School, he was actually not an outlier in the wider American society. The 1960s had caught up with him. It was the police who were out of step with the times.[54]

Reich was not the only one writing about the police problem either. Rexroth pointed to a burgeoning "What's Wrong with the Police" literature and had even read the "well-meaning, mild-mannered" law professor's *Yale Law Journal* essay. But Reich's "code of conduct" for the police seemed both too mild and futile for Rexroth. "Eight points of ordinary legality and courtesy—but strictly belling the cat," he figured. Rexroth was just as troubled as Reich about the overpolicing of American society. But even the self-proclaimed subversive shied from the radical idea of getting rid of the police. The "only thing to do," Rexroth concluded, was "to adopt the protective behavior of the common criminal: 'Keep your nose clean and don't volunteer.' Carry the phone number of a lawyer and a bondsman." Litigate, in other words.[55]

Considering where Reich, Douglas, and Rexroth ended, the turn to proceduralism may seem all but inevitable. This is one way to tell the story, about a vision unrealized, with a legal revolution in privacy rights that did not come to fruition. Reich's right to privacy in public had dissolved into a list of rules. Douglas's wanderers and nonconformists were still subject to vagrancy laws, albeit more specific ones. Rexroth hunkered down for his day in court. The police carried on with their duty to maintain order and security using discretionary authority.

But a narrative of futility, failure, or lost opportunity would short-change the social and cultural transformations that did take place. It was remarkable that Douglas and Reich, white men at the elite levels of the legal profession, imagined themselves as outsiders, as vagabonds rebelling against the Establishment.[56] Their understanding of their position in midcentury America reveals a revolution that brought the top and bottom of society closer together. The

law-abiding citizens became a bit groovier, and they, too, were policed. The avant-gardes and bohemians in Greenwich Village and the
Lower East Side in New York, North Beach in San Francisco, and
Halsted and Maxwell Streets in Chicago had once been disciplined
without much mainstream opposition. When the Emma Goldmans
of the new middle class embraced those lifestyles and also came
under police scrutiny—usually while in their cars, "the only way in
which an average citizen comes in frequent contact with the police,"
Rexroth noticed—proceduralism became the way for individuals to
claim some rights. They were subject to discretionary policing, but
at least they could fight its abuses, and their challenges amounted to
a legal revolution.

Placing the growth of criminal procedure rights alongside the development of policing can illuminate the breathtaking changes and
stubborn continuities in the twentieth century. One case that illustrates this change-amid-continuity is *Katz v. United States*, decided
in 1967, one year after the publication of "Police Questioning." The
Supreme Court held that federal agents needed to procure a warrant
before installing a recording device "to the outside of the public telephone booth" to listen in on the phone conversations of a suspected
bookmaker. The decision actually reconceived a public space—in
this case, a public telephone booth—as private. In doing so, the Court
formulated a new test for determining the scope of the Fourth
Amendment's protection: whether the police violated a "reasonable
expectation of privacy." This standard seemed attuned to Reich's
concerns and, in fact, according to law professor David Sklansky, the
justices may have secretly intended for *Katz* to end the "patrolling
for homosexual sodomy by spying on men in toilet stalls."[57]

And yet, the Court held onto the traditional public/private framework by tying privacy expectations to the physical home. Justice
Stewart's opinion stated that the Fourth Amendment guarantee did
"not vanish when the search in question is transferred from the setting of a *home*, an *office*, or a hotel *room* to that of a telephone *booth*."
In a string of analogies, Stewart associated public telephone booths
with the ultimate symbol of the private sphere. Justice Harlan ad-
vanced this analysis even more forcefully in his concurring opinion,
which, significantly, is cited as the holding of the case. Harlan clarified

that he read the opinion of the Court "to hold only . . . that an enclosed telephone booth is an area . . . like a home." When a person "occupies" the booth and "shuts the door behind him," he explained, that booth becomes "a temporarily private place."[58]

On one hand, *Katz* presented an important move from a property analysis to a privacy analysis. But on the other hand, it seems to have made little difference in subsequent case law. One way to make sense of *Katz* is to see the reconceptualization of the telephone booth as an effort to protect individuals from overweening police officers who had taken their authority too far. At the same time, the Court retained the public/private framework, thus also preserving the public sphere, the sphere of discretionary policing. Even under the new *Katz* standard, courts held that individuals had a lesser expectation of privacy in their cars than in their homes. Once courts conceded the primacy of public order and security on the road, a fully substantive right to privacy existed only as a theoretical possibility.[59]

Midcentury Americans referred to the awesome power of the police as an "anomaly" or a "challenge" in a free society. American law resolved that dilemma with a conception of freedom that accommodated discretionary policing. Freedom meant not just the right to be free from policing in the private sphere, subject only to the system of warrants. Freedom could also be had in the public sphere, which was protected by increasingly detailed procedural rights. Indicative of the choices that made proceduralism essential, due process was both a cause for celebration and a source of anxiety. In 1958, President Eisenhower proclaimed May 1 as Law Day, a "national dedication to the principle of government under laws." In observance, newspapers published opinions focusing on "due process of law" as the "very heart" of "liberty under law." Yet, the proceduralization of the Fourth Amendment revolved around a fundamental unease. In 1965, Judge Henry Friendly of the Second Circuit made this point as well, quoting from Learned Hand's 1952 book on the judiciary, that "constitutions must not degenerate into vade mecums [manuals or handbooks] or codes; when they begin to do so, it is a sign of a community unsure of itself and seeking protection against its own misgivings." The proliferation of codes reflected a society increasingly uncertain about its reliance on the police to provide security.[60]

6

The Fourth Amendment Tool
in Criminal Patrol

> The problem is always one of weaving paper triumphs—
> the words of judges—into the fabric of human conduct.
> That process is long and wearisome.
>
> NAACP, *The Legal Front:*
> *Some Highlights of the Past Year* (1940)

> You either already are or want to be a 5%er—one of the
> *exceptional* minority committed to outstanding perfor-
> mance on patrol. . . . You know search-and-seizure laws
> inside-out because they are your tools—and you know how
> to use them.
>
> Charles Remsberg, *Tactics for Criminal Patrol* (1995)

FOLLOWING THE Due Process Revolution, the US Supreme Court
heard more and more car cases and decided them with increasingly nuanced holdings. The justices ruled on questions such as
whether the police may, without a warrant, examine tires and take
exterior paint samples, disassemble a gas tank at a border checkpoint, or search a car parked at an impound lot. The "passenger
compartment"—that is, the interior of the car that includes at least

231

the front and back seats, the precise scope of which was also litigated—
produced its own collection of case law addressing all manner of
details, such as whether the police may reach inside, bend down for
a better view, look inside when the driver is not in the vehicle, grab
a weapon protruding from under the driver's seat, or rummage
through a jacket lying on the seat. The trunk of the automobile created another cluster of decisions. There were also cases on whether
procedures concerning drivers should also apply to passengers and
whether rental cars should have different rules. The nation's highest
court had taken upon itself the task of refereeing encounters between motorists and the police in which every square inch of the
automobile, and every factual permutation, was up for grabs.[1]

The judicial management of these disputes produced a body of
constitutional laws regulating the police, which scholars refer to as
the "modern regime of criminal procedure."[2] It also presented a
puzzle. The proliferation of procedural rules—proceduralism, in a
word—suggested that many criminal defendants, while perhaps not
a sufficient number, have been able to challenge the police and get
their day in court.[3] At the same time, however, the contentiousness
in the law of car stops and searches pointed to serious problems.
Abuses of civil asset forfeiture—a legal action that allows law enforcement officers to seize property and cash that they believe are
connected to criminal activity, even without having to prove the
owner's guilt—often began when a police officer pulled over a car.
Driving While Black has highlighted the issue of racial profiling on
the road, and traffic stops have been especially harrowing encounters for minorities. These practices have contributed to one of the
highest incarceration rates in the world, and police violence and unequal protection have even attracted the critical attention of the UN
Human Rights Council.[4] This was the paradox of American procedures: *why have they been inadequate in achieving justice for all?*

Decades before any organized movement came together to protest
Driving While Black, a white farmer complained about pretextual
stops. In 1952, shortly after midnight on a January morning, two
Oklahoma State highway patrolmen pulled over Virgil Brinegar—the

same Virgil of *Brinegar v. United States*—for passing a truck in a no-passing zone on Route 66. The facts strongly suggested, however, that they had stopped him because he was by then a known "habitual whiskey runner" in a state that had remained steadfastly dry. Brinegar's previous bootlegging conviction had occurred less than a year after he had moved to Vinita, Oklahoma, from Arkansas. It may also have been that his status as a newcomer who dared to take his case all the way to the US Supreme Court had branded him in the eyes of local law enforcement. In the 1950s, Vinita was a small farming town of fewer than 6,000 where a Supreme Court litigant would stand out.[5]

During the stop for the alleged traffic violation, the officers searched the glove compartment and found an opened half-pint bottle of liquor. They also wanted to search the trunk, but Brinegar claimed not to have the key on him. So the officers informed him that he was under arrest for passing in a no-passing zone and instructed him to drive his car to the courthouse. Once there, Brinegar continued to maintain that he did not have the key to the trunk, so then the officers ordered him to take a cab home and return with the key. When Brinegar replied that he had probably lost the key and would not be able to find it until daylight, the officers put him in jail. The next morning, without getting a warrant, they impounded the car and pried open the trunk, which, as they expected, contained alcohol.

By the time Brinegar's case reached Oklahoma's highest criminal appeals court, the legal question centered on whether the police could search the "turtle-back" of the car as part of an arrest for a traffic infraction that had nothing to do with liquor and may even have been, the court acknowledged, "a subterfuge for a search." The doctrine at issue was the "search incident to arrest," which permitted an officer, upon making an arrest, to search the arrestee and the immediate surroundings as a safety precaution. The court discovered that this well-established exception to the warrant requirement had somehow led judges and treatise writers down a line of precedent that ultimately permitted the "search of the entire motor vehicle as incident to an arrest for a minor traffic violation." Brinegar argued that this "extension of the exception" had gotten "far out of hand," to the point that the police, he further claimed, were engaging in a "general practice of stopping motorists and searching their cars, and pretending that the motorist had violated some traffic regulation."[6]

The judges were in a predicament. Despite their clear lack of sympathy for Brinegar's "habit of violating with impunity that very constitution for which he now expresses so great concern," they found that his argument could "not be lightly cast aside." They noted that "traffic regulations as a whole are so complicated now in cities and towns and even out on highways that it requires a very alert person indeed to escape violating some of the rules and regulations at some time." Moreover, the opinion continued, "the violation of the minor ones subjects one to arrest." It was unfortunate that "not very nice people," as Justice Frankfurter once put it, were usually the ones who defended the constitution's guarantees. The court's desire to uphold Brinegar's conviction conflicted with the realization that in an automotive society, its decision would have implications far beyond the bootlegger before them. The rule of decision set forth in *Brinegar v. State* would also apply to "a physician hurrying to a call, . . . a minister of the Gospel on his way to serve the sick or mentally ill, or school girls with their bags packed and on their way to their campus"—essentially, the "most substantial and law-abiding citizenship." Permitting the search of Brinegar's trunk might be "literally construed" to authorize exploratory searches, which would convert traffic regulations into general warrants—the epitome of arbitrary power in US history—to search anyone's car. The "more we have studied the question," the judges admitted, "the more convinced we have become that a re-examination of the subject" was necessary.[7]

Upon review, the court concluded that a traffic infraction no longer entitled officers to search the trunk. This holding placed a limit on the police that, conversely, granted individuals a right to privacy in the back storage spaces of their cars. *Brinegar v. State* triggered a reconsideration of precedents set during the first wave of car search cases in the 1920s. By 1960, commentators observed that state courts were beginning to rein in officers' power to search a car by requiring the search to be related to the crime of arrest. If a motorist was arrested for burglary or murder, for example, it would be reasonable for the police to search the vehicle for stolen goods or the murder weapon. But traffic offenses did not usually have criminal accessories. Evidence of passing in a no-passing zone, for instance, could not be concealed inside a car. Legal scholars agreed that underlying the developments in case law lay the "fear . . . that no respectable citizen is able to drive without some possibility and, in fact, probability, of violating a traffic law." But law professors questioned whether the new restrictions adequately considered "society's interest in crime prevention and detection." This debate mirrored the Oklahoma court's bind. Deciding the case with the more "substantial and law-abiding citizenship" in mind would also set Brinegar free. The law of car searches had to take account of the fact that most Americans drove, the innocent and the guilty alike. The democratization of automobility that democratized policing created a thorny problem: how could the Fourth Amendment enable the police to pursue criminal suspects while also shielding ordinary citizens from police harassment?[8]

In the end, the court found a way to affirm Brinegar's conviction. According to its opinion, the "accused's downfall here was having the liquor in a place convenient for rapid procurement and use of firearms or other weapons." Because officers were entitled to conduct a protective search of the immediate surroundings as part of an arrest, the glove compartment, which was within Brinegar's grabbing distance, was searchable. The whiskey found inside then "opened the gate for a quest otherwise barred." The opinion was quick to qualify that "not every arrest of a motorist for a traffic violation would justify a search of the seats and glove compartment for weapons." It depended on whether the officer reasonably believed that the person was armed, dangerous, or likely to escape. Only with such a suspicion could an officer search parts of the car where a weapon could be tucked away but within reach. The court, however, neglected to explain how the suspected rumrunner appeared armed, dangerous, or intent on escape. After all, the officers had allowed Brinegar to drive himself to the courthouse and, once there, had ordered him to take a taxi home and return with the key to the trunk.[9]

This was the usefulness of the reasonableness standard, the touchstone of Fourth Amendment jurisprudence ever since *Carroll v. United States*. In researching the scope of the police's search powers as part of a traffic arrest, the Oklahoma court looked all the way back to the US Supreme Court's first car search case and its progeny. "The lesson to be learned from the cases," the court concluded, boiled down to one question: "*Was it reasonable?*" The opinion recited Fourth Amendment boilerplate, taken from *Carroll*, that whether warrantless searches were constitutionally "unreasonable" was "a judicial question to be determined in each case in view of *all the facts and circumstances.*" Because of its fact-intensive nature, there was "no formula for the determination of reasonableness," according to another early Supreme Court opinion decided in 1931.[10]

Over time, requiring the consideration of "all the facts and circumstances" had littered the doctrine of searches and seizures with relentlessly litigated, factually nuanced rules of decision. As one commentator described it in 1963, "'unreasonable' in the context of the Fourth Amendment is a term of art," explaining that "a certain amount of such vagueness is rather of the essence." Theoretically, all the reasonableness determinations would coalesce into a body of case law that could guide officers and citizens encountering each other on the street as well as judges deciding cases with similar facts. The *Brinegar* court ended up surveying more than fifty cases, both state and federal. Having fallen into a rabbit hole of car search cases, the opinion reported that the court had "searched in vain for a case" that was on point. The judges were thus unconstrained by precedent and free to apply the reasonableness standard according to the particular circumstances of Brinegar's case.[11]

Ultimately, a standard that depended on a fact-specific inquiry allowed courts to tailor rulings for individual cases, even without seeming to contradict prior cases. It enabled judges to decide whether to let the police do their job, even when an officer skirted constitutional bounds. It offered a method of sorting the guilty from the innocent. To be sure, judges could, and sometimes did, side with defendants. But criminal law scholars have noticed that the reasonableness standard, by and large, has been "highly deferential" to the police. Even Professor Joseph Simeone (and later Judge Simeone of the Missouri Supreme Court), who wrote in favor of the new limits on search powers, made allowances for "unusual circumstances." He approvingly cited *Brinegar v. State* as an example, which goes to show how easy it was to find justification for the police's actions, particularly after the fact, when the question was whether to suppress evidence of guilt.[12]

When a search uncovered criminal evidence, enterprising cops soon learned what was expected of them: an additional fact besides the violation of some traffic law. Articulating something out of the ordinary—a nervous glance, shaking hands, a revealing smell—when asked for one in a court of law was especially easy when they caught someone red-handed. Requiring an "unusual" fact did little to eliminate pretextual stops. In practice, more often than not, "all the facts and circumstances" rationalized discretionary policing of people who were, in fact, guilty.

By the 1960s, criminals like Virgil Brinegar began to seem quaint. Upticks in violent crimes and urban riots, as well as a series of high-profile assassinations, thrust the traditionally local matter of crime control into the national spotlight for the first time since the lawless Prohibition years. The fear of guns also gripped the country, matching anxiety levels felt in the 1930s when gangsters and bank robbers began wielding submachine guns. In 1964, presidential candidate Barry Goldwater ran on a law-and-order platform with a message that proved so compelling that his opponent who won the election, Lyndon Johnson, subsequently called for a "war on crime." Congress considered a slew of laws, including the Gun Control Act and the Omnibus Crime Control and Safe Streets Act, both of which passed in 1968. Courts were not immune to national concerns either. When trial judges decided motions to exclude evidence or when appellate judges reviewed the constitutionality of searches and seizures of guns and criminal evidence, they thought about how Fourth Amendment doctrine might interfere with police efforts to fight crime.[13]

At the same time that government leaders were looking to bolster law enforcement, civil rights activists, student protestors, and a new generation of Emma Goldmans were denouncing the police. The two contingents confronted each other often, whether during political demonstrations or on a patrol officer's beat. With the police arguing for more latitude to deal with crime and with individuals willing to question every move, Fourth Amendment precedents both old and new—including the relatively recent *Brinegar* decision—were open for renegotiation.

In 1973, the Supreme Court heard two cases on the search of
a person incident to arrest—an issue, according to the Court, that
had "remained virtually unchallenged until the present." What had
changed since "time immemorial" was the willingness of down-
and-out defendants to object to how the police had acquired evidence
against them. At the same time, the police were still making the argument, heard since the first decades of the twentieth century, that
the automobile had changed the Fourth Amendment stakes. Not only
did police encounters with criminals usually transpire on the road,
they pointed out, but cars also provided cover for attackers and were
outfitted with hidden compartments for concealing weapons. Vehicle
stops were thus one of the most routine and yet most treacherous
aspects of the job, they maintained. The police sought greater search
powers in the face of growing defiance against their authority, and
one flash point in this clash culminated with two cases that, in defining the scope of searches of arrestees, revealed a remarkable judicial consensus on the necessity of police discretion.[14]

The first case began when D.C. Metro police officer Richard Jenks
saw Willie Robinson Jr. driving his 1965 Cadillac on the night of
April 23, 1968. Officer Jenks knew from a "routine" checkpoint four
days earlier that Robinson was driving with a revoked driver's license.
Jenks had an uncanny ability to spot drivers with revoked or fraudulent licenses, earning him the title "revocation doctor." In 1968
alone, he made more than 200 such arrests, compared with his colleagues' annual average of twenty-five. He attributed his "Supercop"
abilities to a "sixth sense." Jenks had a photographic memory for
faces. He could look through thousands of mug shots, then plant
himself behind a tree and pick out wanted felons from the line of
cars that stopped at the light. That worked well until the city chopped
the tree down. When Jenks first encountered Robinson at the checkpoint, he had noticed discrepancies on the two identification cards
that Robinson presented. Jenks later checked Robinson's traffic and
criminal records and discovered that Robinson's temporary operator's permit had the wrong date of birth.[15]

When Jenks recognized Robinson on the road four days later,
he arrested Robinson and proceeded to conduct a search. This
search was more intrusive than a frisk, which the Supreme Court

had defined in *Terry v. Ohio* as a "carefully limited search of the *outer* clothing." Jenks reached *into* Robinson's pockets to pull out, according to his testimony, a "crumpled up cigarette package." Because the objects inside felt nothing like cigarettes, Jenks opened the packet and found fourteen gelatin capsules of white powder, which he suspected was, and later was proven to be, heroin.[16]

United States v. Robinson would have been identical to the second Fourth Amendment case the Supreme Court heard that year if Washington, D.C., were swapped for Eau Gallie, Florida; a 1965 Cadillac for a 1953 Cadillac; driving with a revoked license for driving without a license; and heroin for marijuana. *Gustafson v. Florida*, however, did not have its version of Supercop. Rather, Lieutenant Paul Smith was more like the officers in *Papachristou v. City of Jacksonville*, the vagrancy case from Florida. It was 2:00 in the morning when Smith noticed a Cadillac weaving across the center line. Although more than justified in pulling over a possible drunk driver, Smith later testified that he did not think that the driving constituted an offense and that he would not have pulled the car over "had he known the occupants." The occupants turned out to be students who had been out on a Saturday night and were returning to their dorms. If not for the missing driver's license, Smith admitted that he would have instead arrested James Gustafson for disorderly conduct, a variation of a vagrancy charge. Like Officer Jenks, Smith reached into Gustafson's coat pocket, removed a cigarette package, looked inside it, and discovered marijuana.[17]

In both *Robinson* and *Gustafson*, the police encounter began with a traffic stop and concluded with an arrest for drug possession. This was not an uncommon occurrence, which reflected the ubiquity of traffic offenses more than an orchestrated drug enforcement strategy. Developing that strategy would take another decade. Although American society had long criminalized heroin and marijuana, the various iterations of its drug wars treated narcotics as a health problem as much as a crime problem until the early 1970s. One turning point was New York's Rockefeller drug laws, enacted in 1973 and named after the state's governor, who had presidential ambitions. The laws established a mandatory minimum of fifteen years to life for possession of four ounces of prohibited substances—the same sentence for second-degree murder. Systematized enforcement and severe penalties gained ground in the 1980s and have ramped up since then. But back in the late 1960s, Robinson's and Gustafson's drug busts were more incidental to the ubiquity of traffic stops, a cop's superhuman memory, and a patroller's routine watch for "vagrant" teenagers.[18]

The opinion in *Robinson*, which stated the holding for *Gustafson* as well, concluded that incident to a lawful arrest, an officer could search any "containers" found inside the pockets of an arrestee's clothes. Dangers that lurked in each uncertain moment of a traffic stop plus the fear of guns undoubtedly motivated the Court's broad grant of authority. The government had presented data from the FBI's Uniform Crime Reports, acknowledged in Justice Rehnquist's opinion, that in the first three months of that year, eleven out of thirty-five slain officers were killed during a traffic stop. The opinion also cited a study finding that "approximately 30% of the shootings of police officers occur when an officer stops a person in an automobile." Robinson's lawyer cast doubt on the probative value of the government's numbers, pointing out that the statistics did not indicate the percentage of *all* traffic stops that resulted in officer deaths.[19]

Compared to the total number of traffic stops, the likelihood of police casualties was small, but a group of police organizations informed the Supreme Court that traffic stops were "one of the most dangerous aspects of police work." This perspective permeated a 1968 police training video, titled *Outnumbered*. The narrator began with the truism that "vehicle stops are routine," which lulled many a highway patroller into thinking that the driver "may be a traffic violator, nothing more." But he immediately disabused trainees of that complacency, warning, "It may also be the last traffic violator he ever stops." To illustrate the unknown possibilities, he queried, "Who is waiting inside the protective shell of that car? Felon: neurotic, dangerous, and erratic? Or plain citizen: thoughtful and resigned?" The narrator gave the only safe answer, that "there is no answer, only potential danger for the officer." This was precisely the tone of the law enforcement groups' amici brief, which argued that a "*Terry*-type frisk" provided "insufficient protection" in the context of a traffic arrest.[20]

Stoking fears about surprise attacks was the government's strategy in Robinson's case all along. During the hearing on the defense's motion to suppress evidence, the prosecutor called as an expert witness a contractor who worked in the National Bomb Data Center of the International Association of Chiefs of Police, one of the three police organizations that filed the amici brief. Charles Newhouser was a retired sergeant in the Air Force, where he had specialized in "clandestine weaponry." On the witness stand, he divulged that he had, at present, "twenty-five weapons on my person that could kill or incapacitate." The judge, not expecting or not believing what he had just heard, sputtered, "I am sorry. I didn't hear that." The defense lawyer, Joseph Gartlan, piped up, "The witness has just admitted to what is a crime in the District of Columbia." After the court reporter read back the question and answer, Gartlan protested that the proceedings were "getting a little bit lurid." His Honor responded, "I will give you assurance you won't be hurt."[21]

The judge then allowed the expert to remove and display all twenty-five weapons concealed on his person. Newhouser pulled out, to give just a few examples, a surgeon's scalpel from his eyeglasses, a crochet needle (its "general usage is to attack a soft portion of the body," he explained) and a "hypodermic needle with a poison sac" from his shirt collar, a knife with an eight-inch blade from his coat lapel, a "kidney puncher" contained inside a Bic pen from his shirt pocket, a .22 caliber pistol in a cigarette package ("Lark King-Size"), a blowgun with a poison dart from his necktie (made out of a McDonald's straw and a sewing needle), and two more knives from his belt buckle. Out of modesty, Newhouser stepped aside from view to take out a .22 automatic pistol inside his jockey shorts and a Dutch-made hand grenade "located behind my testicles." In response to the defense's cross-examination, Newhouser testified that an officer doing a *Terry*-type frisk would probably find only the pocket-knife inside his pocket. Newhouser expressed doubt that even a "more detailed search," the kind of search that Officer Jenks had performed, would unearth many of the items. Swayed by this testimony, the trial judge specifically referenced Newhouser's "demonstration" when ruling that "the law does not prohibit a search such as conducted by Officer Jenks."[22]

Although the Supreme Court's *Robinson* opinion did not mention this line of testimony, a majority of the justices did accept the threat to officers at face value. Surely, the Court reasoned, the Fourth Amendment could not prevent officers from protecting themselves in the line of patrol duty. The dissent did not deny the government's statistics or the validity of the police's fear. Instead, it marshaled the same evidence to support its position that almost all officer deaths were inflicted with guns and knives—weapons that normally could not fit inside a cigarette packet.

On one level, *Robinson* involved a substantive disagreement about the appropriate scope of the police's search powers. Parallel to this argument ran a jurisprudential disagreement on the appropriate kind of rule for regulating the police. The majority favored "bright-line" rules that functioned like a binary system—arrest/no arrest, search/no search—that determined rights based on prespecified conditions. The *Robinson* holding was such a rule: an arrest (the condition) entitled the police to search all items found on the arrestee (the right). The attraction of bright lines was ease of application and predictability. Officers had to act quickly, with little time to go through reasonableness determinations with the deliberation that judges could afford in the quiet of their chambers. They also needed certainty about the constitutionality of their actions, lest they risk losing key evidence and, with it, the entire case. Proponents of clear-cut rules liked to quote criminal procedure expert Wayne La-Fave that a "highly sophisticated set of rules, qualified by all sorts of ifs, ands, and buts and requiring the drawing of subtle nuances and hairline distinctions," hindered law enforcement officers in the field. In line with this view, *Robinson* held that it was reasonable during every arrest—including non-traffic arrests—for an officer to search every pocket, everything inside those pockets, and everything inside any containers inside those pockets.[23]

The *Robinson* rule did not exempt wallets or sealed envelopes, which, the dissent pointed out, were particularly private objects and, anyway, could not conceivably contain a knife or gun. This was precisely why the justices in the minority preferred a rule that required "case-by-case" judicial review. They maintained that searching a wallet, an envelope, or a cigarette packet would be reasonable only if it was necessary to an officer's safety; otherwise, it was an unjustified intrusion on individual privacy. Judges had to consider the "totality of the circumstances" to determine whether danger had existed, which meant that each case had to be considered individually and could potentially result in a rule of decision based on its unique set of facts.

Importantly, the nature of Fourth Amendment rules, whether categorical or nuanced, did not necessarily align with a specific position on the relative rights of individuals and the police. After all, it was possible to set forth a hard-and-fast rule that was *more* protective of individual rights, such as a rule flatly prohibiting officers from searching inside containers found in the pockets of an arrestee's clothing. This would have satisfied the majority's preference for bright-line rules, and it would have shielded people's privacy in their pockets from the police. But the dissent did not demand a more protective bright-line rule. The heart of the jurisprudential debate, then, was not simply about the extent of the police's power but more centrally was about how courts ought to deal with the inevitability of police discretion. The "welter of life," as one Fourth Amendment scholar put it, was "constantly churning up situations" that made it difficult to establish fixed rules governing the police. Given the uncertainties, especially during traffic stops, should courts give the police the flexibility to exercise their judgment without having to worry about how judges might second-guess their decisions? Or did a democratic society demand that an impartial judicial figure review each instance of discretionary police action?[24]

According to the *Robinson* opinion, this was the "fundamental disagreement," argued over even more fiercely than the substantive question also at stake. The dissent denounced the bright, clear-cut rule of *Robinson* as "a clear and marked departure from our long tradition of case-by-case adjudication of the reasonableness of searches and seizures." The majority pointedly responded that neither the "long line of authorities" nor "the history of practice in this country and in England" mandated "such a case-by-case adjudication." Both were right. Under a longer arc of history, the Fourth Amendment had not always been fractured into factual gradations. But ever since the development of modern police forces that attended mass automobility, Fourth Amendment jurisprudence had become increasingly atomized with the proliferation of constitutional challenges.[25]

In addition to generating litigation, the shift to policing as a mode of governance exposed tensions in the concept of the rule of law. One widely held tenet of this fundamental precept of American liberty mandated clearly defined rules. Only when people know in advance what the government expects of them, the reasoning went, can they live without fear of arbitrary government intrusion. As Justice Scalia once declared, "Predictability . . . is a needful characteristic of any law worthy of the name. There are times when even a bad rule is better than no rule at all." The certainty of bright-line rules fit this bill, whereas the ad hoc quality of *ex post* judicial rulemaking did not. But another well-accepted rule-of-law principle required judicial review of all police action. According to this theory, in a totalitarian state, the police decided individual guilt, while in a free society, a court of law overseen by a neutral magistrate supervised the entire criminal process. If a court did not examine how the police had gathered evidence in their pursuit of prosecution, then the police could effectively determine the outcome of a trial with whatever evidence they turned up. The case-by-case method that evaluated each police search addressed this concern better than a one-size-fits-all rule.[26]

On the rule-of-law question, the conservative justices could not claim the principled position. Then Justice Rehnquist—he was promoted to chief justice in 1986—wrote the *Robinson* opinion notwithstanding his predilection for case-by-case adjudication in other areas of constitutional law. His support for law and order apparently overrode his jurisprudential preference. Even more, jurists in favor of general rules seemed not to notice that while such rules might provide predictability, the rules that they set forth in Fourth Amendment cases worked to enhance the power of officers at the expense of citizens' privacy rights. In American history, jurisprudes had embraced clear and preestablished rules to constrain the discretion of officials in "big government." But by the mid-twentieth century, judges sought such rules to *allow* the discretion of law enforcement officers. No justice holding this inconsistency explicitly addressed the police exceptionalism in their theory of law. Instead, the justices described the risks that officers faced and, like Rehnquist, emphasized the "quick ad hoc judgment" that those risks necessitated, implying that the police function was inherently different from administration. Bureaucrats worked in offices, read files, and could take their time deciding matters. Police officers, by contrast, worked the streets and often found themselves having to respond to developing situations that required them to think and act on their feet. And in the context of cars, time seemed especially compressed and the unexpected all the more perilous. For these justices, the challenges of maintaining order presented a special need for discretion that warranted judicial deference. To the justices in dissent, this amounted to an abdication of the judicial role in a free society.[27]

At the same time, the jurisprudential dispute revealed a profound transformation in the liberal understanding of freedom. Justice Thurgood Marshall wrote in his *Robinson* dissent that "the intensive, at times painstaking, case-by-case analysis characteristic of our Fourth Amendment decisions bespeaks our 'jealous regard for maintaining the integrity of individual rights.'" In writing of the *jealous regard for maintaining the integrity of individual rights*, Marshall was quoting *Mapp v. Ohio*, which actually had nothing to do with bright-line rules or case-by-case adjudication. Rather, the point of that line from the *Mapp* opinion was to justify the incorporation of the exclusionary rule by appealing to a flexibly progressive interpretation of the Constitution. But it was fitting that Marshall looked to *Mapp*, a landmark case along the path to proceduralism. In the automotive century, the ability to challenge the police in a court of law had become essential to individual liberty as definite limits on policing became untenable in a world of danger and uncertainty. What if an arrestee had a safety pin or razor blade inside a wallet? Marshall conceded this possibility, which explains why he did not insist on a wholesale prohibition on warrantless searches of small containers. In that situation, such a rule would have undermined "society's interest that police officers not take unnecessary risks in the performance of their duties," Marshall granted. Forcing Marshall's concession was an acceptance of discretionary policing as a way of governing American society, a position that all the justices, conservative and liberal alike, shared. Their jurisprudential disagreement had to do with how closely to manage discretion, not whether it should be allowed.[28]

The unquestioned reliance on law enforcement, and the conse-·
quent need for rules to govern the police, also informed the scholarship of Kenneth Culp Davis, a prominent administrative law
professor who tried to apply the principles of his field to policing.
He recognized that the police "make far more discretionary determinations in individual cases than any other class of administrators."
But he did not call for less policing. Instead, he argued for "discretionary justice," a term that reflected the simultaneous need for
discretionary power and police accountability. By "discretionary justice," Davis meant a regulatory system in which police departments
set policies to govern their line officers on the beat. Just as agency
rulemaking procedures provided legitimacy to the modern administrative state, Davis believed that the same format could provide a
way to harness good uses of police discretion while hemming its
abuses. He essentially sought to transfer the task of "policing the
policing" from the courts to the police themselves. Whether the
policymaking that Davis had in mind or the case-by-case adjudication that Marshall favored, the desire for rules accompanied the shift
to policing as a mode of governance. Freedom, as liberal jurists conceived it, no longer meant simply the right to be left alone in private
spaces. Freedom also depended on a process for setting rules.[29]

Marshall also argued that a totality-of-the-circumstances analysis
served another important function, which was to screen for pretext. Even Professor LaFave—who had railed against a "highly
sophisticated set of rules, qualified by all sorts of ifs, ands, and buts"—
hesitated upon reading *Robinson*. With the prevalence of traffic
offenses, the "specter of the pretext arrest loom[ed] so large" that he
worried that the decision would "open the way to widespread abuse
of the power of arrest and to a wholesale invasion of the privacy of
ordinary citizens." LaFave's concern could have been taken from a
page out of the dissent. "There is always the possibility," Marshall
wrote, "that a police officer, lacking probable cause to obtain a search
warrant, will use a traffic arrest as a pretext to conduct a search." He
did not mean "to impugn the integrity of our police, but merely to
point out that case-by-case adjudication will always be necessary to
determine whether a full arrest was effected for purely legitimate reasons or, rather, as a pretext for searching the arrestee."[30]

Virgil Brinegar would have found Marshall's point ironic. The Oklahoma court that affirmed his conviction had teased out specific facts to justify the pretextual search of his car, not to smoke it out. Anthony Amsterdam, a leading Fourth Amendment scholar, put it plainly that "in practice," the reasonableness standard meant that "appellate courts defer to trial courts and trial courts defer to the police." "What other results should we expect?" he continued. "If there are no fairly clear rules telling the policeman what he may or may not do," Amsterdam explained, "courts are seldom going to say that what he did was unreasonable." For case-by-case adjudication to work as Marshall intended, judges had to be as discerning and wary as the great crusader himself, and perhaps also as removed from the actual people involved in the case. It took discipline to uphold the Fourth Amendment by dismissing evidence of guilt—the liquor, the heroin, the marijuana—that prosecutors brought before the court. It took resolve to discount in-court testimonies of local police officers. It took faith to face the guilty and let them go free. For Supreme Court justices who never met the prosecutors, the officers, or the defendants, sifting through the facts and circumstances for pretext was a more detached affair.[31]

The distance separating the nine justices sitting at the top of the American judicial system and the judges in county seats and municipal courts reflected the disconnect between the ideals of case-by-case adjudication and its implementation. In the pages of Supreme Court opinions, considering the totality of the circumstances was a way to maintain "the integrity of individual rights." In trials that took place throughout the country, however, all the facts and circumstances were mustered, just as often as not, to condone discretionary, even pretextual, policing.

Six weeks after the Supreme Court issued its decision in *United States v. Robinson*, Professor Anthony Amsterdam gave the Oliver Wendell Holmes Lecture, the most prestigious talk given every three years at Harvard Law School, on the Fourth Amendment. Like Kenneth Culp Davis, Amsterdam preferred police rulemaking over constitutionalizing criminal procedure. The reason, he explained, was that formulating a "single, comprehensive theory" of the Fourth Amendment was impossible. On the one hand, the effort "to categorize or pigeon-hole situations for the purpose of enforcing a discipline of rules upon the richness of events" seemed hopeless. On the other hand, "if some categorization is not done, if the understandable temptation to be responsive to every relevant shading of every relevant variation of every relevant complexity is not restrained, then we shall have a fourth amendment with all of the character and consistency of a Rorschach blot." The difficulty of finding equilibrium between these two impulses augured what was to come in the law of car searches, which by the 1980s dissolved into finely spun, contradictory doctrines.[32]

The Court tried to untangle the threads in *New York v. Belton*. The case began on the morning of April 9, 1978. State Trooper Douglas Nicot pulled over a two-door Chrysler traveling twenty miles per hour over the speed limit on the New York Thruway. When the driver rolled down the window, Nicot caught a waft of burnt marijuana. He also noticed a small manila envelope with the stamp "Supergold," which he knew was a brand name for pot. The license and registration handed to him indicated that neither the driver nor the other three passengers owned the car or were related to the owner. He ordered all four men out of the car, frisked each of them, and arrested them for marijuana possession. Because he had only one set of handcuffs, Nicot kept them separated along the highway. He then picked up and opened the envelope and found what he had suspected. Nicot also retrieved several marijuana butts from the ashtray. On the backseat lay a black leather jacket. Inside the pockets, Nicot found an identification card for a Roger Belton, a twenty-dollar bill rolled with white powder, and a plastic bag containing the same powdery substance.[33]

Belton, who had sat behind the driver's seat, was charged with criminal possession of cocaine. He tried to exclude from evidence the contents inside the pockets of his leather jacket, without which the prosecution would no longer have a case. Pointing out that a jacket could contain private belongings—"papers and effects" in Fourth Amendment terminology—Belton argued that the warrantless search was unconstitutional. To distinguish the *Robinson* precedent that authorized the police to search the pockets of a coat as an incident to arrest, Belton argued that a better analogy existed: a jacket found lying on the backseat of a car was more like a suitcase.

Just one year earlier, the Supreme Court had decided whether the search-incident-to-arrest exception applied to a search of a double-locked footlocker located in the trunk of a car. *United States v. Chadwick* concluded that it did not and, accordingly, that a warrant was necessary. But the decision nevertheless allowed warrantless searches of the area within an arrestee's "immediate control," also known as a person's "grabbing distance." Taking the phrase "grabbing distance" literally, it was hard to imagine a scenario where this warrant exception might apply to things inside cars. An arrest typically took place outside the car, and even assuming that the arrestee was not handcuffed, the longest arms would still have difficulty reaching inside the car to grab a weapon or destroy evidence. Given the near impossibility of this feat, *Chadwick* could be said to require, for all intents and purposes, a warrant for a search incident to arrest of containers found inside cars. So when Belton needed a case to support his argument that the warrantless search of his leather jacket was unlawful, he relied on *Chadwick*. His jacket, he argued, was more like the double-locked footlocker than the overcoat in *Robinson*.[34]

When the case came before New York's highest court, a divided bench reversed Belton's conviction. The Court of Appeals ruled that because the arrestees were "effectively neutralized" and because the leather jacket was "within the exclusive control" of Trooper Nicot, the search-incident-to-arrest exception did not apply. They would have decided differently had Belton been wearing the jacket at the time of his arrest per *Robinson*, but the jacket had been lying on the back seat. Citing *Chadwick*, the majority found it "difficult to imagine a more private receptacle where one might place one's most personal items than the zippered recesses of a jacket." Left inside the car, the leather jacket had become a container and, thus, a Fourth Amendment–protected property.[35]

In response, the dissent argued that the majority held a narrow perspective of the circumstances in which the officer found himself. Nicot was alone, on the highway, with four men who were in a car they did not own and who had used, and still possessed, an uncertain quantity of illegal drugs. "The situation was still fluid," the dissent continued. The men had been told that they were under arrest, but they were not handcuffed. They outnumbered the officer. They knew that it was just a matter of time before the officer would find criminal evidence in the car. It was a naïve understanding of human nature to assume that simply because the suspects were told that they were under arrest, they had been "effectively neutralized" and the car "within the exclusive control" of the officer, as the majority had concluded. "Although one might well wish that all criminal suspects could so readily be subdued," the dissent wrote, "I cannot agree with a decision that requires a police officer to stake his very life upon the validity of such a questionable presumption."[36]

Both sides had a point. Belton, who stood some distance from the car, could not physically reach for his jacket. At the same time, Nicot could have reasonably believed that the four men might overpower him and take command of the situation. The search-incident-to-arrest exception could come down either way precisely because "the facts and circumstances" could be marshaled for either position. That the dissent also relied on the totality of the circumstances to make its case on behalf of the police demonstrated that the debate over the nature of Fourth Amendment rules did not line up with a particular position on the substantive matter of the police's search powers. Just as significantly, it also revealed how police discretion made judicial review and thus proceduralism unavoidable. Even if a judge disfavored case-by-case adjudication, either the defendant or the police would find a point of contention requiring judicial resolution.

Frustration with the idiosyncrasies of a factually nuanced Fourth Amendment prompted the Supreme Court to issue a bright-line rule in *Belton*: Incident to "a lawful custodial arrest," the police could search the car *and* "examine the contents of any containers found in the passenger compartment." *Belton* allowed officers to search everything—envelopes, clothing, handbags, luggage. Even if there was just one arrestee, not four, standing outside the car. Even if officers outnumbered arrestees. Even if the arrest was for a traffic offense. "It is true," the opinion acknowledged, "that these containers will sometimes be such that they could hold neither a weapon nor evidence of the criminal conduct for which the suspect was arrested." But it was

more important, the Court maintained, to provide "a straightforward rule, easily applied, and predictably enforced." Otherwise, a
criminal would go free just because the constable did not know how a
judge might later rule on a motion to suppress evidence.[37]

Belton launched round two of *Robinson*'s jurisprudential debate, this
time with Justice Brennan attacking the majority's effort to cover a
multitude of scenarios with just one rule. And this time, the dissent
sought to undermine the entire enterprise and expose the illusion of
bright lines with a long list of factual hypotheticals that the Court's
seemingly well-defined rule failed to address. One issue was time:
"Would a warrantless search incident to arrest be valid if conducted
five minutes after the suspect left his car? Thirty minutes? Three
hours?" Another set of questions involved types of cars: "Are special
rules necessary for station wagons and hatchbacks, where the luggage compartment may be reached through the interior, or taxicabs,
where a glass panel might separate the driver's compartment from
the rest of the car?" Still more questions dealt with the passenger
compartment, the area inside the car: "Does it include locked glove
compartments, the interior of door panels, or the area under the floor-
boards?" Brennan listed several more questions to emphasize that
bright-line rules did not exist. Professor Amsterdam also voiced this
perspective in his Holmes Lecture when he insisted that there were
"no sharp lines in the nature of the things that police do or of
the requirements that can be imposed upon them." In fact, Justice
Scalia, adherent of general rules, more or less resigned himself to this
view in *his* Holmes Lecture, delivered in 1989, confessing, "We will
have totality of the circumstances tests and balancing modes of
analysis with us forever—and for my sins, I will probably write some
of the opinions that use them." Defining boundaries marking where
the police's right to search ended and where the individual's right to
privacy began, *Belton*'s critics asserted, was an exercise in futility.[38]

The dissent continued. The more serious defect with bright-line
rules was that they provided "*no guidance to the police officer seeking to
work out these answers for himself*." This was a point that Brennan himself underscored. Brennan argued that judging reasonableness based
on "all the facts and circumstances" was actually not a hindrance to
law enforcement as the majority claimed; to the contrary, it aided the

police. In a world of discretion, guiding principles, not an incomplete set of rules, better enabled the police in "exercising their judgment" whenever they confronted a situation for which there was no predefined law. This argument was meant to highlight the inadequacies of the majority's approach, but it also revealed the contours of Brennan's understanding of freedom. Notwithstanding his recognition that in some situations the police had to exercise their judgment, Brennan seemed not to realize, or at least did not mention, how much American society had come to depend on discretionary policing, to the point that it informed how *he* thought about the requirements of the Fourth Amendment. Rather than demanding definite limits on policing, Brennan defended the standard of reasonableness because of its ability to guide the police in their exercise of discretion.[39]

To be sure, Brennan also denounced the *Belton* rule for coming down too heavily in favor of the police. In criticizing *Belton*'s formulation, the dissent called out its "fiction" that "the interior of a car is *always* within the immediate control of an arrestee who has recently been in the car." This fiction essentially eliminated *Chadwick*'s grabbing-distance limitation for searches of cars incident to arrest. In the dissent's view, the *Belton* majority erred not only by attempting to set a bright-line rule but also by giving the police too much power.[40]

Belton did grant the police significant power. Untethered to the facts of *Belton*, the rule permitted them to search the entire passenger compartment and everything found inside as an incident to arrest. Because the opinion did not limit its holding to serious or violent offenses, the police could arrest a driver for a minor traffic violation as a way to search the car for non-traffic-related crimes. *Belton* essentially abrogated the *Brinegar* line of case law establishing that arrests for traffic offenses could permit searches only for the officer's safety and not for the purpose of gathering evidence of unrelated crimes. And given that it was not too difficult to come up with a violation of the traffic code that could justify an arrest, the probable-cause requirement for warrantless car searches also became meaningless. *Belton* had outrun *Carroll*.

Subsequent cases went even further. In 1982, the Supreme Court in *United States v. Ross* clarified the scope of the automobile exception by confirming that it included containers found in the car's trunk. Justice Marshall wrote in dissent that the Court had spurned its holding in *Chadwick* requiring warrants for containers. But the majority found a way to distinguish the two cases. In *Chadwick*, the police had probable cause to search only the luggage inside the trunk; in *Ross*, the police had probable cause to search the entire trunk for a bag of heroin. But what was the difference between a container inside a car and a car transporting a container? "The line between probable cause to search a vehicle and probable cause to search a package in that vehicle is not always clear," the Court admitted a decade later; it was a "curious line" between "the search of an automobile that coincidentally turns up a container and the search of a container that coincidentally turns up in an automobile." Where that line was drawn came down to case-specific facts, which often resulted in anomalous results. As Justice Blackmun put it, "the more likely the police are to discover drugs in a container, the less authority they have to search it."[41]

The Court attempted to straighten out the anomaly in the 1991 case *California v. Acevedo*. It did so by explicitly overruling *Chadwick*. The opinion explained that it was "better to adopt one clear-cut rule to govern automobile searches." But the ruling did not rid Fourth Amendment jurisprudence of all its contradictions, revealing, once more, the doctrinal messiness when dealing with discretionary policing. As the dissent pointed out, *Acevedo* created a new anomaly: the police would need a warrant to search a briefcase if the owner was carrying it—and then would be free to search it without a warrant once the owner placed the briefcase in a car.[42]

The state of the law sparked a good deal of ridicule from the legal academy. Law professors mocked the doctrinal inconsistences. One pointedly called it an "embarrassment," while still another declared that "Fourth Amendment theory [was] in tatters." Whether the justices embraced ad hoc proceduralism or reluctantly engaged in pragmatic proceduralism, Fourth Amendment doctrine resulted in complexities and contradictions that exhibited the absence of a coherent theory.[43]

Proceduralism also did not eliminate the problem of pretextual policing. Actually, an increasingly proceduralized Fourth Amendment made it easier. Although *Acevedo* eliminated the warrant requirement to search a container in a car, the Court "reaffirmed" the "principle" that probable cause to search just the container—a brown paper bag in the case of *Acevedo*—did not further justify a search of the entire car. What the opinion framed as a limiting principle was, really, an invitation for additional facts showing probable cause to search the rest of the car. Virgil Brinegar understood exactly how this principle played out in the real world. He knew that all it took was one valid search to open "the gate for a quest otherwise barred," as the Oklahoma court explained to him. The police might have initially had legal justification to search only the bag—or the glove compartment in Brinegar's case—but the drugs or liquor found inside could then provide probable cause to search the rest of the car.

By century's end, the logic of *Carroll* had reached its fullest potential. *Belton*, *Ross*, and *Acevedo* established brighter-line rules that gave the police a great deal of discretionary authority. The inevitability of case-by-case adjudication under the standard of reasonableness also favored the police, especially when evidence of guilt could slant the ex post facto narrative told in court. Individuals, indeed, had "a lesser expectation of privacy in a motor vehicle," as the Supreme Court was wont to declare when justifying the police's search powers. To synthesize a decade's worth of cases, it was not "unreasonable" under the Fourth Amendment for the police to use an arrest for a minor traffic violation as the starting point to search the entire car.

In the mid-1980s, Charles Remsberg, a journalist who had earned his bachelor's and master's degrees at the Medill School of Journalism at Northwestern University, learned about the enterprising patrol operations of Harrison County, Mississippi. He was soon convinced that patrollers could be "the most vital resource available against narcotics traffickers." Over the next decade, the award-winning and best-selling author on the subject of officer safety refined the methods that would go into his third textbook, *Tactics for Criminal Patrol: Vehicle Stops, Drug Discovery and Officer Survival*, which he used to train local police throughout the country. At the same time that Remsberg was discovering the full potential of routine patrol, the drug war took a sharp, punitive turn under President Reagan's direction. In 1986, Congress passed the Anti–Drug Abuse Act, which established mandatory minimum sentences for dealers; it updated the act two years later to extend the same harsh consequences to users as well. Also in 1986, the US Drug Enforcement Administration (DEA) launched Operation Pipeline, which relied on state highway patrols, rather than special forces, to intercept trafficked drugs. The reporter-turned-textbook-author and the federal-state partnership employed the same strategy: they turned the Fourth Amendment into a law-enforcement tool in the War on Drugs.[44]

Remsberg's *Tactics for Criminal Patrol* spelled out how "a clear working knowledge of search-and-seizure law" could transform an officer's "most common activities—vehicle stops—into on-site investigations that lead to significant felony arrests." What Remsberg called "Criminal Patrol," a term that reflected the complete merger of crime fighter and traffic cop, typically began with "a traffic infraction or equipment violation as [the] legal basis for pulling [a car] over." This was because chancing upon probable cause that a car's occupants were violating drug laws did not happen frequently enough. Relying on traffic offenses to expand drug patrol operations was especially reliable when a uniformed patroller's "mere presence can provoke a stoppable violation." According to veteran officers, drivers, upon seeing a patrol car, often committed a technical violation, like stopping suddenly. When their mere presence did not do the trick, officers could stop for "more trivial violations or public safety considerations," such as

> having a taillight out or a cracked windshield, changing lanes without signaling, impeding traffic, following too closely, failing to dim lights, speeding 3 to 5 mph over the limit, wearing no seatbelt, allowing air hoses on trucks to rub against metal or liquid to drip onto the roadway from under the back doors of semi-trailers, and so on.

Given the volumes of traffic laws and an equal number of possible violations, the federal government also trained highway patrollers in forty-eight states to use pretextual stops in Operation Pipeline.[45]

To aid patrol officers in determining which drivers to pull over, the DEA composed the "drug courier profile"—basically, a list of characteristics believed typical of people transporting illegal drugs. Significantly, many of the supposedly telltale traits, like dreadlocks and wearing "lots of gold" jewelry, had distinctly racial overtones. If officers missed the point, they could not have misunderstood the charge to pay attention to "ethnic groups associated with the drug trade." It was also clear which groups warranted extra scrutiny. In an Operation Pipeline training video, all the drug suspects had Hispanic names. Another film, *Jamaican Posse*, cast only black people in the role of trafficker. With even more specificity, the federal agency's intelligence reports, circulated to local officials, listed the nationalities and ethnicities that allegedly dominated the drug trade. Although racial ideas and imagery permeated policy decisions, it would be too simplistic to attribute the practice of investigatory vehicle stops to purely racist motivations. As Professor James Forman has pointed out, calls for pretextual policing also came from those in the black community who feared that depredations of addiction and violence would end with "group suicide." Regardless of intentions, enough people failed to consider how the drug courier profile would subject innocent people to coercive and invasive police tactics just because of their skin color.[46]

With a lawful traffic stop in progress, "Criminal Patrol" entered its "investigative phase." This was when the officer looked for, in Fourth Amendment parlance, facts and circumstances to determine whether an individual was "'just' a traffic violator . . . or a felony suspect." If the latter, then those facts and circumstances could "blossom eventually into reasonable suspicion" to justify an investigation. An entire chapter was devoted to which facts and circumstances counted; actually, "virtually *everything*," according to Remsberg, was "subject to interpretation." Trained officers saw "potential" in cues that would seem ordinary to the less observant. Fabric softener, carpet freshener, heavy perfume, and mustard might be humdrum, but they were also "commonly used" to mask drug odors. A "lived-in look," with "beverage cans and fast-food wrappers on the seats or floor, suggesting meals grabbed on the run from drive-up windows," could be evidence of someone's busy life or, from the elite "5 percenter's" perspective, of a drug courier's "long hours of straight-through driving." Vacationers may have a "road map open for reference," but so did traffickers "hitting backroads in hopes of avoiding state-police interdiction teams." Even "'good guy' symbols," like a Bible—the "Number 1 indicator" according to one midwestern trooper—or antidrug materials were open to interpretation.[47]

If a driver or passenger justified what Remsberg dubbed "the full Criminal Patrol treatment," then the officer entered the "treacherous ground of the Fourth Amendment." But *Tactics* revealed a way around that terrain. The officer could ask for consent to search the car, and the subject's assent opened "a passageway . . . through the Fourth Amendment's impediments." Surprising even experienced Criminal Patrollers, nearly every drug seizure in an automobile—92 percent nationwide at the time—began with a consent search. Some seasoned troopers claimed that they had never been turned down. According to Remsberg, most drivers did not know that they could say no. In 1973—the same year that *United States v. Robinson* was decided—the Supreme Court had ruled that a valid consent search did not require knowledge of the right to refuse consent and, further, that officers need not inform individuals of that right before seeking consent. Like *Robinson*, *Schneckloth v. Bustamonte* was not foremost a car case; *Robinson* dealt with a search of a person incident to arrest, while *Bustamonte* involved consent searches. But both cases arose in the context of a vehicle stop, as did many constitutional issues involving the police in the twentieth century. In *Robinson*, the police stopped the driver for a revoked driver's license; in *Bustamonte*, it was for a busted headlight. And as in *Robinson*, law enforcement needs during car stops motivated the *Bustamonte* opinion, which explained that requiring informed consent would "impose" on searches that "normally occur on the highway." Legal scholars have repeatedly criticized the decision for the same reason that *Tactics* called this "the magic moment": a driver's "freedom to disregard [a cop's] questions and split simply don't occur to him."[48]

If a savvy driver rebuffed a request to search, the officer still had a range of options. The go-to alternative was a custodial arrest, which triggered a search incident to arrest, which then opened the passenger compartment for warrantless inspection pursuant to *Belton*. Helpfully, the arrest need not be a felony. "Even a misdemeanor will do," *Tactics* instructed. In some jurisdictions, Remsberg pointed out, "certain minor traffic infractions—like seatbelt violations in Iowa—can qualify for in-custody arrests."[49] A search incident to arrest, whether for felonies or for trivial violations of the traffic code, led to the penultimate goal of "Criminal Patrol," a warrantless search. This, in turn, could lead to the ultimate goal of discovering "serious criminal conduct, especially drug offenses." The steps from traffic stop to felony arrest were nearly foolproof, Remsberg guaranteed, if patrollers focused on "working traffic in an investigative frame of mind" and on "making the most of what [they] *can* do legally than in feeling paralyzed by what [they] can't do."[50]

When police officers' discretionary authority ranged from giving a warning to conducting the "full Criminal Patrol treatment," those who were profiled experienced completely different police encounters from the nonprofiled. For Everyman, traffic stops followed a routine. A flashing siren meant pull over. An officer asked for a license and registration, and the driver handed them over. The stop ended with either a warning or a ticket, and both parties went their separate ways. Pleasantries, annoyances, or appeals for mercy might have been exchanged. But in general, Everyman knew what to expect. In 1978, a former San Diego policeman published *The Ticket Book* because during his five years on the force, he "couldn't help but notice" that most motorists were "confused about why they were stopped" and what they could do about the ticket they received. So he wrote a layperson's bible on the "traffic law enforcement system," from the moment an officer flashed the siren to trial in traffic court. Notwithstanding the questions that many citizens apparently had ("How much training does a cop have in ticket writing?" "Do cops get tickets too?" "Which excuses work?"), *The Ticket Book* assumed that most people did in fact know what to do when pulled over. It was really a handbook for those who wanted to know how to beat a speeding citation. Several chapters dealt with speed traps and radars. In contrast, just one paragraph consisting of three sentences responded to the question, "Can he search my car?" The answer:

The law allows the officer to search your vehicle providing that he has the "probable cause" that we previously mentioned. Whether or not a search was legal is something for you and your attorney to work out in your defense. Probable cause is not a subject for amateurs, and most attorneys charge you enough to qualify them as experts.

Given the unlikelihood that its intended audience would need a lawyer for such a situation, *The Ticket Book* spared details. As traffic stops became routinized, the policing of cars became an accepted, even tolerated, part of American life. By the end of the twentieth century, no one speaking on behalf of Everyman complained that traffic stops raised constitutional issues.[51]

Not so for people of color. Investigatory traffic stops became such a salient experience for black Americans that it inspired Jay-Z's rap song "99 Problems." "The year is '94 and in my trunk is raw / in my rearview mirror is the motherfucking law," verse 2 began, although when Jay-Z was pulled over in real life, the drugs were stashed in a hidden compartment in the sunroof. "Well you was doing fifty-five in a fifty-four" was the lyrical way of explaining that Jay-Z's character had been pulled over for no good reason. When the "jake"— disparaging slang for cop—asks, "Do you mind if I look round the car a little bit?" the author surrogate responds, "I know my rights so you go'n need a warrant for that." The rapper was actually wrong about that point of law—*Carroll v. United States* exempted cars from the warrant requirement—but he was correct about a driver's right to refuse consent. Jay-Z later recalled that when he was "living my version of this story," he was allowed to leave because the K-9 unit that had been called was running late. "It would've changed my life," Jay-Z reflected, if the drug-sniffing dog had arrived just a few minutes earlier.[52]

Law professors were not immune from the full Criminal Patrol treatment either. Almost four decades after Charles Reich wrote about his experience with car stops, Devon Carbado, of UCLA Law School, published a law review article about his. Professor Carbado recounted how years before he had become an American citizen in 2000, the identity of black American had already been foisted on him.

His first "racial episode with over-policing" occurred during a traffic stop, only two weeks after he had purchased his first car, a convertible Triumph Spitfire. After he pulled over, he found himself, as Reich had once described, staring into the blinding beam of a flashlight. But the mistreatment that Carbado suffered went beyond the series of intrusive questions that Reich endured. Instead of responding to his inquiries about what he had done wrong, the officers ordered Carbado and his brother out of the car with their hands on their heads. As the two men sat on the curb as commanded, the officers proceeded to question them on their origins; as black men with British accents, they did not fit the stereotypes their interrogators held. Then, without consent, the officers combed the entire car for drugs, weapons, or stolen goods—anything to justify their actions. After finding nothing, the officers pressed the two brothers against the side of the patrol car and frisked them. Again, the officers found nothing. No apology was given before letting them go.[53]

The ordeal left Professor Carbado wondering, what if the officers had found something? Under the Fourth Amendment—as practiced, not written—the discovery of drugs or incriminating evidence would have legitimized the police's conduct. It would have been easy for the officers to manufacture cause or consent for the car search and frisk. Prosecutors could also help translate their hunches into legalese. Courts, for their part, would have been more likely to credit the officers' version of "all the facts and circumstances." Carbado's questioning of authority could have made the officers leery. That his brother, who had been in the United States for less than a month, did not have any identification on him would have been downright suspicious. The "predominantly black neighborhood south of Los Angeles" could be turned into what Fourth Amendment doctrine called a "high crime area," where the police were given even more deference in exercising their judgment. Officers knew that these "facts and circumstances" could support a finding of reasonableness.[54]

The Carbados' experience was not a one-off; rather, it was part of a policy, even if its foot soldiers came from local, autonomous sheriff's offices and police departments. The federal government coordinated their efforts, and entrepreneurs like Remsberg compiled and disseminated the techniques. Targeted prosecutions of specific individuals had evolved over the years into standardized procedures used against a class of people who fit a certain description. The professor and his brother did not have a known reputation for transporting illicit goods, as did Virgil Brinegar. The officers did not have special skills for remembering revoked licenses, as did Officer Jenks. What made the surveillance of profiled drivers possible was the same combination of a hyperregulated public-safety regime and a hyperproceduralized Fourth Amendment that had ensnared Brinegar and Robinson decades earlier. But now, law enforcement learned how to scale up their operations.

Given the Fourth Amendment's broad grant of discretion, the only argument left to challenge the police was that an unlawful motive tainted an otherwise lawful traffic stop. In the late 1970s and early 1980s, some state and federal appellate courts, recognizing the problem of discriminatory pretextual stops, began to allow inquiries into the officer's motivation: did the officer profile the driver based on race, or did the officer serendipitously find the drugs in the car? But the police knew better than to reveal the real reasons for their actions. As Remsberg disclosed in *Tactics*, "officers rarely utter the 'P word'"—profiling—"except among themselves." In case a new recruit did not realize this was a matter of circumspection, the book explicitly advised, "Never use red-flag buzzwords like 'profile' and 'profiling' to explain in your report or testimony why you became suspicious or stopped a given driver. Avoid these terms on the radio, too; tapes may be subpoenaed." To preempt allegations of pretext, *Tactics* recommended keeping logbooks showing that "pulling over motorists for 'stickler' reasons is part of your customary pattern—not a glaring exception conveniently dusted off in the defendant's case." This made it "difficult if not impossible for the defendant to claim that the stop was unfairly targeted against just him or her as part of inappropriate selective law enforcement." The textbook confirmed Professor Amsterdam's description of motivation as "a self-generating phenomenon"; if knowledgeable officers know that racial profiling is unlawful, then they will seldom admit to it. Their strategic reticence made it hard to peer into their mind to untangle the mix of intents, some lawful, some unlawful.[55]

The Supreme Court rendered that task impossible by limiting the Fourth Amendment inquiry to just the objective, external facts and circumstances of the police encounter. *Whren v. United States*, decided in 1996, was a classic case of an investigatory stop that began with minor traffic infractions and ended with drug convictions. The arguments in *Whren* highlighted how the police problem had changed over the second half of the twentieth century. To challenge pretextual stops, the petitioners' lawyer pointed to the ubiquity of traffic violations, just as Justice Jackson did in his 1949 dissent in *Brinegar v. United States*, and just as the Oklahoma court did in its 1953 opinion in *Brinegar v. State*. The justices deciding *Whren* in 1996 also recognized the singularity of traffic laws. Justice O'Connor remarked during oral argument, "I don't know of any other area that works" like traffic violations, which presented "the reality that sooner or later most of us are going to commit some traffic violation for which we could get a ticket." The lawyer seized on this point, declaring that because "the universe of persons" subject to a traffic stop encompassed "all motorists," the police had unlimited discretion to stop anyone—the very definition of arbitrariness. But in a span of fifty years, the problem of arbitrary policing had narrowed to discriminatory policing. Although Whren's lawyer began with "the universe of persons," her argument quickly focused on particular people. "Unfortunately," she continued, "all the evidence" indicated that "individuals singled out for arbitrary enforcement" were "disproportionately minorities." In the "game" of pretextual stops, "not everyone [got] the same odds."[56]

The nature of the game had changed as well. At midcentury, the problem was the potential for police action without basis in law, so Everyman needed the exclusionary rule to deter unlawful policing. At century's end, the problem had become police action that *did* have a basis in law but that departed from normal practice. Put simply, police treated minorities differently. While earlier jurists like Sam Warner, Jerome Hall, and Justice Jackson feared that the exercise of discretion could lead to arbitrary power, late twentieth-century scholars worried, as Professor William Stuntz argued, that "discretionary justice too often amounts to discriminatory justice."[57]

Regardless, the *Whren* Court ruled that an officer's motive had no bearing on the constitutionality of police action. According to the opinion, "the Fourth Amendment's concern with 'reasonableness' allows certain actions to be taken in certain circumstances, *whatever* the subjective intent." So long as there was a violation of the traffic code, an officer could stop a car, full stop.[58]

The opinion was unanimous. No justice could be persuaded that an officer who stopped minorities at a greater rate than the departmental average violated the Fourth Amendment. It also did not matter to the Court that in *Whren*, police policy actually forbade the officer's actions; plainclothes officers driving unmarked cars could not make traffic stops for infractions that did not pose an "immediate threat to the safety of others." But in the Court's view, the officer was enforcing a valid law even if he had violated his department's rules. In fact, it was those rules that conflicted with the law. To make noncompliance with policy a constitutional violation, the justices reasoned, would render traffic laws "a dead letter at the option of the police department." As one of the justices stated at oral argument, "the police don't have the authority to tell the legislature which traffic laws are to be repealed."[59]

The Court, however, did not consider how police departments did effectively repeal traffic laws when they issued a policy or adopted a general practice of non-enforcement. Just as significantly, the Court also did not discuss how selective enforcement was unavoidable because the laws as well as their violations were so numerous.[60] The *Whren* opinion acknowledged this conundrum only in passing by stating that the unanimous justices were "aware of no principle that would allow [them] to decide at what point a code of law becomes so expansive and so commonly violated that infraction itself can no longer be the ordinary measure of the lawfulness of enforcement." The Court's rejection of disparate racial impact as one such principle amounted to a disavowal of judicial review of the reasonableness of the traffic enforcement regime as a whole. In short, *Whren* dictated that neither police nor courts had the authority to second-guess lawmakers in the domain of vehicular traffic. Revealing their deference to legislative supremacy, several justices pointed out during argument that drug offenders would not be the only ones claiming a violation of the Fourth Amendment based on an officer's departure from standard procedures. So could drivers challenging a speeding ticket. That, they

believed, went too far. In fact, the *Whren* opinion specifically dis-
claimed the evidentiary problems of proving an officer's state of mind
as a basis for the decision. For the justices, upholding the regulatory
scheme of street and highway safety as legislators constructed it, in
however piecemeal or haphazard fashion, precluded them from scruti-
nizing selective, even discriminatory, enforcement of traffic laws.[61]

After the Supreme Court decided *Whren*, legal scholar David
Sklansky noted that even though the Court had "given vehicle stops
an unusual amount of attention," what was "missing" in Fourth
Amendment doctrine was "a recognition that car stops and similar
police actions may raise special concerns for Americans who are not
white." His observation was a reflection of law's lag. The Fourth
Amendment had not evolved over the twentieth century to deal
with lawful, but racially motivated, policing. It developed to allow
"reasonable" investigations during vehicle stops. But by enabling
discretionary policing, the Fourth Amendment had also created
opportunities for racial profiling.[62]

If the profusion of car cases since *Carroll v. United States* manifested
an area of constitutional law without a coherent theory of jurisprudence, then the car cases decided in the era of mass incarceration
betrayed a Fourth Amendment without a theory of justice. To be
sure, the Supreme Court in *Whren* did recognize discriminatory
policing as a constitutional issue. "We of course agree with petitioners," the opinion stated, "that the Constitution prohibits selective enforcement of the law based on considerations such as race."
But a discrimination claim, Justice Scalia instructed, arose under the
Fourteenth Amendment's equal protection clause, not the Fourth
Amendment guarantee against unreasonable searches and seizures.[63]

Defense attorneys had already anticipated the Supreme Court's
stance. In 1996, just months before the Court decided *Whren*, a New
Jersey court excluded evidence of drugs against seventeen black motorists based on the equal protection and due process clauses of the
Fourteenth Amendment. The defense had compiled data showing
disparities in traffic law enforcement "so wide, so big" that the computer would not even "spit out a number," recalled the professor
who had conducted the survey. Nearly every driver sped past legal

limits, but blacks were stopped at a disproportionate rate—to be precise, between 16.35 and 22.1 standard deviations above the median, depending on the segment of the New Jersey Turnpike. The opinion helpfully explained that statisticians consider standard deviations over 2 to be statistically significant. To put this in layman's terms, it was "highly unlikely [that] such statistics could have occurred randomly or by chance." Even more damning, the defense's expert demonstrated that state troopers using radar stopped black drivers in proportion to their motoring population, while troopers not using radar arrested many more blacks. The witness commented, "As they got more discretion, they stopped more blacks." Discrimination on the turnpike could not hide behind the numbers.[64]

The ruling in *State v. Soto* had an immediate impact, leading to the dismissals of more than 150 drug cases in New Jersey. To manage the deluge of profiling-related claims, one Superior Court judge was assigned to handle them all. Yet, notwithstanding its legal breakthrough, the case garnered only a few headlines, mostly within the state. The *New York Times* recognized *Soto*'s "novel legal strategy"—six years later. Six months of trial with dueling statisticians as star witnesses who slogged through standard deviations and distribution tails failed to capture the public's attention—until 1998.[65]

On April 23, 1998, two New Jersey state troopers pulled over a black teenager driving a minivan with three friends, two black and one Hispanic. What was supposed to be a routine traffic stop for speeding ended violently when the van slowly started rolling backward, prompting the troopers to fire eleven shots, which wounded three of the boys. The troopers explained that the driver had backed up, knocked one of them over, and bumped into their cruiser before reversing across the turnpike's three lanes. The victims denied that they were speeding in the first place and recounted how they had accidentally gone into reverse and could not stop before the volley of gunshots ambushed them. They were, they added, just on their way to a basketball tryout. A year later, three of them still had bullets lodged inside their bodies.[66]

It was the turnpike shooting of four unarmed teenagers that finally got reporters to write about Driving While Black and forced the state's attorney general to admit that racial profiling was "real—not imagined." As part of that concession, the state also dropped its appeal of the *Soto* ruling. While the tragedy on the turnpike brought greater public attention to the *Soto* case, *Soto*, in turn, reframed the shooting from an isolated event to a methodical War on Drugs against minority drivers. "I hate to sound callous," the defense lawyer in *Soto* remarked, "but it would have been another set of minorities shot by police, their word against police—but for *Soto*." As he put it, "The shooting stood out in relief because of *Soto*. *Soto* stood out in relief because of the shooting." The statistics that the *Soto* team put together provided the connection between police violence and a policy of discrimination.[67]

Challenging pretextual stops as a violation of equal protection, as *Whren* directed, accomplished significant reforms in New Jersey. Defendants were able to exclude evidence. The state agreed to install video cameras in its patrol cars, which could be used to challenge the police's version of "all the facts and circumstances." Promising changes came out of the turnpike shooting, which raises a historical and legal question. Did it matter that claims of discriminatory policing were brought under the equal protection clause rather than the Fourth Amendment?[68]

The history told in this book would suggest so. Conceiving of discrimination only as an issue of equal protection reflected a change in how American society thought about the police problem, from the policing of Everyman to the policing of racial minorities. This shift, in turn, has obscured an important normative question about how much power the police should have in a free society. The problem with pretextual policing is not only that the police treat groups differently; it is, just as importantly, that they have that much discretionary power at all. Substantive questions require attention in addition to concerns about racialized policing. Should the police be able to search the entire car during a routine traffic stop? Should minor traffic violations be able to lead to an unrelated criminal investigation? Given that nearly a third of police shootings in 2015 began with a traffic stop, what can the government do to make that encounter safer for both officers and citizens?[69] How would our policies and our laws, as well as our interpretation of the Fourth Amendment, change if these police practices happened to Everyman?

Epilogue

The history of American freedom is, in no small measure,
the history of procedure.

Justice Felix Frankfurter, *Malinski v. New York* (1945)

THE HISTORY OF CARS, policing, and the Fourth Amendment de-
scribes a past that is becoming increasingly foreign in the twenty-
first century. Journalists and policymakers have already announced
the decline of the car's central role in American life as younger generations prefer urban lifestyles and Uberization. Concerns about the
arbitrary policing of Everyman sound out of touch with a racialized
War on Drugs, Driving While Black, and Black Lives Matter. Public
discussion is now focused on discriminatory policing.[1]

Although the concerns of the past may seem distant today, we are
still grappling with the fallout from developments that occurred in
the first few decades of the twentieth century. In response to the automotive revolution, American society shifted to policing as a mode
of governance and updated its laws to sanction police discretion. The
consequences of granting the police vast powers were worked out
during the most paranoid spell of the Cold War. Yet many of the issues that midcentury jurists struggled to resolve still confound us
today. With new technologies that are altering our experiences of
freedom and privacy, litigants are still arguing over how the Fourth
Amendment should take both public and private rights into account.
Criminal defendants are still questioning the limits of the police's
discretionary authority to enforce laws enacted for public safety.
Those who seek redress for police abuse are still left wondering

whether existing remedies are sufficient to secure a free and democratic society.

Earlier legal scholars from Sam Warner to Charles Reich and past jurists from Chief Justice Taft to Justice Douglas settled on procedural rights to reconcile discretionary policing with their understandings of the rule of law. Now the cross-currents between law's history and present-day injustices have raised questions about the adequacy of our inherited constitutional norms. As twenty-first-century litigants sustain a legal culture of proceduralism—in 2018 alone, the US Supreme Court decided three Fourth Amendment cases—each challenge they bring offers another opportunity to reconsider what is "due" in our understanding of due process and whether that is enough.

In 2012, Justice Scalia resurrected Fourth Amendment classical legalism in *United States v. Jones*. He concluded that when the FBI attached a GPS device to the defendant's Jeep Grand Cherokee as part of an ongoing narcotics investigation, the government "physically occupied *private property* for the purpose of obtaining information"—a conclusion that overlooked every case that not only distinguished cars from other types of private property but also described all the ways that cars were more like public property. But Scalia, also an adherent of originalism, was looking past twentieth-century cases to the founding era. "It is beyond dispute," he claimed, "that a vehicle is an 'effect' as that term is used in the Amendment" and, moreover, would have been so considered "when it was adopted" had cars existed at the time James Madison drafted the Bill of Rights.[2]

In a concurring opinion, Justice Alito poked fun at Scalia's anachronistic attempt to analogize an electronic tracking instrument to an eighteenth-century policeman, asking: "Is it possible to imagine a case in which a constable secreted himself somewhere in a coach and remained there for a period of time in order to monitor the movements of the coach's owner? The Court suggests that something like this might have occurred in 1791, but this would have required either a gigantic coach, a very tiny constable, or both—not to mention a constable with incredible fortitude and patience." The quip highlighted the irrelevance of Scalia's preferred legal analysis in the modern world, a point that Justice Sotomayor elaborated further in a separate opinion. With factory-installed vehicle-tracking devices and GPS-enabled smartphones, she explained, the police do not have to physically touch, or trespass, the car to follow a suspect for extended periods of time. The government can simply request information from the company that compiles the data because under current case law, individuals do not have a Fourth Amendment right of privacy to information held by third parties. Technology had rendered the *Jones* ruling obsolete on arrival.[3]

As expected, it did not take long for a smartphone case to reach the Supreme Court. The material facts of *Carpenter v. United States*, decided in 2018, were similar to those of *Jones* but without the physical trespass; instead of attaching a GPS device to a car, the FBI subpoenaed T-Mobile for the defendant's "cell-site location information" (CSLI) recorded from his cell phone's minute-by-minute contacts with the wireless network. Justice Gorsuch wrote separately in *Carpenter* in a concurring opinion that picked up where Scalia had left off in *Jones*. Like his predecessor, Gorsuch preferred the "traditional" approach, grounded in private property, to protect "modern analogues" of "specific rights known at the founding." But in trying to specify how the property analysis would work in the twenty-first century, Gorsuch ended up admitting that he could "not begin to claim all the answers today." Originalism and formalism, Gorsuch realized, were unhelpful when technologies created new forms of property that were neither wholly private nor public, and not even *real* in the legal sense of the word. GPS tracking devices, smartphones, and social media platforms produce staggering amounts of personal information that are not physical and not owned by individuals themselves. Calls for regulation on how Facebook, Google, and other Internet and telecommunications companies handle those data have further clouded the meaning of privacy not just from one another but also from the government—including the police. *Carpenter* squarely presented a question about the Fourth Amendment's applicability to a new type of property that, as a solicitor general once said of the automobile back in 1925, "has not heretofore existed."[4]

For the majority of the justices in *Carpenter*, electronically gathered personal data were so "unique" in how much they revealed about a person's private life that the Court decided not to apply twentieth-century precedents. Chief Justice Roberts, who wrote the opinion, also made clear that the ruling was "a narrow one" that did not overturn prior case law; in other words, CSLI was sui generis. The police could still obtain bank or phone records without asking permission from a judge, but cell-site locational records would require a warrant based on probable cause. Even though that information was also owned by third parties and subject to government regulation, the Court classified it as private. In response, the dissent pointed out the incongruity of privileging records that "disclose a person's location only in a general area" over documents that detail a person's purchases or call history.[5]

The *Carpenter* decision was a culmination of a series of cases beginning with *Jones* that hinted that the Court would treat smartphones differently for Fourth Amendment purposes. In her *Jones* concurrence, Sotomayor had worried that with a "precise, comprehensive record of a person's public movement" sourced from electronic devices, the government could gather "a wealth of detail about her familial, political, professional, religious, and sexual associations." In *Jones*, the FBI was seeking to prove that the defendant had stopped by a stash house. But similar searches could also disclose constitutionally protected activities like trips to an abortion clinic or AIDS treatment center, or visits to a mosque, synagogue, or church.[6]

The next case after *Jones* revealed the justices' unease that more was in jeopardy than a person's locational information. Chief Justice Roberts outlined the potential privacy intrusions in a digital world in *Riley v. California*, a 2014 case involving the twenty-first-century version of *United States v. Robinson*. The police stopped David Riley for driving with expired registration tags and arrested him upon discovering that he was also driving with a suspended license. During the search incident to arrest, instead of a cigarette package in the arrestee's pocket as in *Robinson*, the police retrieved a smartphone. After looking through the photos, videos, texts, and contacts—analogous to looking inside a cigarette packet, the government argued—officers found evidence that Riley had been involved in a gang-related shooting a few weeks earlier. In ruling that the *Robinson* precedent did not apply to the case at hand, Roberts described the breadth and richness of personal information that cell phones contain. "Even the most basic phones that sell for less than $20 might hold photographs, picture messages, text messages, Internet browsing history, a calendar, a thousand-entry phone book, and so on," he explained. With this information, the government could easily piece together an individual's political affiliation, daily routines, reading habits, romantic interests, medical issues, and more. "Indeed," he concluded, "a cell phone search would typically expose to the government far *more* than the most exhaustive search of a house." In making the comparison to a "house," the preeminent private sphere in American constitutional law, the chief justice was indicating the strength of the privacy interests at stake. Although the technology may be twenty-first century, the themes were from the twentieth. But that was the point. Roberts was trying to fit modern contraptions into old paradigms. Even if the use of mobile devices is public in the sense that it interfaces with the World Wide Web largely enabled by third parties, Roberts emphasized many Americans' understanding that individuals still have an expectation that what they do on their phones is not the police's business.[7]

Yet, recognizing privacy interests, as Sotomayor and Roberts did, or finding a private property interest, as Scalia and Gorsuch did, does not end the matter. Recall that even the private home could be turned into a public nuisance, and become subject to the police power, if the welfare of the community required it. Houses, cars—anything at all really—acquired the status of "private" or "public" after judges considered competing rights. The exigencies of automobility may have changed the nature of the analysis; instead of deciding whether *every* car search needed a warrant, judges now decide whether the circumstances of a *particular* car search require one. But, importantly, cars did not eliminate the necessity of weighing the public's claims against private rights. If the history of the automotive Fourth Amendment can offer any insight today, it is this: As new forms of property and objects of government regulation migrate from vehicular highways to the information superhighway, delineating the boundary between public and private will remain circumstantial, inconsistent, and highly proceduralized so long as American society continues to depend on discretionary policing. In short, more litigation is in store.

In *Riley v. California*, Chief Justice Roberts summoned Justice Jackson's argument in *Brinegar v. United States* that a search of Riley's phone must be regarded as a search of the phone of Everyman. "Now it is the person who is not carrying a cell phone, with all that it contains, who is the exception," he declared. Invoking the history of general warrants and "the arbitrary claims of Great Britain," Roberts had in mind the possible privacy threats to "every" American. The opinion did not mention the defendant's race or that he was a member of a predominantly black gang. It omitted the reality that most individuals who are stopped for a traffic violation and then searched are racial minorities.[8]

Notwithstanding Roberts's omission, recent cases and reports indicate that the police are still using traffic stops as a prelude to criminal investigations that target minorities. In 2017, an en banc Seventh Circuit decided *United States v. Johnson*, a case that shows that the police are continuing to take full advantage of Fourth Amendment doctrines to maximize the effectiveness of what Charles Remsberg had called "Criminal Patrol." Just after 7:30 P.M. on January 8, 2014, two squad cars from the Milwaukee Police Department pulled up to a parked Toyota Highlander, one right beside and the other right behind. Within seconds, five police officers jumped out and "bathed the parked car in bright light" with their headlights, spotlights, and flashlights, according to the court's description of the scene. One officer saw a backseat passenger, Randy Johnson, make suspicious movements and ordered all occupants out of the car. The door ajar, the officer noticed a gun on the floor. Johnson was subsequently handed to the federal government for prosecution on the charge of possessing a weapon as a felon.[9]

The Milwaukee police were not investigating a specific case or looking for a specific individual. They were part of the "Neighborhood Task Force Street Crimes Unit" assigned to patrol "hot spots," or "high crime" areas, which are often in minority neighborhoods. According to the testimony of a Task Force officer, "part of [their] initiative is to look for smaller infractions and hope that possibly they may lead to bigger and better things." In this case, the progression from traffic stop to felony charges against a car passenger began with a *suspected parking violation*. "Everything else," according to the Seventh Circuit, "followed naturally (and legally)." As the court noted, the Fourth Amendment, as interpreted over the past century, allowed officers to stop a car for minor traffic violations, including non-moving offenses. It permitted officers to order the car's occupants out. *Terry v. Ohio* and subsequent cases authorized "frisks" of cars for weapons. To cap it off, *Whren v. United States* condoned pretextual stops by forbidding inquiries into officers' subjective motives. After putting all of these precedents together and reciting the axiom that the "Fourth Amendment requires searches and seizures to be reasonable," the court concluded that the police actions were lawful.[10]

It is stunning to consider how the authority to stop cars for minor traffic offenses, combined with the authority to stop people for brief questioning, has burgeoned into a full-fledged crime-control strategy involving multiple patrol officers equipped with squad cars, guns, and lights. In a potential sign of change, the Supreme Court recently attempted to separate regulatory enforcement from criminal investigation. In the 2015 case *Rodriguez v. United States*, a K-9 officer stopped the defendant after seeing him swerve on the highway, issued a warning for driving on the shoulder, and then requested to walk his drug-sniffing dog around the vehicle. When the defendant refused, the officer detained him until a second officer arrived on the scene to provide assistance. The K-9 alerted the officers to the presence of drugs, which provided probable cause for a warrantless car search pursuant to *Carroll v. United States*, which, in turn, led to the discovery of a large bag of methamphetamine. The Court ruled that prolonging a stop beyond the conclusion of the tasks related to the traffic mission requires an independent individualized suspicion. In other words, the authority to pull over a car for a traffic violation could not be rolled into a justification for a dog sniff, which lacked a "close connection to roadway safety" since its only purpose was to detect evidence of crime.[11]

In a dissent echoing earlier criticisms that Fourth Amendment doctrine had become a nonsensical compilation of rules, Justice Alito asserted that the *Rodriguez* "holding is not only arbitrary; it is per-verse." The officer's mistake, it appeared, was not his actions per se but their sequence. If he had conducted the dog sniff before com-pleting the traffic warning, he would not have run afoul of the Court's new rule. But because the officer, out of concern for his safety, chose to wait for another policeman to arrive—for a total waiting time of five to six minutes—he had potentially violated the Fourth Amend-ment. In the future, Alito pointed out, officers could easily get around the *Rodriguez* rule by waiting to hand over the driver's license and ticket until after they finish the investigatory portion of the stop.[12]

If the *Johnson* case exposed the regulatory roots of the carceral state, then *Rodriguez* illustrated the difficulty of severing traffic en-forcement and crime control when the police are assigned both tasks. This may explain why the Supreme Court declined to hear Johnson's appeal. As the Seventh Circuit maintained, once there is a traffic violation, the police may then take many actions "naturally (and legally)." The Supreme Court's denial of certiorari in *Johnson* and the futility of its rule in *Rodriguez* both reaffirmed its unwillingness to scrutinize the administration of street and highway safety. By allowing the Seventh Circuit's decision to stand, the Court also left the tactics of Criminal Patrol intact, with the imprimatur of the law.[13]

On November 9, 2015, the US Supreme Court issued a per curiam decision—meaning that the Court may have viewed the issue as un-controversial, notwithstanding Justice Sotomayor's dissent—denying damages against a Texas state trooper. The case began when state and local authorities pursued Israel Leija in an eighteen-minute, high-speed chase. Leija, reportedly intoxicated, called the police dis-patcher twice, claiming to have a gun and threatening to shoot at the officers if they did not abandon the pursuit. To stop the car, the police set up tire spikes beneath a bridge on the interstate highway, where Leija was expected to pass. Minutes before Leija's arrival, Trooper Chadrin Mullenix came up with the idea of shooting at Lei-ja's car. He asked several supervisors for permission to shoot and, disregarding instructions to wait and see if the spikes would work, he fired six shots. Not only did his plan fail—the car did not stop until it hit the spike strip and rolled over—but Mullenix also killed Leija. The deceased's estate sued for damages under Section 1983 of the 1871 Civil Rights Act, alleging that Mullenix used excessive force in violation of Leija's Fourth Amendment rights.[14]

The issue on appeal concerned qualified immunity, a doctrine that shields officials from civil liability if their conduct "does not violate clearly established statutory or constitutional rights of which a reasonable person would have known." In addressing this question, the *Mullenix* opinion revealed how proceduralism has come to eviscerate police officer accountability. According to the per curiam, Mullenix's actions did not violate a *clearly established* constitutional right because existing cases were either "at a high level of generality" that failed to consider "the specific context of the case" or "too factually distinct to speak clearly to the specific circumstances here." In effect, unless the precise factual circumstances had already been litigated, police officers enjoy immunity.[15]

The Fourth Amendment has come a long way since this book's opening case of *Wiley v. State* in 1916 involving the Arizona deputy sheriff found guilty of murder when his shots at the Bateses' vehicle killed Mrs. Bates. The law has reached the point where proceduralism is now too proceduralized. We can view this overdevelopment with cynicism; what was supposed to be a safeguard against abuse of discretion has ended up protecting officers from liability. But the history of the twentieth-century Fourth Amendment should also provide a dose of realism. After all, proceduralism was intended to enable discretionary policing as well. American law may have settled on a solution to the paradox of police discretion in a society committed to the rule of law. But one era's answers may not be sufficient to solve another generation's problems, a challenge that may require defining freedom anew.

Abbreviations

Organizations and Publications

ABA	American Bar Association
ACLU	American Civil Liberties Union
ACLUSC	American Civil Liberties Union of Southern California
BPD	Berkeley Police Department
DAS	New York County District Attorney Scrapbook
DOC	Department of Commerce
DOJ	Department of Justice
HLR	*Harvard Law Review*
IACP	International Association of Chiefs of Police
LAPD	Los Angeles Police Department
LAT	*Los Angeles Times*
NAACP	National Association for the Advancement of Colored People
NACC, *Facts & Figures*	National Automobile Chamber of Commerce, *Facts and Figures of the Automobile Industry*
NCLOE	National Commission on Law Observance and Enforcement

NCSHS	National Conference on Street and Highway Safety
NSC	National Safety Council
NYCLC	New York Civil Liberties Committee
NYT	*New York Times*
PM	*Popular Mechanics Magazine*
TAC	*The American Chauffeur*
The Beat	*The Los Angeles Police BEAT*
TOPE	*The Oakland Post Enquirer*
TNPJ	*The National Police Journal*
WSJ	*Wall Street Journal*
YLJ	*Yale Law Journal*

Archives

ACLU Records	American Civil Liberties Union Records, Seeley G. Mudd Manuscript Library, Princeton University, Princeton, New Jersey
ACLUSC Records	American Civil Liberties Union of Southern California Records, ca. 1935–, Special Collections, Charles E. Young Research Library, University of California, Los Angeles, California
ASL	Arizona State Library, Archives and Public Records, Phoenix, Arizona
AVP	August Vollmer Papers, Bancroft Library, University of California, Berkeley, California
Benson	Benson Ford Research Center, Dearborn, Michigan
BPD Records	Berkeley Police Department Records, 1909–1932, Bancroft Library, University of California, Berkeley, California
Harlan Papers	John Marshall Harlan Papers, Seeley G. Mudd Manuscript Library, Princeton University, Princeton, New Jersey

HHPL	Herbert Hoover Presidential Library, National Archives and Records Administration, West Branch, Iowa
Jackson Papers	Robert H. Jackson Papers, 1816–1983, Manuscript Division, Library of Congress, Washington, D.C.
LACA	Los Angeles City Archives and Records Center, Erwin C. Piper Technical Center, Los Angeles, California
NAACP Papers	National Association for the Advancement of Colored People Papers, ProQuest History Vault
NARA Denver	Records of the US District Court of Colorado, National Archives and Records Administration, Denver, Colorado
NICB	National Insurance Crime Bureau, Des Plaines, Illinois
NYCMA	New York City Municipal Archives, Records and Information Services, New York, New York
OWP	Orlando Winfield Wilson Papers, Bancroft Library, University of California, Berkeley, California
Rutledge Papers	Wiley Rutledge Papers, 1912–1984, Manuscript Division, Library of Congress, Washington, D.C.
Taft Papers	William H. Taft Papers, 1784–1973, Manuscript Division, Library of Congress, Washington, D.C.

Notes

Introduction

Epigraph (Hillenbrand): *Seabiscuit: An American Legend* by Laura Hillenbrand, copyright © 2001 by Laura Hillenbrand. Used by permission of Random House, an imprint and division of Penguin Random House LLC and HarperCollins Publishers Ltd. All rights reserved.

1. Wiley v. State, 19 Ariz. 346, 348–352 (1918); Abstract of Record, Wiley v. State, 19 Ariz. 346 (1918) (No. 429), ASL. For cases with similar facts, see McAdams v. State ex rel. Sullivan, County Attorney, 101 Okla. 267 (1923); Pales v. Paoli, 5 F.2d 280 (1st Cir. 1925); Taylor v. State, 36 Okla. Crim. 431 (1927); Copeland v. Dunehoo, 36 Ga. App. 817 (1927); Eubank v. State, 115 Tex. Crim. 112 (1930); "Chicago Police to Use Shotgun," *TNPJ* 8, no. 1 (May 1921): 30.

2. On early cars, see "Cure for Rattling Doors," *TAC* 4, no. 1 (January 1916): 16; "Haste to Fly for Money May Balk Progress," *PM* 15, no. 6 (June 1911): 836.

3. *Wiley,* 19 Ariz. at 354; Monty McCord, *Police Cars: A Photographic History* (Iola, WI: Krause Publications, 1991), 303; O. W. Wilson, "Dallas Police Department" (n.p., [1934?]), 43, 49, box 1, OWP.

4. On common-law arrests, see Christopher G. Tiedeman, *A Treatise on the Limitations of Police Power in the United States Considered from Both a Civil and Criminal Standpoint* (St. Louis: F. H. Thomas, 1886), 83–85; Kurtz v. Moffitt, 115 U.S. 487, 498–499 (1885).

5. *Wiley,* 19 Ariz. at 355; Brief of Appellant, Wiley v. State, 19 Ariz. 346 (1918) (No. 429), ASL.

6. Debbie Nathan, "What Happened to Sandra Bland?" *Nation* 302, no. 19/20 (May 9, 2016): 12–18.

7. Nick Selby, Ben Singleton, and Ed Flosi, *In Context: Understanding Police Killings of Unarmed Citizens* (St. Augustine, FL: Contextual Press, 2016), 39; US DOJ, Civil Rights Division, *Investigation of the Ferguson Police Department* (n.p., March 4, 2015), 2, 9; Charles R. Epp, Steven Maynard-Moody, and Donald

Haider-Markel, *Pulled Over: How Police Stops Define Race and Citizenship* (Chicago: University of Chicago Press, 2014), 2; see also Franklin E. Zimring, *When Police Kill* (Cambridge, MA: Harvard University Press, 2017), 51–53.

8. K. K. Rebecca Lai, Haeyoun Park, Larry Buchanan, and Wilson Andrews, "Assessing the Legality of Sandra Bland's Arrest," *NYT,* July 22, 2015, https://perma.cc/9QW7-J7U3. For Supreme Court opinions that allow Officer Encinia's actions, see Whren v. United States, 517 U.S. 806 (1996); Pennsylvania v. Mimms, 434 U.S. 106 (1977); Tennessee v. Garner, 471 U.S. 1 (1985); Scott v. Harris, 550 U.S. 372 (2007).

9. Lai et al., "Assessing"; Manny Fernandez and David Montgomery, "Perjury Charge Dropped against Ex-Trooper in Sandra Bland Case," *NYT,* June 28, 2017.

10. Edwin H. Sutherland and C. E. Gehlke, "Crime and Punishment," in President's Research Committee on Social Trends, *Recent Social Trends in the United States,* vol. 2 (New York: McGraw-Hill, 1933), 1139–1146.

11. Robert S. Lynd and Helen Merrell Lynd, *Middletown: A Study in Contemporary American Culture* (New York: Harcourt, Brace, 1929), 251–253; US DOC, Bureau of the Census, *Historical Statistics of the United States 1789–1945: A Supplement to the Statistical Abstract of the United States* (Washington, DC, 1949), 223; NACC, *Facts & Figures* (New York, 1926), 80; William Ashdown, "Confessions of an Automobilist," *Atlantic Monthly* 135, no. 6 (June 1925): 789; see also Jan Jennings, "Housing the Automobile," in *Roadside America: The Automobile in Design and Culture,* ed. Jan Jennings (Ames: Iowa State University Press, 1990), 95–106. On *Middletown,* see Sarah E. Igo, *The Averaged American: Surveys, Citizens, and the Making of a Mass Public* (Cambridge, MA: Harvard University Press, 2007), 68–102.

12. Willard Hurst, quoted in William J. Novak, "Law Capitalism, and the Liberal State: The Historical Sociology of James Willard Hurst," *Law and History Review* 18, no. 1 (2000): 109–110; see also Lawrence Van Gelder, "Willard Hurst, 86, Legal Scholar and Pioneer in History of Law," *NYT,* June 20, 1997.

13. Frank H. Easterbrook, "Cyberspace and the Law of the Horse," *University of Chicago Legal Forum* (1996): 208; Stephen Dunn, *Between Angels: Poems* (New York: W. W. Norton, 1989), 55; Sinclair Lewis, "The Sacred," *Free Air* (New York: Harcourt, Brace and Howe, 1919); Vincent Bryan and Gus Edwards, "In My Merry Oldsmobile," in *Favorite Songs of the Nineties: Complete Original Sheet Music for 89 Songs,* ed. Robert A. Fremont (New York: Dover, 1973), 150–151; Bruce Springsteen, "Thunder Road," *Born To Run* (1975; New York, Columbia Records, 2015); see also E. L. Widmer, "Crossroads: The Automobile, Rock and Roll, and Democracy," in Jennings, *Roadside America,* 82–91. On creation narratives justifying "motordom," see Peter D. Norton, "Of Love Affairs and Other Stories," in *Incomplete Streets: Processes, Practices, and Possibilities,* ed. Stephen Zavestoski and Julian Agyeman (New York: Routledge, 2015), 17–35.

14. James B. Jacobs, *The Eternal Criminal Record* (Cambridge, MA: Harvard University Press, 2015).

15. See Markus Dirk Dubber, *The Police Power: Patriarchy and the Foundations of American Government* (New York: Columbia University Press, 2005), 126–127.

16. The question of enforcement has been a source of debate between William Novak and Harry Scheiber, who, in his review of Novak's *The People's*

Welfare, questioned how vigorously regulatory laws were enforced. While that question may be debatable for the nineteenth century, the compliance problem was impossible to ignore in the twentieth-century automotive society. See Harry N. Scheiber, "Private Rights and Public Power: American Law, Capitalism, and the Republican Polity in Nineteenth-Century America," review of *The People's Welfare: Law and Regulation in Nineteenth-Century America*, by William J. Novak, *YLJ* 107, no. 3 (1997): 850–856.

17. Novak, *People's Welfare*, 163–171; see also Brian Balogh, *The Associational State: American Governance in the Twentieth Century* (Philadelphia: University of Pennsylvania Press, 2015); Christopher Capozzola, *Uncle Sam Wants You: World War I and the Making of the Modern American Citizen* (New York: Oxford University Press, 2008), 21–54, 83–143; William J. Novak, "The Legal Transformation of Citizenship in Nineteenth-Century America," in *The Democratic Experiment: New Directions in American Political History*, ed. Meg Jacobs, William J. Novak, and Julian E. Zelizer (Princeton, NJ: Princeton University Press, 2003), 94–105.

18. William S. Harlow, *Duties of Sheriffs and Constables* (San Francisco: Sumner Whitney, 1884).

19. In an 1854 prohibition case, for instance, three citizens brought a complaint before the justice of the peace, who then issued a warrant for the constable to search and seize all liquor found in the defendant's house and to summon him to appear in court. A committed temperance advocate remarked that "all that was needed to make prohibition work was three good temperance men, a loyal constable, and an efficient magistrate." Fisher v. McGirr, 1 Gray 1 (Mass. 1854); Neal Dow, quoted in Novak, *People's Welfare*, 181.

20. Jerome Hall, "Legal and Social Aspects of Arrest without a Warrant," *HLR* 49, no. 4 (1936): 579. On private policing and prosecution, see, for example, David Sklansky, "The Private Police," *UCLA Law Review* 46, no. 4 (1999): 1205–1221; Allen Steinberg, "From Private Prosecution to Plea Bargaining: Criminal Prosecution, the District Attorney, and American Legal History," *Crime & Delinquency* 30, no. 4 (1984): 570–577. On special policemen, see "The Chester, Pa., Police Force," *TNPJ* 1, no. 3 (December 1917): 31; "For Better Protection," *Los Angeles Sunday Times*, December 20, 1903; Sidney L. Harring, *Policing a Class Society: The Experience of American Cities, 1865–1915* (New Brunswick, NJ: Rutgers University Press, 1983), 91–92.

On police history, see, for example, Allen Steinberg, *The Transformation of Criminal Justice, Philadelphia, 1800–1880* (Chapel Hill: University of North Carolina Press, 1989); Eric H. Monkkonen, *Police in Urban America: 1860–1920* (New York: Cambridge University Press, 1981); David R. Johnson, *Policing the Urban Underworld: The Impact of Crime on the Development of the American Police, 1800–1887* (Philadelphia: Temple University Press, 1979); Samuel Walker, *A Critical History of Police Reform: The Emergence of Professionalism* (Lexington, MA: Lexington Books, 1977).

21. NACC, *Facts & Figures* (New York, 1927), 39; see also James J. Flink, *The Automobile Age* (Cambridge, MA: MIT Press, 1988), 130–135. For numbers of farmer-owned passenger cars, see NACC, *Facts & Figures* (New York, 1921), 17. On the significance of the independent farmer, see Victoria Saker Woeste, "Agriculture and the State, 1789–2000," in *The Twentieth Century and After*

(1920–), vol. 3 of *The Cambridge History of Law in America*, ed. Michael Grossberg and Christopher Tomlins (Cambridge: Cambridge University Press, 2008), 522–562; Bruce H. Mann, *Republic of Debtors: Bankruptcy in the Age of American Independence* (Cambridge, MA: Harvard University Press, 2002), 127–128.

22. Pennsylvania Coal Co. v. Mahon, 260 U.S. 393, 417–422 (1922) (Brandeis, J., dissenting); Carroll v. United States, 267 U.S. 132 (1925); Maul v. United States, 274 U.S. 501, 524–525 (1927) (Brandeis, J., concurring); Olmstead v. United States, 277 U.S. 438, 478 (Brandeis, J., dissenting); Samuel D. Warren and Louis D. Brandeis, "The Right to Privacy," *HLR* 4, no. 5 (1890): 193–220; Charles E. Colman, "About Ned," *HLR Forum* 129, no. 3 (2016): 128, 128n5, 148–151. On substantive due process and the right to privacy, see, for example, David E. Bernstein, *Rehabilitating* Lochner: *Defending Individual Rights against Progressive Reform* (Chicago: University of Chicago Press, 2011), 107–124; Barry Cushman, "Justice Brandeis and Substantive Due Process," *Green Bag 2d* 19 (2016): 145–156. On decriminalization, see, for example, Risa L. Goluboff, *Vagrant Nation: Police Power, Constitutional Change, and the Making of the 1960s* (New York: Oxford University Press, 2016), 149, 399n8; Peggy Pascoe, *What Comes Naturally: Miscegenation Law and the Making of Race in America* (New York: Oxford University Press, 2009); Lawrence M. Friedman, *Crime and Punishment in American History* (New York: BasicBooks, 1993), 341–354; Dubber, *Police Power*, 202–203.

23. On the Warren Court, see, for example, William J. Stuntz, *The Collapse of American Criminal Justice* (Cambridge, MA: Belknap Press of Harvard University Press, 2011), 216–227; Dan M. Kahan and Tracey L. Meares, "The Coming Crisis of Criminal Procedure," *Georgetown Law Journal* 86, no. 5 (1998): 1153–1159; Morton J. Horwitz, *The Warren Court and the Pursuit of Justice* (New York: Farrar, Straus and Giroux, 1998), 91–98; Friedman, *Crime and Punishment*, 294–304.

24. See Wesley MacNeil Oliver, "The Neglected History of Criminal Procedure, 1850–1940," *Rutgers Law Review* 62, no. 2 (2010): 447–525; Robert Post, "Federalism, Positive Law, and the Emergence of the American Administrative State: Prohibition in the Taft Court Era," *William and Mary Law Review* 48, no. 1 (2006): 1–183; Michael J. Klarman, "The Racial Origins of Modern Criminal Procedure," *Michigan Law Review* 99, no. 1 (2000): 48–97; Morgan Cloud, "The Fourth Amendment during the *Lochner* Era: Privacy, Property, and Liberty in Constitutional Theory," *Stanford Law Review* 48, no. 3 (1996): 555–631.

25. Warren and Brandeis, "Right to Privacy," 214. In fact, many of the newly created rights that were called "fundamental" were not absolute. The state continued to subject the right to privacy to regulation, even when it concerned marriage or reproductive freedom. Compare Loving v. Virginia, 388 U.S. 1, 12 (1967) ("Marriage is one of the 'basic civil rights of man,' fundamental to our very existence and survival"), with Virginia Code (1975), sec. 20-38.1, "Certain Marriages Prohibited." In *Roe v. Wade*, the Supreme Court established a right of privacy "broad enough to encompass a woman's decision whether or not to terminate her pregnancy." But to the claim that "the woman's right is absolute," the Court responded, "With this we do not agree." 410 U.S. 113, 153 (1973).

26. Kahan and Meares, "Coming Crisis," 1171; Stuntz, *Collapse*, 210–212. Although the Supreme Court has primarily taken the procedural path, they have invalidated laws that criminalized drug addition, the failure of convicted felons to register with the police, and the sale or use of contraceptives. See Robinson v. California, 370 U.S. 660 (1962); Lambert v. California, 355 U.S. 225 (1957); Griswold v. Connecticut, 381 U.S. 479 (1965). On the substance / procedure distinction, see, for example, William J. Stuntz, "Substance, Process, and the Civil-Criminal Line," *Journal of Contemporary Legal Issues* 7, no. 1 (1996): 1–41; William J. Stuntz, "The Substantive Origins of Criminal Procedure," *YLJ* 105, no. 2 (1995): 393–447; Anthony G. Amsterdam, "The Void-for-Vagueness Doctrine in the Supreme Court," *University of Pennsylvania Law Review* 109, no. 1 (1960): 67–116; David Wolitz, "Herbert Wechsler, Legal Process, and the Jurisprudential Roots of the Model Penal Code," *Tulsa Law Review* 51, no. 3 (2016): 633–687.

CHAPTER 1 • A Mystery of Traffic

1. Francis V. Greene, "An Account of Some Observations of Street Traffic," *Transactions of the American Society of Civil Engineers* 15 (February 1886): 123–138; Clay McShane and Joel A. Tarr, *The Horse in the City: Living Machines in the Nineteenth Century* (Baltimore: Johns Hopkins University Press, 2007), 54; J. E. Wright, "Automobiles Transforming City Thoroughfares," *TAC* 4, no. 3 (March 1916): 121; Herbert Hoover, "Fair Automobile Safety Regulation," *Insurance Field* 49, no. 16-A (April 17, 1924): 5; G. V. Straus, "The Newark, N.J., Police," *TNPJ* 7, no. 5 (March 1921): 3.

2. William Junkin Cox, "Why Automobile Accidents?," *Harper's Monthly Magazine* (June 1935): 54. On automobile accidents, see Miller McClintock, *Street Traffic Control* (New York: McGraw-Hill, 1925), 6–8; "Berkeley Auto Deaths Alarm," newspaper article, n.d., box 48, BPD Records; "Auto Kills Girl; Police Save Driver," *NYT*, September 5, 1921; see also Peter D. Norton, *Fighting Traffic: The Dawn of the Motor Age in the American City* (Cambridge, MA: MIT Press, 2008), 21–32, 65–79.

3. NSC, *Accident Facts* (Chicago, 1933), 10 table 5; NSC, *The New War on Accidents* (Chicago, 1936): 16; David Van Schaack, "Automobile Accidents and Their Prevention," *TNPJ* 6, no. 6 (September 1920): 10; William Phelps Eno, "Highway Traffic Regulation and Control with Particular Reference to the Prevention of Accidents" (paper, Conference on Motor Vehicle Traffic, Yale University, April 9–11, 1924), 1–2, box 157, folder 2765, HHPL; August Vollmer, "National Conference on Street and Highway Safety, Washington" (press release, September 26, 1931), carton 2, AVP; August Vollmer, "The Police and the Traffic Problem" (n.p., December 15, 1930), carton 2, AVP; August Vollmer, "Notes on Address to Japanese Police Officials" (n.p., 1932), 2, box 46, AVP.

4. See Christopher G. Tiedeman, *A Treatise on the Limitations of Police Power in the United States Considered from Both a Civil and Criminal Standpoint* (St. Louis: F. H. Thomas, 1886), 1–5; Commonwealth v. Alger, 61 Mass. 53, 85 (1851); see also William J. Novak, *The People's Welfare: Law and Regulation in*

Nineteenth-Century America (Chapel Hill: University of North Carolina Press, 1996), 121–131; Markus Dirk Dubber, *The Police Power: Patriarchy and the Foundations of American Government* (New York: Columbia University Press, 2005).

5. Iowa State Highway Commission, "Speed Limit—Drive Moderately," *Service Bulletin* 4, no. 7 (July 1916): 11; "Honor Plan for Speeders Abandoned by County," *PM* 26, no. 4 (October 1916): 550; "'Prudence' Will Be Speed Limit in Iowa under New Honor System," *Cape Girardeau Southeast Missourian*, June 7, 1929.

6. Roscoe Pound, "The Growth of Administrative Justice," *Wisconsin Law Review* 2, no. 6 (1924): 334–335. On the "discovery and reinvention of jaywalking" in the battle for the streets between pedestrians and motorists, see Norton, *Fighting Traffic*, 71–78. On torts, see G. Edward White, *Tort Law in America: An Intellectual History* (New York: Oxford University Press, 1980), 3–62. Notably, White's 1980 edition on the history of tort law does not cover automobile liability, while the expanded 2003 edition includes it in the discussion of no-fault automobile insurance.

7. *Revised Statute Laws of Louisiana* (Voorhies 1876), sec. 2274; Homer B. Cross, "Out of the Past," *Guardian* (Los Angeles, 1937): 33, box C2013, LACA; LAPD, *Annual Report* (1902), box B-2294, LACA. On nineteenth-century police power over streets and traffic, see, for example, *Revised Ordinances of 1892 of the City of Boston* (Boston: Rockwell and Churchill, 1892), chap. 6, sec. 7; City of St. Louis v. Green, 7 Mo. App. 468 (1879); Parish of St. Martin v. Delahoussaye, 30 La. Ann. 1092 (1878); Hall v. Ripley, 119 Mass. 135 (1875); Beisiegl v. New York Cent. R. Co., 40 N.Y. 9 (1870); Parish of West Baton Rouge v. Robertson, 8 La. Ann. 69 (1853); McClintock, *Street Traffic Control*, 185; see also David Thacher, "Olmsted's Police," *Law and History Review* 33, no. 3 (August 2015): 594; Richard C. Wade, *The Urban Frontier: The Rise of Western Cities, 1790–1830* (1959; reprint, Illini Books ed., 1996), 86, 285–286.

8. For negligence cases, see, for example, *Hall*, 119 Mass. 135; Eugene McQuillin, *A Treatise on the Law of Municipal Corporations*, vol. 3 (Chicago: Callaghan, 1912), sec. 932. On the lack of a traffic enforcement regime before cars, see McShane and Tarr, *Horse in the City*, 37–55; Anne Norton Greene, *Horses at Work: Harnessing Power in Industrial America* (Cambridge, MA: Harvard University Press, 2008), 178; Norton, *Fighting Traffic*, 48.

9. Roscoe Pound, *Criminal Justice in America* (New York: Henry Holt, 1930), 11, 123, 130; see also James Willard Hurst, *Law and the Conditions of Freedom in the Nineteenth-Century United States* (Madison: University of Wisconsin Press, 1956), 3–32; Barbara Young Welke, *Recasting American Liberty: Gender, Race, Law and the Railroad Revolution, 1865–1920* (New York: Cambridge University Press, 2001), 3–8; Susanna L. Blumenthal, *Law and the Modern Mind: Consciousness and Responsibility in American Legal Culture* (Cambridge, MA: Harvard University Press, 2016), 4–5, 26–58.

10. Pound, *Criminal Justice*, 123; De Witt C. Blashfield, *Blashfield's Cyclopedia of Automobile Law and Practice*, 14 vols. (1927; St. Paul, MN: West, 1946); Pound, "Growth of Administrative Justice," 334–335.

11. *The General Laws of the Commonwealth of Massachusetts* (1921), chap. 90, sec. 7; "Massachusetts Enforces Headlight Law," *Motordom* 14, no. 1

(June 1920): 10; Leon J. Pinkson, "Plan for Marking Turns Is Now Suggested," *San Francisco Chronicle*, December 21, 1913; Howard S. Abbott, *A Treatise on the Law of Municipal Corporations*, vol. 1 (St. Paul: Keefe-Davidson, 1905), sec. 126; McQuillin, *Law of Municipal Corporations*, secs. 935–936; "The Traffic Officers and Motor Lights," *TNPJ* 6, no. 2 (May 1920): 13; E. V. Wilcox, "Overproduction of Laws," in *Selected Articles on Law Enforcement*, ed. Julia E. Johnsen (New York: H. W. Wilson, 1930), 152; August Vollmer, *The Police and Modern Society* (Berkeley: University of California Press, 1936), 144; see also Neal Dow Becker, *Road Rules and the Law of Automobiles* (New York: Erle W. Whitfield, 1910), sec. 17; Blashfield, *Cyclopedia*, vols. 1–5.

12. "A Mystery of Traffic," newspaper article, November 1927, DAS, roll 48, vol. 333, NYCMA; Charles J. Rosebault, "The Right to Drive an Automobile," *NYT*, September 11, 1921; Vollmer, *Police and Modern Society*, 144 (traffic study).

13. Pound, *Criminal Justice*, 15–17, 23; see also Julia E. Johnsen, explanatory note in Johnsen, *Law Enforcement*, 11; Elihu Root, "The Citizen's Part in Government," in *Addresses on Government and Citizenship*, ed. Robert Bacon and James Brown Scott (Cambridge, MA: Harvard University Press, 1916), 10–12; see also Edwin H. Sutherland and C. E. Gehlke, "Crime and Punishment," in President's Research Committee on Social Trends, *Recent Social Trends in the United States*, vol. 2 (New York: McGraw-Hill, 1933), 1116–1123.

14. Increased Penalties (Jones-Stalker) Act, 27 U.S.C. §§ 91, 92 (1929); Arthur D. Greenfield, "Malum Prohibitum," *ABA Journal* 7, no. 9 (1921): 495; "Religion and Social Service: The Reformation of Herrin," *Literary Digest* (August 1, 1925): 28; see also Michael A. Lerner, *Dry Manhattan: Prohibition in New York City* (Cambridge, MA: Harvard University Press, 2007), 7–39; Daniel Okrent, *Last Call: The Rise and Fall of Prohibition* (New York: Scribner, 2010), 317; Lisa McGirr, *The War on Alcohol: Prohibition and the Rise of the American State* (New York: W. W. Norton, 2016).

15. *Inaugural Address of Herbert Hoover* (Washington, DC, 1929), 3, 5; William Howard Taft, "Enforce Prohibition," February 5, 1919, in *William Howard Taft: Collected Editorials, 1917–1921*, ed. James F. Vivian (New York: Praeger, 1990), 173; Taft to Hon. James R. Sheffield, July 8, 1923, reel 255, Taft Papers; William Howard Taft, "Is Prohibition a Blow at Personal Liberty?," *Ladies' Home Journal* (May 1919): 78; see also John H. Clarke, "Observations and Reflections on Practice in the Supreme Court," *ABA Journal* 8, no. 5 (May 1922): 267; Root, "Citizen's Part," 11–12.

16. State v. Pauley, 192 N.W. 91, 97 (N.D. 1922) (Robinson, J., dissenting); see also Kellen Funk, "Shall These Bones Live? Property, Pluralism, and the Constitution of Evangelical Reform," *Journal of Law & Social Inquiry* 41, no. 3 (2016): 744–756; Lerner, *Dry Manhattan*, 127–147, 171–188.

17. "Reckless Drivers Like Gunmen, Says Executive," *Ford News* 2L, no. 10 (March 15, 1922): 8; District of Columbia v. Colts, 282 U.S. 63, 71, 73 (1930); see also State v. Rodgers, 91 N.J.L. 212 (1917).

18. Newspaper clipping from *Washington News*, August 14, 1925, box 157, folder 2768, HHPL; "Secretary Hoover Just Escapes Auto as He 'Jaywalks,'" newspaper article, August 15, 1925, box 157, folder 2768, HHPL; "Who's to Blame?" *Ford News* 2, no. 5 (January 1, 1922): 7.

19. Sidney J. Williams, Director of Public Safety Division, NSC, "We Can Reduce Traffic Accidents if We Want To," *American City* 43, no. 3 (September 1930): 117; Vollmer, *Police and Modern Society*, 142; see also August Vollmer, "Traffic Safety Meeting" (n.p., January 23, 1929), table "Arrests for Traffic Violations," box 48, BPD Records.

20. Jessie Carney Smith and Carrell Peterson Horton, eds., *Historical Statistics of Black America*, vol. 1 (New York: Gale Research, 1995), 126; Richard Sterner, *The Negro's Share: A Study of Income, Consumption, Housing and Public Assistance* (New York: Harper & Brothers, 1943), 144–149; Kathleen Franz, "'The Open Road': Automobility and Racial Uplift in the Interwar Years," in *Technology and the African-American Experience: Needs and Opportunities for Study* ed. Bruce Sinclair (Cambridge, MA: MIT Press, 2004), 131–141; Peggy Pascoe, *What Comes Naturally: Miscegenation Law and the Making of Race in America* (New York: Oxford University Press, 2009), 164–165; John Eligon and Michael D. Shear, "Trump Pardons Jack Johnson, Heavyweight Boxing Champion," *NYT*, May 24, 2018; "Mystery of Traffic."

21. Vollmer, *Police and Modern Society*, 137; Rosebault, "Right to Drive."

22. Vollmer, "Traffic Safety Meeting," 3; Vollmer, "Police and the Traffic Problem," 3; see also Cox, "Why Automobile Accidents," 54–55.

23. DOC, NCSHS, "Clinics Needed for Reckless Drivers" (press release, September 29, 1925), box 157, folder 2768, HHPL; see also NCSHS, *Report to NCSHS* (Washington, DC, December 1924), 7, box 157, folder 2766, HHPL; Mitchell May, "Cites Arguments for Examinations of Motorists," *TAC* 4, no. 4 (April 1916): 170.

24. "Mystery of Traffic"; BPD, no title (press release, December 31, 1923), box 6, BPD Records; Vollmer, "Traffic Safety Meeting," 2; Vollmer, "Police and the Traffic Problem," 3; "Says Providence Cares for 'Man on Street,'" *TNPJ* 6, no. 6 (September 1920): 45.

25. Vollmer, "Traffic Safety Meeting," 3–4; F. Scott Fitzgerald, *The Great Gatsby* (New York: Scribner, 1925); Vollmer, *Police and Modern Society*, 140, 142.

26. Pound, *Criminal Justice*, 12, 169.

27. Larry McKilwin, "Keeping the Land Yacht Shipshape," *Harper's Weekly* 53, no. 2715 (January 2, 1909): 10; Otto Bierbaum, quoted in Diane Bailey, *How the Automobile Changed History* (Minneapolis: Abdo, 2016), 20; see also James J. Flink, *The Automobile Age* (Cambridge, MA: MIT Press, 1988), 137–138. On automobile speed, see "Getting Automobile Sense," *PM* 36, no. 3 (September 1921): 348; David P. Billington and David P. Billington Jr., *Power, Speed, and Form: Engineers and the Making of the Twentieth Century* (Princeton, NJ: Princeton University Press, 2006), 201.

28. "Freedom for the Woman Who Owns a Ford" (October 1924), Object ID 64.167.19.6, Benson; driving tip, quoted in Scott M. Fisher, *Iowa State Patrol* (Charleston, SC: Arcadia, 2013), 11; "Many Women Good Drivers of Motor Cars," *PM* 25, no. 1 (January 1916): 28; "Women at the Wheel," newspaper article, 1928, DAS, roll 48, vol. 333, NYCMA; NACC, *Facts & Figures* (New York, 1930), 79. On the challenges of driving, see "Get Acquainted with the Inside of Your Motor Car," *TAC* 4, no. 11 (November 1916): 518; "A Safety Device," *TAC* 4, no. 3 (March 1916): 134; John Chapman Hilder, "O Tempora! O Motors!,"

Harper's Monthly Magazine 164 (December 1931): 76–77, 79–80. On women and cars, see Carol Sanger, "Girls and the Getaway: Cars, Culture, and the Predicament of Gendered Space," *University of Pennsylvania Law Review* 144, no. 2 (1995): 711–714; Virginia Scharff, *Taking the Wheel: Women and the Coming of the Motor Age* (New York: Free Press, 1991), 54, 67–88, 135–142; Flink, *Automobile Age*, 162–164. On covered cars, see David L. Lewis, "Sex and the Automobile: From Rumble Seats to Rockin' Vans," in *The Automobile and American Culture*, ed. David L. Lewis and Laurence Goldstein (Ann Arbor: University of Michigan Press, 1983), 131. In 1925, US manufacturers for the first time produced more closed cars than open cars. "Production of Cars by Body Type," NACC, *Facts & Figures* (New York, 1930), 8.

29. Franz, "Open Road," 133–135; Arthur F. Raper, *Preface to Peasantry: A Tale of Two Black Belt Counties* (Chapel Hill: University of North Carolina Press, 1936), 174–175; Cotten Seiler, *Republic of Drivers: A Cultural History of Automobility in America* (Chicago: University of Chicago Press, 2008), 67.

30. H. B. Brown, "The Status of the Automobile," *YLJ* 17, no. 4 (1908): 226; Brush Runabout advertisement, in *Collier's* 46, no. 16 (January 7, 1911): 29; "Ford the Universal Car," Ford Model T Catalog, 1916–1917, Object ID 64.167.175.85, http://perma.cc/2FF8-2J8W; People v. Case, 220 Mich. 379, 388 (1922); "Glare Shield for Auto Folds Like Blades of Fan," *PM* 41, no. 4 (April 1924): 565; "New Automobile Cap and Goggles," *PM* 18, no. 3 (September 1912): 360. On standardization, see Bruce W. McCalley, *Model T Ford: The Car that Changed the World* (Iola, WI: Krause Publications, 1994), 171–177. On sunglasses, see "Dark Glasses Are New Fad for Wear on City Streets," *Life* 4, no. 22 (May 30, 1938): 31–33.

31. Pound, *Criminal Justice*, 169–172. On the culture of consumption, see Seiler, *Republic of Drivers*, 33–35; Warren I. Susman, *Culture as History: The Transformation of American Society in the Twentieth Century* (New York: Pantheon Books, 1984), 271–285; William R. Leach, "Transformations in a Culture of Consumption: Women and Department Stores, 1890–1925," *Journal of American History* 71, no. 2 (September 1984): 319–342. On car loans, see Robert S. Lynd and Helen Merrell Lynd, *Middletown: A Study in Contemporary American Culture* (New York: Harcourt, Brace, 1929), 255; Lendol Calder, *Financing the American Dream: A Cultural History of Consumer Credit* (Princeton, NJ: Princeton University Press, 1999), 184–199.

32. Pound, *Criminal Justice*, 14; Michael Grossberg, *Governing the Hearth: Law and the Family in Nineteenth-Century America* (Chapel Hill: University of North Carolina Press, 1985), 289; see also William J. Novak, "The Legal Transformation of Citizenship in Nineteenth-Century America," in *The Democratic Experiment: New Directions in American Political History*, ed. Meg Jacobs, William J. Novak, and Julian E. Zelizer (Princeton, NJ: Princeton University Press, 2003), 94–105; Michael Willrich, *City of Courts: Socializing Justice in Progressive Era Chicago* (New York: Cambridge University Press, 2003); Novak, *People's Welfare*, 19–50.

33. Hoover, "Fair Automobile," 5; August Vollmer, untitled (speech, Police Conference, University of Chicago, November 20, 1930), 1, carton 4, AVP; Pound, *Criminal Justice*, 13–14, 168–169; Lynd and Lynd, *Middletown*, 254. On voluntarism and vigilantism, see Christopher Capozzola, *Uncle Sam Wants You:*

World War I and the Making of the Modern American Citizen (New York: Oxford University Press, 2008), 83–143. On the diffusion of the automotive society, see, for example, Flink, *Automobile Age*, 129–157; Michael L. Berger, *The Devil Wagon in God's Country: The Automobile and Social Change in Rural America, 1893–1929* (Hamden, CT: Archon Books, 1979), 207–210. On nineteenth-century mobility, see, for example, Hendrik Hartog, *Man and Wife in America: A History* (Cambridge, MA: Harvard University Press, 2000), 20.

34. Lynd and Lynd, *Middletown*, 254n6, 259, 362.

35. DOC, "Secretary Hoover Calls National Conference on Street and Highway Accidents for December 15th" (press release, October 27, 1924), box 157, folder 2764, HHPL; Lew R. Palmer, Conservation Engineer, The Equitable Life Assurance Society, to Hoover, April 10, 1924, box 157, folder 2765, HHPL. On associational governance, see Brian Balogh, *The Associational State: American Governance in the Twentieth Century* (Philadelphia: University of Pennsylvania Press, 2015), 2–3, 23–40.

36. NCSHS Report (1924), 24, 27; Van Schaack, "Automobile Accidents," 28; "'Death Meter' Urges Drivers to Make Streets Safe," *PM* 41, no. 4 (April 1924): 590; "Signboard Gives Auto Drivers Pause," *Ford News* 3L, no. 13 (May 1, 1923): 7.

37. Alfred Reeves, General Manager, NACC, to Hoover, March 28, 1924, box 157, folder 2765, HHPL; Stokes to Greenwood, June 11, 1926, box 158, folder 2771, HHPL; Greenwood to Stokes, June 12, 1926, box 158, folder 2771, HHPL.

38. Safety Pledge, box 157, folder 2768, HHPL.

39. "The Courtesy Plan," *Ford News* 5L, no. 21 (September 1, 1925): 2.

40. DOC, "Would Find Whether Illiteracy Is Auto Accident Factor" (press release, August 24, 1924), box 159, folder 2781, HHPL; NCSHS, *Report of NCSHS* (Washington, DC, March 25, 1926), 6, box 159, folder 2784, HHPL; "Hurry Slowly," *Ford News* 1, no. 8 (February 15, 1921): 5; see also DOC, NCSHS, *Summary Report of Committee on Education* (December 7, 1924), box 159, folder 2781, HHPL; NSC, *Bulletin of the Education Section* 1, no. 1 (April 1, 1924): 1–2, box 157, folder 2765, HHPL; NSC, *War on Accidents*, 13; Eno, "Highway Traffic Regulation," 4–5; Ralph Winslow, Better Traffic Committee of Pittsburgh, to Hoover, December 11, 1926, box 158, folder 2772, HHPL; "Hoover's Drive to Make Roads Safe for Everybody," *Boston Transcript*, November 15, 1924, box 158, folder 2776, HHPL; "Good Drivers' League," *Ford News* 20, no. 4 (April 1940): 94. On early twentieth-century "safety-first campaigns" in the context of railroad accidents, see Welke, *Recasting*, 35–42.

41. "New Form of Punishment," *Ford News* 5L, no. 11 (April 11, 1925): 2; McClintock, *Street Traffic Control*, 199–200; William M. Tudor, District Manager, Public Safety Department, East Bay District, California State Automobile Association, to B. E. Martenstein, December 31, 1923, box 6, BPD Records; see also Rules and Regulations of the Citizen Police of Berkeley, carton 4, AVP.

42. BPD press release (December 31, 1923); "Decreasing Street Accidents, Police Work of Many Cities," *Ford News* 2L, no. 15 (June 1, 1922): 7; Van Schaack, "Automobile Accidents," 26.

43. Vollmer, *Police and Modern Society*, 140; see also NSC, *War on Accidents*, 14.

44. Roscoe Pound, "Criminal Justice and the American City," in *Criminal Justice in Cleveland: Reports of the Cleveland Foundation Survey of the Administration of Criminal Justice in Cleveland, Ohio*, ed. Roscoe Pound and Felix Frankfurter (Cleveland: Cleveland Foundation, 1922), 560–561; Pound, *Criminal Justice*, 213. On Pound and the problem of free will, see Thomas A. Green, *Freedom and Responsibility in American Legal Thought* (New York: Cambridge University Press, 2014), 55–96.

45. On Prohibition, see, for example, Richard F. Hamm, *Shaping the Eighteenth Amendment: Temperance Reform, Legal Culture, and the Polity, 1880–1920* (Chapel Hill: University of North Carolina Press, 1995); Lerner, *Dry Manhattan*.

46. See Morris R. Cohen, "Positivism and the Limits of Idealism in the Law," *Columbia Law Review* 27, no. 3 (1927): 237–250.

47. Vollmer, "Traffic Safety Meeting," 2; Vollmer, *Police and Modern Society*, 143, 145; Vollmer, "National Conference on Street and Highway Safety," 3; Wilcox, "Overproduction of Laws," 151–152; see also Robert Post, "Federalism, Positive Law, and the Emergence of the American Administrative State: Prohibition in the Taft Court Era," *William and Mary Law Review* 48, no. 1 (2006): 72–77.

48. BPD, "Minutes of Special Meetings Called for the Purpose of Organization and Education Held in the Cities of Fresno, Oakland and Los Angeles" (June 10, 1919), 2, box 48, BPD Records; J. Allen Davis and Harry V. Cheshire Jr., "California Motor Vehicle Legislation," *West's Annotated California Codes* 66 (St. Paul, MN: West, 1960), 14; California Motor Vehicle Act (1919), chap. 147, sec. 20(o); see also McClintock, *Street Traffic Control*, 104–110.

49. Ward v. Clark, 232 N.Y. 195, 198 (1921); McClintock, *Street Traffic Control*, 124.

50. Vollmer, *Police and Modern Society*, 138; Vollmer, "Police and the Traffic Problem," 2, 4; Miller McClintock, Paul G. Hoffman, and Rockwell Kent, "The Traffic Problem," *Life* 5, no. 1 (July 4, 1938): 43; James Willard Hurst, *The Growth of American Law: The Law Makers* (Boston: Little Brown, 1950), 10; see also "The White Line on the Road," *Ford News* 2L, no. 4 (April 1941): 91, 107.

51. McClintock, *Street Traffic Control*, 86–87; Vollmer, *Police and Modern Society*, 145; "Getting Automobile Sense," 348; Ben Connally, "Constitutional Law—Declaring a Statute Unconstitutional Because of Indefinite Terminology," *Texas Law Review* 11, no. 2 (1932–1933): 216; NCSHS, no title (press release, March 25, 1926), box 160, folder 2792, HHPL.

52. "Hoover Adjures Highway Safety," newspaper article, May 28, 1930, box 88, folder 1294, HHPL.

53. Connally, "Constitutional Law," 216; "Getting Automobile Sense," 348; McClintock, *Street Traffic Control*, 88. On radar technology, see Pagan Kennedy, "Who Made That Traffic Radar?" *NYT Magazine*, August 30, 2013; Rod Dornsife, *The Ticket Book* (La Jolla, CA: The Ticket Book, 1978), 94–205; *State*

Trooper: America's State Troopers and Highway Patrolmen, ed. Marilyn Olsen (Paducah, KY: Turner, 2001), 28–29.

54. California Motor Vehicle Act, sec. 22(a); McQuillin, *Law of Municipal Corporations*, sec. 932; "Safety, not Speed Rate, Consideration in New Traffic Rules," *TNPJ* 5, no. 6 (March 1920): 55; *Hall*, 119 Mass. 135; see also "New York Law Didn't Limit," *Ford News* 7L, no. 10 (March 15, 1927): 7.

55. John W. O'Connor, "The All-Important Traffic Problem," *TNPJ* 8, no. 6 (November 1921): 8; Herbert Hoover, "Address before NCSHS" (Washington, DC, December 15, 1924), 7, box 157, folder 2766, HHPL; Vollmer, *Police and Modern Society*, 145; Herbert Hoover, foreword to *Final Text of Uniform Vehicle Code*, by NCSHS (Washington, DC, 1926), v; see also McClintock, *Street Traffic Control*, 176–177.

56. Ex Parte Daniels, 183 Cal. 636, 639 (majority), 642–643, 647, 650 (Shaw, J., dissenting) (1920).

57. Meigs O. Frost, "Toll Mounts under Farce of State Control," newspaper article, September 18, 1927, box 158, folder 2773, HHPL; Herbert Hoover, "Opening Remarks before Second NCSHS" (Washington, DC, March 23, 1926), 8, box 159, folder 2784, HHPL; "Untangling Our Automobile Laws," *Scientific American* 130, no. 4 (April 1924): 232; NACC, *Facts & Figures* (New York, 1924), 18, 83.

58. Calvin Coolidge, *Address of the President of the United States to NCSHS* (n.p., December 1924), 5, box 37, folder 422, HHPL; Hoover, "Opening Remarks," 8; Herbert Hoover, "Address at the Closing Session of NCSHS" (Washington, DC, March 26, 1926), 3, box 49, folder 564, HHPL; Herbert Hoover, "Announcement of Calling of Third NCSHS" (Washington, DC, April 23, 1930), box 87, folder 1272, HHPL.

59. Hoover, "Address at the Closing Session," 3; Hoover, "Address before NCSHS," 8; NCSHS, "Press Summary of the Report of the Committee on Highway Engineering and Construction" (press release, November 28, 1924), 1, box 157, folder 2764, HHPL; NCSHS, *Model Municipal Traffic Ordinance* (Washington, DC, 1930), sec. 10; Richard F. Weingroff, "From Names to Numbers: The Origins of the U.S. Numbered Highway System," *AASHTO Quarterly* 76, no. 2 (1997): 11; see also McClintock, *Street Traffic Control*, 215–216; NCSHS, *Uniform Vehicle Code*, 90.

60. August Vollmer, "Traffic Control" (n.p., April 4, 1922), 4, carton 2, AVP; see the President's Highway Safety Conference, *Preliminary Revised Report of Committee on Laws and Ordinances* (Washington, DC, 1949), 18–19; A. B. Barber, "How the States Are Working towards a Uniform Motor Vehicle Code," *American City Magazine* 35, no. 6 (December 1926): 851–854; see also Norton, *Fighting Traffic*, 193.

61. Hoover, "Opening Remarks," 4; NACC, *Facts & Figures* (New York, 1927), 58; Hoover, "Announcement . . . Third NCSHS."

62. Hoover, "Opening Remarks," 3; Bertram Briggs, "The Protectors of Jamestown, N.Y.," *TNPJ* 10, no. 4 (October 1922): 17; Ernest Greenwood to Hoover, December 6, 1926, box 158, folder 2771, HHPL; see also "National Highway Safety Council's Traffic Law Enforcement Proposals Outlined," *U.S.*

Daily, March 13, 1926; "Auto Death Toll Fast Increasing," *New York American*, December 18, 1924.

63. John Hertz, "Address to NCSHS" (Washington, DC, n.d.), 3–5, box 160, folder 2793, HHPL.

64. Underhill Moore and Charles C. Callahan, "Law and Learning Theory: A Study in Legal Control," *YLJ* 53, no. 1 (1943): 3–5; Charles E. Clark, "Underhill Moore," *YLJ* 59, no. 2 (1950): 191; William O. Douglas, "Underhill Moore," *YLJ* 59, no. 2 (1950): 188. Underhill Moore was one of twenty on Karl Llewellyn's 1931 list of realists. Morton J. Horwitz, *The Transformation of American Law, 1870–1960: The Crisis of Legal Orthodoxy* (New York: Oxford University Press, 1992), 180–181; see also F. S. C. Northrop, "Underhill Moore's Legal Science: Its Nature and Significance," *YLJ* 59, no. 2 (1950); John Henry Schlegel, *American Legal Realism and Empirical Social Science* (Chapel Hill: University of North Carolina Press, 1995), 115–146. On 1930s criticisms of legal realism and empiricism as trivial, see Edward A. Purcell Jr., *The Crisis of Democratic Theory: Scientific Naturalism and the Problem of Value* (Lexington: University Press of Kentucky, 1973), 163.

65. Moore and Callahan, "Law and Learning Theory," 1–2, 7, 61, 78.

66. Moore and Callahan, "Law and Learning Theory," 21.

67. Root, "Citizen's Part," 11; Gveinbjorn Johnson, "Do We Need a Code of Ethics for the Public," in Johnsen, *Law Enforcement*, 213; August Vollmer and Alfred E. Parker, *Crime and the State Police* (Berkeley: University of California Press, 1935), 43. Other experiments in "nonpunitive control" took place around the same time as Moore's study. O. W. Wilson, *Police Administration* (New York: McGraw-Hill, 1950), 171–177.

68. Hoover, "Opening Remarks," 3; "Coolidge Deplores Increase in Crime: He Tells the Congregational Council that Religion Is the Only Remedy," *NYT*, October 21, 1925; see also "Hoover Urges Uniform Laws," *Washington Herald*, December 16, 1924, box 158, folder 2776, HHPL.

69. John A. Harriss, "Tower Flash System of Traffic Regulation," *National Police Bulletin* 1, no. 4 (October 31, 1921): 6–7, 11; "'Millionaire Deputy' Solves Traffic Problem for New York: Discoveries May Improve Local Street Travel System," *San Francisco Chronicle*, September 19, 1921.

70. Harriss, "Tower Flash," 6, 11.

71. Michel Foucault, "Panopticism," in *Discipline & Punish: The Birth of the Prison*, trans. Alan Sheridan (New York: Vintage Books, 1977), 195–228.

72. Laura A. Smith, "Yankee Traffic Cop a Wizard beside Frenchman," *TNPJ* 6, no. 2 (May 1920): 13.

73. "New York Police Determined to Make Towers Artistic," *TNPJ* 8, no. 6 (November 1921): 17; "Traffic Towers," *NYT*, November 22, 1921; see also George Warren, *Traffic Courts* (Boston: Little, Brown, 1942), 6–7 (Gallup poll showing 80 to 90 percent of those surveyed favoring "thorough enforcement of traffic laws").

74. William Renwick Riddell, "The Psychology of the Automobile," *TNPJ* 3, no. 4 (January 1919): 19. On contributory negligence, see, for example, Charles Fisk Beach Jr., *A Treatise on the Law of Contributory Negligence* (New

York: Baker, Voorhis, 1885), secs. 7, 25–31; Beisiegl v. New York Cent. R. Co., 40 N.Y. 9 (1870).

75. Crosby to Hoover, report, 1926, box 158, folder 2772, HHPL.

76. Daniel T. Rodgers, *Atlantic Crossings: Social Politics in a Progressive Age* (Cambridge, MA: Belknap Press of Harvard University Press, 1998); Report from Crosby to Hoover; Riddell, "Psychology," 19; "Hoover Starts Something Else," newspaper article, box 158, folder 2773, HHPL.

CHAPTER 2 • From Lumbering Foot Patrolmen to Motor-Mounted Policemen

1. Editor's foreword to "Forty Fighting Years: The Story of August Vollmer," by Robert Shaw, *TOPE*, May 24, 1938; Robert Shaw, "August Vollmer Risks Life in Raid on Bay Vice Den," *TOPE*, May 28, 1938. On Vollmer, see Alfred E. Parker, *The Berkeley Police Story* (Springfield, IL: Thomas, 1972), 5–39; O. W. Wilson, "August Vollmer," *Journal of Criminal Law and Criminology* 44, no. 1 (1953): 94, 97–100. On uniforms, see Eric H. Monkkonen, *Police in Urban America: 1860–1920* (New York: Cambridge University Press, 1981), 46, 53, 162–168.

2. Shaw, "Vollmer Risks Life"; Robert Shaw, "Marshal Installs New System, Sets Trap for Thief," *TOPE*, June 2, 1938; Robert Shaw, "Young Marshal in Hot Pursuit of Store Bandit," *TOPE*, June 3, 1938; see also "Signal Lamps Call Police," *LAT*, August 12, 1904; Gene E. Carte and Elaine H. Carte, *Police Reform in the United States: The Era of August Vollmer, 1905–1932* (Berkeley: University of California Press, 1975), 22.

3. On progressivism and expertise, see Thomas C. Leonard, *Illiberal Reformers: Race, Eugenics and American Economics in the Progressive Era* (Princeton, NJ: Princeton University Press, 2016), 27–54. On the Progressive Era generally, see, for example, Barbara Young Welke, *Law and the Borders of Belonging in the Long Nineteenth Century United States* (New York: Cambridge University Press, 2010); Michael Willrich, *City of Courts: Crime, Law, and Social Policy in Chicago, 1880–1930* (New York: Cambridge University Press, 2003); Nayan Shah, *Contagious Divides: Epidemics and Race in San Francisco's Chinatown* (Berkeley: University of California Press, 2001); Daniel T. Rodgers, *Atlantic Crossings: Social Politics in a Progressive Age* (Cambridge, MA: Belknap Press of Harvard University Press, 1998); Robyn Muncy, *Creating a Female Dominion in Reform, 1890–1935* (New York: Oxford University Press, 1991); William E. Nelson, *The Roots of American Bureaucracy* (Cambridge, MA: Harvard University Press, 1982); Stephen Skowronek, *Building a New American State: The Expansion of National Administrative Capacities* (New York: Cambridge University Press, 1982).

4. August Vollmer, "Police Progress in Practice and Theory," *American City* 43, no. 3 (September 1930): 111–112; August Vollmer, "The Future Policeman" (n.p., May 9, 1931), box 48, BPD Records. On Vollmer's vision, see August Vollmer, "Police Progress in the Past Twenty-Five Years," *Journal of Criminal Law and Criminology* 24, no. 1 (1933): 161–175. On Vollmer and police professionalism, see Samuel Walker, *A Critical History of Police Reform: The Emergence of Professionalism* (Lexington, MA: Lexington Books, 1977), 53–78.

5. Vollmer to George Martin, August 13, 1924, box 40, AVP; F. M. Kreml, Director, Department of Police, Bureau of Accident Prevention, City of Evanston, Illinois, to Vollmer, April 4, 1933, box 36, AVP; Stuart M. Chambers, "Duluth's Military Police Force," *TNPJ* 8, no. 3 (July 1921): 4; J. E. Regan, "Chief Girvin's Buffalo Police," *TNPJ* 2, no. 4 (July 1918): 7; see also W. L. Rook, "Youngstown's Police, with Watkins at the Head," *TNPJ* 1, no. 6 (March 1918): 24.

6. "The 'Traffic Cop,'" *TNPJ* 6, no. 6 (September 1920): 23; Ernest Greenwood, "The Traffic Problem," *Evening Star, Washington, D.C.*, September 8, 1924; Miller McClintock, *Street Traffic Control* (New York: McGraw-Hill, 1925), 193; LAPD, *Annual Report* (1913), 48, box B-1061, LACA; see NACC, "Sweeping Reductions in Motor Fatalities" (press release, February 27, 1925), box 157, folder 2767, HHPL; NCSHS, *Report of NCSHS* (Washington, DC, March 25, 1926), 5, box 159, folder 2784, HHPL.

7. Regan, "Buffalo Police," 7; A. B. Ogle, "Detroit—The Police Force Efficient," *TNPJ* 2, no. 7 (October 1918): 3, 6; "Cleveland's 'Finest,' under Chief Smith," *TNPJ* 3, no. 5 (February 1919): 3–4; G. V. Straus, "The Newark, N.J., Police," *TNPJ* 7, no. 5 (March 1921): 3–4; S. Lee McBride, "The Pittsburgh Bureau of Police," *TNPJ* 3, no. 4 (January 1919): 5; Greenwood, "Traffic Problem" (NYC police); G. G. Evans, "The Police Force of Seattle, Queen City of the Northwest," *TNPJ* 5, no. 3 (December 1919): 6. Detroit's allotment of 20 percent appears to have been the norm. The National Automobile Chamber of Commerce reported in 1925 that cities with a population between 25,000 and 100,000 assigned between 17 and 18 percent of their police forces to traffic duty. NACC, *Facts & Figures* (New York, 1925), 77. On the expansion of state police forces, see Edwin H. Sutherland and C. E. Gehlke, "Crime and Punishment," in President's Research Committee on Social Trends, *Recent Social Trends in the United States*, vol. 2 (New York: McGraw-Hill, 1933), 1140–1141.

8. "The Traffic Officers and Motor Lights," *TNPJ* 6, no. 2 (May 1920): 13 (my italics); August Vollmer, *The Police and Modern Society* (Berkeley: University of California Press, 1936), 146. On the costs of hiring traffic cops, see Peter D. Norton, *Fighting Traffic: The Dawn of the Motor Age in the American City* (Cambridge, MA: MIT Press, 2008), 57.

9. Spencer D. Irwin, "The Columbus, O., Police Department under Chief French," *TNPJ* 9, no. 5 (May 1922): 8; see also R. C. Jones, "The Police Bulwark of the Gateway to the West," *TNPJ* 9, no. 3 (March 1922): 77; "National Highway Safety Council's Traffic Law Enforcement Proposals Outlined," *U.S. Daily*, March 13, 1926 (hereafter, "Proposals Outlined"); McClintock, *Street Traffic Control*, 191.

10. August Vollmer, "Vice and Traffic—Police Handicaps," *Southern California Law Review* 1, no. 4 (1928): 329; "Policewomen's Work Is Praised," newspaper article, n.d., box 48, BPD Records.

11. Vollmer, "Vice and Traffic," 326.

12. Vollmer, "Vice and Traffic," 327–329.

13. Vollmer, "Vice and Traffic," 327; Vollmer, "Practice and Theory," 111. On politics and the LAPD, see "Our City Government: No. 8—The Police Department," *LAT*, October 5, 1924.

14. *Inaugural Address of Herbert Hoover* (Washington, DC, 1929), 5. On Prohibition enforcement, see Michael A. Lerner, *Dry Manhattan: Prohibition in New York City* (Cambridge, MA: Harvard University Press, 2007), 61–95; Lisa McGirr, *The War on Alcohol: Prohibition and the Rise of the American State* (New York: W. W. Norton, 2016), 121–155.

15. NCLOE, *Report on Lawlessness in Law Enforcement*, vol. 11 of *U.S. Wickersham Committee Reports* (Washington, DC, 1931).

16. NCLOE, *Report on Police*, by August Vollmer, vol. 14 of *U.S. Wickersham Committee Reports* (Washington, DC, 1931); NCLOE, *Report on the Enforcement of the Prohibition Laws*, vol. 1 of *U.S. Wickersham Committee Reports* (Washington, DC, 1931), 126–130, 146; Pierre du Pont, quoted in David E. Kyvig, *Repealing National Prohibition* (Chicago: University of Chicago Press, 1979), 113.

17. "The Cost of Enforcement," newspaper article, December 7, 1928, DAS, roll 48, vol. 334, NYCMA; see also Alfred E. Smith, "The Governor's Statement," *NYT*, June 2, 1923. On police abuse during prohibition, see, for example, McGirr, *War on Alcohol*, 67–102.

18. Iowa State Highway Commission, "Should Sale of High Speed Automobiles Be Prohibited by Law in Iowa," *Service Bulletin* 4, no. 7 (July 1916): 12–13; Warren G. Harding, "Address of the President to a Joint Session of Congress," 67th Cong., 1st sess., *Congressional Record* (April 12, 1921), 61, pt. 1:1921; Herbert Hoover, "Address before NCSHS" (Washington, DC, December 15, 1924), box 157, folder 2766, HHPL; "A Safety Conference," *Evening Star*, Washington, D.C., October 27, 1924; LAPD, *Annual Report* (1913), 49, box B-1061, LACA; LAPD, *Annual Report* (1937–1938), 43, box B-1061, LACA.

19. August Vollmer, "Police Problems" (speech, February 26, 1932), 5, box 46, AVP; *Revised Statute Laws of Louisiana* (Voorhies 1876), sec. 2274; Frank M. Cochran, "Chief Jenning's Toledo Police," *TNPJ* 9, no. 6 (June 1922): 137, 144; "Bill Proposes Removal of Speed Limit," *Coshocton Tribune*, January 18, 1929.

20. August Vollmer, "Depriving Criminals of Police Assistance," interview by University of California Radio Service (September 10, 1935), 3–5, carton 2, AVP.

21. Vollmer, "Depriving Criminals," 7. On the Pinkerton agency's anti-union activities, see, for example, J. Anthony Lukas, *Big Trouble: A Murder in a Small Western Town Sets Off a Struggle for the Soul of America* (New York: Simon & Schuster, 1997), 81–87; David A. Sklansky, "The Private Police," *UCLA Law Review* 46, no. 4 (1999): 1212–1217.

22. August Vollmer and Alfred E. Parker, *Crime and the State Police* (Berkeley: University of California Press, 1935), 24–26, 143; see also "To Organize Nation for Traffic Safety," *NYT*, April 11, 1924; Bruce Smith, *The State Police: Organization and Administration* (New York: Macmillan, 1925) 8–10; New York, Legislative Document No. 37, Special Message of the Governor to the Legislature, *Recommendations for the Improvement of Criminal Law Enforcement* (1936), 11, carton 5, AVP. On the history of American highways, see Earl Swift, *The Big Roads: The Untold Story of the Engineers, Visionaries, and Trailblazers Who Created the American Superhighway* (Boston: Houghton Mifflin Harcourt, 2011); Tom Lewis, *Divided Highways: Building*

the Interstate Highways, Transforming American Life (New York: Viking Penguin, 1997).

The automobile also increased the federal government's involvement in criminal matters that were traditionally within the states' domain. The trope of the interstate bandit, driving from town to town, prompted President Franklin D. Roosevelt to launch a "War on Crime." Within six months of his inaugural address, Congress introduced 105 crime bills, many of which passed. See Daniel Richman, "The Past, Present, and Future of Violent Crime Federalism," *Crime and Justice* 34, no. 1 (2006): 387–388; Claire Bond Potter, *War on Crime: Bandits, G-Men, and the Politics of Mass Culture* (New Brunswick, NJ: Rutgers University Press, 1998), 118–125; Kenneth O'Reilly, "A New Deal for the FBI: The Roosevelt Administration, Crime Control, and National Security," *Journal of American History* 69, no. 3 (1982): 638–658; see also Arthur C. Millspaugh, *Crime Control by the National Government* (Washington, DC: Brookings Institution, 1937).

23. Vollmer and Parker, *State Police*, 49–57; *State Trooper: America's State Troopers and Highway Patrolmen*, ed. Marilyn Olsen (Paducah, KY: Turner, 2001); Scott M. Fisher, *Iowa State Patrol* (Charleston, SC: Arcadia, 2013), 8–9, 18–20, 23–24.

24. A. D. Jacobson, "Minneapolis's Courageous Police Force," *TNPJ* 8, no. 4 (August 1921): 4; "For Better Protection," *LAT*, December 20, 1903; LAPD, *Annual Report* (1912), 5, box B-1061, LACA; see also *A Few Pointers Regarding Police, Both Special and Regular* (n.p., n.d.), box 48, BPD Records.

25. Harry McCormick, "Boston's One-Year-Old Police Force," *TNPJ* 6, no. 6 (September 1920): 7; L. F. McMahon, "Chief Schmidt Popular with His Men," *TNPJ* 7, no. 5 (March 1921): 22; DOC, "Public School Superintendents Aid Safety Campaign" (press release, May 5, 1925), box 160, folder 2792, HHPL; DOC, NCSHS, *Summary Report of Committee on Education* (December 7, 1924), 2, box 159, folder 2781, HHPL; Robert Shaw, "'Problem Boys' Made Members of Police Force," *TOPE*, June 20, 1938; see also F. H. Bargee, Principal, Scarritt School, Kansas City, "The Street Patrol of the Junior Safety Council," *Bulletin of the Education Section* 1, no. 1 (April 1, 1924): 4, box 157, folder 2765, HHPL.

26. Frederick J. Haskin, "Washington's Traffic Squad for Children," *TNPJ* 9, no. 2 (February 1922): 21.

27. H. B. Sommer, "The Police Forces of Tonawanda and North Tonawanda," *TNPJ* 6, no. 2 (May 1920): 3–4; George Brereton, "Looking Back: Ex-Director of the California Department of Justice Remembers His Years as a Patrolman under August Vollmer," interview by Jane Howard Robinson, *August Vollmer: Pioneer in Police Professionalism* (Berkeley: University of California, 1972), 395; August Vollmer, "Traffic Control" (n.p., April 4, 1922), 7, carton 2, AVP. For an account of nineteenth- and early twentieth-century police patrol, see Christopher Thale, "The Informal World of Police Patrol: New York City in the Early Twentieth Century," *Journal of Urban History* 33, no. 2 (2007): 183–216. On the policing of those on the margins of society, see, for example, Risa L. Goluboff, *Vagrant Nation: Police Power, Constitutional Change, and the Making of the 1960s*

(New York: Oxford University Press, 2016); Eric H. Monkkonen, *Police in Urban America, 1860–1920* (New York: Cambridge University Press, 1981).

28. "Says Providence Cares for 'Man on Street,'" *TNPJ* 6, no. 6 (September 1920): 45.

29. Vollmer, "Police Problems," 7; Vollmer, "Vice and Traffic," 330; Vollmer, *Police and Modern Society*, 145–146.

30. Arthur Woods, "Policeman and Public," *TNPJ* 6, no. 1 (April 1920): 13.

31. Bruce Cobb, Associate Magistrate, Traffic Court, New York, *Making the Road Safe* (1923), 20, box 157, folder 2767, HHPL.

32. Mary Sims, "Vollmer's Life and Work," review of "August Vollmer," by O. W. Wilson, *The Los Angeles Police Beat* (December 1953): 7, box B-2283, LACA; DOC, *Summary Report*, 3; J. H. Richmond, "What the Public Expects of the Police Force," *TNPJ* 5, no. 5 (February 1920): 39; "The 'Traffic Cop,'" *TNPJ* 6, no. 6 (September 1920): 23.

33. August Vollmer, *The Police Beat* (draft manuscript, 1929), 9, carton 2, AVP. Insurance organizations like the National Automobile Theft Bureau formed in response to the shortcomings of law enforcement in preventing and recovering stolen motor vehicles. See, for example, National Automobile Theft Bureau, *An Investigative Aid to the Law Enforcement Profession* (Chicago: National Automobile Theft Bureau, n.d.), NICB.

34. McClintock, *Street Traffic Control*, 201.

35. NCSHS, *Suggested Preliminary Draft of Report of Committee on Municipal Traffic Ordinances and Regulations* (Washington, DC, n.d.), 50, box 158, folder 2780, HHPL; NCSHS, *Model Municipal Traffic Ordinance* (Washington, DC, 1930), secs. 4, 53; McClintock, *Street Traffic Control*, 200.

36. Matthew J. Eder, "Second National Police Conference a Tremendous Success," *TNPJ* 10, no. 3 (September 1922): 38; James S. Gibbons, "Lona B. Day, Builder of the Scranton Police Force," *TNPJ* 3, no. 2 (December 1918): 5; McClintock, *Street Traffic Control*, 193–194; Fisher, *Iowa State Patrol*, 24.

37. Fisher, *Iowa State Patrol*, 24.

38. Fisher, *Iowa State Patrol*, 37; see also McClintock, *Street Traffic Control*, 195.

39. NCSHS, *Report to NCSHS* (Washington, DC, December 1924), 23, box 157, folder 2766, HHPL; Robert Shaw, "World Laughs at Schools for Officers," *TOPE*, June 14, 1938; Vollmer and Parker, *State Police*, 109, table 11; Robert E. Ahrens, "An Experimental Investigation of Police-Training Requisites" (Ph.D. diss., University of Southern California, 1938), 13–18; Cochran, "Toledo Police," 139; Vollmer, "Future Policeman." On Vollmer and police education, see "Chief Vollmer Heads U[niversity] of C[alifornia] Police School," newspaper article, n.d., box 48, BPD Records; August Vollmer, "Abstract of the 'Wickersham' Police Report," *Journal of Criminal Law and Criminology* 22, no. 5 (1932): 720–721. On professionalization, see Andrew Abbott, *The System of Professions: An Essay on the Division of Expert Labor* (Chicago: University of Chicago Press, 1988).

40. Kermit Hall, "L. B. Sullivan," in *100 Americans Making Constitutional History: A Biographical History*, ed. Melvin I. Urofsky (Washington, DC: CQ Press, 2004), 189–191; Northwestern Center for Public Safety, About Us, "A

Brief History of NUCPS," https://perma.cc/8X5U-9RZG; *New York Times Co. v. Sullivan*, 376 U.S. 254, 257–259 (1964); Tracey Maclin and Maria Savarese, "Martin Luther King Jr. and Pretext Stops (And Arrests): Reflections on How Far We Have Not Come Fifty Years Later," *University of Memphis Law Review* 49 (June 2018): 1–2. On police reformers and police schools, see Thomas A. Reppetto, *The Blue Parade, 1945–2012*, vol. 2 of *American Police: A History* (New York: Enigma Books, 2012), 32–33.

41. Daniel J. O'Brien, "Police Training and Education," *TNPJ* 9, no. 6 (June 1922): 28.

42. Los Angeles County Grand Jury, Committee on Public Safety, untitled (March 4, 1932), 2–3, box 23, folder 4, ACLUSC (my italics).

43. IACP, Code of Ethics, https://www.theiacp.org/resources/law-enforcement-code-of-ethics; Olsen, *State Trooper*, 116–117, 215; John E. Regan, "The Police Force of Buffalo, Queen City of the Lakes," *TNPJ* 6, no. 1 (April 1920): 45.

44. Robert L. Hofford, "Philadelphia Well-Organized Police Force," *TNPJ* 7, no. 3 (December 1920): 7; "Thank You, Please!," newspaper article, 1928, roll 48, vol. 332, NYCMA; see also "Polished Policemen," newspaper article, 1928, roll 48, vol. 332, NYCMA.

45. "Indianapolis Chief Favors Assessing Offending Motorists," *TNPJ* 9, no. 1 (January 1922): 57.

46. Hofford, "Philadelphia Well-Organized," 7. Nicholas Parrillo has also argued that "the proliferation of elaborate restrictions on conduct" has not led to more rule-bound official behavior, but rather "ever-greater subjective judgment, discretion, and forbearance in imposing—or, more accurately, refraining from imposing—the sanctions for such conduct." That is because, as he quotes a seventeenth-century Parliamentarian, enforcement "to the utmost" would be "unsufferable." In short, "subjective and discretionary decisions *not* to enforce the law . . . were (and are) necessary to sand off the hard edges of modern state power so it can win acceptance by the population." Nicholas Parrillo, *Against the Profit Motive: The Salary Revolution in American Government, 1780–1940* (New Haven, CT: Yale University Press, 2013), 4, 39–40, 278, 282.

47. Neal Dow Becker, *Road Rules and the Law of Automobiles* (New York: Erle W. Whitfield, 1910), secs. 44–49; "Proposals Outlined"; "Indianapolis Chief," 26; Burton W. Marsh, Director, Safety and Traffic Engineering Department, American Automobile Association, to Vollmer, May 8, 1935, box 1, AVP. On the history of traffic citations, see Floyd Feeney, *The Police and Pretrial Release* (Lexington, MA: Lexington Books, 1982), 14–16.

48. August Vollmer, "National Conference on Street and Highway Safety" (press release, Washington, DC, September 26, 1931), 1, carton 2, AVP; "Cleveland's 'Finest,' under Chief Smith," *TNPJ* 3, no. 5 (February 1919): 3. On the golden rule, see "Chief Henry C. Baker, of Racine, Wis.," *TNPJ* 4, no. 6 (September 1919): 14; Spencer Holst, "Toledo's Reorganized Police Force," *TNPJ* 3, no. 6 (March 1919): 3, 5; Walker, *Police Reform*, 95–98; Sidney L. Harring, *Policing a Class Society: The Experience of American Cities, 1865–1915* (New Brunswick, NJ: Rutgers University Press, 1983), 40.

49. O. W. Wilson, *Dallas Police Department* (Wichita, KS, 1934), 3, box 1, OWP.

50. George Warren, *Traffic Courts* (Boston: Little, Brown, 1942), 35–41; Newman F. Baker, "Traffic Tickets," *Journal of the American Institute of Criminal Law and Criminology* 30, no. 3 (1939): 389–395; Ahrens, "Police-Training Requisites," 54–55.

51. O'Brien, "Police Training," 28; "Indianapolis Chief," 26.

52. Raymond B. Fosdick, "European Police Systems," *TNPJ* 2, no. 2 (May 1918): 8, 26, 29.

53. Jerome Hall, "Police and Law in a Democratic Society," *Indiana Law Journal* 28, no. 2 (1953): 139.

54. "Proposals Outlined"; see also McClintock, *Street Traffic Control*, 204; Olsen, *State Troopers*, 19–20.

55. See "To Organize Nation"; "Hoover Urges Uniform Laws," *Washington Herald*, December 16, 1924, box 158, folder 2776, HHPL; Fisher, *Iowa State Patrol*, 35; McClintock, *Street Traffic Control*, 92–93; see also "The Police Motorcycle," *The Beat* (April 1951): 12, box B-2283, LACA.

56. "Speed in Police Work," *American City* 18, no. 1 (January 1918): 42; Taft to Francis Peabody, July 12, 1923, reel 255, Taft Papers; People v. Case, 220 Mich. 379, 388 (1922); "Cars and the Cops," *TNPJ* 6, no. 6 (September 1920): 23; Vollmer, "Practice and Theory," 111.

57. See Robert Shaw, "Berkeley Police Get First Autos and Draw Laugh," *TOPE*, June 14, 1938; "Speed in Police Work," 41; "The World's First Auto Police Patrol," *TNPJ* 4, no. 5 (August 1919): 10. It appears that even as late as 1950, municipalities had different policies on patrol cars. See O. W. Wilson, *Police Administration* (New York: McGraw-Hill, 1950), 101–102, 299.

58. August Vollmer, untitled (speech, Police Conference, University of Chicago, n.d.), 2, carton 4, AVP; "Detroit to Try Radio Phones on Patrol Wagons," *TNPJ* 8, no. 3 (July 1921): 19; Vollmer, "Practice and Theory," 111; see also Vollmer and Parker, *State Police*, 120–123.

59. Vollmer to Wilson, April 8, 1929, box 2, OWP; Vollmer to Wilson, March 31, 1928, box 2, OWP; Vollmer to Wilson, January 26, 1932, box 2, OWP; H. D. Hayes, DOC, Radio Division, Office of US Supervisor of Radio, to Vollmer, March 3, 1930, box 26, AVP.

60. Herbert A. Wilson, Boston Police Commissioner, to Vollmer, February 25, 1930, box 26, AVP; Vollmer to Wilson, January 26, 1932; see also E. H. Barber, Duluth, Minnesota Chief of Police, to Vollmer, February 24, 1930, box 26, AVP; John L. Miles, Kansas City, Missouri, Chief of Police, to Vollmer, February 22, 1930, box 26, AVP.

61. Vollmer, "Practice and Theory," 111; Vollmer, "Abstract," 721; see also Vollmer and Parker, *State Police*, 1–4; State v. Watson, 209 N.C. 229 (1936).

62. Sutherland and Gehlke, "Crime and Punishment," 1128–1129; J. W. Collins, "Policing Dayton, O., the 'Gem City,'" *TNPJ* 1, no. 4 (January 1918): 20. On crime rates, see Clarence S. Darrow, "Crime and the Alarmists," *Harper's Monthly Magazine* 153 (October 1926): 536–537. On Ford squads of other police departments, see, for example, Ogle, "Detroit," 3; John M. Platt, "The Police of Newport News, Va.," *TNPJ* 10, no. 4 (October 1922): 35.

63. William Young, "Combatting the Automobile Thief," *TNPJ* 3, no. 6 (March 1919): 17; LAPD, "Daily Bulletin," November 27, 1922, box B-2280, LACA; see also Homer B. Cross, "Out of the Past," *Guardian* (Los Angeles: 1937): 283, box C2013, LACA; Jerome Hall, *Theft, Law and Society* (Boston: Little, Brown, 1935). On auto theft, see Sutherland and Gehlke, "Crime and Punishment," 1135; see also John A. Heitmann and Rebecca H. Morales, *Stealing Cars: Technology and Society from the Model T to the Gran Torino* (Baltimore: Johns Hopkins University Press, 2014), 12–17; Willrich, *City of Courts*, 290; James J. Flink, *The Automobile Age* (Cambridge, MA: MIT Press, 1988), 160.

64. Heitmann and Morales, *Stealing Cars*, 14; Automobile Protective and Information Bureau, *Annual Report* (Chicago: Automobile Protective and Information Bureau, 1921), NICB; B. W. McCay, "The Auto as a Factor in Crime," *TNPJ* 8, no. 4 (August 1921): 15; *Case*, 220 Mich. at 388; "More about the Smooth Wiles of the Auto Thief," *Literary Digest* 66, no. 3 (July 17, 1920): 78; Lenoir v. State, 132 So. 325, 326 (Miss. 1931).

65. August Vollmer, untitled (speech, International Police Chiefs' Association, n.d.), 4–5, box 48, BPD Records; "Monograms on Radiator Caps Is New Practice," *PM* 25, no. 4 (April 1916): 592; see also Albert Sidney Gregg, "Training Men to Hear and See Straight," *TNPJ* 8, no. 4 (August 1921): 11.

66. National Automobile Theft Bureau, *75th Anniversary 1912-1987* (Palos Hills, IL: National Automobile Theft Bureau, 1987), 56, NICB; Heitmann and Morales, *Stealing Cars*, 17 (1916 insurance company pamphlet), 18 (Bosco ad), 51 (locks); McCay, "Auto as a Factor," 15.

67. Vollmer, "Police Problems," 3 (1932 DOJ statistics); "Chicago Asks for New Crime Laws," *TNPJ* 7, no. 5 (March 1921): 31; National Motor Vehicle Theft (Dyer) Act, 41 Stat. 324 (1919); Morton L. Wallerstein, ed., *Pollard's Code Biennial* (Richmond: Everett Waddey, 1920), chap. 57, sec. 11; "Motors for Police Use Needed," *TNPJ* 6, no. 5 (August 1920): 20.

68. On the Toledo Police Department, see Heitmann and Morales, *Stealing Cars*, 32–33; see also McCay, "Auto as a Factor," 15–16; William B. Naughton, "Policing the Second City of the United States," *TNPJ* 6, no. 5 (August 1920): 5; Young, "Combatting," 17; Don J. Williams, "The Police of the 'Gem City of the Granite State,'" *TNPJ* 5, no. 2 (November 1919): 41; Harvey T. Blakeslee, "Chief Jenkins's Portland, Ore., Police Force," *TNPJ* 9, no. 2 (February 1922): 4; Cochran, "Toledo Police," 11; Automobile Protective and Information Bureau, *Stolen Automobiles (Methods to Employ in Identification and Recovery)* (Chicago: Automobile Protective and Information Bureau, n.d.), NICB.

69. LAPD, *Annual Report* (1956), 18–19, box C2003, LACA.

70. Matthews v. State, 67 Okla. Crim. 203 (1939); Regan, "Buffalo Police," 6.

71. Vollmer, *Police Beat*, 6–7; see also George Allen, "On Patrol," *Guardian*, 49.

72. Vollmer, *Police Beat*, 10–13; BPD, Officers Meeting (minutes, October 12, 1926), box 48, BPD Records. For a description of patrol in New York City, see Christopher Thale, "Assigned to Patrol: Neighborhoods, Police and Changing Deployment Practices in New York City before 1930," *Journal of Social History* 37, no. 4 (2004): 1037–1064. On the "one-man car," see LAPD, *Annual Report* (1954), 12, box C2003, LACA.

73. Vollmer to Wilson, January 26, 1932; Walker, *Police Reform*, 144; Wilson, *Police Administration*, 99.

74. Blakeslee, "Chief Jenkins's," 61; Jack H. Hodgkinson, "The Up-To-Date Police Force of Port Huron, Mich.," *TNPJ* 9, no. 3 (March 1922): 26.

75. NACC, *Facts & Figures* (New York, 1923), 4, 26; Vollmer to Wilson, January 26, 1932; Vollmer to Wilson, April 8, 1929; John Chisholm, "Crime Prevention Problems," *The Beat* (January 1951): 31, box B-2283, LACA.

76. Vollmer, "Future Policeman," 2; BPD, "Minutes of Special Meetings called for the purpose of organization and education held in the Cities of Fresno, Oakland and Los Angeles" (June 10, 1919), 3, box 48, BPD Records; Vollmer to Wilson, September 23, 1936, box 2, OWP.

77. Vollmer, "Practice and Theory," 111; Vollmer to Wilson, April 4, 1928, box 2, OWP; Vollmer to J. A. Greening, June 6, 1933, box 42, folder 3, AVP.

78. Peter J. O'Toole Jr., "Newark's Able Body of Policemen," *TNPJ* 4, no. 1 (April 1919): 3; see also Carl A. Schroeder, "The Fort Wayne Police, under Dayton F. Abbott," *TNPJ* 2, no. 2 (May 1918): 12.

79. Thomas F. Adams, *Police Patrol: Tactics and Techniques* (New Jersey: Prentice-Hall, 1971), 1, 37. On motorization, see Samuel Walker, *The Police in America: An Introduction* (New York: McGraw-Hill, 1983), 13. On 1960s reformers, see Herman Goldstein, "Police Response to Urban Crisis," *Public Administration Review* 28, no. 5 (1968): 417–422; George L. Kelling, "Toward New Images of Policing," review of *Problem-Oriented Policing*, by Herman Goldstein, *Law & Social Inquiry* 17, no. 3 (1992): 554–555. On falling crime rates from 1930s to 1950s, see, for example, William J. Stuntz, "*Bordenkircher v. Hayes:* Plea Bargaining and the Decline of the Rule of Law," in *Criminal Procedure Stories*, ed. Carol S. Steiker (New York: Foundation, 2006), 360, 360n31.

80. Virginia State Police, History, https://perma.cc/43TD-7DCK; Olsen, *State Trooper*, 102; Vollmer and Parker, *State Police*, 52–57, 160; New York, *Message of the Governor*, 11; see also Vollmer, "Past Twenty-Five Years," 174–175; Smith, *State Police*, 42–43; Fisher, *Iowa State Patrol*, 22; Sutherland and Gehlke, "Crime and Punishment," 1140–1141.

81. "The Police Motorcycle," *The Beat* (April 1951): 13; LAPD, *Annual Report* (1953), 5, box C2003, LACA; "The Automobile Peril," *TNPJ* 7, no. 4 (January 1921): 18; Elliot Underwood, "The Edgewater, N.J., Police," *TNPJ* 7, no. 4 (January 1921): 20; see also LAPD, *Annual Report* (1912), 8, box B-1061, LACA; "Highway Protection," *TNPJ* 6, no. 6 (September 1920): 23.

82. LAPD, *Annual Report* (1920), 4, box B-1061, LACA; LAPD, *Annual Report* (1912), 7–8, box B-1061, LACA; LAPD, *Annual Report* (1902), box B-2294, LACA.

CHAPTER 3 • The Automotive Fourth Amendment

Epigraph (Roy): Excerpt from *The Ministry of Utmost Happiness: A Novel* by Arundhati Roy, copyright © 2017 by Arundhati Roy. Used by permission of Arundhati Roy and Alfred A. Knopf, an imprint of the Knopf Doubleday Publishing Group, a division of Penguin Random House LLC. All rights reserved.

1. Carroll v. United States, 267 U.S. 132, 171–174 (1925) (McReynolds, J., dissenting); Transcript of Record, Carroll v. United States, 267 U.S. 132 (1925) (No. 15), 4–5, 7–13; "List Prices and Weights," *Automobile Trade Journal* 25, no. 5 (1920): 105–106.

2. National Prohibition (Volstead) Act, 41 Stat. 305 (1919).

3. Brief of Plaintiffs in Error on Reargument, Carroll v. United States (No. 15), 2 (hereafter, *Carroll*, Petitioners' Brief).

4. Substituted Brief for the United States on Reargument, Carroll v. United States, 267 U.S. 132 (1925) (No. 15), 77 (hereafter, *Carroll*, Government's Brief); *Carroll*, Petitioners' Brief, 13.

5. Even as late as 1937, federal law enforcement personnel numbered about 17,000, and of these, about 10,000 belonged to the Coast Guard. By contrast, the 1930 Census counted 169,270 local law enforcement officers, a number that included detectives, marshals, constables, sheriffs, and policemen. Arthur C. Millspaugh, *Crime Control by the National Government* (Washington, DC: Brookings Institution, 1937), 283. On the relative prevalence of searches before and after Prohibition, see Victor House, "Search and Seizure Limits under the Prohibition Act," *NYT*, February 11, 1923. On customs searches, see Andrew Wender Cohen, *Contraband: Smuggling and the Birth of the American Century* (New York: W. W. Norton, 2015).

6. See People v. Huntington, 1 N.Y.S. 526 (1888); Anderson v. Cowles, 72 Conn. 335 (1899); see also Thomas Y. Davies, "Recovering the Original Fourth Amendment," *Michigan Law Review* 98, no. 3 (1999): 620–627. On state prohibition, see William J. Novak, *The People's Welfare: Law and Regulation in Nineteenth-Century America* (Chapel Hill: University of North Carolina Press, 1996), 171–189.

7. Robert Shaw, "Young Marshal in Hot Pursuit of Store Bandit," *TOPE*, June 3, 1938; see also Smith v. Commonwealth, 197 Ky. 192 (1923).

8. On damages, see, for example, Petit v. Colmary, 4 Penne. 266 (Del. Super. Ct. 1903); Scott v. Donald, 165 U.S. 58 (1897); Cotter v. Plumer, 72 Wis. 476 (1888); Theodore Sedgwick, *A Treatise on the Measure of Damages*, vol. 1 (New York: Baker, Voorhis, 1868), 146–165. Carroll's lawyer pointed to the insufficiency of damages as justification for the exclusionary rule. See *Carroll*, Petitioners' Brief, 15–16.

9. Interstate Commission on Crime, *Handbook on Interstate Crime Control* (Newark, NJ, 1942), 16–17.

10. See, for example, Bowman v. Chicago and Northwestern Railroad Co., 125 U.S. 465 (1888); Leisy v. Hardin, 135 U.S. 100 (1890); State v. Intoxicating Liquors, 95 Me. 140 (1901); State v. Intoxicating Liquors, 101 Me. 430 (1906); State v. Woodland, 89 Kan. 641 (1913; see also Richard F. Hamm, *Shaping the Eighteenth Amendment: Temperance Reform, Legal Culture, and the Polity, 1880–1920* (Chapel Hill: University of North Carolina Press, 1995), 56–91, 203–226.

11. Town of Blacksburg v. Beam, 88 S.E. 441, 441 (S.C. 1916). On forfeiture, see, for example, Skinner v. Thomas, 171 N.C. 98 (1916); Cox v. State, 70 Okla. 131 (1918); Gunn v. Atwell, 148 Ga. 137 (1918); State v. Jones-Hanson-Cadillac Co., 103 Neb. 353 (1919); H. T. Armington & Sons v. State, 24 Ga. App. 75 (1919); State v. Davis, 55 Utah 54 (1919); Landers v. Commonwealth, 126 Va. 780

(1919); State v. Crosswhite, 203 Ala. 586 (1920); Hoover v. People, 68 Colo. 249 (1920). On the founding-era history of civil forfeiture, see Caleb Nelson, "The Constitutionality of Civil Forfeiture," *YLJ* 125, no. 8 (2016): 2462–2467. On the significance of the independent farmer, see Victoria Saker Woeste, "Agriculture and the State, 1789–2000," in *The Twentieth Century and After (1920–)*, vol. 3 of *The Cambridge History of Law in America*, ed. Michael Grossberg and Christopher Tomlins (Cambridge: Cambridge University Press, 2008), 522–562; Bruce H. Mann, *Republic of Debtors: Bankruptcy in the Age of American Independence* (Cambridge, MA: Harvard University Press, 2002), 127–128.

12. John H. Wigmore, "Using Evidence Obtained by Illegal Search and Seizure," *ABA Journal* 8, no. 8 (1922): 479; House, "Search and Seizure." On nineteenth-century regulation, see Novak, *People's Welfare*.

13. Weeks v. United States, 232 U.S. 383 (1914).

14. Asher L. Cornelius, *The Law of Search and Seizure* (Indianapolis: Bobbs-Merrill, 1926), iii; Lamb v. State, 60 P. 2d 219, 219 (Okla. Crim. 1936); Jimmie Lewis Franklin, *Born Sober: Prohibition in Oklahoma, 1907–1959* (Norman: University of Oklahoma Press, 1971), 173–195.

15. House, "Search and Seizure"; see also Robert Post, "Federalism, Positive Law, and the Emergence of the American Administrative State: Prohibition in the Taft Court Era," *William and Mary Law Review* 48, no. 1 (2006): 116–119, 117–118nn395–396.

16. Commonwealth v. Schwanda, 19 Northampton Cty. Rep. 37, 43 (1923); Frederic A. Johnson, "Some Constitutional Aspects of Prohibition Enforcement," *Central Law Journal* 97 (1924): 114, 122–123; Zechariah Chafee Jr., review of *Ill Starred Prohibition Cases: A Study in Judicial Pathology*, by Forrest R. Black, *HLR* 45, no. 5 (1932): 949. On law enforcement failures during Prohibition, see NCLOE, *Report on the Enforcement of the Prohibition Laws*, vol. 1 of *U.S. Wickersham Committee Reports* (Washington, DC, 1931), 44–51. On repeal efforts motivated by law enforcement abuse, see Michael A. Lerner, *Dry Manhattan: Prohibition in New York City* (Cambridge, MA: Harvard University Press, 2007), 227–254.

17. Orick v. State, 105 So. 465, 471 (Miss. 1925); People v. Adams, 176 N.Y. 351 (1903); People v. Defore, 242 N.Y. 13, 21 (1926); see also Wesley MacNeil Oliver, "The Neglected History of Criminal Procedure, 1850–1940," *Rutgers Law Review* 62, no. 2 (2010): 498, 498n279, 503–505.

18. States that adopted the exclusionary rule in prohibition cases are Atz v. Andrews, 84 Fla. 43 (1922); Flum v. State, 193 Ind. 585 (1923); Youman v. Commonwealth, 189 Ky. 152 (1920); Tucker v. State, 128 Miss. 211 (1922); Hoyer v. State, 180 Wis. 407 (1923); State v. Arregui, 44 Idaho 43 (1927); People v. Castree, 311 Ill. 392 (1924); People v. Marxhausen, 204 Mich. 559 (1919); State v. Owens, 302 Mo. 348 (1924); Gore v. State, 24 Okla. Crim. 394 (1923); State v. Gooder, 57 S.D. 619 (1930); Hughes v. State, 145 Tenn. 544 (1922); State v. Gibbons, 118 Wash. 171 (1922); State v. Andrews, 91 W. Va. 720 (1922).

States that adopted the exclusionary rule in nonprohibition cases are State v. Sheridan, 121 Iowa 164 (1903); State v. George, 32 Wyo. 223 (1924).

State courts that rejected the exclusionary rule in prohibition cases are Massantonio v. People, 77 Colo. 392 (1925); State v. Chuchola, 32 W. W. Harr. 133, 120 A. 212 (Del. 1922); State v. Dillon, 34 N.M. 366 (1929); State v. Fahn,

53 N.D. 203 (1925); Commonwealth v. Dabbierio, 290 Pa. 174 (1927); Welchek v. State, 93 Tex. Cr. R. 271 (1923); State v. Aime, 62 Utah 476 (1923); Hall v. Commonwealth, 138 Va. 727 (1924); Banks v. State, 207 Ala. 179 (1922); Benson v. State, 149 Ark. 633 (1921); State v. Reynolds, 101 Conn. 224 (1924); State v. Johnson, 116 Kan. 58 (1924); State v. Schoppe, 113 Me. 10 (1915); Meisinger v. State, 155 Md. 195 (1928); Commonwealth v. Wilkins, 243 Mass. 356 (1923); State v. Pluth, 157 Minn. 145 (1923); Billings v. State, 109 Neb. 596 (1923); State v. Agalos, 79 N.H. 241 (1919); State v. Simmons, 183 N.C. 684 (1922).

States that rejected the exclusionary rule in nonprohibition cases are Argetakis v. State, 24 Ariz. 599 (1923); People v. Mayen, 188 Cal. 237 (1922); State v. Fleckinger, 152 La. 337 (1922); State v. Chin Gim, 47 Nev. 431 (1924); State v. Black, 5 N.J. Misc. 48 (1926); State v. Lindway, 131 Ohio St. 166 (1936); Jackson v. State, 156 Ga. 647 (1923); People v. Defore, 242 N.Y. 13 (1926); State v. Folkes, 174 Or. 568 (1944); State v. Green, 121 S.C. 230 (1922); State v. Stacy, 104 Vt. 379 (1932).

For historical arguments that prohibition led to the development of the twentieth-century state, see Novak, *People's Welfare*, 188–189; Lisa McGirr, *The War on Alcohol: Prohibition and the Rise of the American State* (New York: W. W. Norton, 2016), 189–229.

19. *Beam*, 88 S.E. at 441. The South Carolina precedent that had rejected the exclusionary rule was State v. Atkinson, 18 S.E. 1021, 1024–1025 (S.C. 1894).

20. State v. Harley, 92 S.E. 1034, 1035 (S.C. 1917); *Beam*, 88 S.E. at 441.

21. State v. Green, 114 S.E. 317, 318–319 (S.C. 1922).

22. State v. Pauley, 192 N.W. 91, 96–97 (N.D. 1922) (Robinson, J., dissenting); House, "Search and Seizure."

23. *Carroll*, Petitioners' Brief, 15.

24. See Post, "Federalism, Positive Law," 94–96.

25. *Carroll*, Government's Brief, 20, 42–44.

26. Morton Keller, *In Defense of Yesterday: James M. Beck and the Politics of Conservatism, 1861–1939* (New York: Coward-McCann, 1958), 178.

27. On classical legal thought, see Morgan Cloud, "The Fourth Amendment during the *Lochner* Era: Privacy, Property, and Liberty in Constitutional Theory," *Stanford Law Review* 48, no. 3 (1996): 566–631; Keith D. Revell, "The Road to *Euclid v. Ambler*: City Planning, State-Building, and the Changing Scope of the Police Power," *Studies in American Political Development* 13, no. 1 (1999): 50–145; William M. Wiecek, *The Lost World of Classical Legal Thought: Law and Ideology in America, 1886–1937* (New York: Oxford University Press, 1998); Morton J. Horwitz, *The Transformation of American Law, 1870–1960: The Crisis of Legal Orthodoxy* (New York: Oxford University Press, 1992), 9–31; Thomas C. Grey, "Langdell's Orthodoxy," *University of Pittsburgh Law Review* 45, no. 1 (1983): 1–53; Duncan Kennedy, "The Structure of Blackstone's Commentaries," *Buffalo Law Review* 28, no. 2 (1979): 205–382. But see David E. Bernstein, *Rehabilitating* Lochner: *Defending Individual Rights against Progressive Reform* (Chicago: University of Chicago Press, 2011), 47–49; Christopher Tomlins, "Necessities of State: Police, Sovereignty, and the Constitution," *Journal of Policy History* 20, no. 1 (2008): 59; Markus Dirk Dubber, *The Police Power: Patriarchy and the Foundations of American Government* (New York: Columbia

University Press, 2005), 190–210; Barry Cushman, *Rethinking the New Deal Court: The Structure of a Constitutional Revolution* (New York: Oxford University Press, 1998). On gender, see Barbara Young Welke, *Law and the Borders of Belonging in the Long Nineteenth Century United States* (New York: Cambridge University Press, 2010).

28. Boyd v. United States, 116 U.S. 616, 623 (1886); William G. Webster, *An Explanatory and Pronouncing Dictionary of the English Language* (Philadelphia: Lippincott, 1856), 455. On the classical Fourth Amendment, see Cloud, "Fourth Amendment," 576–577. On the *Boyd* case, see Cohen, *Contraband*, 260–265.

29. NYC police commissioner, quoted in Marilynn S. Johnson, *Street Justice: A History of Police Violence in New York City* (Boston: Beacon, 2003), 120 (my italics); Christopher G. Tiedeman, *A Treatise on the Limitations of Police Power in the United States Considered from Both a Civil and Criminal Standpoint* (St. Louis: F. H. Thomas Law Book, 1886), 83–84 (my italics).

30. Tiedeman, *Treatise*, 84–85; see also Kurtz v. Moffit, 115 U.S. 487, 498–499 (1885); William S. Harlow, *Duties of Sheriffs and Constables* (San Francisco: Sumner Whitney, 1884), sec. 399.

31. Novak, *People's Welfare*, 51–82, 149–171.

32. Not until the twentieth century did courts recognize a warrant exception for houses. The first reported case recognizing the doctrine of hot pursuit of a suspect into a home was decided in 1934. Adkins v. State, 42 Ariz. 534, 543–544 (1934). The US Supreme Court first recognized this doctrine in 1967. Warden, Maryland Penitentiary v. Hayden, 387 U.S. 294, 298–299 (1967).

33. *Carroll*, Government's Brief, 21, 72.

34. Moore v. State, 103 So. 483, 496 (Miss. 1925) (Ethridge, J., dissenting); People v. Case, 220 Mich. 379, 397 (1922) (Wiest, J., dissenting); Park v. United States, 294 F. 776, 789 (1st Cir. 1924) (Anderson, J., dissenting); see also Millette v. State, 148 So. 788, 792 (Miss. 1933); State v. De Ford, 120 Or. 444, 459 (1926). For definition of "effects," see Alexander M. Burrill, *Burrill's Law Dictionary*, vol. 1 (New York: Baker, Voorhis, 1850), 533; Henry Campbell Black, *Black's Law Dictionary*, 3rd ed. (St. Paul, MN: West, 1933), 642.

35. Virginia Scharff, *Taking the Wheel: Women and the Coming of the Motor Age* (New York: Free Press, 1991), 125 (car ads); Robert S. Lynd and Helen Merrell Lynd, *Middletown: A Study in American Culture* (New York: Harcourt, Brace, 1929), 7, 257; Vincent Bryan and Gus Edwards, "In My Merry Oldsmobile," in *Favorite Songs of the Nineties: Complete Original Sheet Music for 89 Songs*, ed. Robert A. Fremont (New York: Dover, 1973), 151. See also Beth L. Bailey, *From Front Porch to Back Seat: Courtship in Twentieth-Century America* (Baltimore: Johns Hopkins University Press, 1988), 86; David L. Lewis, "Sex and the Automobile: From Rumble Seats to Rockin' Vans," in *The Automobile and American Culture*, ed. David L. Lewis and Laurence Goldstein (1980; Ann Arbor: University of Michigan Press, 1983), 125; James J. Flink, *The Automobile Age* (Cambridge, MA: MIT Press, 1988), 160–162.

36. *Carroll*, Government's Brief, 47–48, 50, quoting Laws of the General Assembly of the Commonwealth of Pennsylvania (1923), sec. 23.

37. *Case*, 220 Mich. at 388; Commonwealth v. Street, 3 Pa. D. & C. 783, 790 (Pa. Ct. of Quarter Sessions 1923). On "regulating the running of automobiles,"

see Eugene McQuillin, *A Treatise on the Law of Municipal Corporations*, vol. 3 (Chicago: Callaghan, 1912), sec. 935. On public rights to highways, see Novak, *People's Welfare*, 121–131.

38. Olmstead v. United States, 277 U.S. 438, 457 (1928).

39. Maul v. United States, 274 U.S. 501, 524 (1927) (Brandeis, J., concurring).

40. *Olmstead*, 277 U.S. at 478 (Brandeis, J., dissenting); Samuel D. Warren and Louis D. Brandeis, "The Right to Privacy," *HLR* 4, no. 5 (1890): 214 (my italics); see also Charles E. Colman, "About Ned," *HLR Forum* 129, no. 3 (2016): 128, 128n5, 148–151; Sarah E. Igo, *The Known Citizen: A History of Privacy in Modern America* (Cambridge, MA: Harvard University Press, 2018), 33–44.

41. Melvin I. Urofsky, *Louis D. Brandeis: A Life* (New York: Schocken Books, 2009), 356, 693; David M. Dorsen, *Henry Friendly: Greatest Judge of His Era* (Cambridge, MA: Harvard University Press, 2012), 29–30; see also David E. Bernstein, "From Progressivism to Modern Liberalism: Louis D. Brandeis as a Transitional Figure in Constitutional Law," *Notre Dame Law Review* 89, no. 5 (2014): 2034–2037. For a different theory of Brandeis's contradictory positions in *Carroll* and *Olmstead*, see Post, "Federalism, Positive Law," 124–125n406, 136–137.

42. *Street*, 3 Pa. D. & C. at 788; *Case*, 220 Mich. at 383, 389.

43. United States v. Rembert, 284 F. 996, 1004 (S.D. Tex. 1922); Newton v. State, 223 P. 195, 196 (Okla. Crim. 1923); Volstead Act, secs. 21, 29. Prohibition cases before 1929 usually dealt with misdemeanors. That changed in 1929, when Congress passed the Increased Penalties Act to respond to flagrant violations of the Volstead Act.

44. *Street*, 3 Pa. D. & C. at 791; *Case*, 220 Mich. at 390 (Wiest, J., dissenting); see also *Newton*, 223 P. at 196; United States v. Fenton, 268 F. 221, 222 (D. Mont. 1920).

45. *Case*, 220 Mich. at 383–384; *Fenton*, 268 F. at 222; see also *Newton*, 223 P. at 196.

46. *Case*, 220 Mich. at 390–392, 402, 412 (Wiest, J., dissenting). On the founding-era history, see William J. Cuddihy, *The Fourth Amendment: Origins and Original Meaning, 602–1791* (New York: Oxford University Press, 2009); Davies, "Original Fourth Amendment"; Nelson B. Lasson, *The History and Development of the Fourth Amendment to the United States Constitution* (Baltimore: Johns Hopkins Press, 1937), 13–105.

47. *Street*, 3 Pa. D. & C. at 788, 790.

48. *Carroll*, 267 U.S. at 147, 153–154. See also Peru v. United States, 4 F.2d 881, 883 (8th Cir. 1925), for a list of cases decided before *Carroll* that distinguished cars and houses.

49. *Street*, 3 Pa. D. & C. at 787; *Boyd*, 116 U.S. at 641.

50. *Carroll*, 267 U.S. at 153–154, 156.

51. *Moore*, 103 So. at 499 (Ethridge, J., dissenting).

52. *Carroll*, 267 U.S. at 156.

53. Taft to Charles P. Taft, December 22, 1924, reel 270, Taft Papers; Taft to Van Devanter, December 23, 1924, reel 270, Taft Papers.

54. Chafee, review, 947.

55. *Case*, 220 Mich. at 392–393 (Wiest, J., dissenting); *De Ford*, 120 Or. at 459–462; Robert L. Hofford, "Philadelphia Well-Organized Police Force," *TNPJ* 7, no. 3 (December 1920): 7.

56. "Has the Rest of the Constitution Been Repealed by the Eighteenth Amendment?" *Sun*, Baltimore, March 4, 1925; *Moore*, 103 So. at 497, 498–499 (Ethridge, J., dissenting).

57. *Carroll*, Government's Brief, 68; *Carroll*, 267 U.S. at 160.

58. *Carroll*, Petitioners' Brief, 2; *Carroll*, 267 U.S. at 174 (McReynolds, J., dissenting); Tranum v. Stringer, 216 Ala. 522, 525 (1927).

59. Sam B. Warner, "Investigating the Law of Arrest," *Journal of Criminal Law and Criminology* 31, no. 1 (1940): 111; Council of State Governments, *The Handbook on Interstate Crime Control*, rev. ed. (Chicago, 1949): v, 10, 142. On other state judges' observations on illegal police practices, see, for example, Ketcham v. State, 75 P. 2d 1159, 1160 (Okla. Crim. 1938); Bush v. State, 77 P. 2d 1184, 1187 (Okla. Crim. 1938). On other studies recommending reforms to criminal procedures to facilitate law enforcement, see, for example, NCLOE, *Report on Criminal Procedure*, vol. 8 of *U.S. Wickersham Committee Reports* (Washington, DC, 1931): 5, 18–20, 47.

60. Warner, "Investigating," 111, 115.

61. Sam B. Warner, *Preliminary Report to the Committee on Arrest of Interstate Commission on Crime* (n.p., August 5, 1940), 2, box 166, folder 1, Milton R. Konvitz Papers, Kheel Center for Labor-Management Documentation and Archives, Cornell University Library; Sam B. Warner, "The Uniform Arrest Act," *Virginia Law Review* 28, no. 3 (1942): 319.

62. "Policemen on Trial," *Los Angeles Daily Times*, March 23, 1898.

63. Warner, "Investigating," 115; Warner, *Preliminary Report*, 6.

64. Warner, "Investigating," 119–120.

65. Warner, "Investigating," 120.

66. Warner, "Investigating," 115.

67. Warner, "Investigating," 111; Warner, *Preliminary Report*, 7; Warner, "Uniform Arrest Act," 324.

68. United States v. Bonanno, 180 F. Supp. 71, 78 (S.D.N.Y. 1960); Warner, "Uniform Arrest Act," 320; Jerome Hall, "The Law of Arrest in Relation to Contemporary Social Problems," *University of Chicago Law Review* 3, no. 3 (1936): 373.

69. Warner, "Uniform Arrest Act," 322, 344; Lyon v. Rood, 12 Vt. 233, 238 (1840), quoting Williams v. Jones, 95 Cas. T. Hard. 299, 301 (1736).

70. Warner, "Uniform Arrest Act," 325.

71. Warner, "Uniform Arrest Act," 322–323.

72. Warner, "Uniform Arrest Act," 325; James M. Hepbron, review of *Our Lawless Police*, by Ernest Jerome Hopkins, *HLR* 45, no. 7 (1932): 1289.

73. John W. Polcyn, foreword to *Arrest, Search and Seizure*, by Hubert E. Dax and Brooke Tibbs (Milwaukee: Hammersmith-Kortmeyer, 1946), iii; Elliott B. Barnett, Lehigh University, to Roger N. Baldwin, ACLU, July 14, 1953, box 1073, folder 11, ACLU Records; Herbert Monte Levy, Staff Counsel, ACLU,

to Elliott B. Barnett and Karl A. Gabler, Lehigh University, July 10, 1953, box 1073, folder 11, ACLU Records; Paula R. Markowitz and Walter I. Summerfield Jr., "Philadelphia Police Practice and the Law of Arrest," *University of Pennsylvania Law Review* 100, no. 8 (1952): 1213.

74. "Uniform Arrest Law Adoption Urged by Roll," *LAT*, May 13, 1955; see also S. Ernest Roll, "Proposed Changes in the California Law of Arrest" (draft bill, August 1955), box 23, folder 4, ACLUSC.

75. Bernard Weisberg, General Counsel, Illinois Division, ACLU (address, Biennial Conference, Plenary Session on Police Authority and Civil Liberties, April 22, 1960), 2, box 23, folder 3, ACLUSC; see Richard M. Leagre, "The Fourth Amendment and the Law of Arrest," *Journal of Criminal Law, Criminology, and Police Science* 54, no. 4 (1963): 393n3. On the unlikelihood of obtaining tort remedies for unlawful arrests, see Caleb Foote, "Tort Remedies for Police Violations of Individual Rights," *Minnesota Law Review* 39, no. 5 (1955): 500. On the perception of the Uniform Arrest Act as "a substantial expansion of police power," see Herbert L. Packer, "Two Models of the Criminal Process," *University of Pennsylvania Law Review* 113, no. 1 (1964): 8.

76. Kimmis Hendrick, "Los Angeles Seeks Liberties-Police Balance," *Christian Science Monitor*, February 15, 1957; Douglas Dales, "12 Bills Prepared on Police Search," *NYT*, January 21, 1964; Herman Goldstein, interview by author, Madison, WI, June 18, 2015; see also "Recent Statute: Criminal Law—New York Authorizes Police to 'Stop-and-Frisk' on Reasonable Suspicion," *HLR* 78, no. 2 (1964): 473–477.

77. Terry v. Ohio, 392 U.S. 1, 30 (1968).

78. *Terry*, 392 U.S. at 4, 9; *Carroll*, 267 U.S. at 154.

79. On public apathy toward unlawful police practices, see Markowitz and Summerfield, "Philadelphia Police Practice," 1207.

80. United States v. Place, 462 U.S. 696, 721–722 (1983) (Blackmun, J., dissenting); Thomas F. Adams, *Police Patrol: Tactics and Techniques* (New Jersey: Prentice-Hall, 1971), 26–27. On riots, see, for example, Eduardo Obregón Pagán, *Murder at the Sleepy Lagoon: Zoot Suits, Race, and Riot in Wartime L.A.* (Chapel Hill: University of North Carolina Press, 2003).

81. Pennsylvania v. Mimms, 434 U.S. 106, 108–109 (1977); Edward Hirsch, preface to *Drive, They Said: Poems about Americans and Their Cars*, ed. Kurt Brown (Minneapolis: Milkweed Editions, 1994), xv. For more cases that refer to reasonableness as the touchstone of the Fourth Amendment, see, for example, Brigham City, Utah v. Stuart, 547 U.S. 398, 398 (2006); Heien v. North Carolina, 135 S. Ct. 530, 536 (2014); Birchfield v. North Dakota, 136 S. Ct. 2160, 2186 (2016).

82. Brief for the N.A.A.C.P. Legal Defense and Educational Fund, Inc., as Amicus Curiae, Terry v. Ohio, 392 U.S. 1 (1968) (Nos. 63, 67, and 74), 56–57, 64, 68; Roy Wilkins, Executive Director, NAACP, to Honorable George Edwards, US Court of Appeals for the Sixth Circuit, May 24, 1966, 009056-007-0154, NAACP Papers.

CHAPTER 4 • It Could Happen to You

Epigraph: Excerpt from *The Long Goodbye* by Raymond Chandler, copyright ©
1953 by Raymond Chandler, copyright renewed 1981 by Mrs. Helga Greene.
Used by permission of the estate of the author c/o Rogers, Coleridge & White
Ltd., 20 Powis Mews, London W11 1JN and Vintage Crime/Black Lizard, an
imprint of Penguin Random House LLC. All rights reserved.

1. J. Lieberman to ACLU, July 20, 1948, box 25, folder 2, ACLUSC. On
midcentury views of the ACLU, see, for example, A. C. Germann,
"The A.C.L.U.—A Comment" (Long Beach State College, California, 1961),
box 23, folder 4, ACLUSC.

2. Heist to Lieberman, July 22, 1948, box 25, folder 2, ACLUSC.

3. Heist to Police Commission, July 22, 1948, box 25, folder 2, ACLUSC.

4. Esther M. Sharpe to Heist, August 20, 1948, box 25, folder 2, ACLUSC.

5. Heist to Sharpe, August 24, 1948, box 24, folder 9, ACLUSC.

6. People v. Cahan, 44 Cal. 2d 434, 447 (1955); Jerome Hall, "Police and
Law in a Democratic Society," *Indiana Law Journal* 28, no. 2 (1953): 143. On
Hall, see Thomas A. Green, *Freedom and Criminal Responsibility in American
Legal Thought* (New York: Cambridge University Press, 2014), 151–157,
189–195.

7. On the American Way of Life, see Wendy L. Wall, *Inventing the "Amer-
ican Way": The Politics of Consensus from the New Deal to the Civil Rights
Movement* (New York: Oxford University Press, 2008); Lizabeth Cohen, *A
Consumer's Republic: The Politics of Mass Consumption in Postwar America* (New
York: Alfred A. Knopf, 2003), 112–129; Jackson Lears, "A Matter of Taste:
Corporate Cultural Hegemony in a Mass-Consumption Society," in *Recasting
America: Culture and Politics in the Age of Cold War*, ed. Lary May (Chicago:
University of Chicago Press, 1989), 48–54.

8. For another version of this characterization of the Fourth Amendment,
see Anthony G. Amsterdam, "Perspectives on the Fourth Amendment," *Minnesota Law Review* 58, no. 3 (1974): 377.

9. Wolf v. Colorado, 338 U.S. 25, 28 (1949); Brinegar v. United States, 338
U.S. 160, 180 (1949) (Jackson, J., dissenting).

10. *Wolf*, 338 U.S. at 27–28; see also Clerk "SLT," cert memo, n.d., box 173,
folder 1, Rutledge Papers.

11. In his dissent in *Roe v. Wade*, then Justice Rehnquist tried to defend the
anti-abortion law by framing the case as involving a "transaction resulting in
an operation," which, he argued, "is not 'private' in the ordinary usage of that
word." By failing to make the medical procedure the most salient portrayal of
the activity in question, Justice Rehnquist had already lost half the battle. The
image at the center of the opinion of the Court was "the woman and her
responsible physician . . . in consultation." In this scene, the decision to terminate a pregnancy takes place in the doctor's office, an established private sphere.
Roe, in turn, relied on *Griswold v. Connecticut*, which located the decision to use
contraceptives in "marital bedrooms," another hallmark private space. Roe v.
Wade, 410 U.S. 113, 153 (majority), 172 (Rehnquist, J., dissenting) (1973); Griswold v. Connecticut, 381 U.S. 479, 485 (1965).

12. See Willis v. Warren, 17 How. Pr. 100, 101–102 (N.Y. Ct. Com. Pl. 1859). A contemporary example of this argument is the legal holding that a sealed package loses Fourth Amendment protection and can be searched without a warrant if it is known to contain contraband. See United States v. Jacobsen, 466 U.S. 109, 120–121 (1984); Illinois v. Caballes, 543 U.S. 405, 408–409 (2005).

13. Olmstead v. United States, 277 U.S. 438, 464 (1928); see also Amsterdam, "Perspectives," 357. On the criminalization of abortions, see Leslie J. Reagan, *When Abortion Was a Crime: Women, Medicine, and Law in the United States, 1867–1973* (Berkeley: University of California Press, 1997).

14. *Wolf,* 338 U.S. at 27–28.

15. *Wolf,* 338 U.S. at 27 (majority), 41 (Murphy, J., dissenting).

16. *Wolf,* 338 U.S. at 28; handwritten notes by Rutledge from October 23, 1948, conference, box 173, folder 1, Rutledge Papers.

17. *Wolf,* 338 U.S. at 41–42 (Murphy, J., dissenting). On the lack of remedies, see Jerome Hall, "The Law of Arrest in Relation to Contemporary Social Problems," *University of Chicago Law Review* 3, no. 3 (1936): 346–353; Paula R. Markowitz and Walter I. Summerfield, "Philadelphia Police Practice and the Law of Arrest," *University of Pennsylvania Law Review* 100, no. 8 (1952): 1206–1212; Hall, "Police and Law," 173; Caleb Foote, "Tort Remedies for Police Violations of Individual Rights," *Minnesota Law Review* 39, no. 5 (1955): 493–508, 513.

18. *Brinegar,* 338 U.S. at 164.

19. *Brinegar,* 338 U.S. at 162–171.

20. *Brinegar,* 338 U.S. at 171; conference voting sheet, Brinegar v. United States, box 149, folder 1, Jackson Papers; Wiley to Jackson, memo, January 28, 1949, box 149, folder 2, Jackson Papers; see also Justice Burton, memorandum for the conference, February 4, 1949, box 167, folder 10, Rutledge Papers.

21. *Brinegar,* 338 U.S. at 188 (Jackson, J., dissenting); see also memorandum by Jackson, November 6, 1948, 9, box 149, folder 1, Jackson Papers.

22. Wiley to Jackson, January 28, 1949; *Brinegar,* 338 U.S. at 170; Frankfurter to Jackson, memo, n.d., box 149, folder 1, Jackson Papers.

23. [?] to Jackson, memo, n.d., box 149, folder 1, Jackson Papers; *Brinegar,* 338 U.S. at 176 (Rutledge, J.), 179 (Burton, J., concurring); typewritten memo from Murphy to Jackson, n.d., box 149, folder 1, Jackson Papers.

24. *Brinegar,* 338 U.S. at 171, 175–176.

25. *Brinegar,* 338 U.S. at 175–176.

26. *Brinegar,* 338 U.S. at 183, 188 (Jackson, J., dissenting).

27. *Brinegar,* 338 U.S. at 181–182 (Jackson, J., dissenting).

28. *Brinegar,* 338 U.S. at 181.

29. Hall, "Police and Law," 133, 152–153, 156–157; see also Sarah A. Seo, "Democratic Policing before the Due Process Revolution," *YLJ* 128 (forthcoming 2019).

30. Memorandum from Walter White to Roy Wilkins, November 10, 1937, 001530-014-0623, NAACP Papers; Jesse W. M. DuMond to Board of City Directors of Pasadena, California, January 23, 1950, box 23, folder 4, ACLUSC.

In 1929, the NAACP petitioned the Wickersham Commission, which had been tasked with investigating the causes of lawlessness during Prohibition, to also look into lynchings, arguing that the "lawlessness against the Negro [was] one of the tap-roots of lawlessness generally." The commission appears not to have responded to the request. Walter White to Charles H. Tuttle, US Attorney, September 11, 1929, 001422-016-0838, NAACP Papers.

31. "Rights of Arrest," *Boston Traveler,* February 17, 1960; "You? Arrested?," *Boston Herald,* February 9, 1960; see also Illinois State Bar Association, Committee on Civil Rights, *Your Rights When Arrested* (Illinois, 1951), box 23, folder 4, ACLUSC. For discussions on unlawful policing of innocent people, see Hall, "Police and Law," 141; Albert R. Beisel Jr., *Control over Illegal Enforcement of the Criminal Law: Role of the Supreme Court* (Boston: Boston University Press, 1955), 7–8.

32. Frederick G. Brownell, "It Could Happen to You," *American Magazine* 147, no. 5 (May 1949): 24–25, 130–131.

33. Heist to International City Managers Association, March 26, 1947, box 25, folder 2, ACLUSC; "4800 Cars Searched in Blockade," *Daily News,* May 8, 1947; "Blockade of Sunset Strip Nets—1 Drunk," *Daily News,* April 14, 1947; see also "Road Blocks Net Weapons," *LAT,* March 16, 1947; "Net 64 in L.A. Crime Drive Blockade," *Herald Express,* March 15, 1947, LAPD, *Public Relations Scrapbook,* LACA.

34. "L.A. Police Revive Road Blocks in War on Crime," newspaper article, March 15, 1947, box 25, folder 2, ACLUSC; see also "Road 'Blocks' Trap Many in Crime Wave," *Los Angeles Examiner,* March 16, 1947, LAPD, *Public Relations Scrapbook,* LACA.

35. Edward J. Kelly, Executive Secretary, IACP, to Heist April 10, 1947, box 25, folder 2, ACLUSC; Romaine L. Poindexter, Letters from Readers, "Police Blockades," *LAT,* August 18, 1948.

36. Requesting waivers appears to have been a common practice. See Alan Gartner, *The Police and the Community: Police Practices and Minority Groups* (Brandeis University, n.d.), 12, box 1079, folder 7, ACLU Records and 001475-015-0481, NAACP Papers.

37. "Innocent Road Block Victim Held 40 Hours," *Los Angeles Examiner,* June 29, 1947.

38. Risa Goluboff's *Vagrant Nation* tells a revealing story. In the early 1960s South, clerks in the federal district courts applauded when African Americans filed lawsuits against local justices of the peace because they themselves "had suffered at the hands of j.p.'s [justices of the peace] when they tried to contest unfair traffic tickets." Anthony Amsterdam, quoted in Risa Goluboff, *Vagrant Nation: Police Power, Constitutional Change, and the Making of the 1960s* (New York: Oxford University Press, 2016), 131.

39. ACLU, memo on Conference of New York Police Committee, February 17, 1950, box 575, folder 23, ACLU Records; George E. Rundquist, Assistant Director, ACLU, to Friends, February 28, 1950, box 575, folder 23, ACLU Records.

40. NYCLC, "The Police and the Community" (memo of meeting of the Police Practices Committee, October 2, 1950), 1, box 575, folder 23, ACLU

Records; E. M. Slaughter, "As the Twig Is Bent," *The Guardian* (Los Angeles: LAPD, 1937): 255, box C2013, LACA.

The Chicago and Southern California branches of the ACLU formed standing committees on police problems in 1947. One year later, the national ACLU established the Committee on Police Practices. By 1951, the New York City and Philadelphia affiliates followed suit. Samuel Walker, *In Defense of American Liberties: A History of the ACLU* (1990; Carbondale: Southern Illinois University Press, 1999), 247.

41. National Popular Government League, *To the American People: Report upon the Illegal Practices of the United States Department of Justice* (Washington, DC, 1920), 4–5; NCLOE, *Report on Lawlessness in Law Enforcement*, vol. 11 (Washington, DC, 1931), 4; see also Marilynn S. Johnson, *Street Justice: A History of Police Violence in New York City* (Boston: Beacon, 2003), 125, 133, 149–180; Walker, *In Defense*, 87. On how the ACLU compromised its radical origins to focus on constitutional law claims, see Laura Weinrib, *The Taming of Free Speech: America's Civil Liberties Compromise* (Cambridge, MA: Harvard University Press, 2017).

42. Arthur Laurents, Leonard Bernstein, and Stephen Sondheim, "Gee, Officer Krupke," *West Side Story* (New York: Random House, 1958), 114–117.

43. Goluboff, *Vagrant Nation*, 12–73; Weinrib, *Taming*, 99, 121.

44. "A Tentative Outline for Agreement and Procedure" (n.p., April 29, 1957), box 24, folder 1, ACLUSC. El Congreso identified a similar problem in Los Angeles. Edward Escobar has argued that hostility between Mexican Americans and the LAPD emerged in the postwar years, when the professionalism of the LAPD coincided with the racialization of crime. Edward J. Escobar, *Race, Police, and the Making of a Political Identity: Mexican Americans and the Los Angeles Police Department, 1900–1945* (Berkeley: University of California Press, 1999), 3–6.

45. NYCLC, "Police and the Community," 1–2.

46. California DOJ, *Police Training Bulletin: A Guide to Race Relations for Police Officers* (California, 1946), 2, box 24, folder 13, ACLUSC; The International City Managers' Association, *The Police and Minority Groups*, by J. E. Weckler and Theo E. Hall (Chicago, 1944), 8, box 24, folder 13, ACLUSC; Hall, "Police and Law," 148; see also Joseph T. Kluchesky, Chief of Police, Milwaukee, WI, *Police Action in Minority Problems* (New York: Freedom House, n.d.), box 24, folder 13, ACLUSC. On postwar riots, see, for example, Thomas J. Sugrue, *The Origins of the Urban Crisis: Race and Inequality in Postwar Detroit* (1996; Princeton, NJ: Princeton University Press, 2005), 29; Eduardo Obregón Pagán, *Murder at the Sleepy Lagoon: Zoot Suits, Race, and Riot in Wartime L.A.* (Chapel Hill: University of North Carolina Press, 2003).

47. California DOJ, *Police Training Bulletin*, 23–25, 29; Weckler and Hall, *Minority Groups*, 9; Walker, *In Defense*, 247.

48. Automobile Manufacturers Association, *Automobile Facts and Figures* (Detroit, 1950), 23; R. C. Combes, "Frankenstein on Wheels," in *Guardian*, 77–79; Edythe I. Copeland, "Credit Is Due," *Southside Journal*, January 5, 1946, LAPD, *Public Relations Scrapbook*, LACA.

49. Robert Allan Arends to ACLU, August 12, 1959, box 1075, folder 13, ACLU Records.

50. Whether a vehicle stop amounted to an arrest was a common question that confused even Supreme Court justices. In one 1959 case, the Court described a car stop as an arrest that required probable cause; the following year, it raised the possibility that a similar car stop might *not* be an arrest. This issue would soon become largely irrelevant as officers realized that they could justify any stop with a traffic violation. Henry v. United States, 361 U.S. 98, 98–104 (1959), but see Rios v. United States, 364 U.S. 253, 261–262 (1960).

51. Robert Allan Arends to ACLU, August 12, 1959, box 1075, folder 13, ACLU Records; Melvin L. Wulf to Robert A. Arends, August 19, 1959, box 1075, folder 13, ACLU Records.

52. T. R. Mathews to "Allen" Reitman, February 18, 1959, box 1075, folder 1, ACLU Records.

53. Alan Reitman, ACLU, to T. R. Mathews, February 24, 1959, box 1075, folder 1, ACLU Records.

54. Duncan E. Hilton to ACLU, July 28, 1958, box 67, folder 9, ACLUSC.

55. Eason Monroe, Executive Director, to Duncan E. Hilton, August 1, 1958, box 67, folder 9, ACLUSC; Board of Police Commissioners to Aki Aleong, February 5, 1970, box C-289, LACA; see also Board of Police Commissioners to Jewel Dean Lyons, November 26, 1969, box C-0288, LACA.

56. Eugene Weiner to Police Commissioner Howard R. Leary, March 4, 1964, box 1079, folder 19, ACLU Records.

57. Gilbert King, *Devil in the Grove: Thurgood Marshall, the Groveland Boys, and the Dawn of a New America* (New York: Harper, 2012), 14–20; NAACP, "Florida Police Arrest, Beat State NAACP Chief" (press release, October 4, 1956), 001487-012-0711, NAACP Papers.

58. NAACP, "Young Physician Beaten by Texas Highway Cop" (press release, July 16, 1953), 001459-020-0115, NAACP Papers; Joseph H. Hayes (affidavit, August 19, 1946), 1–2, box 24, folder 1, ACLUSC. On midcentury observations of police abuse against black Americans, see William A. Westley, "Violence and the Police," *American Journal of Sociology* 59, no. 1 (1953): 40; Foote, "Tort Remedies for Police Violations," 501.

59. Untitled report by Dr. Singleton, n.d., 001530-014-0569, NAACP Papers.

60. Carter W. Wesley to Thurgood Marshall, May 7, 1940, 001455-009-0051, NAACP Papers. On the "etiquette of race" in Jim Crow Mississippi, see Neil R. McMillen, *Dark Journey: Black Mississippians in the Age of Jim Crow* (Urbana: University of Illinois Press, 1989), 23–28.

61. NAACP, "NAACP Asks Justice Dept. to Probe Georgia Assault" (press release, June 30, 1955), 001459-020-0115, NAACP Papers.

62. Memorandum from Walter White to Mr. Carter, July 1, 1953, 001459-019-0751, NAACP Papers; Edward J. Bruce to Walter White, February 24, 1939, 001530-014-0967, NAACP Papers.

63. New Jersey State Conference of the NAACP, *Report of the Investigation of the Shooting of Stanley Jackson*, by Melvin D. Halsey (Plainfield, NJ, 1937), 001530-014-0643, NAACP Papers; "Trooper Shoots Local Youth," *Perth Amboy Evening News*, February 1, 1937, 001530-014-0643, NAACP Papers; see also Alfred Jackson to NAACP, February 1, 1937, 001530-014-0643, NAACP Papers.

On midcentury views on joyriding, see LAPD, *Annual Report* (1950), 25, box C2003, LACA; Leonard D. Savitz, "Automobile Theft," *Journal of Criminal Law and Criminology* 50, no. 2 (1959): 132.

64. Unsigned letter to Carlton B. Norris, President, Newark Branch, NAACP, September 11, 1961, 001487-013-0148, NAACP Papers; NAACP, Detroit Branch, *Police Brutality: Study of Complaints in Detroit* (Detroit, MI, October 1958), 488, box 23, folder 7, ACLUSC. Interestingly, the pattern of police abuse skewed male. Only eighteen of the cases in the Detroit study involved women; given that most of the letters to the ACLU were also written by men, gender seems to have tempered citizen-police encounters.

65. National Museum of American History, Smithsonian Institution, "Simler Turn Signal," *America on the Move*, https://perma.cc/G99L-4BT4.

66. Notarized letter from William Thomas Phillips to Board of Police Commissioners, March 9, 1953, box 24, folder 1, ACLUSC; William Thomas Phillips, notarized statement, March 17, 1953, box 24, folder 1, ACLUSC.

67. "Tyler Allison Given Release," newspaper article, August 28, 1939, 001530-014-0967, NAACP Papers; "A Bid for Optimism," *Atlanta World*, n.d., 001422-004-0201, NAACP Papers; "All-White Jury Frees Sheriff in 23 Minutes," *New York Post*, August 8, 1958; American Jewish Congress, "Brooklyn NAACP Asks to Examine Grand Jury Minutes in Case of Officer Who Killed Negro Motorist; Police 'Reign of Terror' against Negroes Charged" (press release, July 27, 1949), 001459-005-0001, NAACP Papers; William Pickens Jr. to Thurgood Marshall, November 13, 1939, 001530-016-0935, NAACP Papers; see also Lloyd M. Smith, President, ACLU of Southern California, "Police Malpractice against Racial Minorities" (speech, hearing of the California Advisory Committee of the US Commission on Civil Rights, Los Angeles, CA, 1962), box 63, folder 9, ACLUSC.

68. American Jewish Congress press release; Brownell, "It Could Happen," 132; see also "A Task Grows in Brooklyn for DA," *New York Age*, June 4, 1949.

69. "Widowed by Cop, Must Get 50G's," *New York Age*, October 27, 1951; Ferguson v. City of New York, 107 N.Y.S.2d 534, 534 (N.Y. App. Div. 1951); Ferguson v. City of New York, 303 N.Y. 936, 937 (1952); "Nab 4 Dope Users in $10,000 Theft," *Brooklyn Daily Eagle*, January 22, 1954.

70. "FBI Arrests Minnick in Shooting of Negro," newspaper article, February 12, 1953, 001459-020-0001, NAACP Papers; "Arrest Florida Patrolman for Christmas Day Killing," newspaper article, February 21, 1953, 001459-020-0001, NAACP Papers; The Inter-Citizens Committee, *Document No. 7 on Human Rights in Alabama* (Birmingham, AL, 1960), 001487-012-0637, NAACP Papers.

71. Frederick Woltman, "FBI Civil Rights Inquiry Blocked by Monaghan," *New York World Telegram and Sun*, February 16, 1953; Ella J. Baker, President, and Edward W. Jacko Jr., Chairman, Legal Redress Committee, New York Branch, NAACP, to Vincent R. Impolliteri, Mayor of New York City, February 16, 1953, 001459-019-0751, NAACP Papers; Roy Wilkins to Police Commissioner George P. Monaghan, February 16, 1953, 001459-019-0751, NAACP Papers.

72. Norman H. Moore, Sergeant, LAPD, "'Police Review Boards,'" *California Peace Officer* 11, no. 2 (November–December 1960): 5, box 23, folder 3,

ACLUSC; Esther M. Sharpe, Acting Secretary, Board of Police Commissioners, Los Angeles, to Edwin P. Ryland and A. A. Heist, October 3, 1946, box 24, folder 1, ACLUSC; Editorial, "Police Review Board Is a One-Sided Plan," *Star-News*, June 2, 1960; "ACLU Blasted on Police Review Plan," *Los Angeles Herald & Express*, June 16, 1960; Gartner, *Police and the Community*, 15–25; James R. Hudson, "Police Review Boards and Police Accountability," *Law and Contemporary Problems* 36, no. 4 (1971): 522, 527, 531n71. On the NAACP and civilian review boards, see Roy Wilkins, NAACP Executive Director (statement, July 16, 1965), 001487-013-0148, NAACP Papers; Joseph Harvey Johnson, Chairman, Legal Redress Committee, to Gloster B. Current, Director of Branches, NAACP, March 28, 1960, 001487-013-0296, NAACP Papers.

73. California DOJ, *Police Training Bulletin*, 11, 13; City and County of San Francisco Police Department Rules and Regulations (San Francisco, 1951), rule 502; IACP, Code of Ethics, https://www.theiacp.org/resources/law-enforcement-code-of-ethics; Kluchesky, *Minority Problems*, 3.

74. California DOJ, *Police Training Bulletin*, 20, 29; Calvin Banks to Dr. Morsell, memo, April 8, 1964, 001487-013-0148, NAACP Papers; see also Stephen P. Kennedy, Police Commissioner of NYC, *The Police and Community Relations* (remarks, Brotherhood Week Luncheon, National Conference of Christians and Jews, February 13, 1958), 001487-013-0148, NAACP Papers.

75. California Highway Patrol, *"Routine" Traffic Stop Police Training Film* (1962), https://perma.cc/J9CS-6MUZ.

76. "Claims Officers Awakened Him in His Room," newspaper article, n.d., box 25, folder 2, ACLUSC; Mathews to Reitman.

77. After *Wolf* and *Irvine v. California*, 347 U.S. 128 (1954), the exclusionary rule came before five state courts, and all five declined to adopt the rule. Those states were Georgia, New York, New Hampshire, Pennsylvania, and Maryland. See Huff v. State, 82 Ga. App. 545 (1950); Clemons v. State, 84 Ga. App. 551 (1951); People v. Vieni, 301 N.Y. 535 (1950); State v. Mara, 96 N.H. 463 (1951); Commonwealth v. Montanero, 173 Pa. Super. 133 (1953); Commonwealth v. Rich, 174 Pa. Super. 174 (1953); Stevens v. State, 202 Md. 117 (1953).

78. "New York Police Commissioner Asks Guidance on Search-Seizure Problems" (n.p., n.d.), box 23, folder 4, ACLUSC.

79. *Cahan*, 44 Cal. 2d at 439–449.

80. LAPD, *Annual Report* (1958), 18, box C2003, LACA; "Judge Mosk Says No Increase in Crime since Cahan Decision," newspaper article, March 8, 1956, box 24, folder 9, ACLUSC.

81. Memorandum from Herbert Monte Levy to Free Speech—Association Committee, February 1, 1956, box 24, folder 9, ACLUSC.

82. Levy memorandum; Brownell, "It Could Happen," 133; see also LAPD, *Annual Report* (1952), 23, box C2003, LACA.

83. "Judge Mosk Says"; "Changes Urged in Search and Seizure Laws," *LAT*, March 4, 1957; see California Penal Code (1957), sec. 833; see also "[Attorney General] Brown Scorns Arrests under Antiquated Law," *LAT*, June 4, 1957; Kimmis Hendrick, "Los Angeles Seeks Liberties-Police Balance," *Christian*

Science Monitor, February 15, 1957. On nonuse of warrants, see, for example, Markowitz and Summerfield, "Philadelphia Police," 1183–1184.

84. Mapp v. Ohio, 367 U.S. 643, 643 (1961).

85. Justice Clark to Justice Harlan, memo, May 4, 1961, box 125, folder 236, Harlan Papers; Carolyn N. Long, Mapp v. Ohio: *Guarding against Unreasonable Searches and Seizures* (Lawrence: University Press of Kansas, 2006), 82–85; Justice Clark, quoted in Paul R. Baier, "Justice Clark, the Voice of the Past, and the Exclusionary Rule," *Texas Law Review* 64, no. 2 (1985): 419n19. Justice Harlan had joined the majority in *Mapp* when the reversal of the state's judgment was supposed to be based on the First Amendment.

The ACLU and its Ohio affiliate participated in *Mapp v. Ohio* as amici, arguing that it was unconstitutional to criminalize "mere possession" of obscene literature. Brief Amici Curiae on Behalf of ACLU and Ohio Civil Liberties Union, Mapp v. Ohio, 367 U.S. 643 (1961) (No. 236), 1–2. The entire brief focused on this argument, save for one short paragraph on the illegal search and seizure. During oral argument, the ACLU lawyer spent nearly all of his fifteen minutes challenging the constitutionality of the statute. Bernard A. Berkman to Rowland Watts, April 1, 1961, box 1514, folder "Mapp v. Ohio," ACLU Records.

86. This provision is now found in 42 U.S.C. § 1983.

87. Myriam E. Gilles, "Police, Race and Crime in 1950's Chicago: *Monroe v. Pape* as Legal Noir," in *Civil Rights Stories,* ed. Myriam Gilles and Risa Goluboff (New York: Foundation, 2008), 46–52.

88. Appendix A, Brief for Petitioner, Monroe v. Pape, 365 U.S. 167 (1961) (No. 39), 67–76.

89. Oral argument transcript, Monroe v. Pape, 365 U.S. 167 (1961) (No. 39); see also Sheldon Nahmod, "Section 1983 Is Born: The Interlocking Supreme Court Stories of *Tenney* and *Monroe,*" *Lewis & Clark Law Review* 17, no. 4 (2013): 1039–1040.

90. Lawrence P. Tiffany, Donald M. McIntyre Jr., and Daniel L. Rotenberg, *Detection of Crime: Stopping and Questioning, Search and Seizure, Encouragement and Entrapment* (Boston: Little, Brown, 1967), 100; Sidney E. Zion, "Detectives Get a Course in Law," *NYT,* April 28, 1965; Gartner, *Police and the Community,* 13; Markowitz and Summerfield, "Philadelphia Police," 1184.

91. On the coining of the phrase "due process revolution," see Gray A. Debele, "The Due Process Revolution and the Juvenile Court: The Matter of Race in the Historical Evolution of a Doctrine," *Law & Inequality* 5, no. 3 (1987): 516n25; Fred P. Graham, *The Self-Inflicted Wound* (New York: Macmillan, 1970), 26. On "modern" criminal procedure, see, for example, Dan M. Kahan and Tracey L. Meares, "The Coming Crisis of Criminal Procedure," *Georgetown Law Journal* 86, no. 5 (1998): 1158–1159.

92. Stringer v. Dilger, 313 F.2d 536, 538–540 (10th Cir. 1963); Stringer v. Dilger, No. 7073 (D. Colo. May 6, 1963), box 879, NARA Denver (hereafter, "Trial Record").

93. Stringer Deposition, Trial Record, 9–15; Stringer Trial Transcript, Trial Record, 264–274.

94. The trial judge instructed the jury that the verdict must be unanimous. Stringer Deposition, Trial Record, 5, 29–30.

95. Stringer's lawyer discussed the *Monroe* opinion in his brief opposing defendant's motion to dismiss. See Brief Opposing Motion to Dismiss, Trial Record. Several years later, the district judge wrote an opinion maintaining that an action under Section 1983, as interpreted by *Monroe v. Pape*, requires a wrongful act. Baxter v. Birkins, 311 F. Supp. 222, 224–225 (D. Colo. 1970).

96. *Stringer*, 313 F.2d at 540–541.

CHAPTER 5   •   The Right to Privacy in Public

Epigraph (Chauncey): From *Gay New York: Gender, Urban Culture, and the Making of the Gay Male World, 1890–1940* by George Chauncey, copyright © 1994. Reprinted by permission of Georges Borchardt, Inc. and Basic Books, an imprint of Hachette Book Group, Inc. All rights reserved.

Epigraph (L'Engle): From a draft of *A Wrinkle in Time* by Madeline L'Engle published by the *Wall Street Journal*, April 16, 2015, by permission of Charlotte Jones Voiklis.

1. Charles A. Reich, "Police Questioning of Law Abiding Citizens," *YLJ* 75, no. 7 (1966): 1161–1162.

2. Papachristou v. City of Jacksonville, 405 U.S. 156, 156n1, 158–160 (1972).

3. *Papachristou*, 405 U.S. at 168; Reich, "Police Questioning," 1165, 1172.

4. See William N. Eskridge Jr., *Dishonorable Passions: Sodomy Laws in America, 1861–2003* (New York: Viking, 2008), 124–127; Charles A. Reich, "Keeping Up: Walking with Justice Douglas" (unpublished, 2016), on file with author.

5. Charles A. Reich, *The Sorcerer of Bolinas Reef* (New York: Random House, 1976), 22–24, 55–83. On the importance of the suburban home to freedom during the Cold War, see Sarah E. Igo, *The Known Citizen: A History of Privacy in Modern America* (Cambridge, MA: Harvard University Press, 2018), 108–112. On heteronormativity and homosexuality at midcentury, see Elaine Tyler May, "Cold War—Warm Hearth: Politics and the Family in Postwar America," in *The Rise and Fall of the New Deal Order 1930–1980*, ed. Steve Fraser and Gary Gerstle (Princeton, NJ: Princeton University Press, 1989), 153–181; Lynn Spigel, *Make Room for TV: Television and the Family Ideal in Postwar America* (Chicago: University of Chicago Press, 1992); Margot Canaday, *The Straight State: Sexuality and Citizenship in Twentieth-Century America* (Princeton, NJ: Princeton University Press, 2009). On the lavender scare, see David K. Johnson, *The Lavender Scare: The Cold War Persecution of Gays and Lesbians in the Federal Government* (Chicago: University of Chicago Press, 2004); K. A. Cuordileone, "'Politics in an Age of Anxiety': Cold War Political Culture and the Crisis in American Masculinity, 1949–1960," *Journal of American History* 87, no. 2 (2000): 515–545; John D'Emilio, "The Homosexual Menace: The Politics of Sexuality in Cold War America," in *Passion and Power: Sexuality in History*, ed. Kathy Peiss and Christina Simmons (Philadelphia: Temple University Press, 1989), 226–240.

6. Reich, *Sorcerer*, 46–47, 79–80.

7. Reich, *Sorcerer*, 80; Reich, interview with author, April 20, 2017.

8. Reich, interview with author, April 13, 2017.

9. Reich, interview with author, April 13, 2017; Reich, *Sorcerer*, 140, 155.

10. Reich, *Sorcerer*, 125. Reich did not mention or cite the legal historian who immortalized this phrase. See James Willard Hurst, *Law and the Conditions of Freedom in the Nineteenth-Century United States* (1956; Madison: University of Wisconsin Press, 1984), 3.

11. Reich, *Sorcerer*, 125, 140; Charles A. Reich, *The Greening of America* (1970; New York: Bantam Books, 1971). On the 1960s and the counterculture, see, for example, Terry H. Anderson, *The Movement and the Sixties* (New York: Oxford University Press, 1995), 241–291.

12. See Christine Stansell, *City of Women: Sex and Class in New York, 1789–1860* (1986; Urbana: University of Illinois Press, 1987), 185–191; George Chauncey, *Gay New York: Gender, Urban Culture, and the Making of the Gay Male World, 1890–1940* (New York: BasicBooks, 1994), 179–205.

13. Reich, "Police Questioning," 1172.

14. Reich, "Police Questioning," 1167, 1172; *Papachristou*, 405 U.S. at 164, 164n6.

15. See *Drive, They Said: Poems about Americans and Their Cars*, ed. Kurt Brown (Minneapolis: Milkweed Editions, 1994); Stephen Dunn, "The Sacred," *Between Angels: Poems* (New York: W. W. Norton, 1989), 55; *Papachristou*, 405 U.S. at 164. Historian Amy Dru Stanley has highlighted a radical understanding of human rights in the Civil Rights Act of 1875 that protected, among other things, "the right to experience amusement in a public sphere." Though Reich and Douglas's notion of freedom evokes this earlier idea, what was different in the mid-twentieth century was the emphasis on nonconformity, on bucking conventional desires. Amy Dru Stanley, "Slave Emancipation and the Revolutionizing of Human Rights," in *The World the Civil War Made*, ed. Gregory P. Downs and Kate Masur (Chapel Hill: University of North Carolina Press, 2015), 271.

16. *Papachristou*, 405 U.S. at 156–157n1 (ordinance), 158–160; Risa L. Goluboff, *Vagrant Nation: Police Power, Constitutional Change, and the Making of the 1960s* (New York: Oxford University Press, 2016).

17. Charles A. Reich, "The New Property," *YLJ* 73, no. 5 (1964): 734; Fred R. Shapiro and Michelle Pearse, "The Most-Cited Law Review Articles of All Time," *Michigan Law Review* 110, no. 8 (2012): 1489; Charles A. Reich, "Midnight Welfare Searches and the Social Security Act," *YLJ* 72, no. 7 (1963): 1347; Reich, *Sorcerer*, 81.

18. Reich, quoted in Laura Kalman, *Yale Law School and the Sixties: Revolt and Reverberations* (Chapel Hill: University of North Carolina Press, 2005), 50; Reich, "New Property," 756, 768–769; Reich, "Midnight Welfare Searches," 1360. On the Harvard incident, see Rodger D. Citron, "Charles Reich's Journey from the *Yale Law Journal* to the *New York Times* Best-Seller List: The Personal History of *The Greening of America*," *New York Law School Law Review* 52, no. 3 (2007): 392.

19. Reich, "New Property," 733; Automobile Manufacturers Association, *Automobile Facts and Figures* (Detroit, MI: Automobile Manufacturers Association, 1961), 34, 36; Reich, "New Property," 737, 740, quoting Lee v. State, 187 Kan. 566, 570 (1961).

20. The Supreme Court recently held that the police may administer a breath test, but not a blood test, without a warrant as a search incident to arrest for drunk driving. Birchfield v. North Dakota, 136 S. Ct. 2160 (2016).

21. Reich, "New Property," 741–742, 748–749, 754, 776.

22. This is still true today. Some states suspend driver's licenses for unsatisfied debts stemming from criminal cases and traffic fines, creating a cycle of debt. People with suspended licenses are forced to drive anyway in order to commute to work to pay off those debts, but then they get hit with more fines for "driving while suspended." For the undocumented, the choices are just as limited and the consequences especially dire. Shaila Dewan, "Driver's License Suspensions Create Cycle of Debt," *NYT*, April 14, 2015.

23. On the necessity of cars in American society, see Andres Duany, Elizabeth Plater-Zyberk, and Jeff Speck, *Suburban Nation: The Rise of Sprawl and the Decline of the American Dream* (New York: North Point, 2000), 115–133.

24. Wall v. King, 206 F.2d 878, 882 (1st Cir. 1953); Argersinger v. Hamlin, 407 U.S. 25, 48 (1972) (Powell, J., concurring). In *Cruzan by Cruzan v. Director, Missouri Department of Health*, Justice Scalia also recognized a liberty interest in driving cars. But he argued that the equal protection clause, not the due process clause, protected that right. 497 U.S. 261, 300 (1990) (Scalia, J., concurring). On driving and democratic citizenship, see Charles R. Epp, Steven Maynard-Moody, and Donald P. Haider-Markel, *Pulled Over: How Police Stops Define Race and Citizenship* (Chicago: University of Chicago Press, 2014), 17–19.

25. Reich, April 13 interview; Thomas F. Adams, "Field Interrogations," *Police* (March–April 1963): 28.

26. Reich, "Police Questioning," 1162–1163, 1166. On roadblocks, see Richard M. Leagre, "The Fourth Amendment and the Law of Arrest," *Journal of Criminal Law, Criminology, and Police Science* 54, no. 4 (1963): 416.

27. In an article about Justice Black's judicial philosophy, Reich discussed the related problem that "the same due process clause that subjected state criminal procedure to Supreme Court scrutiny . . . was also used by the Court to review and invalidate state economic regulation." He continued: "The two-edged sword of the due process clause, which by its literal wording gives coextensive protection to property rights and individual liberty, posed a dilemma for Black, who was reluctant to accord the same degree of protection to the former as to the latter." According to Reich, Justice Black began his tenure with a restrictive view of the Fourth Amendment, but questioned that view as he became increasingly disillusioned with the police. He finally changed his mind in 1960. Charles A. Reich, "Mr. Justice Black and the Living Constitution," *HLR* 76, no. 4 (1963): 690–691.

28. Reich, "Police Questioning," 1166.

29. Reich, "Police Questioning," 1163–1164, 1166.

30. Brief for the N.A.A.C.P. Legal Defense and Education Fund, Inc., as Amicus Curiae, Terry v. Ohio, 392 U.S. 1 (1968) (Nos. 63, 67, and 64), 36; Arthur L. Johnson, Executive Secretary, Detroit Branch, NAACP, "Police Brutality against Negroes in Detroit" (statement, December 15, 1960), 8, 001487-012-0864, NAACP Papers.

31. John L. Mitchell, "The Bitter, 14-Year Legacy of a Slaying," *Washington Post*, September 3, 1980; see also Arthur S. Black, Chairman, Central Branch, The Legal Redress Committee, NAACP, *Special Report on Coroner's Case # 66-4983* (May 1966), 009056-006-0082, NAACP Papers.

32. Joe Saltzman, *Black on Black* (1968), accessed July 9, 2018, https://perma .cc/5FE8-WVJW; Joe Saltzman, "An Introduction to *Black on Black*" (presentation, USC Annenberg School for Communication, October 27, 2008), https://perma.cc/PU25-SA5G.

33. Reich, "Police Questioning," 1164–1165; Reich, April 20 interview.

34. Reich, "New Property," 760, 778, 785.

35. Reich, "New Property," 787; Reich, quoted in Kalman, *Yale Law School*, 50; Goldberg v. Kelly, 397 U.S. 254, 262n8 (1970).

36. State v. Shack, 58 N.J. 297 (1971); Javins v. First National Realty Corp., 428 F.2d 1071 (D.C. Cir. 1970); Reich, "Mr. Justice Black," 733. Laura Kalman has portrayed Reich as a scholar whose "head lay with legal liberalism." Kalman, *Yale Law School*, 63; see also Citron, "Reich's Journey," 400.

In 1963, Reich wrote about Justice Black's living constitutionalism in a law review article that secured his tenure at Yale Law School. When Reich asked Black for his thoughts on the article, the justice remarked that it seemed to describe "Charlie Reich's judicial philosophy more than his." Indeed, by the time Reich clerked for Black, the justice had adopted a more classical approach in his constitutional interpretation. Reich, interview with author, April 6, 2017.

37. Reich, "New Property," 771–774.

38. Reich, "Police Questioning," 1170; Griswold v. Connecticut, 381 U.S. 479, 485–486 (1965). On *Griswold*, see Igo, *Known Citizen*, 154–170.

39. Reich, "Police Questioning," 1170.

40. Reich, "Police Questioning," 1165, 1171.

41. Reich, "Police Questioning," 1170.

42. Reich, "Police Questioning," 1170–1171.

43. On the illusory distinction between substance and procedure, see, for example, William J. Stuntz, "Substance, Process, and the Civil-Criminal Line," *Journal of Contemporary Legal Issues* 7, no. 1 (1996): 1–41; William J. Stuntz, "The Substantive Origins of Criminal Procedure," *YLJ* 105, no. 2 (1995): 393–447; Anthony G. Amsterdam, "The Void-for-Vagueness Doctrine in the Supreme Court," *University of Pennsylvania Law Review* 109, no. 1 (1960): 67–116.

44. Reich, "Police Questioning," 1172; Alan Reitman to Spencer Coxe, August 5, 1959, box 1075, folder 9, ACLU Records.

45. Reich, "Police Questioning," 1171–1172. On the concept of security at midcentury, see Jerome Hall, "Police and Law in a Democratic Society," *Indiana Law Journal* 28, no. 2 (1953): 162; Stephen P. Kennedy (press release, 63rd Annual Conference of the IACP, September 10, 1956), box 1074, folder 2, ACLU Records. On security and the Cold War, see May, "Cold War—Warm Hearth," 160–161.

46. Madeleine L'Engle, deleted excerpt in Jennifer Maloney, "A New 'Wrinkle in Time,'" *WSJ*, April 16, 2015, https://perma.cc/7FVB-3TFZ;

322 NOTES TO PAGES 223–227

William H. Whyte, *The Organization Man* (New York: Simon & Schuster, 1956); Malvina Reynolds, "Little Boxes," *The Malvina Reynolds Songbook* (Berkeley, CA: Schroder Music, 1974), 44–45.

47. "Legality of United States Participation in the Viet Nam Conflict: A Symposium," *YLJ* 75, no. 7 (1966): 1084; Neil H. Alford Jr., "The Legality of American Military Involvement in Viet Nam: A Broader Perspective," *YLJ* 75, no. 7 (1966): 1111, 1121; Richard A. Falk, "International Law and the United States Role in the Viet Nam War," *YLJ* 75, no. 7 (1966): 1124–1125, 1135; Office of the Legal Adviser, US Department of State, "The Legality of United States Participation in the Defense of Viet Nam," *YLJ* 75, no. 7 (1966): 1085; Reich, April 6 interview; Kalman, *Yale Law School*, 62.

48. *Papachristou*, 405 U.S. at 164. On Douglas's draft opinions in *Papachristou*, see Goluboff, *Vagrant Nation*, 318–322.

49. *Papachristou*, 405 U.S. at 168; Florida Statutes Annotated (West 1972), sec. 856.021 (my italics). Florida courts upheld the constitutionality of the new vagrancy statute. State v. Ecker, 311 So.2d 104, 109 (Fla. 1975), cert. denied, Bell v. Florida, 423 U.S. 1019 (1975).

50. Henry M. Hart Jr. and Albert M. Sachs, *The Legal Process: Basic Problems in the Making and Application of Law*, "Tentative Edition" (Cambridge, MA, 1958); J. D. Hyman, "Constitutional Jurisprudence and the Teaching of Constitutional Law," *Stanford Law Review* 28, no. 6 (1976): 1286n70; Willard Hurst to Herman Goldstein, December 11, 1963, on file with author; "How I Got Here," *Gargoyle* (Winter / Spring 2008): 17–19; see also Geoffrey C. Shaw, "H. L. A. Hart's Lost Essay: *Discretion* and the Legal Process School," *HLR* 127, no. 2 (2013): 677, 697; William N. Eskridge Jr. and Philip P. Frickey, "The Making of *The Legal Process*," *HLR* 107, no. 8 (1994): 2031–2055; Kenneth Culp Davis, *Discretionary Justice: A Preliminary Inquiry* (1969; Urbana: University of Illinois Press, 1973), 222.

51. Reich, April 6 interview; Shaw, "Lost Essay," 679.

52. For the few cases that did create substantive rights, see William J. Stuntz, *The Collapse of American Criminal Justice* (Cambridge, MA: Belknap Press of Harvard University Press, 2011), 210.

53. Reich, "Police Questioning," 1171. On the inevitability of police discretion with selective enforcement, see Herman Goldstein, "Police Discretion: The Ideal versus the Real," *Public Administration Review* 23, no. 3 (September 1963): 140–147. Reich should not be judged too harshly for his compromise, especially by today's standards. We now have "electric eyes and computers," and the experiences of municipalities that have installed cameras that can detect every speeding violation and automatically issue tickets suggest that Reich is not alone in his acquiescence to discretionary policing. Public outcry against speed cameras has prompted local and state governments to take them down or guarantee a human officer to oversee the ticketing process. Nassau County, New York, after much protest, replaced cameras with more police patrols. The sector of the motoring public that wanted discretionary enforcement of traffic laws was presumably not from minority populations that tended to experience a much different, more harrowing traffic stop. See Lori Bordonaro, "Nassau Shuts Down Controversial School Zone Speed Cameras," *NBC New*

York, December 15, 2014, https://perma.cc/55XM-CASV; "Montgomery's Speed Car Cams Gone, but New Plan Will Triple Cost of Fines," *WSFA.com,* updated July 6, 2016, https://perma.cc/897X-PFGX; William Petroski, "Iowa Senate Oks Ban on Traffic Enforcement Cameras as Foes Predict More Traffic Deaths," *Des Moines Register,* updated February 28, 2018, https://perma.cc/98JA -2NQJ; Elizabeth E. Joh, "Discretionless Policing: Technology and the Fourth Amendment," *California Law Review* 95, no. 1 (2007): 199–234.

54. Kenneth Rexroth, "The Fuzz," *Playboy* 14, no. 7 (June 1967): 76, 118, 123, 126.

55. Rexroth, "Fuzz," 129.

56. Indeed, it is telling that both Reich and Douglas appear prominently in this history about the policing of Everyman and Risa Goluboff's history about the policing of people "out of place." On how the rebel outsider "can be simultaneously both inside and outside," see Grace Elizabeth Hale, *A Nation of Outsiders: How the White Middle Class Fell in Love with Rebellion in Postwar America* (New York: Oxford University Press, 2011), 7.

57. Katz v. United States, 389 U.S. 347, 348 (majority), 360 (Harlan, J., concurring); David Alan Sklansky, "'One Train May Hide Another': *Katz,* Stonewall, and the Secret Subtext of Criminal Procedure," *U.C. Davis Law Review* 41, no. 3 (2008): 879.

58. *Katz,* 389 U.S. at 359 (majority opinion, my italics), 360 (Harlan, J., concurring).

59. On car searches under the *Katz* standard, see, for example, Cardwell v. Lewis, 417 U.S. 583, 590 (1974); Sklansky, "One Train," 885.

60. Herman Goldstein, *Policing a Free Society* (Cambridge, MA: Ballinger Publishing, 1977), 1; President's Commission on Law Enforcement and Administration of Justice, *The Challenge of Crime in a Free Society* (New York: E. P. Dutton, 1968); "Proclamation No. 3221, Law Day, 1958," *Code of Federal Regulations,* title 3 (1958): 143, currently codified in Law Day, U.S.A., 36 U.S.C. § 113 (1961); "Due Process and Freedom," *Indianapolis Times,* May 4, 1959; Henry J. Friendly, "The Bill of Rights as a Code of Criminal Procedure," *California Law Review* 53, no. 4 (1965): 954, quoting Learned Hand, "The Contribution of an Independent Judiciary to Civilization," in *The Spirit of Liberty,* ed. Irving Dilliard (New York: Knopf, 1952), 179.

CHAPTER 6 • The Fourth Amendment Tool in Criminal Patrol

1. See Cardwell v. Lewis, 417 U.S. 583 (1974); United States v. Flores-Montano, 541 U.S. 149 (2004); South Dakota v. Opperman, 428 U.S. 364 (1976); Michigan v. Thomas, 458 U.S. 259 (1982). On the passenger compartment, see New York v. Class, 475 U.S. 106 (1986); Texas v. Brown, 460 U.S. 730 (1983); Michigan v. Long, 463 U.S. 1032 (1983); Thornton v. United States, 541 U.S. 615 (2004); Belton v. New York, 453 U.S. 454 (1981), overruled by Arizona v. Gant, 556 U.S. 332 (2009). On the trunk, see California v. Acevedo, 500 U.S. 565 (1991), overruling Arkansas v. Sanders, 442 U.S. 753 (1979), and United States v. Chadwick, 433 U.S. 1 (1977). On passengers, see Rakas v. Illinois, 439 U.S. 128 (1978); Maryland v. Wilson, 519 U.S. 408 (1997); Wyo-

ming v. Houghton, 526 U.S. 295 (1999); Arizona v. Johnson, 555 U.S. 323 (2009). On rental cars, see Byrd v. United States, 138 S. Ct. 1518 (2018).

2. Dan M. Kahan and Tracey L. Meares, "The Coming Crisis of Criminal Procedure," *Georgetown Law Journal* 86, no. 5 (1998): 1158–1159.

3. According to the World Justice Project, an initiative of the American Bar Association that began in 2006, the United States has one of the fairest and most transparent criminal justice systems in the world. Critical legal theorist Mark Tushnet has written about its Rule of Law Index as an ideological project. See "Rule of Law Index: 2017–2018," World Justice Project, https://perma.cc/QFJ3-RH22; Mark Tushnet, "Critical Legal Studies and the Rule of Law" (working paper, updated June 6, 2018), https://perma.cc/PDQ6 -2W3T.

4. United Nations, General Assembly, Human Rights Council, *Draft Report of the Group on the Universal Periodic Review: United States of America* (Geneva: United Nations, May 21, 2015), https://perma.cc/P2ZD-2SXM. On civil asset forfeiture, see Sarah Stillman, "Taken," *New Yorker*, August 12 and 19, 2013. For a definition of "Driving While Black," see Kenneth Meeks, *Driving While Black: Highways, Shopping Malls, Taxi Cabs, Sidewalks: How to Fight Back if You Are a Victim of Racial Profiling* (New York: Broadway Books, 2000), 4–5.

5. Brinegar v. State, 97 Okla. Crim. 299, 306 (1953); Jimmie Lewis Franklin, *Born Sober: Prohibition in Oklahoma, 1907–1959* (Norman: University of Oklahoma Press, 1971), 173–195; Brinegar obituary, *Vinita Daily Journal*, July 2, 1990; US DOC, Bureau of the Census, *Characteristics of the Population*, vol. 2 of *Census of Population: 1950* (Washington, DC, 1952), 36–18, table 7; Debra Westbrook, interview with author, September 29, 2016.

6. *Brinegar*, 97 Okla. Crim. at 307, 312.

7. *Brinegar*, 97 Okla. Crim. at 306–308, 316; United States v. Rabinowitz, 339 U.S. 56, 69 (1950) (Frankfurter, J., dissenting).

8. Burton C. Agata, "Searches and Seizures Incident to Traffic Violations—A Reply to Professor Simeone," *Saint Louis University Law Journal* 7, no. 1 (1962): 16; see also Joseph J. Simeone, "Search and Seizure Incident to Traffic Violations," *Saint Louis University Law Journal* 6, no. 4 (1961): 509–519.

9. *Brinegar*, 97 Okla. Crim. at 314–315.

10. *Brinegar*, 97 Okla. Crim. at 313, citing Go-Bart Importing Co. v. United States, 282 U.S. 344, 357 (1931).

11. Richard M. Leagre, "The Fourth Amendment and the Law of Arrest," *Journal of Criminal Law, Criminology, and Police Science* 54, no. 4 (1963): 396, 420.

12. Simeone, "Search and Seizure," 517. On reasonableness as a deferential standard, see Tracey Maclin, "The Central Meaning of the Fourth Amendment," *William and Mary Law Review* 35, no. 1 (1993): 199–200; Cynthia Lee, "Reasonableness with Teeth: The Future of Fourth Amendment Reasonableness Analysis," *Mississippi Law Journal* 81, no. 5 (2012): 1147; Devon W. Carbado, "Blue-on-Black Violence: A Provisional Model of Some of the Causes," *Georgetown Law Journal* 104, no. 6 (2016): 1505–1508. On Judge Simeone, see "Remembering Joe Simeone," Saint Louis University School of Law, May 5, 2015, https://perma.cc/2C3K-NAGW.

13. Franklin E. Zimring, "Continuity and Change in the American Gun Debate," in *Guns, Crime, and Punishment in America*, ed. Bernard E. Harcourt (New York: New York University Press, 2003), 29–30; see also Elizabeth Hinton, *From the War on Poverty to the War on Crime: The Making of Mass Incarceration in America* (Cambridge, MA: Harvard University Press, 2016); Michael W. Flamm, *Law and Order: Street Crime, Civil Unrest, and the Crisis of Liberalism in the 1960s* (New York: Columbia University Press, 2005). On gun control laws in the 1930s, see Adam Winkler, *Gunfight: The Battle over the Right to Bear Arms in America* (New York: W. W. Norton, 2011), 181–224.

14. United States v. Robinson, 414 U.S. 218, 224 (1973); United States v. Mills, 185 F. 318, 319 (S.D.N.Y. 1911). Searches incident to arrest have vastly outnumbered warrant searches. See Wayne A. Logan, "An Exception Swallows a Rule: Police Authority to Search Incident to Arrest," *Yale Law & Policy Review* 19, no. 2 (2000): 382–383.

15. Brief for Respondent, United States v. Robinson, 414 U.S. 218 (1973) (No. 72-936), 2–3n2; Dan Morgan, "Police Pvt. Jenks, Revocation 'Doctor,' Wins Another Case," *Washington Post*, March 22, 1964; Marion Clark, "Supercop," *Washington Post Potomac*, December 8, 1968.

16. Terry v. Ohio, 392 U.S. 1, 30 (1968); *Robinson*, 414 U.S. at 223; Appendix, United States v. Robinson (No. 72-936) (Supplemental Hearing on Defendant's Motion to Suppress), 37.

17. Brief for Petitioner, Gustafson v. Florida, 414 U.S. 260 (1973) (No. 71-1669), 4; see also *Gustafson*, 414 U.S. at 261–262.

18. See Julilly Kohler-Hausmann, *Getting Tough: Welfare and Imprisonment in 1970s America* (Princeton, NJ: Princeton University Press, 2017), 79–111; Kathleen J. Frydl, *The Drug Wars in America, 1940–1973* (New York: Cambridge University Press, 2013), 313–326; Doris Marie Provine, *Unequal under Law: Race in the War on Drugs* (Chicago: University of Chicago Press, 2007), 93–94; David F. Musto, *The American Disease: Origins of Narcotic Control* (1973; New York: Oxford University Press, 1999), 273–293.

19. *Robinson*, 414 U.S. at 234n5; see also Robinson Brief, 13–15.

20. Brief *Amici Curiae* in Support of the Petitioner of Americans for Effective Law Enforcement, Inc., International Association of Chiefs of Police, Inc., and the Metropolitan Police Department of the District of Columbia, United States v. Robinson, 414 U.S. 218 (1973) (No. 72-936), 11, 16; "Outnumbered," Police Science Productions, 1968, https://perma.cc/FD5M-M6TW. On the fear of guns during the War on Drugs, see James Forman Jr., *Locking Up Our Own: Crime and Punishment in Black America* (New York: Farrar, Straus and Giroux 2017), 47–77.

21. Robinson supplemental hearing, 60, 64.

22. Robinson supplemental hearing, 59–77; Petition for a Writ of Certiorari, Appendix B, oral decision of Judge Jones, United States v. Robinson, 414 U.S. 218 (1973) (No. 72-936).

23. Wayne R. LaFave, "'Case-by-Case Adjudication' versus 'Standardized Procedures': The Robinson Dilemma," *Supreme Court Review* (1974): 141.

24. Anthony G. Amsterdam, "Perspectives on the Fourth Amendment," *Minnesota Law Review* 58, no. 3 (1974): 351.

25. *Robinson*, 414 U.S. at 235 (majority), 239 (Marshall, J., dissenting).

26. Antonin Scalia, "The Rule of Law as a Law of Rules," *University of Chicago Law Review* 56, no. 4 (1989): 1179; Sarah A. Seo, "Democratic Policing before the Due Process Revolution," *YLJ* 128 (forthcoming 2019).

27. *Robinson*, 414 U.S. at 235. On Rehnquist's jurisprudence, see, for example, Jay S. Bybee and Tuan N. Samahon, "William Rehnquist, the Separation of Powers, and the Riddle of the Sphinx," *Stanford Law Review* 58, no. 6 (2006): 1735–1762. On his law-and-order legacy, see, for example, Madhavi M. McCall and Michael A. McCall, "Chief Justice William Rehnquist: His Law-and-Order Legacy and Impact on Criminal Justice," *Akron Law Review* 39, no. 2 (2006): 323–372. In the latter half of the twentieth century, the justice most vocal on the importance of general rules was Scalia. But he did not discuss how bright-line Fourth Amendment rules actually undermined individual privacy. See Scalia, "Rule of Law"; Richard A. Brisbin Jr., *Justice Antonin Scalia and the Conservative Revival* (Baltimore: Johns Hopkins University Press, 1997), 294–295.

28. *Robinson*, 414 U.S. at 238, 254 (Marshall, J., dissenting).

29. Kenneth Culp Davis, *Discretionary Justice: A Preliminary Inquiry* (1969; Urbana: University of Illinois Press, 1973), 222.

30. LaFave, "Case-by-Case Adjudication," 141, 153, 162; *Robinson*, 414 U.S. at 248 (Marshall, J., dissenting).

31. Amsterdam, "Perspectives," 394.

32. Amsterdam, "Perspectives," 352, 375. On the incoherence of Fourth Amendment jurisprudence, see, for example, Chapman v. United States, 365 U.S. 610, 622 (1961) (Clark, J., dissenting); Rios v. United States, 364 U.S. 206, 238–239 (1960) (Frankfurter, J., dissenting).

33. New York v. Belton, 453 U.S. 454, 455–456 (1981).

34. United States v. Chadwick, 433 U.S. 1, 15 (1977); see also Albert W. Alschuler, "Bright Line Fever and the Fourth Amendment," *University of Pittsburgh Law Review* 45, no. 2 (1984): 273.

35. People v. Belton, 50 N.Y.2d 447, 451–452 (1980).

36. *Belton*, 50 N.Y.2d at 451–452, 454–455 (Gabrielli, J., dissenting).

37. *Belton*, 453 U.S. at 454, 459, 461.

38. *Belton*, 453 U.S. at 470 (Brennan, J., dissenting); Amsterdam, "Perspectives," 394; Scalia, "Rule of Law," 1187.

39. *Belton*, 453 U.S. at 470, 472 (Brennan, J., dissenting).

40. *Belton*, 453 U.S. at 466 (Brennan, J., dissenting).

41. United States v. Ross, 456 U.S. 798 (1982); California v. Acevedo, 500 U.S. 565, 574, 580, 597 (1991).

42. *Acevedo*, 500 U.S. at 579 (majority), 598 (Stevens, J., dissenting).

43. Akhil Reed Amar, *The Constitution and Criminal Procedure: First Principles* (New Haven, CT: Yale University Press, 1997), 1; Morgan Cloud, "The Fourth Amendment during the *Lochner* Era: Privacy, Property, and Liberty in Constitutional Theory," *Stanford Law Review* 48, no. 3 (1996): 555.

44. Charles Remsberg, *Tactics for Criminal Patrol: Vehicle Stops, Drug Discovery and Officer Survival* (Northbrook, IL: Calibre, 1995), 1, 15. Remsberg liked to italicize, but I quote him throughout without the underscoring. On Remsberg, see Americans for Effective Law Enforcement, Charles Remsberg

biography, accessed July 7, 2018, https://perma.cc/67KN-GLG6; Northwestern University, Medill School, About Us, Awards, Hall of Achievement, Charles Remsberg, accessed July 7, 2018, https://perma.cc/XB43-Q4QU. On Reagan's War on Drugs, see Provine, *Unequal under Law*, 103–117; Michelle Alexander, *The New Jim Crow: Mass Incarceration in the Age of Colorblindness* (New York: New Press, 2012), 53–54; Daniel Richman, "The Past, Present, and Future of Violent Crime Federalism," *Crime and Justice* 34, no. 1 (2006): 393–400.

45. Remsberg, *Tactics*, 1, 6, 68–69.

46. Charles R. Epp, Steven Maynard-Moody, and Donald P. Haider-Markel, *Pulled Over: How Police Stops Define Race and Citizenship* (Chicago: University of Chicago Press, 2014), 33–34; David A. Harris, ACLU Special Report, "Driving While Black: Racial Profiling on Our Nation's Highways," June 1999, https://perma.cc/DUB9-GS5W; David Kocieniewski, "New Jersey Argues that the U.S. Wrote the Book on Racial Profiling," *NYT*, November 29, 2000; State v. Soto, 324 N.J. Super. 66, 80–81 (1966); Alexander, *New Jim Crow*, 70–72; Forman, *Locking Up*, 194–211. For a critique of race-based critiques of the War on Drugs, see Randall Kennedy, *Race, Crime, and the Law* (New York: Pantheon Books, 1997), 351–386.

47. Remsberg, *Tactics*, 134–144.

48. Remsberg, *Tactics*, 134, 211–228; Schneckloth v. Bustamonte, 412 U.S. 218, 231–232 (1973).

49. In 2008, the Supreme Court ruled that the illegality of an arrest did not invalidate a search incident to that arrest. In other words, a law forbidding an officer from making an arrest for a minor traffic violation did not determine the constitutionality of the search incident to arrest. Virginia v. Moore, 553 U.S. 164 (2008).

50. Remsberg, *Tactics*, 9, 15, 25, 234.

51. Rod Dornsife, *The Ticket Book* (La Jolla, CA: The Ticket Book, 1978), v, 1–2, 12, 24, 45, 49, 69–205.

52. Jay-Z, *Decoded* (New York: Spiegel & Grau, 2010), 60–61; see also Caleb Mason, "Jay-Z's *99 Problems*, Verse 2: A Close Reading with Fourth Amendment Guidance for Cops and Perps," *Saint Louis University Law Journal* 56, no. 2 (2012): 567–585.

53. Devon W. Carbado, "(E)Racing the Fourth Amendment," *Michigan Law Review* 100, no. 5 (2002): 947–958.

54. Carbado, "(E)Racing," 953. On the role of prosecutors, see Daniel Richman, "The Process of *Terry*-Lawmaking," *St. John's Law Review* 72, no. 3 (1998): 1044–1045.

55. Remsberg, *Tactics*, 45, 66, 70; Amsterdam, "Perspectives," 437. For an example of a case allowing inquiries into motivation, see United States v. Cruz, 581 F.2d 535, 541–542 (5th Cir. 1978) (en banc); see also Brief of California District Attorneys Association, as *Amicus Curiae* in Support of Respondent, Whren v. United States, 517 U.S. 806 (1996) (No. 95-5841), 26; Brian J. O'Donnell, "Whren v. United States: An Abrupt End to the Debate over Pretextual Stops," *Maine Law Review* 49, no. 1 (1997): 211–214.

56. Whren v. United States, 517 U.S. 806, 808–809 (1996); Oral Argument Transcript, Whren v. United States, 517 U.S. 806 (1996) (No. 95-5841), 30;

Brief for Petitioners, Whren v. United States, 517 U.S. 806 (1996) (No. 95-5841), 13–14.

57. William J. Stuntz, *The Collapse of American Criminal Justice* (Cambridge, MA: Belknap Press of Harvard University Press, 2011), 5.

58. *Whren*, 517 U.S. at 814.

59. *Whren*, 517 U.S. at 815 (D.C. police regulation); *Whren* Transcript, 8.

60. Kenneth Culp Davis also made this point when he wrote, "In the total system of police discretion, one fundamental failure is the continued enactment of statutes which go far beyond the limits of effective law enforcement." Davis, *Discretionary Justice*, 91.

61. *Whren*, 517 U.S. at 817.

62. David A. Sklansky, "Traffic Stops, Minority Motorists, and the Future of the Fourth Amendment," *Supreme Court Review* (1997): 272, 309.

63. *Whren*, 517 U.S. at 813.

64. John Kifner, "Van Shooting Revives Charges of Racial 'Profiling' by New Jersey State Police," *NYT*, May 10, 1998; *Soto*, 324 N.J. Super. at 70–71.

65. Steve Strunsky, "In Person: Pursuing Justice, Rewriting Law," *NYT*, June 30, 2002; see also "Praise for Ruling on Race-Based Traffic Stops," *Central New Jersey Home News*, March 10, 1996.

66. David M. Herszenhorn, "11 Miles of Turnpike Shut to Re-Create a Shooting," *NYT*, April 12, 1999; Amy Waldman, "Describing a 'Hard-Fought Year,' 4 Men in Turnpike Shooting File Lawsuit," *NYT*, April 23, 1999; David Kocieniewski, "A Former Trooper's Take on His Race Profiling Case," *NYT*, April 5, 2006.

67. David M. Herszenhorn, "Reversal Has Some Questioning Attorney General's Motives," *NYT*, April 21, 1999; Strunsky, "In Person."

68. "Metro News Briefs: Video Cameras Installed on 650 Trooper Vehicles," *NYT*, December 8, 1998.

69. See Pagan Kennedy, "Why Are Police Officers More Dangerous than Airplanes?" *NYT*, August 11, 2017; Nick Selby, Ben Singleton, and Ed Flosi, *In Context: Understanding Police Killings of Unarmed Citizens* (St. Augustine, FL: Contextual, 2016), 39.

Epilogue

1. See Marc Fisher, "Cruising toward Oblivion," *Washington Post*, September 2, 2015; Elisabeth Rosenthal, "The End of Car Culture," *NYT*, June 29, 2013; Tony Dudzik, Jeff Inglis, and Phineas Baxandall, *Millennials in Motion: Changing Travel Habits of Young Americans and the Implications for Public Policy* (n.p., U.S. Public Interest Research Group Education Fund and Frontier Group, October 2014), 24, 30, https://perma.cc/Z8JE-KZZ5.

2. United States v. Jones, 565 U.S. 400, 404–405 (2012) (my italics).

3. *Jones*, 565 U.S. at 420, 420n3 (Alito, J., concurring), 415 (Sotomayor, J., concurring).

4. Carpenter v. United States, 138 S. Ct. 2206, 2268, 2271–2272 (2018) (Gorsuch, J., dissenting); Substituted Brief for the United States on Reargument, Carroll v. United States, 267 U.S. 132 (1925) (No. 15), 72.

5. *Carpenter*, 138 S. Ct. at 2217, 2220 (majority), 2232 (Kennedy, J., dissenting).

6. *Jones*, 565 U.S. at 415 (Sotomayor, J., concurring).

7. Riley v. California, 134 S. Ct. 2473, 2489, 2491 (2014).

8. *Riley*, 134 S. Ct. at 2490, 2494.

9. Joel Rubin and Ben Poston, "L.A. County Deputies Stopped Thousands of Innocent Latinos on the 5 Freeway in Hopes of Their Next Drug Bust," *LAT*, October 4, 2018; United States v. Johnson, 874 F.3d 571, 574 (7th Cir. 2017) (en banc).

10. United States v. Johnson, 823 F.3d 408, 410 (7th Cir. 2016); *Johnson*, 874 F.3d at 576 (Hamilton, J., dissenting).

11. Rodriguez v. United States, 135 S. Ct. 1609, 1611 (2015).

12. *Rodriguez*, 135 S. Ct. at 1624 (Alito, J., dissenting).

13. US Supreme Court, No. 17-1349, 2018 WL 1470947 (Mem) (October 1, 2018).

14. Mullenix v. Luna, 136 S. Ct. 305, 306–307 (2015).

15. *Mullenix*, 136 S. Ct. at 308, 312.

Acknowledgments

This is the hardest part of the book to write because words are inadequate to communicate my gratitude. But it is also a joy to acknowledge the people and institutions that have supported me in writing this history.

Archivists are unsung heroes, and I begin with them. My deepest thanks go to the staffs at Arizona State Library; Bancroft Library at the University of California, Berkeley; Benson Ford Research Center; Herbert Hoover Presidential Library; Los Angeles City Archives and Records Center; the Manuscript Division at the Library of Congress; Mudd Manuscript Library at Princeton University; the National Archives at Denver and Washington, D.C.; New York City Municipal Archives; and Charles E. Young Library at the University of California, Los Angeles.

Finishing this book would have taken many more years if not for the generous financial support of the Beach Law Faculty Opportunity Fund at Iowa Law School, the American Philosophical Society's Franklin Research Grant, the William Nelson Cromwell Foundation Grant, the Charles W. McCurdy Fellowship at UVA Law School, and the Samuel I. Golieb Fellowship at NYU Law School.

My thinking has benefited immeasurably from presenting chapters at conferences and faculty workshops. I am grateful to the organizers and participants at the American Bar Foundation's Legal History Workshop, American Society for Legal History's 2017

Annual Meeting, Emory Law School's Faculty Colloquium, Iowa Law School's Junior Faculty and Legal Studies Workshops, Law and Society Association's 2018 Annual Meeting, Southeastern Association of Law Schools' 2017 Conference, University of Chicago Law School's Legal Theory Workshop, University of Maryland Law School's Con Law Schmooze, University of Minnesota's Faculty Works-in-Progress and Legal History Workshops, and University of Oregon Law School's Race, Ethnicities, and Inequalities Colloquium.

Many people provided substantive feedback and friendship that went above and beyond the standard of collegiality, and I want to specially acknowledge Curtis Austin, Jamal Greene, Cynthia Lee, Joe Lowndes, Michelle McKinley, Sarah Milov, Cynthia Nicoletti, Angela Onwuachi-Willig, Reuel Schiller, Christopher Schmidt, David Sklansky, David Thacher, Laura Weinrib, and Barbara Welke. Thomas Green, Dirk Hartog, and Michael Willrich also read the manuscript in its entirety and enriched each chapter. I also thank Herman Goldstein, Charles Reich, and Debra Westbrook for speaking with me at length and sharing photographs.

Chapter 5 builds on ideas I first discussed in "The New Public," *Yale Law Journal* 125, no. 6 (2016). Jonas Wang and the journal's team of student editors asked many insightful questions that improved the essay substantially.

This book began with Dirk Hartog's wise counsel and steadfast support. I was lucky to have him as a mentor, and it is a blessing to have him now as a good friend. I was also privileged to receive guidance from Dan Rodgers, Margot Canaday, and Risa Goluboff. Whenever I encountered difficulty, Dan managed to turn the struggle into a virtue. Margot gave me the encouragement to believe I had something to say, which meant the world to me. Risa continues to be my model of a scholar, teacher, and colleague.

I have been the beneficiary of an unending source of intellectual camaraderie and encouragement at the University of Iowa College of Law. My colleagues inspire me daily, the people in the administration make it a joy to come to work every day, and my students deepen my thinking about life and the law. I especially want to thank Stella Burch Elias, Daria Fisher-Page, Paul Gowder, Alison

Guernsey, Emily Hughes, Todd Pettys, Anya Prince, Sean Sullivan, and Christina Tilley for reading chapters. Visiting professors Wendy Greene and César Rosado Marzán have also given invaluable feedback. Without my research assistants Kayla Deloach, Joseph Hinrichs, and Michael Stern, it would have taken me twice as long to finish this book. The law librarians, and especially Amy Koopmann and Eric Earhart, were gracious with countless requests. Amanda Bibbs and Sara Clark supported me day to day. Dean Emerita Gail Agrawal will always be my first dean, who enthusiastically supported my work as a legal historian. She, in cahoots with Derek Pendergast, matched me with Robert and Jane Beach, whose generous giving funded many of my archival trips. Our new dean, Kevin Washburn, saw me through the end of the book-writing process, for which I am grateful.

I finished writing this book at Columbia Law School, where I spent a semester as a scholar in residence at the Center for Contemporary Critical Thought. For this hospitality and intellectual enrichment, I owe Bernard Harcourt. Anna Krauthamer and Khamla Pradaxay ensured that I felt welcome. I was especially humbled when my alma mater hosted a manuscript workshop for me. Monica Bell, Deborah Dinner, Jeffrey Fagan, Bernard Harcourt, Jeremy Kessler, Kate Levine, Tracey Meares, Dan Richman, and Alice Ristroph read the manuscript and spent an entire day huddled in a conference room to talk about it—all on a month's notice.

The people at Harvard University Press have provided me with much reassurance and guidance. Andrew Kinney spent countless hours with me, and Timothy Jones, Stephanie Vyce, and Olivia Woods made sure the entire process went smoothly. The suggestions of my two outside readers enhanced every part of the book.

On a more personal note, I am indebted to my parents, who believed in me. We immigrated to this country when I was five years old. When my parents dropped me off on my first day of kindergarten, just months after we had arrived, they wondered how long it would take me to learn enough English to get by. Today, my parents laugh with delight every time they think about their daughter as a scholar of United States history and law. For this turn of events, my family and I give much of the credit to the public school teachers and professors who showed me much kindness and fostered my love of history. I hope that my parents also recognize their crucial role in my journey.

Finally, this book is for Mike, who never fails to make me laugh. That would be enough. But he has also read every word in these pages and devoted much of our daily time walking Grimke listening to my musings about this or that part of the book. Only the most patient and abiding love could have done all this so joyfully.

Index